THEORETICAL PERSPECTIVES IN SOCIAL PSYCHOLOGY

THEORETICAL PERSPECTIVES IN SOCIAL PSYCHOLOGY

CLYDE W. FRANKLIN, II
Ohio State University

LITTLE, BROWN AND COMPANY
Boston   Toronto

Library of Congress Cataloging in Publication Data

Franklin, Clyde W.
  Theoretical perspectives in social psychology.

  Bibliography: p.
  Includes index.
  1. Social psychology.   I. Title.
HM251.F6763   302   81–23643
ISBN 0–316–29199–4   AACR2

ISBN 0–316–291994

9 8 7 6 5 4 3 2 1

HAL

Published simultaneously in Canada
by Little, Brown & Company (Canada) Limited

Printed in the United States of America

For my children
Coy, Sean, Clyde III, and ''Miss'' Alison
and their grandparents
Coy and Bernice Franklin and Eli and Rozelle Pickett

CONTENTS

PREFACE

During the middle and late 1960s, I had the privilege of assisting three professors at the University of Washington in teaching Sociology 240, the undergraduate introductory social psychology course. The professors were Frank Miyamoto, the symbolic interactionist, Richard M. Emerson, the social exchange theorist, and Robert L. Burgess, the behavioral sociologist. The manner in which they taught the course (usually two of the professorial team taught, for example Miyamoto and Emerson, Emerson and Burgess) has remained vivid in my mind down through the years.

Frank Miyamoto did much more than define "self-concept" when he discussed it; he also talked about the symbolic interaction assumptions underlying the hypothetical construct. Dr. Emerson presented his "power-dependence relations" formulation but never without explaining its link to Homans' *Social Behavior: Its Elementary Forms* and Blau's *Exchange and Power in Social Life*. Bob Burgess, in discussing "differential reinforcement," "positive reinforcement," and "negative reinforcement," always referred to basic assumptions underlying operant theory. The perspectives these teachers employed in teaching topical interests in social psychology were surely diverse, but there was one line of commonality: each presented both *theoretical perspectives* and *topical interests*. Some students may not have agreed with

Bob's contention that much criminal behavior could be seen in a behavioral light, but they did know the basic assumptions underlying his contention. The knowledge students gained from the course was unified, systematized, and had potential for integration; it was not disparate or haphazard. I should like to thank my former professors for this orientation, which has been essential to me in the preparation of this book.

A volume of this kind should promote pedagogical approaches similar to the ones described above, I believe, the result being a better comprehension of social psychological subject matter and an increased interest in the discipline. Rather than simply memorizing basic elements of a particular study, concept, or principle, students seem in this way to learn the relationships *between* studies, concepts, and principles; certainly this has been the case at Ohio State University in Sociology 470 and Sociology 770, our introductory social psychology courses at the undergraduate and graduate levels. I would like to express my appreciation to the members of these classes for aiding me in clarifying my own thoughts and ideas about the perspectives included in this volume. I would like to thank also those who have read or criticized portions of this manuscript: Laurel W. Richardson, Timothy J. Curry, Stephen Pfohl, Judi DiIorio, and Ethel Mayo. I am grateful to Mary Brooks, Cindy Brown, Marsha Hronek, Jane McCoy, and Laurie Taress for their invaluable assistance in preparing the manuscript; and to Brenda Phillips for assistance in preparation of the index. Finally, deep appreciation is extended to my former professor Robert (Bob) Leik, for teaching me to place methodology in its proper perspective in social psychology.

THEORETICAL PERSPECTIVES IN SOCIAL PSYCHOLOGY

THE
FIELD
OF
SOCIAL
PSYCHOLOGY:
AN
INTRODUCTION

1

A young man, having just seen his favorite professional football team win the Super Bowl, suddenly dashes off to the nearest department store to buy a sweater with the team's insignia. An executive, newly divorced from his wife of seven years, seemingly overnight changes his attitude toward marriage, begins to treat women as sex objects, and becomes cold toward his old friends. A black woman and a white woman from different social backgrounds employed by the same firm, develop an intense friendship over a period of time. People outside the field of social psychology are likely to offer a variety of explanations for behavior like this, but they are unlikely to recognize that all three hypothetical situations are the subject matter of social psychology. What makes all three incidents social psychological should become apparent in the next few pages as the nature of social psychology is explored.

To many laymen social psychology, unlike its ancestral disciplines sociology, psychology, anthropology and economics (to mention a few), remains an esoteric or specialized field of study with questionable relevance for everyday life. Those studying social psychology should not be surprised to hear inquiries such as "Why are you studying *that*?" "What *is* social psychology?" "What do social psychologists do?" Part of the reason social psychology has remained a mystery to many may, in fact, be the past doubts and uncertainties expressed by those working within the field, as we shall see. There is at present, however, an emerging agreement about the nature of the discipline. This does not mean that all social psychologists do the same thing: they do not. It does mean that all social psychologists expect to do things of "mutual relevance." This chapter is devoted to what social psychology is, what it is related to, what social psychologists do, and what they *can* do.

SOCIAL PSYCHOLOGY DEFINED

Social psychology is recognized by many within the field as multi-disciplinary and interdisciplinary (Liska, p. 2; Burgess, p. 12; Hill, p. 19). Many scholars feel that social psychology is, or should be, an enterprise undertaken cooperatively by sociologists, psychologists, economists, anthropologists, political scientists, and others, and that this specialized field has broad and far-reaching implications for disciplines such as sociology, psychology, economics, anthropology and political science. It is perhaps due to the multidisciplinary nature of social psychology that questions have arisen regarding its subject matter. The questions have centered around definitions of the field, usefulness of the field, and the future of the field. Moreover, ignorance of work in other disciplines by those supposedly engaged in cooperation across disciplines may result in confusion, uncertainty and disillusionment. Out of all this, however, there may be emerging clarification.

An examination of several leading textbooks in social psychology will show that the discipline has been defined in numerous ways. For example, Schellenberg conceives of it as "the study of interpersonal behavior" (p. v); Secord and Backman suggest that social psychologists study "the behavior of individuals in social contexts"(p. 1); Shaw and Costanzo consider social psychology "the scientific study of individual behavior as a function of social stimuli" (p. 3); Lindesmith, Strauss and Denzin state that social psychology is concerned "with the relationship between individuals and social structures . . ." (1975, p. 3); Vander Zanden, following Gordon Allport, defines social psychology in the glossary of his first chapter as "a scientific attempt to understand and explain how the thoughts, feelings and behavior of individuals are influenced by the actual, imagined or implied presence of others" (p. 27); and, finally, in an earlier and immensely popular textbook in some academic circles, social psychology is defined as "the study of those aspects of human personal behavior which are developed and controlled by the interaction which takes place between the individual and

his small intimate circle of association known as the primary group"
(Faris, 1952. p. iii).[1]

While the definitions of social psychology presented here all contain different concepts, there are some striking similarities between certain sets of definitions. Specifically, Schellenberg and Vander Zanden
conceive of social psychology as the study of interpersonal interaction.
Shaw and Costanzo, and Faris, feel that the subject-matter of social
psychology is the individual's behavior occurring as a *consequence* of
social factors, situations, social interaction and the like. Secord and
Backman, and Lindesmith, Strauss and Denzin, have broader definitions of social psychology than the others. Their conception of it as the
study of the individual's behavior in social environments implies two
things. First, a concern with the effect of *social environments* on individuals' behaviors, and second, a concern with the effect of *individuals' behaviors* on social environments. Using this view of social
psychology, the field seems to cover *all* individual behavior in social
situations as well as relationships *between* the individual and his or her
environment. As Lindesmith, Strauss and Denzin state, two fundamental questions concern social psychologists: "How is man (woman) affected by the social order?" and "How does man (woman) create the
social order that shape and mold his (her) environment?" (1975, p. 3).

The distinction made here between these sets of definitions may
not seem important at first glance. But the three sets of definitions imply different conceptions of the source of much of human behavior.
Shaw and Costanzo, with Faris, seem to agree that a person's behavior
is determined by social factors, while Lindesmith and the others emphasize the relationship between the individual and his or her environment without the view that behavior is necessarily determined by social
factors. The broadness of the latter conception of social psychology is
important, since one variety of a major perspective in social psychology
(symbolic interactionism, as well as several of its offshoots) assumes a
rather indeterministic view of individual behavior. That is, behavior is
viewed as emergent or constructed, rather than simply as released or
determined by such factors as role expectations, internalized values, and
so on. Such a perspective, then, would fall within the purview of social
psychology as defined by Lindesmith, Strauss and Denzin, Secord and
Backman, Schellenberg, and Vander Zanden, but not necessarily of
Shaw and Costanzo's and Faris' definitions of the field.

Two recent works on theories in social psychology offer little in the
way of a definition. Slawski has no formal definition. West and Wick-

---

1. Faris' book for many years was thought of by many social psychologists as one
of the major textbooks written from the symbolic interaction perspective.

lund also avoid formally defining social psychology. Instead, they discuss six general areas of theorizing in social psychology. The areas covered in their volume include: (1) *derivations from learning theory,* (2) *cognitive consistency,* (3) *attribution,* (4) *self-evaluation and self-explanation,* (5) *achievement and leadership,* and (6) *reactions to loss of control.* Following their discussion, West and Wicklund ask whether or not the theories to be discussed within the areas are social psychological. They conclude that an answer depends upon how social psychology is defined, and although their subject index lists a *definition* of social psychology, a formal one is not to be found. If a definition *can* be gleaned from West and Wicklund, it appears to be one that stresses the *approaches* that persons who define themselves as social psychologists have found useful in problem formulation and solution (p. 7).

Reluctance to define the field, and discrepant views regarding the appropriate units of cognition were in all likelihood the impetus for two recent papers on social psychology and the "state of the field": James S. House's "The Three Faces of Social Psychology" and Sheldon Stryker's "Developments in 'Two Social Psychologies': Toward an Appreciation of Mutual Relevance." These papers, I believe, provide the basis for an encompassing and contemporary definition of social psychology which resembles the discipline as we know it today.

Stryker suggests two definitions, the boundaries of which are determined by the predominant professionals within the discipline. There is *psychological social psychology,* defined by "its focus on psychological processes of individuals: the task is to understand the impact of social stimuli on individuals (done primarily by psychologists)." *Sociological social psychology* (done mainly by sociologists) "is defined by the reciprocity of society and the individual"; its task is "the explanation of social interaction." A major point made by Stryker is that these two social psychologies, generally using different methodologies (experimental and naturalistic observation), for years have been on different courses, each only occasionally influencing the other. Yet, he contends, they remain mutually relevant. Noting that part of the "crisis of confidence" in social psychology expressed by some psychological social psychologists could be termed "emerging disaffection" with experimentation, Stryker concludes that there seem to be some general trends toward convergence of the two social psychologies. The emphasis throughout the society on relevance, the increasing recognition that social structure affects the individual and that the individual affects the social structure, the growing respectability of subjectivity in social psychological analyses, and the recognition of commonalities between perspectives within social psychology all seem to portend greater interaction between the two historically diverse social psychologies.

Closely akin to Stryker's discussion of the state of social psychology is James House's article. House suggests three distinct social psychologies which have emerged during the past twenty years: *psychological social psychology* which is concerned with "psychological processes in relation to social stimuli"; *symbolic interactionism* which focuses on "the study of face-to-face social interaction via naturalistic observation"; and *psychological sociology*, which is the study of the relationship between the social structure and its aspects and individual psychological attributes and behavior (p. 161). Recognizing that the three social psychologies often appear to be estranged from each other, House feels that they can actually strengthen each other and social psychology as a whole if there is greater interchange between them. This interchange, however, must be accompanied by clarification of (1) the focuses that shaped each face, (2) the nature of the social psychologies, and (3) the potential relations between the three faces (p. 174).

Given the definitions of social psychology previously cited and the relatively recent work just mentioned, the following definition of social psychology is proposed: *Social psychology is the scientific study of social interaction between individuals; of individual processes in social stimulus situations; and the social structure in relation to the individual.* This definition should satisfy proponents of all three of the "faces" of social psychology. More important, though, is the fact that it is broad enough to encompass most, if not all, of the work being done today by persons who call themselves social psychologists. Now this does not mean that any *one* social psychologist has to do all three aspects of social psychology that constitute its definition. It implies, however, that social psychology, or combinations of social psychologies, should be produced with some cognition of the efforts being made in the other areas.

The definition of social psychology stated here is similar to recent ones given by Cartwright (1979, p. 91) and Lindesmith, Strauss and Denzin (1977, p. 4). Cartwright states ("as a first approximation") that social psychology is "that branch of the social sciences which attempts to explain how society influences the cognition, motivation, development, and behavior of individuals, and in turn, is influenced by them." For Lindesmith, Strauss and Denzin, social psychology

concerns itself with the phases of social experience that derive from individuals' participation in the ongoing worlds of social groups, with their interactions with other people and with the effects upon them of what is broadly designated as the cultural environment.

There is a major difference between this definition of social psychology and the one I have offered, in that Lindesmith, Strauss and Denzin do not include a focus on individual processes in social settings (psychological social psychology). The inclusion of this aspect of social psychology is important, I believe, because it emphasizes the multidisciplinary nature of the field, and it defines the main focus of many social psychologists—including those whose parent discipline is sociology!

Defining social psychology as I have, let us turn to a discussion of its relationship to several of the social sciences including sociology, psychology, anthropology and economics.

THE RELATIONSHIP BETWEEN SOCIAL PSYCHOLOGY AND OTHER SOCIAL SCIENCES

"Social psychology" as a distinctive field of study was formally introduced with the publication in 1908 of psychologist William McDougall's *Social Psychology* and sociologist E. A. Ross' *Social Psychology*. Both books had a major influence on the development of social psychology in psychology and sociology. In fact, some textbooks credit McDougall and Ross with having written the first books on social psychology. This is not quite accurate, as Borgatta noted when he pointed out that Charles Horton Cooley's book entitled *Human Nature and the Social Order*, although somewhat moralizing, may have been just as influential in the emergence of social psychology as those by McDougall and Ross. Moreover, Cooley's work was published in 1902—six years before the appearance of McDougall's or Ross' volumes.

Undoubtedly there will continue to be some controversy over the issue of the first major writings in social psychology. From my position the controversy is unimportant. Regardless of which book first carried the title "Social Psychology," or who authored the first major social psychological work, social psychology did emerge as a field of study in the early twentieth century. It had then, and still has now, broad implications for social life, and is accepted by many scholars to be a vital and exciting part of the social and behavioral sciences.

If social psychology owes a debt to predecessors, then many disciplines should file claims for payment, because the roots of social psychology can be found in many disciplines. The most important influences, however, seem to have come from sociology and psychology.

Sociology and Social Psychology

The unit of analysis in sociology is "forms of social interaction among individuals." As Light and Keller point out, "the sociological eye looks beyond individual psychology and unique events to the predictable pattern and regular occurrences of social life" (p. 5). Typically, sociologists concern themselves with relationships between individuals and patterns of social interaction between groups. Such a focus leads inevitably to a concern with structural factors such as statuses, roles and norms, as well as the relationships between these factors. Due, in part, to the subject matter of sociology, social psychology from a sociological point of view has meant "studying social interaction processes in an effort to understand, among other things, how groups, institutions or social structures manage to function . . ." (Lindesmith, Strauss and Denzin, 1975, p. 17). Social psychology has always been central in sociological thought. Men like Emile Durkheim, Georg Simmel, W. I. Thomas, Max Weber and Gabriel Tarde, among others, took the individual into account in their attempts to understand patterns or forms of social interaction. This should not be surprising since, as Deutsch and Krauss state, "the human being is from birth the terminal focus of the action of others, and understanding human behavior requires comprehension of this individual in his relations with others" (p. 2).

Psychology and Social Psychology

The psychological approach has been different. Psychologists have been concerned with social psychological phenomena in terms of individual behavior (Secord and Backman, p. 3). The subject matter of social psychology in psychology has consisted primarily of feelings, cognitions, perceptions, beliefs, memories and other individual properties. Of course sociologists who specialize in social psychology have studied these properties, just as some psychologists have delved into the "group process." Group dynamics as a topic in social psychology, for example, was initiated by the psychologist Kurt Lewin. Nevertheless, the predominant concerns of psychologists and sociologists in social psychology have been diverse (Liska). In fact, it can be said that of the five perspectives examined in this book, behaviorism, gestalt and field have been influenced largely by the contributions of psychologists while the roots of symbolic interactionism and social exchange lie in the works of sociologists.

With social psychology being so firmly rooted in both psychology and sociology, it is little wonder that the discipline has been thought of as a hybrid behavioral science—a result of the merging chiefly of sociology and psychology, although contributors have come from other social sciences.

Anthropology and Social Psychology

Anthropology is another field in the social and behavioral sciences which has had a major impact on social psychology, but compared to sociology and psychology, anthropology's influence has been relatively recent. In fact, prior to the 1930s anthropologists devoted little attention to social psychology and concentrated instead on cultural factors thought to be common to all societies. The writings of Edward Shapiro, Ralph Linton, Ruth Benedict, Margaret Mead, and others marked a turning point in anthropology. In addition to its traditional emphases, the discipline began to be concerned with the study of personality and roles as well as with culture. More specifically, it can be said that anthropology at this juncture became "the study of man in relation to distribution, origin, classification of races, environmental and social relations, physical characteristics and culture" (Shaw and Costanzo, p. 6). In addition, anthropologists aided the development of social psychology through their presentations of ethnographic findings (from several societies) which contradicted single society findings.[2]

Given the way anthropology was viewed in the past, and the present concerns of numerous anthropologists, it should be easy to see why the discipline is thought to be extremely important by most social psychologists. Many social psychologists (especially sociological social psychologists) recognize and appreciate the work by anthropologists in the areas of roles, socialization, cultural aspirations, values, motives and so on. Such work contributes immensely to the social psychologist's con-

2. Shaw and Costanzo have noted that because we learn in a specific culture, we may have biased views of the behaviors of others in cultures different from our own. Anthropology may rectify problems caused by this bias.

ceptions of human nature, the nature of the social environment and the relationship between humans and their social environments.

Economics and Social Psychology

Finally (but this by no means exhausts the discipline's roots) economics has been another source of contributions to social psychology. While the relationship between economics and social psychology has not been as integrated as the other relationships discussed, at least one of the perspectives dealt with in this book, the social exchange orientation, owes its existence, in part, to economics. Economics, being concerned with the study of humans and patterns of social interaction in relation to production, distribution and use of goods and services, remains an essential discipline for social exchange adherents. Borrowing heavily from such concepts as direct costs, indirect costs, profit, going rate of exchange, fair rate of exchange, and numerous others, social exchange theorists have developed a perspective which integrates key ideas and principles from behavioral psychology and economics. Scholars such as George Homans, Peter Blau, George Thibaut, H. H. Kelley, Richard Emerson and others have been at the forefront of the development of the social exchange orientation and acknowledge the impact of economics on their work.

A brief discussion of the perspectives in social psychology which are at the center of this volume follows.

PERSPECTIVES IN SOCIAL PSYCHOLOGY

Some persons reading recent articles on the state of social psychology (for example, those by Elms; House; Stryker; Liska; Hewitt; Archibald) may feel that a discussion of schools of thought and their distinctive concepts, units of analysis, assumptions and even methodologies only serves to further fractionalize the field. In contrast, I feel that such a discussion may serve an integrative function, in that points of potential convergence can become apparent, possibly leading to the general theoretical framework that many social psychologists feel is necessary at this point in the subject's history. See Liska (p. 4) and Cartwright (1979, pp. 89–90). It is important, however, to recognize that the controversy and concerns that have arisen in the past decade can be pictured as a perceived *lack of unanimity* among social psychologists in their theoretical perspectives and methodologies. This is unfortunate; an analogous situation would be if all medical researchers doing research on sickle cell anemia were uniform in their theory and methodology. The likelihood of major breakthroughs on the pathology would be greatly diminished. Moreover, if the heart specialist were required to have full working knowledge of sickle cell anemia research, limits on time, effort and energy might affect his or her efficiency as a specialist. Of course the problem I am referring to in social psychology is slightly different if the problem *actually* revolves around persons doing different kinds of social psychology *and* simultaneously ignoring the works of social psychologists with different substantive interests, approaches and methodologies. Understandably, it can be tempting to be ethnocentric about one's favorite social psychology. However, this can impede progress. While a general theoretical framework in social psychology seems to be most desirable for many scholars, it may also be desirable that we begin to develop *specialists* devoted to *integrating* the field. Such a development, I believe, would attenuate much of the controversy surrounding the ''state'' of social psychology. Of course, the specialist would have to have a working knowledge of the major perspectives and methodologies in the field. One of the major purposes of this volume is to provide some of the rudiments to such a potential student. These rudiments, I believe, take the form of basic ideas about major perspectives in social psychology.

Symbolic Interactionism

Symbolic interactionism is the first perspective discussed. Perhaps the most popular social psychological perspective in sociology, symbolic interactionism has been nourished by the contributions of men like John Dewey, Charles Cooley, W. I. Thomas, George H. Mead, Herbert Blumer, Manford Kuhn, Erving Goffman and others too numerous to mention. From the writings of these scholars, a set of concepts, ideas and assumptions has developed which is centered around several major principles: (1) the individual and society are inseparable; (2) individuals are reflective and interactive beings who have selves; and (3) individuals react to things in their social environments on the basis of the meanings that things have for them. These and several other assumptions are presented and discussed in this book and, in addition, diversity within symbolic interactionism is explored. Other features of the chapter on symbolic interactionism are an outline of the concerns and debates in the perspective as well as its positive and negative features.

Behavioral Social Psychology

Behavioral social psychology had its beginnings in the contributions of men like Pavlov, Thorndike, Becheterev and Skinner among others. In Chapter 4, I discuss the contributions of these men as well as those of contemporary scholars such as S. W. Bijou and D. M. Baer, J. H. Kunkel, R. Nagasawa, R. L. Burgess, R. L. Akers and D. Bushell.

The major point of departure in behavioral social psychology is the distinction between infrahuman and human behavior. This distinction is reflected in differences between stimulus-response psychology and response-stimulus response psychology (the operant orientation). Behavioral social psychology is based on the latter model, which presupposes that humans are active beings who emit responses. Such responses are felt to operate on the environment in such a way as to alter their probabilities of future occurrences. While all of this may seem extremely technical, an attempt is made to present the behavioral social psychological perspective as clearly as possible.

The Social Exchange Perspective

Chapter 5 is devoted to a discussion of what has become known as the "Social Exchange Perspective." According to its proponents, this is essentially oriented toward structural features of social life. It avows concern with the simple social processes out of which structures of social associations evolve (Blau, 1964, p. 2). Social exchange is an approach in social psychology which is emergent in nature and dependent upon a particular kind of social interaction. To fall within the purview of social exchange, human behavior must be voluntary and motivated by the extrinsic returns that the exchange is expected to bring. The essential feature of social exchange seems to be that behavior must be directed toward certain ends which can only be achieved through social interaction. In other words, behavior must be goal-oriented in order for it to be considered social exchange. Contributions by scholars such as Georg Simmel, George Homans, George Thibaut, H. H. Kelley, Peter Blau, Richard Emerson and Elaine Walster are discussed.

The Gestalt Orientation

Max Wertheimer, Wolfgang Kohler and Kurt Koffka are generally considered to be the founders of the gestalt orientation. All wrote important statements about it. These statements seem to center around two key ideas, the first being that social psychological phenomena should be thought of as "whole" entities. Because of this holistic approach, social psychological elements are viewed as parts of "a system of coexisting and mutually interdependent factors having certain properties as a system that are not deducible from knowledge" of its isolated parts. The second idea stresses the simplicity and orderly nature of certain psychological states and proposes that certain psychological processes "act to make the state of the field as good as prevailing conditions allow" (Deutsch and Krauss, p. 16).

While Wertheimer, Kohler and Koffka were responsible for the initial attention directed toward gestalt principles, broad development of the perspective could not have taken place if it had not been for scholars like Kurt Lewin, Fritz Heider, Solomon Asch, Leon Festinger and Theodore Newcomb, among others. In fact, Deutsch and Krauss, in 1965, were so impressed with gestalt contributions that they suggested the gestalt perspective was the most pervasive influence in social psychology at that time. Today the claim would be extremely difficult to substantiate; however, as is shown in Chapter 6, the gestalt influence remains strong in social psychology.

The Field Theory Orientation

Kurt Lewin, a student of several of the founders of gestalt psychology, is recognized as the founder of field theory. Having been a member of the gestalt group in Berlin, Lewin's thinking was influenced by the basic notions of gestalt psychology. His break from the gestalt perspective was one which was more of topical concern than anything else. Lewin, being interested much more in problems of personality and behavioral actions than in perceptual phenomena (the latter is the chief concern of gestaltists), felt that gestalt psychology did not address issues which he deemed of vital interest. One of the issues which intrigued Lewin was motivation. Therefore, when Lewin broke with the gestalt group, he turned his attention chiefly to the study of motivation. Some of the areas of investigation in social psychology benefitting from Lewinian analyses include levels of aspiration, group leadership, group conformity, group decision-making, and social power.

An interesting feature of field theory is that many of its basic principles have been used in experimental studies without ever being defined as field theory principles. For example, studies by Exline (1963), Nachshon and Wapner (1967), Hastorf, Kite, Gross and Wolfe (1965), and much work in cognitive theory were all influenced by field theory ideas. Chapter 7 is designed to illuminate some of field theory's contributions to social psychology, and in addition, to contribute further to its development as a theoretical perspective in social psychology and to the field as a whole.

SUBSTANTIVE SOCIAL PSYCHOLOGY IN THIS BOOK

An adequate understanding of the various perspectives and orientations used by those doing social psychology today is imperative for students in the field. However, understanding the perspectives alone is not enough. The aspiring social psychologist should have some idea about how to apply the perspectives to the substantive topics and concerns of everyday life. Several such topics and concerns, which I feel cover a wide spectrum of social life, are used here to show how the book's perspectives can be applied. Topics and concerns such as socialization, attitude formation and change, group processes, group maintenance, social influence and social aggression, when appropriate, are explored within the perspectives to show their utility. A brief discussion of some of these topics follows.

Socialization

Socialization is defined by Secord and Backman as "a process of change occurring throughout the life career of the individual as a result of his (her) interaction with other persons" (p. 564). Another popular definition is that socialization "is the process of an individual's adjustment to living with other people, including adjustment to individuals, to groups, and to the culture as a whole" (Schellenberg, pp. 352–353). Both definitions suggest that socialization is a dynamic process that begins at birth and continues through adulthood until some debilitating mental impairment or death. Elaborations of the socialization concept usually include numerous functions of the process, among which are status learning and social control.

The definitions of socialization stated here are consistent with present-day research and theory in the area, which emphasize a developmental approach in adulthood just as exists in childhood. Levinson et al. have stated that "when our work began, there was little theory and even less research evidence regarding adult phases in the life cycle and the nature of adult development" (p. ix). While few social psychologists have felt as Freud did about adulthood—"a scene in which the early unconscious conflicts were re-enacted, rather than as time of further development" (Levinson et al., p. 4)—the area has been ignored and constitutes a new area of interest for many in the field. Discussions on socialization throughout this book will include both childhood and adult socialization when deemed appropriate.

Socialization is discussed most extensively in two of the five perspectives explored, symbolic interactionism and behavioral social psychology. Additionally, while the other perspectives do not permit systematic discussions of socialization, significant contributions have been made on the topic through the use of such perspectives and these are presented in the appropriate sections.

Attitude Formation and Attitude Change

Attitudes generally are defined in social psychology as cognitive, affective and behavioral predispositions toward a physical, abstract or social object. Defined in this way, an attitude is different from the lay meanings of the term, which often suggest that attitudes are "feelings" toward objects. From a social psychological perspective, feelings constitute only one dimension of an attitude. Other dimensions such as *beliefs* about the object and tendencies to *behave* toward the object are usually included in definitions of the concept attitude. Thus, an attitude held by person *A* towards person *B* involves person *A*'s thoughts and beliefs about person *B*, his or her feelings about person *B* (which may be related to but separate from the thoughts and beliefs), and how person *A* is likely to act toward person *B*.

Attitude formation refers to the process whereby there is an emergence of a set of beliefs, feelings and tendencies to act toward some object. *Attitude change,* on the other hand, means alteration or modification in a set of beliefs, feelings and tendencies to act toward some object. Both topics are critical issues in the field of social psychology and are discussed, in some form, in all of the perspectives. The emphases, however, vary from one perspective to another. In symbolic interactionism, behavioral social psychology and the social exchange approach, relatively little attention is devoted specifically to attitude formation and attitude change. Nevertheless, one does find within these perspectives emphases on topics related to the phenomenon, such as attitude maintenance, pressure to change, cognitive prejudice, etc. Additionally, attitude formation and attitude change may be such integral features of a given perspective itself until little effort is made to study the phenomena as substantive areas for research. A case in point is the symbolic interaction approach. An underlying assumption of this perspective is that attitude formation and attitude changes are vital features of all individual action since human action is dependent, in part, on the individual's interpretative mechanism. The interpretative mechanism can be found in all individuals as they build up courses of action which involve making judgments, suspending judgments, checking and rechecking information, forming attitudes and changing attitudes.

Attitude formation and attitude change are also important concerns (for vastly different reasons) in both behavioral social psychology and the social exchange perspectives. Yet the concerns discussed in the perspectives are not directed specifically to attitude formation and attitude change. Attitude formation and attitude change *are* discussed more specifically in the gestalt orientation and the field approach. In fact, theoretical formulations and research efforts related to attitude formation and attitude change make up a fairly great proportion of the work in the gestalt and field perspectives, as will be seen.

Group Formation

Group formation is the process whereby two or more persons began to engage in social interaction in order to act in concert. The process, as described by various textbooks in social psychology, seems to differ from one perspective to another. Yet, there are few contradictions and the various conceptions of group formation appear to be complementary. It may be the case that the complementary nature of different conceptions of group formation will serve, in the future, as a point of departure for integration and synthesis of several perspectives. For example, symbolic interactionists discuss group formation from a point of view in which persons come together to coordinate and join lines of action. Little attention is paid to the inducements which often are vital aspects of group formation. While they are not main considerations in symbolic interactionism, they are indispensable considerations in behavioral social psychology and social exchange perspectives. Moreover, gestalt and field orientations also deal with certain aspects of group formation like attraction, preference for balanced states, group processes, group structures and group products.

Social Influence

Social influence is a central problem in social psychology. The term refers to the process which goes on when there is a modification in the cognition, affectivity and/or behavior of an individual as a result of the action of another or others. In other words, when the actions of others alter, in any way, the thoughts, feelings or actions of an individual, social influence is in operation. Defined in this way, social influence can be viewed as a vital process in nearly every aspect of social psychology. For example, social influence plays a crucial role in socialization, conformity, group formation, attitude change, social perception, interpersonal attraction, social power, communication, leadership and numerous other units of analysis in social psychology. Secord and Backman have pointed out that most topics in social psychology are dependent upon our understanding social influence processes and vice versa. This rather interesting relationship between social influence and social psychology can be understood easily in view of the concerns of one type of social psychology specified earlier; that is, the study of the individual in relationship to his or her environment.

As noted above, social influence seems to be regarded by many social psychologists as a core feature of social psychology. Because of the pervasiveness of social influence, one might be inclined to feel that most, if not all, of the major perspectives in the field would be concerned with the topic. To a certain extent this is true. It is possible to discern elements of social influence in all the perspectives discussed in this book. However, it has not been a central focus in behaviorism, although it is assumed to be in operation in the perspective. This point should become apparent in later discussions of behavioral social psychology.

Social Aggression

Social aggression may be generally defined as behavioral acts which are meant to harm or injure others, physically, mentally, emotionally or otherwise. Such acts may range from verbal and nonverbal gestures to physical violence. In modern society, aggression has become a topic of great concern, for rather obvious reasons. There is hardly a geographical area in the United States that is untouched by increased instances of violence and crime (specific forms of aggression) against persons and/or property.

Social psychologists have been interested in the topic of aggression for many years. Much of the social psychological research has been devoted to (1) the link between frustration and aggression; (2) aggressive models and other aggressive cues; and (3) interpersonal relations and participation in violence. Early research on aggression supported the idea that frustration is related causally to aggression. Later studies, however, have suggested that the relationship between the two variables is more complex; and, in addition that frustration does not always lead to aggression. A great deal of research has also been devoted to studying learned aggressive behavior by observation of aggressive individuals. Some findings have supported the contention that much aggression directed toward persons has been learned from observation of others. However, the evidence is inconclusive on this point. In recent years, research on aggression has taken a different direction. Researchers have begun to study interpersonal violence and participation in mass aggression phenomena such as riots and mobs. Some of their findings are considered later in the book.

Social aggression as a topic of study has been treated most often in behavioral social psychology and social exchange perspectives, as this book reflects. However, other perspectives such as field theory, symbolic interactionism and the gestalt orientations also are feasible perspectives to be used in investigations of aggression. An attempt is made to show some of the directions which research studies of this kind can take and to discuss aggression as a topic of concern in the various social psychological perspectives.

ISSUES IN SOCIAL PSYCHOLOGY

Stryker and House published their reflections on the field of social psychology in *Sociometry* vol. 40, no. 2 (1977). Earlier the same year an exchange between several social psychologists regarding the state of the discipline appeared in *The American Sociologist* vol. 12 (February 1977). A brief summary of the exchange is given below.

Allen Liska suggests at the outset of his article entitled "The Dissipation of Sociological Social Psychology" that, in his opinion, social psychology is becoming psychologized—shifting from a multidisciplinary endeavor to a psychological one (p. 2). Agreeing that there is no dearth of sociological social psychological research, Liska nevertheless feels that it is spread out over a wide variety of subfields within sociology. This possibly accounts for his contention (though he does not say so) that much research which could be classified "social psychological'' is not. Several other indicators of the dissipation of the discipline are discussed. They include: (1) the absence of cross-citations in social psychological works by scholars in different subfields; (2) the lack of reciprocal influence between social psychologists in sociology and those in psychology; (3) a paucity of sociological social psychology textbooks; and (4) the failure of sociological social psychologists to develop a general social psychological framework. With respect to the latter, Liska calls for the development of a general sociological social psychological framework (including both theory and methods) which he feels would be organizing and revitalizing for the discipline.

Both W. Peter Archibald and John P. Hewitt in their articles echo Liska's concerns about the state of social psychology. Archibald, in addition, suggests that sociological social psychology may not *need* general frameworks because the theories already may be too general if social exchange, functionalism and symbolic interactionism are the dominant ones in the field. Questioning the usefulness of these ''general theories'' because of their highly abstract conceptions of ''human nature,'' ''society,'' and the like (p. 10), Archibald asserts that perhaps some of the best social psychological theories have been ignored. A succinct statement of his proposed solution to the dissipation of social psychology is that marxist theory is a viable alternative.

John Hewitt, too, agrees that social psychology is ''withering away.'' An explanation for this unfortunate process lies with the sociological social psychologists. Many (including sociologists in other subfields) have ''a mostly erroneous conception of social structure and its relationship to social process'' (p. 14). According to Hewitt, because of the reification of social structure (i.e., treating the structures as though they are real) by many sociologists (in spite of the fact that social structure is a result of perspective), the appropriate subject-matter of social psychology is often missed. This subject matter is ''the analysis of conduct formation'' which is facilitated by a concentration on symbolic interactionism—the general theory which can enhance processual and structural analyses.

In contrast to the arguments proposed by Liska, Archibald and Hewitt, Robert L. Burgess and Richard J. Hill take different stances regarding present-day social psychology. Taking issue with Liska's division of social psychology into sociological and psychological camps, and implying that his concern about the dissipation of social psychology may reflect lack of academic self-confidence, Burgess dismisses most of what he perceives as Liska's argument. A key point made by Burgess is that social psychology may be being dissipated by infiltrating itself into various subfields in sociology and psychology (pp. 13–14). Burgess sees this as a measure of the success of social psychology.

Hill, in his response to Liska, implies that the diffusion of social psychological concepts is sufficient evidence that the discipline is pragmatic and characterized by vitality. Citing "social exchange" and "expectation states" as social psychological theories of wide applicability, Hill admits that social psychology lacks a general theoretical framework but feels that other theories in the discipline are alive and well. Questioning Liska's methodology concerning cross-citations, Hill notes that simply counting citations provides a "questionable bias for inferring disciplinary dominance" (p. 18). Hill suggests that if sociologists are concerned with psychological dominance in social psychology, they should make their concerns known through increased support for social psychology programs at the national level. He says, "If we are number two, we simply must try harder." A final observation by Hill is that instead of social psychology being multidisciplinary, it is interdisciplinary. Furthermore, Hill's view is that social psychologists are either sociologized or psychologized, *not* interdisciplinary, and therefore form a distinct discipline.

Liska's "Reply to My Critics" (pp. 19–22) responds to all four scholars, paying special attention to the comments of Burgess and Hill and concluding that low representation in the *Handbook of Social Psychology,* the paucity of sociological social psychology textbooks, the citation bias toward psychological social psychology, and other indicators, together "demonstrate an alarming pattern which should not be casually dismissed" (p. 22).

Dorwin Cartwright, in "Contemporary Social Psychology in Historical Perspective," using participant observation as his method, discusses the state of social psychology and raises vital issues related to the future of the discipline. At the outset of his article, Cartwright notes that social psychology is only about eighty years old. Concentrating on social psychology's development in the past four decades, he views the discipline as "a social system influenced by its properties such as funding agencies, editorial practices of journals and publishing houses, the nature of doctoral programs and the demographic composition of producers within the profession" (p. 82).

Cartwright suggests that the single most important influence on social psychology's development was World War II, and that the person having most impact on the discipline was Adolph Hitler (p. 84). While the first thirty or forty years of social psychology's existence were devoted to making it a legitimate field of scientific endeavor, the last forty years have been characterized by (1) significant research on substantive topics; (2) the response of social psychologists to governmental demands for solutions to the problems of a war-torn society; (3) postwar euphoria about the prospects of social psychology; (4) tremendous growth with the establishment of new research facilities and doctoral programs; and (5) extensive publication of social psychological research.

The rise of nazism in Germany, says Cartwright, also affected social psychology since it resulted in a large exodus of social psychologists, (among others) from Europe. This factor, and the associated political events, made social psychology almost a uniquely American phenomenon in its formative years (p. 85). The result of the Americanization of social psychology on its development can be seen, according to Cartwright, in an analysis of the topics researched and the basic assumptions underlying social psychology as it exists today.

In contrast to those who seemingly fear the demise of the discipline, Cartwright's view is that while the initial enthusiasm about social psychology has declined, progress in the discipline has not slowed. There *are* deficiencies in the field, however, which center around methodological technique worship; the paucity of longitudinal analyses; an emphasis upon cognitive representation rather than the transaction between a person and his or her environment; and the lack of a level of theoretical integration which could give a clear conception of the task for social psychology.

Cartwright concludes on a high note, remarking that current changes in the demographic composition of social psychologists, and the historical capacity of social psychologists to meet challenges within the discipline, portend a thriving future.

Current issues in social psychology center not only around the theoretical ones discussed in this section, but also on methodologies. In Chapter 2, some of these methodological issues are discussed.

SUMMARY

As stated previously, social psychology is the *scientific study of social interaction between individuals; individual processes in social stimulus situations; and, the social structure in relation to the individual.* While this definition specifies the subject matter of the discipline, it does not restrict the variety of approaches used to study and understand social psychological phenomena. In line with the brief statements made earlier characterizing the uniqueness of each perspective presented in this volume, methodological and theoretical differences are also treated as distinguishing features of several perspectives discussed. Comprehending these differences should be facilitated by the theory and methodology discussions which follow. Let us turn to some "Theoretical and Methodological Issues in Social Psychology."

BIBLIOGRAPHY

Archibald, W. Peter "Misplaced Concreteness or Misplaced Abstractness? Some Reflections on the State of Sociological Social Psychology," *The American Sociologist* 12, no. 1 (1977), pp. 8–12.

Allport, Gordon W. "The Historical Background of Modern Social Psychology," in G. Lindzey and E. Aronson, eds. *The Handbook of Social Psychology,* 2nd ed. Reading, Ma.: Addison-Wesley, 1968, pp. 1–80.

Bijou, Sidney W. and Donald M. Baer. *Child Development: A Systematic and Empirical Theory.* New York: Appleton-Century-Crofts, 1961.

Blau, Peter M. *Exchange and Power in Social Life.* New York: Wiley, 1964.

Borgatta, Edgar F. *Social Psychology: Readings and Perspectives.* Chicago: Rand McNally, 1969.

Burgess, Robert L. "The Withering Away of Social Psychology," *American Sociologist* 12, no. 1 (1977), pp. 12–14.

Burgess, Robert L. and Don Bushell Jr. *Behavioral Sociology.* New York: Columbia University Press, 1969.

Cartwright, Dorwin, ed. *Field Theory in Social Science: Selected Theoretical Papers by Kurt Lewin.* New York: Harper & Row, 1951

——. "Contemporary Social Psychology in Historical Perspective," *Social Psychology Quarterly* 42, no. 1 (1979), pp. 82–93.

Cooley, Charles H. *Human Nature and the Social Order.* New York: Scribner's Sons, 1902.

Deutsch, Marton and Robert M. Krauss. *Theories in Social Psychology.* New York: Basic Books, 1965.

Elms, Allan C. "The Crisis of Confidence in Social Psychology," *American Psychologist* (October 1975), pp. 967–975.

Exline, R. V. "Explorations in the Process of Person Perception: Visual Interaction in Relation to Competition, Sex and Need for Affiliation," *Journal of Personality* 31, (1963), pp. 1–20.

Faris, Robert E. L. *Social Psychology.* New York: The Ronald Press, 1952.

Hastorf, A. H., W. R. Kite, A. E. Gross and L. J. Wolfe, "The Perception and Evaluation of Behavior Change," *Sociometry* 28 (1965), pp. 400–410.

Hewitt, John P. "Comment: The Dissipation of Social Psychology," *American Sociologist* 12, no. 1 (1977), pp. 14–18.

Hill, Richard J. "Reply to Professor Liska," *American Sociologist* 12, no. 1 (1977), pp. 17–19.

House, James S. "The Three Faces of Social Psychology," *Sociometry* 40, no. 1 (1977), pp. 161–177.

Kohler, Wolfgang. *Gestalt Psychology.* New York: Liveright, 1947.

Levinson, Daniel J., C. N. Darrow, E. B. Klein, M. H. Levinson and B. McKee. *The Seasons of a Man's Life.* New York: Ballantine Books, 1978.

Light, Donald Jr. and Suzanne Keller. *Sociology.* New York: Knopf, 1979.

Lindesmith, Alfred R., Anselm L. Strauss and Norman Denzin. *Social Psychology,* 4th ed. New York: The Dryden Press, 1975.

———. *Social Psychology,* 5th ed. New York: Holt, Rinehart and Winston, 1977.

Liska, Allen E. "The Dissipation of Sociological Social Psychology" *The American Sociologist* 12, no. 1 (1977), p. 207.

———. "Dissipation of Sociological Social Psychology: A Reply to My Critics," *American Sociologist* 12, no. 1 (1977), pp. 19–21.

McDougall, William. *An Introduction to Social Psychology.* London: Methuen, 1908.

Nachshon, I. and S. Wapner. "Effect of Eye Contact and Physiognomy on Perceived Location of the Other Person," *Journal of Personality and Social Psychology* 7 (1967), pp. 82–89.

Ross, E. A. *Social Psychology: An Outline and Source Book.* New York: Macmillan, 1908.

Schellenberg, James A. *An Introduction to Social Psychology,* 2nd ed. New York: Random House, 1974.

Secord, Paul F. and Carl W. Backman. *Social Psychology,* 2nd ed. New York: McGraw-Hill, 1973.

Shaw, Marvin E. and Philip R. Costanzo. *Theories of Social Psychology.* New York: McGraw-Hill, 1970.

Slawski, Carl J. *Social Psychological Theories: A Comparative Handbook for Students.* Glenview, Ill.: Scott Foresman, 1981.

Staats, Arthur W. and Carolyn K. Staats. *Complex Human Behavior: A Systematic Extension of Learning.* New York: Holt, Rinehart and Winston, 1963.

Stone, Gregory P. and Harvey A. Farberman. *Social Psychology Through Symbolic Interaction.* Waltham, Ma.: Ginn-Blaisdell, 1970.

Stryker, Sheldon. "Developments in 'Two Social Psychologies': Toward an Appreciation of Mutual Relevance," *Sociometry* 40, no. 2 (1977), pp. 145–160.

Thibaut, J. W. and H. H. Kelly. *The Social Psychology of Groups.* New York: John Wiley, 1959.

Vander Zanden, James W. *Social Psychology.* New York: Random House, 1977.

West, Stephen G. and Robert A. Wicklund. *A Primer of Social Psychological Theories.* Monterey, Ca.: Brooks/Cole, 1980.

THEORETICAL
AND
METHODOLOGICAL
ISSUES
IN
SOCIAL
PSYCHOLOGY

2

This chapter is devoted to current theory and methodology in social psychology. Some of the elements of a theory, strategies in theory building, issues in theory, methodological strategies, and methodological issues are discussed. The rationale for including these topics in a volume of this kind is quite simple—it should facilitate better comprehension of the perspectives in the book as well as the total field of social psychology.

Some knowledge of the roles of theory and methodology in social psychology is indispensable to a full understanding of each of the perspectives explored. In addition, unless one begins to see the relationship between assumptions, derivations, concepts, methodological techniques, and so forth, it is quite possible that studying social psychology will be nothing more than an exercise in memorization. On the other hand, if the introductory materials in this chapter are grasped, then one can begin to question assumptions, derivations, and concepts—compare them, contrast them and perhaps, even synthesize them. It is my feeling that when these activities start, the learning process truly is under way. In addition, this chapter should help the reader to place in proper perspective other social psychological literature encountered. There are countless articles and books on the subject, and unless portions of this material can be organized in a systematic fashion, it could very well *remain*, to the student, a hodgepodge of seemingly unrelated methodological techniques, ideas, and findings. This chapter should facilitate systematization of these materials by the student somewhat new to the field of social psychology.

Every field of systematic study has a framework of "theory." In social psychology, as in other fields, theoretical schemes indicate observation, inferences from data and the utilization of conclusions to guide research; in essence, theories are rules. Theories in social psychology, however, are not a *particular set of rules* because there are numerous kinds of formulations including narrative, interpretative, postulational and axiomatic ones. Furthermore, theories in social psychology range in scope from the mini to the grandiose. Interestingly, it is the scope of theories in social psychology that has become important to many scholars in the field, some of whom lament the lack of a unified theoretical framework in the discipline, especially in what has been called sociological social psychology. Missing from our discipline, these scholars state, is a framework under which most, if not all, theories of social psychological import can be encompassed. Supposedly this could be done regardless of topical concerns, subfield orientations or methodological techniques proposed for evaluating theories.

Certainly there is much merit to the argument for systematized and unified social psychology. This kind of social psychology does not exist presently, nor is it likely to in the immediate future, but we *do* have bodies of knowledge which meet the criteria for theory to varying degrees of adequacy. These bodies of knowledge have the elements of theory, use acceptable theorizing strategies and are used by social psychologists in ways that theories ordinarily are used. Let us begin to examine how these bodies of knowledge are used in social psychology by discussing the relationship between theory, explanation, prediction and control.

THEORY, EXPLANATION, PREDICTION AND CONTROL IN SOCIAL PSYCHOLOGY

Theories in social psychology are *bodies of related concepts and propositions about social interaction between individuals; individual processes in social stimulus situations; and, the social structure in relation to the individual.* A particular theory in present-day social psychology can be devoted to any one or some combination of the above aspects of the discipline. Moreover, social psychological theory defined in this way covers most social psychology being done by modern-day social psychologists. The major emphasis is on an *explanation* of phenomena thought to be the subject matter of social psychology.

Explanation in social psychology can be referred to as the construction of a pattern of meanings which establishes certain conclusions as more probable than their negation (Kaplan). Put another way, explanation provides *understanding* by describing relationships between causes and effects. An example of explanation can be seen in Festinger's discussion of the causes and consequences of cognitive dissonance. Briefly (a fuller discussion is presented later), Festinger contends that when the individual experiences conflicting cognitions (thoughts, ideas and the like) about an important issue, object or phenomenon, he or she then feels some psychological discomfort (dissonance). Such a psychological state might characterize an extremely patriotic citizen of the United States who regularly drives a car which consumes large amounts of gasoline, yet who feels that it is the duty of every citizen to conserve gasoline. As a result of this uncomfortable feeling, internal mechanisms operate to reduce the discomfort. Presumably these mechanisms activate certain dissonance reduction mechanisms, such as changes in attitude, changes in behavior, and/or the addition of new cognitive elements. This could mean, among other things, a change in degree of the citizen's patriotism, changes in his or her driving habits, or the pursuit of knowledge about supplies of gasoline in the United States, with the conclusion that they are adequate.

Festinger's formulation generated a great deal of research and, in addition, provided adequate descriptions of the causes and consequences of cognitive dissonance. From an explanatory point of view, cognitive dissonance theory has fared well. Major criticisms directed toward the theory generally have been about its ability to predict. Let us turn our attention to *prediction* in social psychology.

Prediction may be defined as *the provision of systematic connections between variables so as to make possible derivations of some relationships from others.* It involves the establishment of law-like statements which may or may not specify factors in a given situation (Phillips, p. 54).

With respect to our example, cognitive dissonance theory, it has been pointed out that one cannot predict with high accuracy *when* dissonance will occur, nor can it be predicted with accuracy *which* of the dissonance reduction mechanisms will be used if dissonance occurs. In short, while it may be possible to *explain* the causes and consequences of dissonance, highly accurate *predictions* of the phenomenon are not insured.

Dissonance theory is not alone in the category of social psychological theories with little predictive power. In social psychology and in the social sciences in general, predictive power is based on contingencies, many of which are either unknown or uncontrollable (Chafetz, p. 20). Gergen (p. 310) makes this point and in the process questions the scientific label attached to social psychology. While predictions in social psychology can be made on the basis of a specific theory, their accuracy hinges on contingencies which may or may not be a part of the theory. In social psychology our predictions always are of the variety that "under certain conditions," X will lead to Y.

Unfortunately, in most instances, we do not know the "conditions." Moreover, "main effects" of complex and simple interactions between factors in laboratory experiments often render our most dependable generalizations undependable. This occurs because the factors may not be operating beyond the laboratory and thus the findings obtained from laboratory experiments may generalize only to other laboratory-like situations.

Of course, a common response when social psychological theories are thought to be empirically inadequate is that human behavior is indeterminant and therefore the facts of social psychology are largely nonrepeatable. This means that the undependability of laboratory findings may be due as much to the *nature* of human behavior variables as it is to laboratory threats to external validity. Elm's observations (p. 972) are provocative in this regard. He feels that there is a need for new and better theories which could give guidance in a field that up to the time of his article had been largely empirical. All of this leads us to a third concept often associated with theory—*control.*

In social psychology, if the theorist-researcher can control or account for all factors affecting the phenomenon in question, then predicting change is possible. It is precisely because social psychologists have generally lacked control over factors in experimental and nonexperimental studies, or else have failed to account for factors later found to be operating in research endeavors (Campbell, 1969; Gergen, 1973), that many now are beginning to advocate abandoning efforts to control. Control refers to *the manipulation of factors in order to produce meaningful consequences.* Elms argues (p. 969) that social psychologists must understand the difficulties and demands of social psychological research and realize that much effort and creativity are necessary aspects of social psychological theory and research. This means that theoretical pluralism and methodological pluralism may be appropriate for the subject matter of social psychology. Strict adherence to some *positivistic* models in social psychology would mean increasing *control* capabilities which at present is beyond the grasp of social psychologists; and which some feel is inappropriate for our subject matter. Moreover, social psychologists of theoretical and methodological "control persuasion" must come face-to-face with moral and ethical decisions related to the "rightness" or "wrongness" of social intervention. Now this does not mean that social psychologists should *not* strive to construct theories which have "control" power; it *does* mean that they should be aware of the social responsibilities inherent in theory construction and research design. For example, while Sears, Maccoby and Levin's findings (1957) on the relationship between childrearing patterns and achievement levels are provocative and can be constructed in a lawlike manner, caution must be exercised in attempting to control achievement levels in children *literally*. More specifically, serious ethical questions remain to be answered before a conclusion can be reached that social psychologists should advocate that parents use love-withdrawal as a punishment technique in order to induce high levels of achievement in children. These questions must be answered in spite of the fact that empirical regularities have been observed which tend to substantiate the implied relationship between childrearing patterns characterized by love-withdrawal and achievement levels. A case in point was the admission by a famous pediatrician made relatively recently that his earlier suggestions for childrearing (which tended toward extreme liberalism in childrearing practices) might have been in error and that he felt partly responsible for undermining parental authority and thus, contributing negatively to the socialization process in America. While an admission of this type is admirable, it can hardly be thought of as a restitution for the misleading advice and perhaps irrevocable influence exerted over thousands of children and their parents. Thus, while control may be a goal toward which some theorists and researchers strive, consideration must be given to the nature of the variable(s) to be controlled and to the possible ramifications of control procedures. While control in the context of theoretical formulation does not necessarily mean promoting certain views, the consequences can be similar when manipulative research involves human subjects. Elms' statement regarding human subjects in research and ethical considerations (p. 974) is appropriate here. He states:

> Social psychologists are obligated to be attentive to ethical issues, especially because their research is largely directed toward other humans. But their attentiveness should be of the kind that allows them to work through an ethical issue, to arrive at a satisfactory resolution in their own eyes and as much as possible in the eyes of other informed observers, and then go ahead with ethically sound and meaningful research.

Obviously our discussion of prediction and control thus far has been directed toward those who feel that the two concepts are indispensable aspects of theory's functions. The breadth of social psychological theory dictates otherwise. In social psychology, there are explanatory formulations that do not emphasize prediction and control. Moreover, basic assumptions underlying many social psychological theories deny the possibility of prediction and control in social psychology. Now if these kinds of formulations can be referred to as *theory*, then what is the feature of commonality which allows them to be placed in the same category with more precise and formal theories? The feature of commonality is *explanation* manifested by the *structure* of the formulation. This structure is our next concern.

THE STRUCTURE OF SOCIAL PSYCHOLOGICAL THEORY

Theory in social psychology has been defined as bodies of related concepts and propositions about social interaction between individuals; individual processes in social stimulus situations; and, the reciprocal relationship between the individual and the social structure. There is nothing implicit or explicit in the definition that limits the flexibility that social psychologists have enjoyed in constructing and presenting their theories. Social psychological theories can be and have been postulational, axiomatic, and narrative among other forms. There does seem to be *one* requirement in social psychology for a formulation to be called a theory and that is the presence of certain theoretical elements. Schrag explicated certain elements of a theory over a decade ago, and with minor modifications they are still applicable. The elements are: (1) postulates, (2) theorems, (3) nominal definitions, (4) operational definitions, and (5) imagery. Chafetz (1978, pp. 48–51) in a more recent discussion of theory in the social sciences seems to combine imagery with concepts. She also feels that operational definitions are important primarily to the research endeavors rather than in theory construction. Hoover (1980, pp. 73–76), on the other hand, feels that there are few axioms (postulates) in the social sciences and conceives of theory in the social sciences as ''a guide to inquiry—a way of organizing and economizing insight so as to avoid the trivial and isolate the significant.'' Obviously this definition emphasizes the uses of theory rather than its distinguishing features. But, an additional emphasis also seems to be present, and that is flexibility in terms of the forms theories in social psychology might take. Based on these and other current discussions of theory, and what seems to be the current drift in social psychology toward greater flexibility with respect to what is appropriately labelled theory, the following features are suggested as necessary elements of any formulation which is to be labelled a theory in social psychology: *basic assumptions, nominal concepts, propositions, imagery* and *operational definitions*. As stated earlier, theories in social psychology range from formal ones such as those constucted by George Homans, Peter Blau and Richard Emerson, to rather informal ones like those presented by Jack Douglas, Erving Goffman and Herbert Blumer. For this reason, the structure of many theories in the field may not be readily apparent. If labelled a theory, however, it should be possible to glean an understanding of certain elements from the formulation. A discussion of these follows.

Basic Assumptions

All theories in social psychology contain certain assumptions underlying the explanatory system which are untestable and accepted without proof. In some theories, these statements are made explicit by the theorist; in others, they are implicit. Chafetz (p. 34), believes that the theorist should be as explicit about these assumptions as possible. This appears to be the trend in social psychology, although many times the researcher proposing the theory is unaware of the basic assumptions underlying the formulation. Part of the reason for this may be due to the various kinds of basic assumptions that often characterize a social psychological theory. There are basic assumptions related to the scientific process; the general approach to the subject matter; and, the specific approach to the subject matter (Chafetz, pp. 34–91; Gouldner, p. 33). Chafetz argues that all scientists must make assumptions about (1) reality and how we come to know it; (2) observations and measurement of whatever it is under investigation; (3) order in the universe and our abilities to understand it; and (4) topical linkages between events. All of these assumptions are related to social psychological theorizing and therefore are made by social psychological theorists. Another set of assumptions, according to Chafetz, is related to the general approach of the discipline. These assumptions, in addition, require that the discipline consists of one or more paradigms defining *what should be studied, what questions should be asked* and *what rules should be used to interpret the response*. In actuality social psychological theorists may not have this latter set of assumptions if what Elms says is true (1975, p. 970)—that it is at a pre-paradigmatic stage. This means that social psychology does not have a general approach to its subject-matter which defines what should be investigated, the nature of the questions to be asked and the rules which should be followed in interpreting the answers obtained. Elms believes that because social psychologists never have approached unanimity in beliefs, values and techniques, the discipline has failed the test for a Kuhnian paradigm. Others, including House and Stryker do not seem to share this conviction. They feel that social psychology is a multiparadigm field. If this is so, then assumptions related to the particular paradigm used are made by the practicing theorist. According to Gouldner, echoed by Chafetz, assumptions "related to the specific subject matter" are called *domain assumptions.* For social psychology, because of the disagreement over the existence of paradigms, it is indeed possible that these assumptions and general scientific assumptions are the only ones made. In fact, if the discipline is pre-paradigmatic as Elms suggests, this is the only conclusion that can be reached. Yet regardless of whether or not there are two or three kinds of assumptions which are made in social psychological theories, there *are* basic theoretical underpinnings in formulations labelled "theories" in the discipline. These underpinnings often are accepted without proof and, as stated earlier, are not usually subjected to direct empirical test. They perform an important function in conjunction with basic concepts in a theory in that they enable the construction of testable propositions.

Nominal Concepts

Nominal concepts are symbols and/or abstractions which tell us little about the empirical world. Their definitions simply are statements of intentions to use words or phrases as substitute expressions for other words or phrases. For this reason, nominal concepts are never *incorrect* if used consistently within a theory. If, in constructing a theory, I decide to call attitudes "observable behaviors," I am perfectly justified in doing this as long as this phrase and its meaning are used consistently throughout the theory. Any criticism of the theory should be directed toward criteria other than the fact that *my* "attitude" is incorrect! It must be admitted, however, that communication within social psychology and any other discipline is facilitated when there is agreement on nominal concepts and their meanings. At least three properties seem to be important for nominal concepts and their definitions. These are (1) that the meaning of the substitute expression or word used for the original is dependent upon the original, (2) the concept or expression has an arbitrary meaning, and (3) the concept and its meaning have no truth claims.

Given what has been said thus far about nominal concepts, one might wonder about their functions in social psychological theory. They do have functions, very important ones, which were recognized some time ago (Bierstedt, pp. 121–130) and are as follows: (1) to speed up and clarify communication; (2) to introduce new words into a language, that is, new concepts into scientific terminology; (3) to indicate the salience of certain concepts in scientific thinking; and (4) to permit the substitution of new concepts for familiar ones that have emotional or nonlogical meanings. These functions can be seen easily with the concept of "attitude." According to Bem attitudes "are likes and dislikes—they are affinities for and aversions to situations, objects, persons, groups, or other identifiable aspects of our environment including abstract ideas and social policies." While this statement could be used in formal theorizing, it would be somewhat awkward and noncommunicative. As a result, the concept attitude is used as a substitute expression for the aforementioned statement and performs not only a communicative function but also substitutes for "dislikes," "likes," "aversion," and "affinities"—all rather emotional terms.

A final word about nominal concepts is that they provide the content for a particular theory and require definitions in developing and presenting a theory (Chafetz, p. 51). Yet, it must be remembered that they are symbols, abstractions, and in a sense, unreal, except for the purpose of the theory.

Propositions

Propositions consist of concepts and the linkages or relationships between them (Hoover, p. 38). At least two or more concepts varying in degree or value are related to each other. The relationships sometimes take an "if–then" form and are testable. For example, the statement, "If parents have been abused as children they are likely to abuse their own children" is a proposition, albeit a simple one. Two concepts and their values are a part of the proposition. "If parents have been abused as children" and "abuse their own children" are the concepts. "Whether they were abused as children or not" and "whether they abuse their own children or not" are the values the concepts can take. Other propositions may be characterized by their concepts varying on some attributes such as degree and are also testable. In relating the concepts "social interaction" and "attraction between members of a group,'' the statement that ''an increase in social interaction between members in a group leads to an increase in attraction between those members,'' is an example of a proposition containing concepts which each have different values that individuals or other units of analysis might take.

In social psychology, theories vary in form and this sometimes makes it difficult to decipher their propositions. Some theories contain explicitly stated assumptions, concepts and propositions, and others do not. If the formulation is a theory, though, the elements should be present in some discernible form. One fairly explicit form of deductive theorizing which gained popularity in general sociology in the 1950s and 60s and still remains a highly used one is axiomatic theorizing. Axiomatic theorizing involves the construction of concepts, basic assumptions, and logically deriving lower-order testable propositions.

Zetterberg has been the major proponent of axiomatic theorizing, and his work has resulted in numerous explanatory systems utilizing axiomatic theorizing. Here is an example of *deriving* theorems axiomatically, taken from his book *On Theory and Verification in Sociology* (pp. 97–99):

I. If national prosperity increases the middle classes expand.
II. If the middle classes expand, the consensus of values increases.
III. If social mobility increases, the consensus of values increases and vice versa.

The implications of these propositions can now be spelled out in the form of theorems. Postulates II and III combine into the familiar:

Theorem 1. If the middle classes expand, the social mobility increases.
Theorem 2. If national prosperity increases, the consensus of values increases.
Theorem 3. If national prosperity increases, the social mobility increases.

In 1964, ground rules for engaging in axiomatic theorizing in sociology were specifically explicated by Costner and Leik. Basically, they pointed out that the transitive rule in theorizing (as exemplified above where Zetterberg postulates that $A \rightarrow B$, $B \rightarrow C$; and therefore $A \rightarrow C$) could be used only when a certain set of conditions could be met. These conditions are: (1) postulates should be stated in asymmetric form; (2) deductions should be made only from postulates in which the common variable is prior to one or both of the other two variables included in the postulates; and (3) a closed system must be assumed, that is, there are no connections between the variables except those stated or implied in the postulates. With respect to the above examples this would mean, for instance, that: (1) Zetterberg's third postulate would have to be made unidirectional. Either an increase in the consensus of values leads to an increase in social mobility or vice versa, but not both; (2) Zetterberg's third theorem violates Costner and Leik's second rule because the common variable, "the social mobility increases," is not logically prior to the other two variables in the formulation; and (3) Zetterberg's system is closed since no other connections between the variables are stated or implied.

Theories which take the axiomatic form and other forms similar in explicitness are relatively easy to inspect for the essential elements of a theory. Others (less explicit in theoretical form) similar to the abbreviated one that follows are not so easy, as we will see. In defense of including this excerpt from Howard Becker's study of marijuana users and use (1963) as an example of theory, the analytic induction techniques used by Becker are as much a theory construction strategy as they are a methodological technique. This point is discussed later in this chapter. Obviously, a full account of Becker's theory cannot be gleaned from the brief statements below but it is possible to get an idea of the way inspection of "accounts" and other narrative theories contain elements required of theory such as concepts and propositions.

> No one becomes a user without (1) learning to smoke the drug in a way which will produce real effects; (2) learning to recognize the effects and connect them with drug use (learning, in other words, to get high); and (3) learning to enjoy the sensation he perceives. In the course of this process he develops a disposition or motivation to use marihuana which was not and could not have been present when he began use, for it evolves and depends on conceptions of the drug which could only grow out of the kind of actual experience detailed above. (Becker, 1963; p. 58)

Imagery

"Individuals actively attempt to maximize congruency between how they perceive themselves and how others perceive them." This is a well-known proposition in social psychology, and some version of it can be found in numerous theoretical formulations. While the proposition may be valid and may aid in explaining perception, much remains to be known about the reason *why factor* X *can affect perception*. It is necessary in social psychological theory construction *to provide a rationale which explains why a particular cause leads to a specified result*. In other words, it is necessary to provide *imagery*. For example, what is it about increased social interaction that leads to increased instances of social conflict and under what conditions is this likely to obtain? Some feel that answers to these kinds of questions undermine claims that formal theories in social psychology tend to be mechanistic and of little explanatory value. Seen from this perspective, imagery is a crucial factor determining whether or not a set of propositions is feasible. For example, from the biological sciences comes the proposition that sexual intercourse leads to pregnancy. However, the questions that must be asked in order to explain this relationship are, what is it about sexual intercourse that results in pregnancy and under what conditions? Explaining the process of conception whereby the sperm penetrates the ovum should be considered as part of the imagery explaining the relationship between sexual intercourse and pregnancy. *Such imagery is also necessary for social psychological theoretical formulations*.

Operational Definitions

Operational definitions specify the procedures to be employed in obtaining a specific indicator of the theoretical concept. The term ''obtaining'' is substituted for ''measuring'' because measuring implies that the concept has ''degrees.'' Obtaining is used because some theoretical concepts have ''kind,'' and obtaining seems to be a more appropriate term encompassing both degree and kind. Moreover, obtaining seems less value-laden with traditional science meanings of operationalization. Obtaining can include all of the methodological approaches presently used in social psychology, including those less definitive and more sensitizing ones endorsed by Herbert Blumer, Norman Denzin, John Hewitt and many other researchers, especially among that relatively new breed of sociologists concerned with ''sociologies of everyday life.''

Regardless of the social psychological theorist's own predilection for testing propositions, her or his work at some point must be subjected to scientific scrutiny if the uses to which the theories are put are to be met. This means that *theories* have to be tested. How the social psychologist tests theories is the next topic for consideration. The wide range of procedures used certainly cannot be discussed, but the contrast between testing what I call *explicitly structured* and *implicitly structured* theories can be shown.

FORMS AND STRATEGIES OF THEORY CONSTRUCTION IN SOCIAL PSYCHOLOGY

Like theories in the other social sciences, those in social psychology have been largely verbal. Until relatively recently, theories enjoying the greatest esteem in the discipline were patterned after the ones in the natural sciences. In the mid-1950s, Blumer (1954, 1956) called for different forms of social theories and methodological approaches which he felt were more appropriate for the subject matter of social psychology and sociology in general than the natural science biased forms. It has taken over twenty-five years for increasing numbers of social psychologists (psychological ones as well) to recognize the legitimacy of *implicitly structured theory*. By implicitly structured theory, I mean *theory characterized by the presence of theoretical elements but little or no specification of them and loosely structured so as not to predetermine or reify the phenomenon theorized about*. In contrast, explicitly structured theory refers *to theoretical formulations characterized by the presence and specification of the elements of a theory presented in such a way that they are easily subjected to conventional empirical test*. When reading an implicitly structured theory in social psychology, one should not expect to find a set of stated postulates, stated nominal concepts, stated theorems and stated imagery. Generally the form of such a theory is quite open and in a sense, constructed as the reader goes along as in the example cited earlier. Important to remember is that while the elements of a theory are not explicitly pointed out, they are, nevertheless, present, and this is precisely why such formulations are labelled *theory*.

Explicitly structured theory, on the other hand, has a *specified form* indicating the *theoretical elements* which are easily discernible to most persons reading the theory. It has even been said that the phenomena theorized about are modified because of the explicitness of the structure of such theories. For example, a theorist who postulates a specific relationship between persons' attitudes toward abortion and their social class in a given community actually may *create* and reify the class structure of that community if she or he *assumes* the community is divided into upper, middle and lower classes or some variant. In the same vein, the relationship between social class and attitude toward abortion is then created by the theorist. The form of theory most often accused of this kind of reification is deduction, although I suspect that induction and retroduction are equally guilty because preconceived assumptions and hypotheses often creep into the formulations. Three explicitly structured forms of theorizing are presented: induction, deduction, and retroduction. Following this discussion several forms of implicitly structured theories are discussed.

Explicitly Structured Theories

Induction   Induction is a form of theorizing which involves examining lawful relations between events (based on the Aristotelian notion of connecting lawfulness with frequency of occurrence), constructing concepts, and attempting to develop generalizations which explain the empirical regularities. Induction means the construction of theory "through the accumulation and summation of a variety of inquiries" (Hoover, p. 74). It involves a strategy of theorizing whereby one moves from the specific to the general. The "general" is supposed to explain the "specific." For instance, if it is systematically observed that whenever there is a crisis between the United States and a foreign country friendships between natives of the two countries dissolve, a set of principles might be gradually and meticulously devised to explain the phenomenon. Concepts like patriotism, ethnocentricity, loyalty, reference group, and similarity may all be observed, defined and formed into propositions which explain the weakening ties.

Using such an explanation, however, may be faulty in that the theorist may be observing a phenomenon that goes on all the time even when there is no international crisis. If this indeed is the case, then many would say that inductive theorizing would result in biases stemming from several sources including (1) a lack of knowledge, (2) a particular value perspective, (3) the assumption that people know about the crisis and (4) that people have strong feelings about the conflict—all of which enhance the likelihood of arriving at an inductively constructed theory which may *not* be an accurate explanation of dissolving friendships. These are the kinds of preconceived assumptions and hypotheses that often are unknowingly a part of inductive theories.

Despite the position that inductive theorizing can include biases which affect the validity of explanations, it has many merits. The theorist who *induces* maintains a close relationship with the real world, observes empirical regularities, and based on these constructs an explanatory scheme. She or he cannot be accused of being an "ivory tower" theorist because the form of theorizing used means that what is observed, in great part, determines the content of the concepts and generalizations constructed. The content of concepts relates directly to another problem common in other theory and research forms but minimized in induction. The problem is operationalization and the question of validity and reliability of measures of concepts. The inductionist is much less worried about being able to *find* the theoretical concept in the real world (rules of correspondence between nominal concepts and operational definitions) because the theoretical concept is based on features of the empirical regularities observed.

For example, let us consider the concept child abuse. A theorist who observes instances of child abuse, ranging from acts of commission to acts of omission is in an excellent position to develop a nominal definition of child abuse. In fact, the definition of child abuse so arrived at might even include failure to instruct the child in society's moral code. The obvious advantage that the inductive theorists have over many others is that they can mold their definitions to fit the observations. In fact, nominal definitions constructed by inductive theorists should be limited only by the breadth of the observations. Generalizations in the form of propositions should follow a similar pattern of development for inductive theorists.

As attractive as induction might seem as a form of theorizing, it is not without its critics. Schrag argues that induction is basically a mechanical operation, the context of which consisted largely of descriptive facts and generalizations combined in some systematic fashion. Moreover, because the inductionist's primary goal is to provide general principles which will explain the specific events observed, premature closure and/or the inability to move beyond data-based relationships is a possibility that is ever present, and the potential for serendipity (unintended findings) is minimal. This leads us to a final point made by Hoover (p. 74): "The danger in accepting the simple view of science as induction is that the inquiries that form the theory's base may have been undertaken from a value perspective or a commitment to fundamental categories that prejudices the phenomenon—leading in due course to a theory that validates the original biases." If this occurs then the theory in all likelihood explains the phenomenon only partially and from a biased point of view.

Deduction Another form of explicitly structured theorizing which has been used extensively in social psychology is deduction. It involves going from the general to the specific. Deductive theorists form their theories firstly by developing abstract concepts and postulates from which they derive lower-order propositions which are subjected to empirical test. The elements of such a theory generally are quite pronounced, with the theorist explicitly stating concepts, postulates, propositions and sometimes operational definitions. In other words, the deductive theorist presents the structure of the theory in a clearly delineated manner leaving little to the imagination of the reader. Examples of such theoretical formulations in social psychology include cognitive dissonance theory, attribution theory, interpersonal attraction theory, and numerous other formulations.

The popularity of deductive theorizing in social psychology cannot be denied. This is so despite the increasing numbers of social psychologists who seem to have become disenchanted, for one reason or another, with natural science approaches to social phenomena (Gergen). Perusal of the major journals and textbooks in the discipline will reveal that deduction is alive and well in social psychology although quite a few social psychologists have expressed misgivings about this form of theorizing.

Retroduction   Retroduction is still another kind of explicitly structured theoretical strategy. It involves elements of deduction and induction. Schrag has referred to the strategy as a technique of *successive approximations whereby theoretical concepts and assumptions are brought into closer alignment with relevant evidence while simultaneously maintaining the logical consistency required of deductive systems.* The theorist moves constantly between theoretical concerns and empirical data. This strategy differs from induction in that the interplay between theory and data produces explanations not only for the data at hand but also proposes explanations which go beyond the data.

More specifically, retroduction begins with the theorist examining empirical data and inducing a theoretical formulation. During the process of induction, however, additional intervening and/or conditional variables are specified which enable one to go beyond the specific findings and suggest other propositions which should be tested. Both positive and negative features of induction and deduction are present in retroduction. The major advantage of this form of theorizing over the others discussed so far is the potential for developing the formulation beyond boundaries established by either the original data or the original theoretical propositions. Thus, more than the other two, this strategy stresses theory and research as "ongoing enterprises." Figure 2.1 provides a schematic illustration of the three forms of explicitly structured theorizing often used in social psychology.

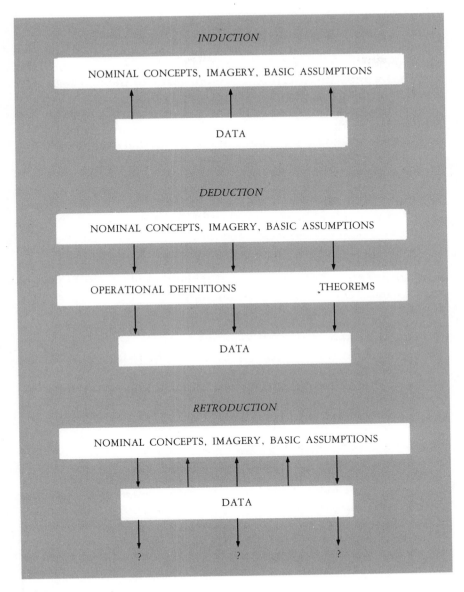

Figure 2.1
Three forms of explicitly structured theorizing in social
psychology

Implicitly Structured Theories

Increasing numbers of social psychologists and other social scientists who attempt explanations of social psychological phenomena are doing so through implicitly structured theories. Many of these scholars have experienced formal academic training which primarily emphasized explicitly structured theory construction and methodological techniques patterned after those in the natural sciences (laboratory experimentation, survey methods, statistical tests of association and significance, etc.). Their acceptance and utilization of the forms of theorizing to be discussed in this section often seem to be as surprising to them as it is to those who remain undaunted by the move of many toward implicitly structured theorizing. Jack Douglas's reflections on his own "emergence" as an implicitly structured theorist in the early pages of his book *Investigative Social Research* is a case in point.

The fact that there has been movement toward implicitly structured theorizing by scholars who at one time felt the form to be the least unconventional does not mean that their specific forms of theorizing are alike. There is diversity within implicitly structured theories just as there is within explicitly structured theories. While a disclaimer against the suggestion that *all* implicitly structured theories can be categorized as one of the following might be in order, many social psychological formulations seem to be one of the following: *expository theories, sensitizing theories* and / or *analytic induction theories*. An examination of the characteristics of each form should show why many implicitly structured social psychological theories fall into one of the categorical forms outlined below.

Expository Theory   Expository theory was the recommended form of theorizing for social psychology and general sociology by Herbert Blumer at the annual meeting in 1953 of the American Sociological Association. This form of theorizing *provides a meaningful, narrative account and illustrations of the phenomena in such a way that the reader is able to interpret the phenomena in terms of his or her own experience.* This means that the reader *participates in the construction of the theory* ("The activities by which theory is produced" [Freeman, p. 129]). The "participation" of the reader in expository theory construction is especially important to the presentation of such theories. Presentation is based upon perceived natural occurrences from experience and observation. When the reader participates in the construction of theory, this adds another dimension which often results in disagreement, conflict, alternative explanations, compromises and the like. Of course this is to be expected since each reader brings different experiences and observations to the situations. The very fact that this occurs epitomizes the dynamic nature of expository theorizing. George Mead's *Mind, Self and Society* is an excellent example of developing and promoting the refinement of aspects of symbolic interactionism (theories originally based on experience and observation) through "reader participation in theory construction." Scholars such as Herbert Blumer, Norman Denzin, John Hewitt and many others have "participated" in this construction.

Sensitizing Theory   Sensitizing theories, named after Blumer's (1954) "sensitizing concepts," are theories that form in direct relationship to "emergent" properties of the phenomena under investigation. In contrast to *expository theory*, sensitizing theory is presented in a form which does *not* call upon the reader to participate in theory construction. Sensitizing theories unfold naturally as the reader progresses through conceptualization and investigation of the phenomena examined by the theorist. In a sense, sensitizing theories are more *structured* than expository ones. Usually beginning with accounts of experience and observation, sensitizing theories develop along the lines pointed to by the investigative techniques and the resulting empirical content emerging from the investigative techniques. One characteristic of the form sensitizing theories takes stands out above all others and that is "process." Sensitizing theories of phenomena are processual even when the phenomena previously have been accorded *structural* properties (Adler and Adler, p. 43). *Boys in White* by Howard Becker et al., Jacqueline Wiseman's *Stations of the Lost*, Sam Wright's *Crowds and Riots* and Sherri Cavan's *Liquor License* are examples of sensitizing theories. Although this form of theorizing is most frequently associated with symbolic interactionism it is not the exclusive property of the perspective. Scholars in such areas as existential sociology, labelling theory and phenomenology have presented formulations taking a sensitizing form.

Analytic Induction Theory   Analytic induction is the *most structured* of the implicitly structured theories considered in this volume. The rationale for including it as a form of implicitly structured theories rather than as solely a methodological technique is that analytic induction "involves the creation of a universal theory intended to fit all cases" (Douglas, p. 38). The creation, however, is loosely structured, empirically based, and follows along naturalistic observation lines. In process, analytic induction is a theory construction strategy which takes a unique form as discussed below.

Florian Znaniecki has been credited with the development of the theoretical strategy in 1934. In 1953, Donald Cressey outlined the steps to be followed in analytic induction. They are:

1. Rough definition of phenomenon.
2. Hypothetical explanation of phenomenon.
3. One case studied in light of hypotheses to see if it is compatible with the hypothesis.
4. Reformulation of hypotheses if necessary *or* the phenomenon is redefined and excluded.
5. Practical certainty may be attained, but if anyone finds exceptions to the hypotheses, then reformulation must occur.
6. A continuation of reformulation until universal rules are established.
7. Cases outside examined to see if final hypotheses apply.

For many implicitly structured theorists, the form taken by analytic induction would seem to be too deterministic given steps 1, 2, and 6. These steps suggest "preconceived hypotheses" and "universal explanation," both of which violate the assumption held by many implicitly structured theorists that such features of theorizing are inappropriate when applied to social behavior. Distinct from many explicitly structured theories, though, are the features of hypothesis reformulation when cases are seen as incompatible with the hypothesis; and the lack of closure even when "universal explanations" seem to be established.

Succinctly, implicitly structured theorizing in social psychology has taken three predominant forms: expository, sensitizing and analytic induction. Such theories are more loosely constructed and the structure does not seem to be as apparent. In addition, *testing* of such theories involves very different procedures from those generally used in testing explicitly structured theories as we will see. In the following section, some issues surrounding the test of explicitly structured theories are presented followed by a discussion of testing implicitly structured theories.

TESTING SOCIAL PSYCHOLOGICAL THEORIES

Explicitly Structured Theories

Developing and Measuring Definitive Concepts   Before the social psychologist can test or construct explicitly structured theories meaning must be given to potential data or actual data. Giving meaning to data involves reducing information to be obtained or already obtained to manageable proportions by specifying how and why such information is to be used in a particular way. This means, in essence, that concepts developed in explicitly structured theories must be definitive and this calls for naming and classifying bits and pieces of information. This is a necessary step in testing explicitly structured theories. *"Definitive concepts refer to fixed and specific procedures designed to isolate stable and definitve empirical contents and are exemplified in the formation of operational definitions, experimental construction of concepts and quantitative indexes"* (Blumer, 1969, p. 145). Therefore, unless it is possible to "capture or isolate definable items in reality" (Hoover, p. 21), explicitly structured theories cannot be tested.

Isolating and grasping definable items are not easy processes in reality regardless of the methodological approach used (for example, survey methods, laboratory experimental methods, field experimental methods). The social psychologist testing explicitly structured theories must be concerned with the validity of concepts constructed, their properties and the levels of measurement used in the definition. Constructing the definitive concept "frustration," for example, may be done via the analysis of subject responses to a questionnaire or through the manipulation of a social situation in the laboratory. The question which remains following the analyses of responses and/or the experimentally induced frustration is, does the measure fulfill its intended purposes? Does it measure or experimentally induce what it intended to measure or experimentally induce? These often are complex questions in social psychology because many times only part of the concept is measured by the *instrument* (in this case, the responses and the experimental induction); and other times, the instrument includes items in addition to those meant by the concept. In experimentation, the latter problem can emerge during the experimental induction process when there is interaction between the induced variable and some other factor like the pretest. As Chafetz points out (p. 54), Guttman scaling and factor analysis are among the techniques used in social research to minimize and/or discover problems of concept validity. Various kinds of experimental designs constructed to minimize contamination of the induced variable could also be added to this list. They include the Solomon 4 group design, after-only experimental designs and numerous types of factorial experimental designs with controls.

Social psychologists also are faced with problems, sometimes unrecognized, regarding the *properties* of concepts to be developed. Whether the concept to be developed has *individual* or *collective* properties is important to the social psychologist in determining what constitutes a case, and reaching conclusions from the study. For example, if *individual opinion change* is a definitive concept in testing a theory in the laboratory, four six-person groups will yield *twenty-four cases*. If the definitive concept is *group opinion change*, four six-person groups will yield only *four* cases. Obviously a decision has to be made regarding the appropriate number of cases thought to be necessary in order to test the theory, and this can be a major problem unless the researcher has unlimited access to large numbers of potential subjects. Also related to individual and collective properties of definitive concepts is the "ecological fallacy" problem, which occurs when inferences are made about individuals from collective data. Equally important—if not more so—in social psychology is the fallacy of inferring group properties from individual data. For instance, if *group opinion change* is the concept to be operationalized and the measure used to assess group opinion change involves the administering of a questionnaire to "individuals" within groups, then the fallacy of inferring group properties from individual data may follow. The researcher, for instance, may attempt to obtain some "average" opinion change score from the "individual" opinion change scores. While this is permissible, conclusions drawn must be about the "average individual" opinion change rather than *group opinion change.* If not, then the researcher is likely to be accused of the fallacy of inferring group properties from individual data.

An analogous problem surrounding properties of cases emerges when experimental induction occurs. Suppose for example that a subject group is exposed to a strong "fear appeal" illustrated lecture about tooth decay, designed to encourage changes in oral hygiene practices. This occurred in the Janis and Feshbach study. If the induction process occurs in a group setting rather than an individual one, would a measure of the validity of the process produce an "individual" phenomenon or some representation of a "group" phenomenon? Is it possible that one of Janis and Feshbach's findings indicating "minimum behavior change" would have been altered significantly if subjects had been exposed *separately* to the strong fear appeal lectures? If so, then conclusions reached about the effects of strong fear appeal lectures on oral hygiene practices in the Janis and Feshbach study must be about *individuals in group settings exposed to strong fear appeals* rather than simply about *individuals exposed to strong fear appeals.* "Individuals in group settings" may imply that such subjects exposed to the treatment reach some *group decision* regarding the "believability" of the appeal *and* patterns of action which might be followed after the appeal. Thus, behaviors which follow such appeals may be those reached and "agreed upon" by the group rather than those individually constructed behaviors. This means, of course, that each individual constitutes a representation of *one* case rather than a *separate* case. This does not minimize the importance of the Janis and Feshbach findings but it does mean that caution must be exercised when interpreting findings. Based on the study, Secord and Backman (1964, p. 136) offer the dissonance interpretation that "strong fear appeal differs from the minimum fear appeal in that it is dissonant with a larger number of cognitive elements that the *subject* already believes." Given the process of inducing strong fear appeal in a collective situation used by Janis and Feshbach and the associated emergent variables, any interpretation would have to be related to individuals in *collective situations* rather than to individuals *alone*. A brief reason would be that some subjects may have been influenced during the lecture by verbal conversation, body movements of others, and the like.

A final issue to be discussed when developing definitive concepts is *level of measurement*. This is a concern of the social psychologist who uses either survey methods or experimental methods to test theories, because both approaches use statistical procedures in analyses. Statistical procedures are not discussed in this volume, but are related to the levels of measurement of definitive concepts. The levels of measurement of concepts in social psychology are discussed below.

NOMINAL LEVELS OF MEASUREMENT   The *nominal scale* is the most simple operation in social psychology (Blalock, p. 12). The aim in developing a nominal scale is to categorize or group elements according to a particular characteristic. For example, if one was interested in determining whether gender is related to attitude in a view of the women's liberation movement, first it would be necessary to group persons according to qualities of masculinity or femininity in a mutually exclusive manner. That is, if a person is assigned to the feminine category, that person cannot be assigned to the masculine category, and vice versa. In addition to mutual exclusiveness, nominal scales are also characterized by symmetry and transitivity. Blalock has made the following statement about the latter two characteristics:

> By symmetry we mean that a relation holding between A and B also holds between B and A. By transitivity we mean that if $A = B$, and $B = C$, then $A = C$ (p. 13).

If "masculine" means only being domineering, and being domineering means being aggressive, then persons defined as masculine should be found to be aggressive. No person found to be nonmasculine could be domineering or aggressive, and, no one masculine could *not* be domineering and aggressive.

Nominal scales include items on a questionnaire such as: What is your religious preference?

_____ Catholic
_____ Methodist
_____ Baptist
_____ Jewish
_____ Other _____

What gender would you assign yourself to?

_____ Masculine
_____ Feminine

ORDINAL LEVELS OF MEASUREMENT   Ordinal scales represent an ordering of categories according to certain characteristics. In addition to assigning objects to mutually exclusive specific categories, an order of the categories occurs (for example, lower, middle, upper) thus implying that some objects possess more or less of a given property than other objects, but not saying precisely how much more. An interesting side note related to this issue, which serves to illustrate the distinction between nominal and ordinal scales, is the women's liberation movement in the United States. Women have attempted to effect changes in the social order's measurement of the sex variable. More specifically, many women have protested against ordinally measuring sex, arguing that sex is and/or should be a nominal variable. These women maintain that males should not be ranked higher than females in the society's value system. On close analysis, one sees that the argument is not against the _exclusivity_ and _transitivity_ characteristics of ordinal scales, but against a third characteristic, which is _asymmetry_. An example of the asymmetrical nature of ordinal scales is easily seen in the ordinal statement that if person A is higher on social power than person B, then person B cannot be higher on social power than person A.

INTERVAL LEVELS OF MEASUREMENT   Interval scales not only imply that some observations have _more_ or _less_ of an underlying property, but also reflect the magnitude of the differences between the observations. In other words, an interval scale of social power allows the researcher to determine how many more units of social power person A has than person B and the differences between the intervals are equal. Moreover, unlike an ordinal scale, it is possible to compare the differences in social power between persons A and B. It can be said that if person A has twelve units of power and person *B* has three units of power that person *A* has nine more units of power than person *B*. But, it cannot be determined that person *A* has four times as much power as person *B* because interval scales are characterized by an arbitrary zero point.

RATIO LEVELS OF MEASUREMENT   Ratio scales have all of the characteristics of interval scales plus a non-arbitrary zero point value. Thus, not only can one compare distances between points on a scale, but it is also possible to suggest that a particular point on a scale represents two or three times more or less of a property than another point. If, for example, there were a ratio measure for social power and two persons were being compared with respect to the variable, it would be possible to reach conclusions that would be more informative than those stated for the interval scale. Not only could one conclude that person *A* had nine more units of social power than person *B*, if person *A* had twelve units of social power while *B* had three units, but it would be possible to state that *A* had four times as much social power as *B*.

Assuming that concepts are adequately defined and measured, the theorist-researcher must now turn to proposition construction. This activity, too, is surrounded by issues and concerns. This brief discussion of levels of measurement has been undertaken because of their implications for statistical techniques frequently used in testing explicitly structured theories. Certain statistical techniques require data at a particular level of measurement. For example, in order to use the Pearsonian product-moment correlation technique or regression analysis, data should be at the interval level of measurement. If data are nominal or ordinal then statistical techniques appropriate to those levels of measurement should be used. If the statistical techniques employed are not appropriate for the levels of measurement of the data, then findings obtaining may be artifacts of the statistical procedures rather than indications of the patterns of the data.

Constructing Propositions   Testing explicitly structured theories in social psychology implies constructing propositions which can be tested. These propositions ordinarily take one of two forms: a correlational form or a causal form.

Correlational propositions are constructed in a way to determine whether or not an association exists between two or more phenomena (variables). While most conventional measures of association require specifying which variable is the independent variable and which one is the dependent variable, only if the propositions are *causal* is it important which variables assume the independent and dependent variable statuses. For example, if I suggest in a theory that there is a strong relationship between "order of birth in a family" and academic success as measured by grade point average among college students, I am *not* saying that birth order causes a certain kind of academic performance even though I might suspect this to be the case. I *am* saying something about a relationship between birth order and academic success without specifying the *nature* of that relationship. Such a proposition might take the following form: "The higher the order of birth in a family, the higher the grade point average." Theoretically, there is no specification of independent and dependent variables.

But, what if I construct the proposition that birth order influences academic success in some way? That is, that high order of birth in a family leads to high grade point averages in college. Or put another way, one's birth order in the family *causes* a certain kind of grade point average in college. The specification of which variables are independent and dependent has occurred. In this case, birth order is the independent variable (cause) and academic success is the dependent variable (result).

Elaborating variables in social psychology is a more difficult activity than simply linking two variables together. More often than not, an explanation of some phenomenon (high grade point average in college) involves more than an independent variable (birth order in the family). Usually, such an explanation involves several variables which may be "explanatory," "interpretive," and/or "conditional" (Hyman). Using birth order as an independent variable and high grade point averages in college as a dependent variable, "amount of parent-child interaction during early childhood" may be posited as an explanatory, interpretative or conditional variable. For instance, many first-born children during early childhood experience greater amounts of interaction with parents than later-born ones do, and those who have high grade point averages in college may also experience high amounts of interaction with parents during early childhood. If the three variables are linked together in an *explanatory* manner, then a high correlation might be hypothesized between birth order and amount of social interaction; and, between amount of social interaction and grade point average in college. However, no relationship is hypothesized between birth order and grade point average in college. Figure 2.2 illustrates this type of variable linkage.

A high correlation is hypothesized between birth order and parent-child interaction during childhood; also a high correlation is hypothesized between parent-child interaction and grade point average in college. However, it cannot be deduced in this example that birth order *causes* a certain kind of grade point average. Instead, parent-child interaction is positively related to birth order and positively related to grade

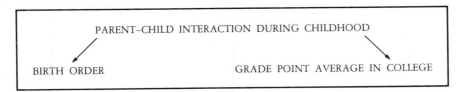

Figure 2.2
Hypothesized explanatory relationship between birth order,
parent-child interaction and grade point average in college

point average in college. The relationship existing between birth order and grade point average in college is hypothesized as spurious in this mode of elaboration.

An interpretive linkage between the three variables would take a different form and different assumptions would be made. Birth order *would* determine the amount of parent-child interaction which *would* in turn determine grade point average in college. This means that a causal relationship is hypothesized between an independent variable (birth order) and a dependent variable (grade point average in college) with an intervening variable (parent-child interaction) *interpreting* the relationship between the former two variables. Figure 2.3 shows this relationship.

A conditional elaboration of the variables would take still another form specifying the conditions under which birth order leads to certain grade point averages in college. A conditional mode of elaboration is illustrated in Figure 2.4.

This hypothesis basically states that under conditions of high parent-child interaction, birth order influences grade point average in college; however, no relationship is proffered between the two variables under conditions of moderate to low parent-child interaction.

These are not the only ways that variables are linked together in social psychology. The literature shows that propositions have been con-

Figure 2.3
Hypothesized interpretive relationship between birth order,
parent-child interaction and grade point average

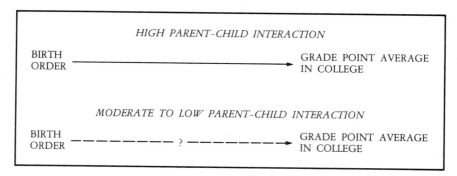

Figure 2.4
Hypothesized conditional relationship between birth order,
parent-child interaction and grade point average

structed in a variety of ways including those specified by Zetterberg in
his book *On Theory and Verification in Sociology.*[1] Regardless of the
specific forms of constructing propositions used, the end result generally is either proposed explanations regarding the *nature* of phenomena or *causes* of the phenomena. The former types of propositions are
correlative in type and the latter types are causally constructed.

Testing Propositions   Propositions in explicitly structured theories in
social psychology have been tested in a variety of ways and using many
different kinds of methodologies. In general though, social psychologists use two major methodological approaches to test theories containing specified propositions stated in falsifiable forms: experimentation
and survey research. *Experimentation* has been used because many
social psychologists, feeling that the establishment of causality is extremely complex, believe that experimental analysis offers the best procedure for controlling extraneous influences, manipulating independent variables and determining the effect of an isolated independent
variable on a dependent variable. All of the many different kinds of experimental and quasi-experimental designs used by social psychologists
are based at least in part on John Stuart Mills' *methods* (Cohen and
Nagel, p. 264). The methods are agreement, difference, concomitant
variation, and residues.

1. Zetterberg presents a listing of varieties of linkages between determinants and
results. The listing includes the following: reversible or irreversible, deterministic or
stochastic, sequential or coextensive, sufficient or contingent and necessary or substitutable. Zetterberg feels that any proposition could be characterized according to this
checklist of attributes (p. 72).

The *method of agreement* argues that when phenomena in evidence are different in all respects except one, that point of agreement is the cause of the phenomenon being evidenced. For example, if two persons who endorse the same political candidate have different political views on all political issues with the exception of views on abortion, then similarity of views on abortion may be seen as cause of their joint endorsement. Mills' *method of difference* suggested that if a phenomenon occurs and it is similar to those that do not occur in all respects except one, then that one respect is the cause of the occurrence.

The method of difference is exemplified in the case of conflict between two persons, their relationship being similar to all other relationships they have where conflict does not occur in all respects except perceptual incongruence, then perceptual incongruence may be seen as the cause of their conflictual social interaction.

The *method of concomitant variation* is rather straightforward in that it states that whenever one phenomenon occurs followed by another, then one is either a cause or an effect or the two are in some way connected through fact or causation. The latter means that they are either one and the same or that both are related to some factor which causes each of them to occur—a troublesome point which has bothered social and behavioral scientists for some time. An example would be if ice-cream consumption rates and crime rates covary in Northern, Midwestern and Eastern sections of the U.S. Both phenomena are related causally to warm weather conditions in the regions of the country but related only in a spurious manner to each other. Warm weather facilitates social interaction (which is directly related to increased crime rates) and changes in human physiological conditions (which are seemingly directly related to increased ice-cream consumption rates). Mills' *method of residues* provides the rationale for a control group in experiments where the experimental group receives "treatment" but the control group does not. If the control group and the experimental group are different in the post-test because of the fact that the experimental group receives "treatment" and the effects of the variation are accounted for, then if upon subtracting this variable, something still remains, this is due to extraneous factors called residues.

All of these methods are implicit in the classical experimental design and some are present in other types of experimental designs. The classical design calls for: (1) an experimental group and a control group, both of which are; (2) pretested with respect to some factor(s) to be observed (later to be called the dependent variable(s)); (3) an exposure of the experimental group to test stimuli (independent variable(s)) while withholding the test stimuli from the control group; and (4) a post-test measure of the observed factor(s) (dependent variables(s)) for the experimental and control groups in order to determine if the independent variable had an effect. The methods of agreement, difference, concomitant variation, and residues are a part of the above steps in the classical experimental process. Other experimental designs may *eliminate* the control group or the pretest, *add* several control groups some of which are not pretested or *vary* from the classical experimental designs in a variety of ways not mentioned here.

Numerous variations of the classical experimental design have been proposed to eliminate threats to both *internal validity* and *external validity*. Internal validity refers to the extent to which extraneous factors are controlled in an experiment and external validity refers to the extent to which experimental findings are generalizable to a larger population.

Regardless of the type or complexity of the design, numerous problems have been associated with experimentation related to the generalizability of results from the laboratory to other settings, the control of extraneous influences and ethical issues. Stryker in response to Gergen's contention that the indeterministic and nonrepetitive nature of behavior defeats generalization, suggests that the social psychological experiment "unroots" persons because they are removed from important social contexts (p. 155). When unrooted, persons experience few interpersonal costs; they are essentially isolated and their behaviors may be unstable. But, Stryker feels this does not imply that behavior, in general, is unstable but that we should be aware of the limitations of generalizing experimental findings often based on "unrooted persons."

Survey methods also are used frequently by social psychologists to test theories. The specific design most often used is the cross-sectional design. This has been referred to as the weakest for testing causal statements, as compared with panel designs and longitudinal designs, because people are studied only at one point in time and subgroups within a total sample are the units of comparison *or* relationships between variables as they are distributed within samples (Chafetz, p. 97). In panel designs, according to Chafetz, data are produced from the same people over time, and in the longitudinal design there is retesting over time although the people tested differ each time. One main problem with cross-sectional designs (a similar problem obtains for longitudinal designs) is that inferring causality is difficult. In order to do so, it is desirable to know the time order of variables since the only relationship that can be found is a correlative one, and because two variables are highly associated does not mean that they are causally related. As Cartwright points out, we may attain a good understanding of the nature of narrative behavior through correlational analysis but learn little about the conditions affecting the formation and decay of social

norms or the determinants of their contents. Panel designs and longitudinal designs are necessary for these kinds of analyses.

Testing propositions using cross-sectional survey methods involves
a number of steps briefly discussed in this section, including sampling
and data production. A lengthy discussion of both would be superfluous. Nevertheless several points about survey methods should be mentioned. First of all, as Chafetz (pp. 98–99) points out, the *definition of
a population* and *representativeness of the sample* are crucial issues in
survey methods. The definition of a population relates to the scope of
the theory and thus, to what population the findings can be generalized. In other words, the units of analysis (individuals or collectives) to
be explained by the findings constitute the population. All males are
not men's liberationists but those who are constitute the population to
be used in testing a theory related to the attitudes of men's liberationists toward sexism in the United States. The representativeness of
the sample is a second key issue according to Chafetz and involves the
question: *are all components of the population represented in the
sample.* For example, men's liberationists may be categorized as never-
married, married and divorced. The sample of men's liberationists must
avoid systematic bias which would result in under-representation or
over-representation of any one category of men's liberationists. There
are a number of types of representative random samples which can be
used to avoid systematic bias. One such sample is the simple random
sample which means that each element of the population has an equal
probability of being selected for the sample. Other varieties of random
sampling include proportional and disproportional stratified samples,
cluster samples and various combinations of these.

Aside from the biased findings which may result if samples are not
representative, many conventional statistical techniques used in data
analyses are based upon this assumption. Data production for explicitly
structured theories in social psychology chiefly has been obtained
through responses to questions put to people. Two major techniques
frequently have been used: the interview and the questionnaire.
Both rely heavily upon the subject's verbal report for information about
the stimuli to which she or he is or has been exposed.

There are crucial differences between the interview and the questionnaire, and while these differences will not be explored here extensively, it may be instructive to discuss some of them. The interview
technique may allow greater flexibility in data collection, since the interviewer (especially in less structured interviews) may deviate from
prearranged inquiries. For example, a subject might be asked to indicate his or her attitude toward women's liberation groups both on a
printed questionnaire and in a verbal interview. The information ob-

tained from the questionnaire will be definitely more limited, even if the subject is allowed to respond in an open-ended, noncategorical manner (for example, a narrative statement expressing his or her views and feelings). In contrast, if an interviewer asks the subject to express his or her attitude toward women's liberation, he or she has the opportunity to observe both the subject and the total situation to which the subject is responding (Selltiz, et al.). Furthermore, there is also the possibility of probing further into the interviewee's attitude toward women's liberation, and thus deriving other relevant information.

The gain, however, of having the interviewer present when a subject responds to questions may be lost due to lack of uniformity from one interview to another. Results may not be comparable. Moreover, anonymity is threatened in this situation. For some kinds of research topics, anonymity of interviewees may not be important, but for others it may be crucial.

In addition to the differences between the questionnaire and the interview mentioned thus far, others such as the expense of one or the other technique, the interpersonal skills required in conducting interviews, and the number of cases which can be obtained, make the decision to use interviews or questionnaires in a given piece of research an extremely important one. Unfortunately, a blueprint for action cannot be presented for each research situation, and the conditions surrounding a given research situation will vary. Nevertheless, perhaps the points raised in this discussion may be used as guidelines in helping the researcher to arrive at a viable decision about which technique to use.

Implicitly Structured Theories

Testing implicitly structured theories, such as those formulated by George H. Mead, Herbert Blumer, Georg Simmel, Max Weber, Emile Durkheim and others, historically has followed the traditional natural sciences approach. Social psychologists have had to pore through the expositions of these scholars and *abstract* what they felt were underlying assumptions and concepts, *derive* propositions and imagery, and *subject* the constructed formulation to "traditional" empirical test. Growing numbers of social psychologists believe that this approach has resulted in the widespread acceptance of socially constructed meanings as concrete reality (reification). This seems to mean that for these scholars (Herbert Blumer and Howard Becker among those at the forefront, followed by others such as Erving Goffman, Jack Douglas, John Hewitt, and Jacqueline Wiseman), the only real test of an implicitly structured theory means inducing through naturalistic observation a theory on the same topic—that is, a replication of a previous study devoid of preconceived hypotheses—even those found in previous naturalistic observations, although Douglas contends these are used (1980, p. 1). There is no difference between *testing* an implicitly structured theory and *constructing* one.

Perhaps it is important that no distinction can be made between testing and constructing the kind of theory of concern in this section. To distinguish between the two activities would add a kind of preconceived structure which is eschewed by the "emergent" theorist. However, constancies do seem to occur. Douglas refers to these constancies as themes which most of these studies seem to share (p. 83). "Emergence," "shared meanings," "definition of the situation" and "multiple realities," among others, seem to characterize the research efforts regardless of the approach. These themes are described in the next chapter and a question which emerges there is, does the method of study *create* process, *destroy* structure and *result* in a kind of reification of "multiple realities"? But the task here is not to criticize the "emergent" approach to theorizing but rather to discuss how it proceeds.

Since it is impossible to distinguish between testing and developing implicitly structured theories of the kind considered here, a general outline of techniques used by Blumer, Becker, Goffman and others of similar persuasions will be discussed. Three general phases seem to characterize their approaches. They are exploration, inspection and generalization.

Exploration   Exploration is the descriptive phase of implicitly structured theory construction. It is characterized chiefly by the development of sensitizing concepts—"concepts which give the user a general sense of reference and guidance in approaching empirical instances" (Blumer, p. 148). The social psychologist, during this phase, realizes in a general way what is important, what is relevant. She or he does *not* attempt to develop definitive concepts, those with specific attributes and objective traits; instead, attempts are made to develop a meaningful expository picture which "enables one to grasp the reference in terms of one's own experience (Blumer, pp. 148–150). Both meaning and sense of concepts are obtained through the above process, which includes testing the concepts against empirical instances rather than taking them for granted (Blumer, p. 150). In brief, exploration provides us with general guidelines which allow us to discuss the direction along which we should look for the variable subject with which we are concerned. Once such guidelines have been found through exploratory inquiries such as direct observation, informal interviewing, reading letters and diaries or through group discussions, the second phase of theory construction can begin.

Inspection   This phase of implicitly structured theory construction is characterized by what Blumer calls "close scrutiny." It is the analysis phase where the discovery of new data shows what methods should be used to complete theory construction. Methods like participant observation and formal interviewing frequently characterize this phase as the theorist looks for emergent qualities, definitions of the situations, shared meanings and other symbolic interaction themes. What Douglas calls "field research" including depth probe field research, investigative reporting, detective work, overt journalism and overt field research all may be used during this phase of theorizing. The chief feature of this phase is that emergent data dictate the methods to be employed in the remainder of the theory construction effort.

Generalization   Following inspection, the theorist will usually move to generalizations. Important during this phase is the presentation of conclusions from multiple realities. This is facilitated by the definition of the situation used in the inspection phase. Generalizations should not be seen as being absolute and objective in presentation, to the extent that there is a preference for portrayals of multiple realities. The question which arises is whether such realities themselves have been reified. In a sense it seems that they have, for the end-result of these kinds of theories seems to be generalizations reflecting all of the elements of "emergent theory," including an "unintended" *structural* one which is "multiple realities"—the existence of which in itself is a perspective which holds a particular type of "ultimate validity."

CRITERIA FOR THEORETICAL FORMULATION

Some argue, as discussed in Chapter 1 and mentioned in this chapter, that there is no systematic and comprehensive *theory* of social psychology. A problem in social psychology that I perceive is that sometimes our theories are inadequate, thus rendering them less usable than they could be potentially—not only in social psychology but also in the world at large. There is a very real fear here for the discipline if usable theories are not produced. Theories are needed in a society at all times, but especially when there are rapid changes, international crises, economic upheavals and numerous other social problems. Social psychological theories should be at the forefront of solutions offered for societal response and stability. This has not been so in the past, and if the discipline continues to be essentially non-contributory to societal problems it may not long endure. Thus, the problem which exists in social psychology is not that it is being dissipated but that it is not dissipated enough, in the sense that few outside the discipline turn to it for aid in problem solving.

Perhaps a greater emphasis on theory evaluation can produce more usable theories in social psychology. While many elements of theory evaluation have been offered, Schrag's criteria for theoretical formulations are still appropriate. Let us examine these criteria as a mode of evaluation for theories in social psychology.

Logical Criteria and Social Psychological Theories

If a social psychological theory meets the criterion of logical adequacy, it means that it has features which include among others consistency, parsimony, non-tautological and non-teleological explanation. In the first place, the theory should be consistent. This requires that the formulation contain no contradictory elements. The propositions should be, instead, complementary. The problem seems simple enough when a theory is constructed through deduction, and the logical rules utilized minimize contradictions in concept formulation and derived propositions.

It is not so simple when theories are tested and revised and when the form of theories is one of *implicit structure*. During testing and revision of theories, contradictions may emerge which call for concept reformulation and proposition reformulation. Also, implicitly structured theories, because of their loose structure, must be formed with special care lest contradictions develop which may render the theoretical formulations logically inadequate.

Parsimony, or the development of a minimum set of principles necessary to explain some phenomenon, is another feature of the *logical criterion.* Again, parsimony is relatively easy to evaluate in explicitly structured theories but rather difficult to evaluate in loosely structured theories. For example, what criteria are to be used in evaluating the brevity and/or conciseness of a sensitizing theory such as the one presented in Blumer's *Symbolic Interactionism: Perspective and Method?* Could Blumer have used fewer words to make the same statement in the volume without sacrificing the content of his formulation? Perhaps the only thing that can be said about parsimony and implicitly structured theories is that such theories should strive for explanation in the most succinct manner possible.

Two additional features of logical adequacy in theories should be their *non-tautological* and *non-teleological* construction. That is, propositions in theories should *not* be constructed so that they are true by definition. When they are, we have circular reasoning. The following statements constitute a tautological explanation of a murder: A woman, after receiving years of physical abuse, killed her husband. Why did she kill him? Because he beat her and she was provoked. How do you know? Because he is dead. Many such spouse homicides, especially when the husband is the victim, are referred to as "victim-precipitated homicide." In many instances there is little evidence to support the contention that victims provoke their own demise, other than the fact that they are dead (Franklin and Franklin, p. 133). The man is a victim-precipitated homicide because he precipitated his death. This explanation of the incident is true by definition and cannot be falsified. But such an explanation does not explain the cause of the victim's death, because precipitating one's death is a part of the definition of victim-precipitated homicide. Social psychologists must avoid such explanations if their theories are to meet the criterion of logical adequacy.

There is also another kind of explanation to be avoided if logical adequacy is to obtain. Consider the following question and answer: Why do parents abuse their children? Because these parents want psychiatric help about their feelings toward their children. Therefore, they physically abuse them, because this increases the likelihood that they will be reported as child abusers and have to undergo psychiatric treatment. This kind of explanation is called a teleology and uses a *consequence* to explain a *cause.* Many child abusers who come to the attention of the courts *are* referred to psychiatrists for treatment. However, it is farfetched to assume that *possibility of referral* to a psychiatrist is the *cause* of child abuse. The etiology of child abuse, a complex phenomenon, in all likelihood involves something more than just a parent "crying out for help."

Operational Criteria and Social Psychological Theories

Regardless of the strategy used in theorizing, major concepts in the formulation essentially must be measured if the theory is to explain anything. In many implicitly structured theories the problem may not seem as great since there is a close relationship between concepts and aspects of "reality." This is only because much operationalization of variables is commonplace in everyday life (Hoover, p. 87). Yet, there are difficulties surrounding the measurement of variables and care must be taken in developing such measures. Hoover (pp. 88–90) discusses two ways of dealing with variables that for one reason or another are difficult to operationalize: substitution and division. *Substitution* involves delineating another variable that isolates key aspects of the concept and which deals directly with the concept in a very familiar way to many people. *Division* means separating the concept into several characteristics, exploring each characteristic independently and then recombining the characteristics into a whole in order to get a single measure of the concept.

For example, the concept "feminist" is rather difficult to measure because it has many features not necessarily agreed upon by those who call themselves feminist or who are interested in the concept. By using substitution in the operationalization of "feminist," it is possible to tap one important element of "feminist" that most people have at least thought about—should women receive equal pay for doing the same work as men? Should women run for public office? To be sure, these are not the *only* elements of "feminist," however, they are important ones and most people deal with them in one way or another. Division of the concept "feminist" might entail separating the concept into categories such as attitudes toward occupational equality between the sexes, attitudes toward child custody, and attitudes toward sexual freedom. Each of these categories may be explored independently and then recombined into a whole to form a single measure. The problem with this procedure is, of course, that interaction between the parts which may contribute to the "whole" concept is lost.

Another issue of great importance in operationalization as referred to earlier, is whether or not concepts in social psychology should be subjected to strict measurement. This debate has been going on for years and obviously has not been won by those opposing strict operationalization nor by those in favor of such procedures. Over twenty years ago a social scientist discussed two elements related to arguments against operationalization: (1) the nature of *social* variables; and, (2) the difficulty of isolating universal categories for social variables (Sjoberg, pp. 617–622). These arguments against strict operationalization of variables are used today. Many argue that because of the complexity and heterogeneity of social variables, it is impossible to reduce them to single dimensions. Moreover, societal forces such as ethical and moral considerations may be barriers to the kinds of information which can be produced and the manner in which they are reported. A related problem concerns the establishment of universal categories for social variables in view of the variability of human behavior. As Sjoberg stated, one never knows if one is comparing apples and apples or apples and oranges.

Recognizing that both the feasibility and possibility of operationalization in social psychology are open to debate, it still must be admitted that if a theory is to obtain operational adequacy, it must be researchable. Researchability, however, may not depend upon the "highly developed" instruments and procedures once deemed necessary by scholars such as William F. Ogburn. Instead, operational adequacy may mean the procedures and techniques endorsed by Blumer years ago, and used by an increasing number of competent and conscientious scholars, such as those mentioned in this chapter.

Empirical Criteria and Social Psychological Theories

An empirically adequate theory is characterized by a close relationship between propositions and the observation of events. While a theory may be logically and operationally adequate, the criterion of empirical adequacy must still be met if the theory is to be a viable explanatory scheme. Numerous theories in social psychology seem plausible and often have assumed important stature in the social psychological literature, but observations have failed to substantiate their theoretical foundations. Instead of discarding those that even with revision are empirically unfounded, we have clung to them with the fervent hope that somehow they will become true. While it is recognized that no theory can ever be exposed to all possible relevant tests and that seeking absolute criteria for the verification of scientific theories is almost futile

(Kuhn, 1962), empirical standards should exist for theories in social psychology. For instance, if through repeated replication and revision, an explicitly structured formulation remains empirically unfounded, then perhaps the theory should be discarded. If an explanatory scheme involving the independent variable "penis envy" as a cause of female anxiety, frustration, and the like, is found to be empirically inadequate, then the explanatory scheme must fall by the wayside in the same manner as those theories suggesting that the world is flat or square.

In addition to the necessity for a close fit between theoretical propositions and empirical data if empirical adequacy is to obtain for a formulation, an issue involving interpretation of research results is relevant here. This is discussed by Freese and Rokeach. Noting that research results may be flawed because of "social-psychological mechanisms or processes other than those posited by investigator," the authors discuss criteria to be used when deciding upon alternative interpretations of research findings in social psychology (pp. 195–201). Their discussion is directly relevant to the empirical adequacy of theoretical formulations since alternative interpretation of research findings can render a theory empirically inadequate.

Freese and Rokeach feel that while many alternative interpretations of social research in social psychology are unwarranted since there exists no direct evidence for them, they could appear to be plausible if they addressed a methodological or substantive defect. *Statistical artifacts* and *faulty research designs* are the sources of methodological flaws, and the *failure to control variables that are theoretically relevant to an investigation* is the source of substantive flaws in empirical investigation. This latter problem fails to eliminate rival hypotheses or theories but must be accompanied by "a body of theory and data to justify the identification of specific variables that were uncontrolled but should have been controlled" (Freese and Rokeach, p. 198).

Pointing out that unflawed research today may be flawed tomorrow, depending on the state of the field, Freese and Rokeach suggest that untested plausible alternative interpretations (characterized by (1) a body of theory and data about the contaminating influence; (2) a body of theory and data applicable to the investigated problem; and, (3) a demonstration that the contaminating influence can operate in the experimental test situation) must be *secondary to supported hypotheses and theories*. If the latter are to be refuted, "alternative hypotheses must be tested and empirically supported" (p. 199). Moreover, "time" of the investigation and its position within a research program are also important aspects to consider. Criticizing specific findings of an existing program when other aspects of the program hold up under close scrutiny may not be sufficient to challenge a total program or to question the empirical adequacy of some theoretical formulations.

Pragmatic Criteria and Social Psychological Theories

The 1960s and early 70s ushered in a new ideology in academe. Students were no longer willing to memorize theoretical formulations without linking them to real world phenomena. In their call for a new or different approach to learning, students demanded, sometimes successfully, that their mentors establish greater congruence between "ivory tower" theorizing and real life situations.

Student demands for greater relevancy in the learning process were compatible with theory construction since pragmatic adequacy has always been an essential—albeit sometimes neglected—part of good theorizing. Part of the reason for this neglect has been due to the line of distinction drawn between pure and applied research—the former being the domain of so-called academically oriented scholars and the latter being the calling of "action researchers." The gap between the two, which has existed for some time, seems to be diminishing as more and more academicians are realizing that the ultimate test of a theory is its use in the real world. Just as theory provides patterns for data interpretations, linkages between studies and frameworks for concepts, it also should "allow us to interpret the larger meaning of our findings for ourselves and others" (Hoover, 1980, p. 39). Theory ensures the criterion of pragmatism. Such a conception of theory in social psychology may be emerging as a legitimate goal more rapidly than some think. Cartwright states:

> Most social psychologists today have come from a restricted segment of American society, and this has limited our theoretical perspective, contributed to an unfortunate degree of ethnocentrism, and greatly influenced the content of empirical research. But these, too, will be overcome as the demographic composition of the field is broadened to include more women, members of various minority groups, scholars from different cultures, and citizens of both the so-called developed and underdeveloped countries. Within the next few years, social psychology should become a truly international

community of scholars, and every effort should be made to facilitate this accomplishment (p. 199).

SUMMARY

Chapter 2 has dealt with some of the theoretical and methodological issues and debates in social psychology. Beginning with a discussion of theory, explanation, prediction, and control in social psychology, the *structure* of social psychological theories was examined. *Theories* in social psychology are labelled as such because they have a *structure* containing the characteristic elements of postulates, concepts, propositions, imagery and empirical indicators (operational definitions). These elements are necessary because otherwise it would be impossible for persons within the field to *agree* that certain formulations are *theories*. What has become increasingly obvious and respected in social psychology is that theories can take different forms and their elements can be presented in varying degrees of explicitness. Many of our theories are *explicitly structured*, clearly delineating the elements of postulates, concepts, propositions, imagery and empirical indicators. Others, an increasing number, are *implicitly structured*, ranging in scope from theories that the reader "participates" in constructing, such as relatively recent ones advanced by Goffman, Douglas, Hewitt and others, to more tightly constructed ones such as those advanced by scholars using analytic induction strategies.

One element of theories on which there has been, and still exists, much debate is operational definitions. The central question is: How should our concepts be operationalized? While many argue that our concepts *should not* be operationalized at all, I believe that this argument is really against those definitions with "fixed and specified procedures designed to isolate stable and definitive contents," (Blumer, 1954). These same scholars would argue *for* the development of "a meaningful expository picture which enables grasping a reference in terms of one's own experience," (Blumer, 1954). This kind of development, I propose, is operationalization also, albeit of the variety that occurs in everyday life. Thus the argument is not against operationalization but against a particular kind of operationalization and its underlying assumptions.

This brings us to a second category of issues discussed, which is the methodological predilections of most social psychologists. Their preferences range from natural science approaches to the study of social phenomena, such as strict experimentation, to the naturalistic observation studies of Blumer, Douglas, Wiseman and others. The position taken in this volume is that both kinds of broad methodologies have merits and the field best advances if there is mutual respect for both approaches. No one method is necessarily superior to another. In fact, the growing acceptance of subjective methodologies by many who previously did not hold such techniques in high esteem suggests that *methodological pluralism* is emerging as the methodological approach with the best promise for social psychology.

Finally, theoretical formulations can be evaluated. Using a model of evaluation developed by Schrag, criteria for theories were explicated, and included logical adequacy, operational adequacy, empirical adequacy and pragmatic adequacy. While these criteria are fairly straightforward for explicitly structured theories in the discipline, they are not as clearly delineated for implicitly structured theories. Greater reliance on and utilization of these kinds of theories in social psychology dictate further development of means by which we can evaluate such explanatory schemes. The rather optimistic view taken here is that this development will occur. Theory and methodology in social psychology have advanced much since the inception of the discipline. The ingenuity and creativity of present-day scholars foreordain even greater advances in the future and this includes clarification of many issues and solutions to many problems in theory and methodology faced by contemporary social psychologists.

BIBLIOGRAPHY

Adler, Peter and Patricia A. Adler. "Symbolic Interactionism," in Jack D. Douglas, Patricia A. Adler, Peter Adler, Andrea Fontana, C. Robert Freeman and Joseph A. Kotarba, eds., *Introduction to the Sociologies of Everyday Life.* Boston: Allyn and Bacon, 1980

Becker, Howard S. "Becoming a Marijuana User," *American Journal of Sociology* 59 (1963), pp. 235–242.

Becker, Howard, Blanche Geer, Everett Hughes, and Anselm Strauss. *Boys in White.* Chicago: University of Chicago Press, 1961.

Bem, Daryl J. *Beliefs, Attitudes and Human Affairs.* Belmont, Ca.: Brooks/Cole, 1970.

Bierstedt, Robert. "Nominal and Real Definitions in Sociological Theory," in Llewellyn Gross, ed., *Symposium on Sociological Theory*. Evanston, Ill.: Row, Peterson, 1959.

Blalock, Hubert M. *Social Statistics*. New York: McGraw-Hill, 1960

Blumer, Herbert. "What is Wrong with Social Theory," *American Sociological Review* 19 (1954).

——. "Sociological Analyses and the Variable," *American Sociological Review* 21 (1956).

——. *Symbolic Interactionism: Perspective and Method*. Englewood Cliffs, N. J.: Prentice-Hall 1969.

Campbell, Donald T. "Prospective: Artifact and Control," in R. Rosenthal and R. Rosnow, eds., *Artifact in Behavioral Research*. N.Y.: Academic Press, 1969.

Cartwright, Dorwin. "Contemporary Social Psychology in Historical Perspective," *Social Psychology Quarterly* 42, no. 1 (1979), pp. 82–93.

Cavan, Sherri. *Liquor License*. Chicago: Aldine, 1966.

Chafetz, Janet Saltzman. *A Primer on the Construction and Testing of Theories in Sociology*. Itasca, Ill.: F. E. Peacock, 1978.

Cohen, Morris R. and Ernest Nagel. *An Introduction to Logic and the Scientific Method*. New York: Harcourt, Brace and World, 1934.

Costner, Herbert L. and Robert K. Leik. "Deductions from Axiomatic Theory," *American Sociological Review* (December 1964), pp. 819–835.

Cressey, Donald. *Other People's Money: A Study of the Social Psychology of Embezzlement*. Glencoe, Ill.: Free Press, 1953.

Douglas, Jack D. *Investigative Social Research*. Beverly Hills, Ca.: Sage Publications, 1976.

Douglas, Jack, Patricia A. Adler, Peter Adler, Andrea Fontana, Robert C. Freeman, and Joseph A. Kotarba. *Introduction to the Sociologies of Everyday Life*. Boston: Allyn and Bacon, 1980.

Elms, Allan. "The Crisis of Confidence in Social Psychology," *American Psychologist* (October 1975), pp. 967–976.

Festinger, Leon. *A Theory of Cognitive Dissonance*. New York: Harper & Row, 1957.

Franklin, Clyde W. and Alice P. Franklin. "Victimology Revisited: A Critique and Suggestions for Future Direction," *Criminology* 14, no. 1 (May 1976), pp. 125–136.

Freeman, C. Robert. "Phenomenological Sociology and Ethnomethodology," in J. D. Douglas, P. A. Adler, P. Adler, A. Fontana, C. R. Freeman and J. A. Kotarba. *The Sociologies of Everyday Life* Boston: Allyn & Bacon, 1980, pp. 113–154.

Freese, Lee and Milton Rokeach. "On the Use of Alternative Interpretation in Contemporary Social Psychology," *Social Psychology Quarterly* 42, no. 3 (1979), pp. 195–201.

Gergen, Kenneth J. "Social Psychology as History," *Journal of Personality and Social Psychology* 26 (1973), pp. 309–320.

Gouldner, Alvin M. *The Coming Crisis of Western Sociology.* New York: Avon, 1970.

Hewitt, John P. "Comment: The Discipline of Social Psychology," *American Sociologist* 12, no. 1 (1977), pp. 14–18.

Hoover, Kenneth R. *The Elements of Social Scientific Thinking,* 2nd ed. New York: St. Martin's, 1980.

House, James S. "The Three Faces of Social Psychology," *Sociometry* 40, no. 2 (1977), pp. 161–177.

Hyman, Herbert. *Survey Design and Analysis.* New York: Free Press, 1955.

Janis, I. L. and S. Feshbach. "Effects of Fear-Arousing Communication," *Journal of Abnormal Social Psychology* 48 (1953), pp. 78–92.

Kaplan, Abraham. *The Conduct of Inquiry: Methodology for Behavioral Sciences.* San Francisco: Chandler, 1964.

Kuhn, Thomas S. *The Structure of Scientific Revolution.* Chicago: University of Chicago Press, 1962.

Mead, George H. *Mind, Self and Society,* Charles Morris, ed. Chicago: University of Chicago Press, 1934.

Phillips, Bernard S. *Social Research: Strategies and Tactics.* New York: Macmillan, 1966.

Schrag, Clarence. "Elements of Theoretical Analysis in Sociology," in Llewellyn Gross, ed., *Sociological Theory: Inquiries and Paradigms.* New York: Harper & Row, 1967.

Sears, R. R., E. E. Maccoby and H. Levin. *Patterns of Child Rearing.* New York: Harper and Row, 1957.

Secord, Paul F. and Carl W. Backman. *Social Psychology.* New York: McGraw-Hill, 1964.

———. *Social Psychology,* 2nd ed. New York: McGraw-Hill, 1974.

Selltiz, Claire, M. Jahoda, M. Deutsch and S. W. Cook. *Research Methods in Social Relations.* New York: Holt, Rinehart and Winston, 1964.

Sjoberg, Gideon. "Operationalization and Social Research," in Llewellyn Gross, ed., *Symposium on Sociological Theory.* Evanston, Ill.: Row Peterson, 1959.

Stryker, Sheldon. "Developments in 'Two Social Psychologies': Toward an Appreciation of Mutual Relevance," *Sociometry* 40, no. 4 (1977), pp. 145–160.

Wilson, T. P. "Conceptions of Interaction and Forms of Sociological Explanations," *American Sociological Review* 35, no. 3 (August 1970), pp. 697–707.

Wiseman, Jacqueline P. *Stations of the Lost.* Englewood Cliffs, N. J.: Prentice Hall, 1970.

Wright, Sam. *Crowds and Riots.* Beverly Hills, Ca.: Sage Publications, 1978.

Zetterberg, Hans. *On Theory and Verfication in Sociology,* 3rd ed. Totawa, N. J.: Bedminster Press, 1965.

THE
SYMBOLIC
INTERACTION
PERSPECTIVE

3

Symbolic interactionism has been the dominant perspective used by American social psychologists to study the behavior of individuals in their social environments. The origins of symbolic interactionism lie in the works of philosophers, economists, psychologists and historians. Stryker (1980, p. 16) has suggested that the origins, in all likelihood, can be traced back to Aristotelian thought. However, Stryker chooses to begin his history of the topic with eighteenth century Scottish moral philosophical principles as the earliest antecedents of symbolic interactionism. Drawing upon Gladys Bryson's volume *Man and Society: The Scottish Inquiry of the Eighteenth Century*, Stryker considers the works of Adam Smith, David Hume and Adam Ferguson to be representative of Scottish moral philosophical thought, which he feels was the forerunner of pragmatic philosophical thought in America. Pragmatic philosophy is recognized as greatly influencing the development of symbolic interactionism.

Scottish moral philosophical thought reflected in the works of Smith, Hume and Ferguson include the following: (1) a commitment to induction as a theoretical strategy and introspection as a methodological technique; (2) a commitment to empiricism emphasizing the significance of experience (Adler and Adler, p. 21); (3) acceptance of the assumption that a source of some human conduct lies in sentiments such as sympathy, habit, moral sense and beliefs; (4) a belief by some, such as Hume and Smith, that sympathy as a major source of human conduct is the basis of shared feelings and consensus among people in society; and (5) a belief by others that habit is a source of human conduct largely acquired through interaction with and communication with others (Stryker, 1980, pp. 17–20). These lines of thought, according to Stryker, are related directly to American pragmatism. Pragmatism is symbolic interactionism's "most direct philosophical antecedent" (Adler and Adler, p. 21).

Philosophical pragmatists such as Charles S. Pierce (1839–1914), William James (1842–1910), John Dewey (1859–1952) and James Mark Baldwin (1861–1934) greatly influenced early symbolic interactionists like Charles H. Cooley (1864–1929), W. I. Thomas (1863–1947) and George H. Mead (1863–1931). An interesting observation here is that most of these scholars were either directly or indirectly associated with the University of Chicago. A philosophy professor stated in 1934 that the atmosphere at the University of Chicago at the turn of the century and for some time afterwards was particularly conducive to the development of social psychology—and more specifically, of symbolic interactionism. Suggesting that there was a "heavily charged psychological air" (Mead, 1934) on the Chicago campus during the late 1800s and early 1900s, Charles Morris implied that George H. Mead's contributions were influenced greatly by the existing intellectual climate. It seems, then, that philosophical pragmatism, with its basic features as enumerated above, combined with the psychological intellectual climate to produce a setting out of which social psychology and one of its major perspectives evolved. This major perspective is symbolic interactionism and its pervasive influence led Arnold Rose in the early 1960s to state that "perhaps half the sociologists of the United States were nurtured, directly or indirectly, on symbolic interactionism conceptions and approaches to research" (1962, p. vii). Given the increased interest in topics considered to be the "sociology of everyday life" by sociologists who previously eschewed some of the guiding theoretical and methodological principles of symbolic interactionism, there is little reason to feel that the influence of symbolic interactionism is waning in the early 1980s.

In the following section important aspects of early behaviorism, evolution theory and philosophical pragmatism are discussed as they relate to the genesis of symbolic interactionism in the United States and thus to the work of the early symbolic interactionists.

THE ANTECEDENTS OF SYMBOLIC INTERACTIONISM

The Influence of Early Behaviorism

It may seem odd to include behaviorism in a discussion of influential lines of thought on the emergence of a perspective to which it is often juxtaposed. Yet, early behavioristic thought *did* influence the development of symbolic interactionism, albeit somewhat negatively. The nature of this influence should be seen in the following discussion.

John B. Watson (1878–1958) seems to have been the behaviorist whose ideas most influenced the development of symbolic interactionism. Watson's approach to the study of human conduct grew out of his disdain for subjective methods of studying individual experience. Vehemently criticizing attempts to understand human behavior by imaginatively "getting inside" other people in order to experience their experiences, Watson advanced what he called an *objective psychology*. Watson's objective psychology was two-fold: it was a way of looking at and understanding human behavior; and, it was a way of using human behavior to explain individual experience without attempting to observe the inner experiences of persons. The nature of this mode of inquiry into social interaction is apparent in some of the following ideas advanced by Watson: (1) language should be viewed as vocal responses, muscular movements and so forth; (2) individuals' social experiences are manifested in their responses; (3) people's private and unobservable experiences fall outside the realm of science—and therefore, do not exist; and (4) a stimulus affects a person, which in turn leads to a response from the person. Watson's view of social interaction between persons, then, is as a *series of stimulus-response sequences of activity*. He is aware of the fact that behaviors exhibited by one person may not be recognized by the other (when one person talks to another in a shared language, the other easily recognizes social experiences, but when a person thinks about another, the other cannot recognize the social experiences as easily). However, when behavioral recognition occurred, Watson felt that the behaviors contained the social experiences, and no further exploration was deemed necessary. Furthermore, for Watson, the behaviors exhibited by one person were stimuli which called out responses in other(s).

Few contemporary social and behavioral scientists would subscribe to this explanation of social interaction. On the other hand, many everyday explanations of social interaction involve stimulus-response reasoning. For example, to suggest that the theft of a person's car occurred because the victim left keys in the ignition is to offer a stimulus-response explanation for a phenomenon which obviously involves many more intervening and/or conditional factors. It was the recognition of this line of thought by early symbolic interactionists that led them to reject stimulus-response explanations in favor of an explanatory model which emphasized the "mind" aspects of human beings and which later would become known as symbolic interactionism.

The Influence of Evolution Theory

Evolutionary principles permeate the work of early symbolic interactionists. Stryker alludes to this by showing how George H. Mead emphasized the essential nature of "cooperation" for human survival (1980, p. 35). Cooperation was felt to be crucial for survival, and behaviors congruent with and enhancing it were thought to be retained, while others "failing to do so, discarded." This was a positive influence on the development of Meadian thought. However, the main proponent of evolution principles, Charles Darwin, expressed ideas about the psychology of human behavior which were not endorsed by early symbolic interactionists. Darwin's explanation of the psychology of human behavior centers around the basic assumption that emotion is a psychological state of consciousness. Social interaction in a two-person group is seen as the result of one person having prior awareness and making a response to the other which, in turn, calls forth a response from another. The series of acts which begin and continue in this manner between two persons is labelled *social interaction* by Darwin.

During social interaction individual social acts are influenced by physiological responses such as muscular changes, facial changes and changes in blood circulation. These and other changes were thought both to *express emotion* and to be an *expression of emotion*. Such changes occur in persons during social interaction because they express some mind content which brings about behavior. Content in the minds of persons is seen as a precondition for their behaviors. Illustratively, if one person loves another, it is manifested by physiological changes in the person who is in love. These are changes which can both inform the other of this love and also indicate the extent of the love. Love in this instance, then, is seen as a psychological state which produces certain physiological behaviors which indicate the psychological state.

Early symbolic interactionists did *not* agree with the idea that prior consciousness brings about behavior from one person and calls it out in the other. Instead, they felt that behavior occurred, and consciousness emerged from the behavior. In our society, when two lovers kiss the gesture itself is an act of love. Kissing is almost an automatic act between lovers and precedes both the awareness of love and deliberate attempts to show love. For early symbolic interactionists, Darwinian notions of prior consciousness were too mentalistic and did not stress the dynamic and constructed nature of much human behavior.

The Influence of Philosophical Pragmatism

Charles Pierce, William James, John Dewey and James Baldwin, among others, greatly influenced early symbolic interactionism. These scholars are responsible for many features of symbolic interactionism, including *the meaning of objects, the development of social selves as a function of social learning rather than instincts, mental activity as processual, humans as active beings, the organism's active role in shaping its environment, societal change through human effort* and an *emphasis on everyday situations.*

From a philosophical pragmatism point of view, *meaning of objects is not inherent in objects but rather derives from the behavior of objects displayed from situation to situation.* Adler and Adler (p. 22) have stated that "this is the original definition of pragmatism as conceived by its founder," Charles Sanders Pierce. It is also a feature, somewhat modified, of symbolic interactionism. Emphasizing that individuals play roles in shaping their environment, many symbolic interactionists submit "that the meaning of objects resides in the behavior directed toward them and not in the objects themselves" (Manis and Meltzer, 1978, p. 3). An explication of this feature of the perspective is offered later in this chapter. Certainly William James' view that humans modify objects with their judgments, ideas, perceptions and feelings toward them contributes significantly to this connotation of the meaning of objects. Rather than emphasizing *the behavior* of objects as Pierce did, James stresses the uses to which objects are put as indication of the meaning of objects, thus leading the way for the "construction of meaning" definition of objects used by many symbolic interactionists today.

The self as "social" also had its genesis in the work of philosophical pragmatist William James, and most contemporary formulations about the self find their fundamental origins in the statements made by him (1890). For James, "the self was the sum total of all that belonged to the person." This included persons' thoughts about themselves, their moods and states, their tangible and intangible possessions and so on. Recognizing four kinds of self (which he named the material self, the spiritual self, the social self and the pure ego), James points out the *social self* as containing the reflexive characteristics central to symbolic interactionist thought. The self, like other objects, can be viewed by the individual. He or she can have cognitions and feelings toward it and behave toward it in the same manner as one can toward external objects. In *Psychology*, James acknowledged two aspects of the social self: the self as knower ("I") and the self as known ("me") both of which must be understood in order to fully understand either one.

The "I" was "that which at any given moment is conscious for the individual": in other words, it is the thinker. It is a passing state of consciousness which is given permanency with further elaboration by James. That is, by his contention that one moment's state of consciousness is replaced by the next moment's state of consciousness, thus establishing a functional relationship between the states. It is because the same objects are known during both states of consciousness that personal unity and sameness occurs. Stated another way, personal unity exists when there are successive knowers (I's) because all of the "knowers" exist with some awareness of what has taken place in the past. To illustrate, as you read these words you are not in the same state of consciousness as you were when starting this chapter. Yet, you experience personal unity because of your awareness of the past.

The "me," regarded by James as "the self as known," in its broadest sense is seen as the "sum total of all that a person can call his or her own," and emerges out of the recognition one received from others. James felt that persons had an innate propensity to gain this recognition and the result was as many social selves for the individual as there were groups significant to him or her and around him or her. These social selves, however, involved both others' recognition and one's own ideas and goals: objective and subjective aspects. One consequence of these many selves is conflict and possible discontinuity of the total self. Usually, however, this is avoided because of the tendency to maintain the social self which evokes esteemed feelings within the person. The self then, for James, is characterized by continuity and variability: continuity is maintained by the *I* and variability is provided by the *me*.

Mental activity as processual is a characteristic of much contemporary symbolic interactionism and it, too, has its origins in pragmatism. The emphasis placed on interpretation of objects, a conspicuous feature of Blumerian symbolic interactionism, is derived directly from the philosophical pragmatist John Dewey's conception of the mind as process. This view of mind as handling and modifying objects and constructing action which contributes to environmental adjustment to role making is central to the symbolic interactionism many of today's scholars endorse. Defining, redefining, developing courses of action are all mental activities which define the mind as process and social interaction as constructed. Dewey, in addition to his conception of mind, also was convinced that the proper direction of the social sciences was toward everyday problem recognition and solution.

Adler and Adler, in comparing Dewey's and James' conception of habit (the former emphasizing building each future course of action on the last and the latter emphasizing repetition and mindless behavior as a connotation of habit) conclude that Dewey's conception leads directly to the view of mind as processual. If, however, James' view of "successive knowers which exist with some awareness of what has occurred in the past" is stressed then a distinction between James and Dewey is much narrower and the processual nature of mental activity also is a part of James' contribution.

A major contribution to contemporary symbolic interactionism by Dewey has been underscored by Stryker (1980, p. 25), and that is Dewey's contention that the activity pursued by a person is part of the definition of a stimulus used to explain human behavior. Stimuli related to the action of an individual must be defined within the context of that action and do not occur prior to and thus act as a cause of that action: "Need for money" causes a person to rob a bank only in the sense that a person outlines a course of bank robbing action. In other words, "need for money" must be defined within the context of robbing a bank and is not prior to and/or a cause of robbing a bank. Among Dewey's contributions to symbolic interactionism, in summary, are: (1) meaning is lodged in social interaction; (2) mental activity is processual; (3) the role of the interpretive process in achieving adjustment in the real world; (4) the emphasis on defining the meaning of objects within the context of the uses to which the object is put (action); and (5) the proposal that the task of the social sciences is to explain everyday life.

Another contribution to symbolic interactionism not previously mentioned was made by James Mark Baldwin (1906). Baldwin, in contrast to James, felt that the self was *totally* social and saw no reason to divide it into parts. The development of the self was seen as occurring through three stages: a projective stage, a subjective stage and an ejective stage. The individual first becomes aware of others, drawing lines of demarcation between others and between others and objects. Following this stage is a subjective one when the child imitates the behavior of others and begins to experience feelings associated with the behavior (self-consciousness). The final stage of self development, according to

Baldwin, is the ejective stage when the child associates feelings with conceptions of this and realizes that others have feeling states. This last stage, according to Meltzer, Petras and Reynolds, and to Stryker, represents a major contribution to sympathetic introspection and role-taking—concepts of great importance to symbolic interactionism.

EARLY SYMBOLIC INTERACTIONISM

William Isaac Thomas

W. I. Thomas (1863–1947) began and nurtured his career at the University of Chicago, first as a graduate student and then as a professor influenced by the "strong center of pragmatism thriving there." Other symbolic interactionists who influenced him included Ellsworth Faris, Robert E. Park, George Herbert Mead and indirectly, Charles H. Cooley.

Meltzer, Petras and Reynolds have stated that the two main contributions W. I. Thomas made to symbolic interactionism were his concept "definition of the situation" and the extension of principles of symbolic interactionism to the adult level.

In terms of theory, Thomas' ideas concerning the definition of the situation stem from his belief that individuals born into social groups are not able to build their own definitions of objects and situations, nor are they able to follow their own wishes, desires and/or whims without some kind of group influence. His feelings about group constraints on the individual are linked to his idea that persons are motivated to act by pleasure, while society is oriented toward resolving conflict between persons who tend to pursue their selfish pleasures. The society, then, is envisioned by Thomas as a regulating agency within which roles and norms develop to guide activity between persons. Another way of saying this is that the society serves to define situations for individuals. Societal agencies such as the family, the church and the community use techniques like gossip, ostracism and jury trials to define situations.

On an *individual level,* Thomas conceives of the definition of the situation as a phase prior to self-determined acts which involve examination and deliberation. This view of the definition of the situation is processual and very similar to what Blumer calls the interpretive process. The definition of the situation is perceived by a decision to act or not to act along a given line which also is preceded by subjective facts of experience. All acts are dependent upon these subjective facts of experience (definition of the situation). Behavior, then, must be analyzed within a context which includes the situation as it exists objectively and the situation as it is subjectively defined by the person involved.

Thomas' methodological predilections stem from his belief that subjective methodological techniques are more appropriate to use in measuring individual definitions and/or subjective facts. He proposed the use of personal documents like diaries, letters, case studies, life histories, etc., to assess individual meanings of situations and thus many of the techniques used by modern symbolic interactionists emerged as viable techniques to be used in social psychological investigation.

Charles Horton Cooley

Most people at one time or another have heard someone make a statement implying that human nature is innate. Charles Horton Cooley (1864–1929), rejected this line of thought in favor of one which stresses social interaction as the ultimate determinant of human nature. In doing this, Cooley constructed an explanation of human nature which stands among the most prominent contributions made by American scholars to early symbolic interactionism. Human nature as manifested in the self, according to Cooley, develops through social interaction with a primary group. The concept "self" is defined by Cooley as that which is designated in common speech by the pronouns "I," "me," "mine," and "myself." More specifically the self is conceived to be "any idea or system of ideas drawn from the communicative life that the mind cherishes as its own."

Primary groups, then, are those responsible for "bringing" the individual into society, as well as providing individuals with their initial experiences and fundamental training. Family, playgroups and neighborhoods are examples of these agencies which give the individual social unity and "social nature." Social nature is seen as being reflected in terms of "the looking glass self" which consists of the imagined appraisals of other persons. The self, from Cooley's perspective, is reflexive and can be termed the looking glass self: (1) through imagination an individual perceives in the minds of others, some thoughts about his appearance for others; (2) the individual imagines how others judge the appearance; and (3) the individual feels pride or mortification as a result of how others judge his or her appearance. Cooley feels that what contributes to the feelings of pride and shame is the imputed sentiment of others' judgments of our appearance (Cooley).

The self, then, is seen as a reflection in the minds of others. It is the person's image of him- or herself, constructed on the basis of perceived reactions of others. An integral aspect of the self is sentiment, seen as having an instinctive base which takes a crude form at the moment of birth, but being modified and refined through social interaction. This means that, for Cooley, society and/or all social life can be viewed as being lodged in the minds of individuals, which makes the task of sociology one of the observation and interpretation of mental activities. These views of society and sociology lead to a methodological technique refined by Cooley and of great importance to social psychologists. The technique is called *sympathetic introspection* and involves imaginatively transferring oneself into the role of others in order to approximate the experience of others. One imagines others' lives and then seeks to recall and describe their experiences (Stryker, 1980, p. 28).

Sympathetic introspection was used by Cooley in developing his conception of the looking glass self. Using his own children as subjects, he noted that children first watch closely the behavior of persons around them, and very soon afterwards are able to see the connection between their own acts and the acts of others. Once the connection is made, the child learns to assume different roles with different people—first for effect, and then to enhance his or her self image. Axiomatically, then, one source of individual behavior lies in the desire to elicit favorable expressions from others, enhancing and maintaining one's self image.

George Herbert Mead

Prior to his death, George Herbert Mead's (1863–1931) influence on the development of symbolic interactionism as a broad and distinctive perspective in social psychology was largely verbal. Through his close association with John Dewey and his lectures at the University of Chicago, Mead cultivated his thoughts about the root ideas of symbolic interactionism. Although Mead published some papers during his tenure at Chicago, primarily in philosophy journals, the ideas and images associated most often with him were not published until after his death in 1931. Following this, A. E. Murphy, M. H. Moore and C. W. Morris edited and published the lecture notes taken in Mead's classes in a series of books, the best-known being Morris' *Mind, Self and Society* (1934).

Two factors perhaps more than any others have been responsible for the spread of Mead's ideas, which continue to influence the development of social psychology. These are (1) the publication of *Mind, Self and Society,* which served as an effective medium for presenting Mead's basic ideas to a larger audience; and (2) the horizontal and vertical mobility of Mead's students in the sociology profession. They dispersed to universities in various geographical regions in the United States, and have enjoyed phenomenally successful sociological careers. It is interesting to note that at least five of them have been presidents of the American Sociological Association.

While these factors have been instrumental in disseminating Meadian thought, the widespread *acceptance* of his ideas came about because of the insight, imagination and creativity displayed in presenting images and conceptions of the individual in his or her social environment.

There are two major ways in which the contributions of Mead have been presented. Some writers have chosen to discuss Mead's work in social psychology by using the general concepts mind, self, and society. Others have used more specific concepts to present his contributions, such as "self," "act," "social interaction," and "joint action." The former approach seems to avoid much of the disorganization and repetition characterizing presentations taking the specific concept approach. Therefore, this more general approach is taken here. The discussion begins with "society" and includes self, mind and social act.

Society as Symbolic Interaction   Infrahumans are said to have "kingdoms," "societies," and "groups." Yet Mead viewed the human being as "social in a distinguishing fashion." He felt this way despite his feeling that there was a "raw stuff"—a physiological basis for human society from which the intelligence of the human social being arises. Distinguishing between humans and infrahumans, Mead felt that instinctive connections characterized relationships between the latter while human societies arose from an organization made possible by the appearance of the self. Succinctly, "it is the self as such that makes the distinctively human society possible" (Mead, p. 240). But *what* is it about the self that contributes to a distinctive association among humans? An answer to this question lies in Mead's position that the human self is reflexive, thus enabling human beings to carry on conversations with significant gestures. Human society "demands individuals who are able to take the role of the other, who possess selves and who use minds" (Charon, p. 157). All of these are deemed necessary if individuals are to engage in cooperative action (become a society).

The self as reflexive means that the individual can become an object unto him or her self. This is accomplished through adopting the position of others and viewing oneself from the standpoint of others. In doing this the person is not only capable of experiencing an overt act he or she directs toward others, but also the *intent* of that act. If I shout vulgar words at a person, I can experience the rage which I intend to evoke in the other person. For Mead, this was the major distinction between humans—who had the ability to engage in a conversation of significant gestures—and infrahumans—who could only engage in a "conversation of non-significant gestures."

> The conversation of gestures is not significant below the human level because it is not conscious, that is, not *self* conscious (though it is conscious in the sense of involving feelings or sensations). An animal as opposed to a human form, in indicating something to, or bringing out a meaning for, another form, is not at the same time indicating or bringing out the same thing or meaning to or for himself; for he has no mind, no thought, and hence there is no meaning here in the significant or self-conscious sense. A gesture is not significant when the reponse of another organism to it does not indicate to the organism making it what the other organism is responding to (Mead, 1934, p. 81).

If the person responds to my initial gesture, I respond not only to the person's overt act but also to the perceived *intention* of the overt act which is ascertained through role-taking. Meltzer has termed this process "responding to others on the basis of interpreted stimuli."(p. 17) For him, Mead implies that humans repond to one another on the basis of meanings of gestures and thus symbols to be interpreted. Thus I do *not* respond directly to other's overt act, but rather, to *my interpretation* of the overt act. If my interpretation of the act (assessment of meaning of the gesture) is synonymous with the meaning attached to the act by other, then concerted action can result. Because I can respond to my own gestures from other's standpoint, and because other can respond to his or her own gestures from other's standpoint, it is possible for us to experience shared meanings of gestures. When persons experience meanings in this way, they are imaginatively sharing responses through role-taking, which enables them to understand the lines of action of others and to fit together their own behavior with others' behavior. An important point made by Meltzer is that when humans share one another's experience as a result of responding to their own gestures, they incorporate other's behavior into their own, and behavior truly becomes social (p. 18). Society, then, according to Mead and interpretations of his work, appears to be *symbolic interaction in process.*

The Self as Process   The self, as we have seen, is a very important concept in Mead's conceptualization of society. Yet society was viewed by him as "cooperative activity which antedates the self" (p. 239). Mead contends that: (1) the self emerges through social interaction and (2) only those possessing a self were capable of symbolic interaction—a necessary feature of cooperative activity.

> The process out of which the self arises is a social process which implies interaction of individuals in the group, implies the pre-existence of the group. It implies also certain cooperative activities in which the different members of the group are involved (Mead, p. 164).

The human infant is seen as devoid of a self. Absent is the ability to interact with itself. It cannot chastise, love, hate, promise and reward itself. Instead, "at birth humans, like animals, are instinct-motivated, unreflective creatures" incapable of engaging in symbolic interaction (Adler and Adler, p. 32). Only through *social interaction* does the self emerge and become defined and redefined. It is an object which is social in origin and undergoes modifications through social interaction.

The self develops through several stages. The *stage of imitation* is the earliest stage, and has also been referred to as the preparatory stage (Charon, p. 65). This stage has been called a presymbolic period, where the interactions with others that characterize infant and toddler behavior seem to lack meaning. During this stage the child merely copies the behavior of those around without any understanding of its meaning or of the relationship between itself and others. This latter point is significant because the stage of imitation presupposes that objects are not yet defined with words and thus the child does not see itself as separate from others. During the later phases of this stage the child may be on the verge of role-taking and in this sense becomes prepared for entrance into the play stage.

The *play stage* is characterized by role-assumption and role-playing. As a child acquires language, it also acquires an ability to arouse in itself the same responses it arouses in others, and an ability to respond to its own responses from the standpoint of others. Because of this, the child becomes able to act toward objects (including itself) on the basis of at least partially shared meanings. Thus the child can play (and typically does) mother, father, brother, aunt or some other significant other, and directs responses toward itself, responds to the role assumed, and uses the latter response as a stimulus to the role he or she has assumed, and so on. How the child plays roles during the play stage is based on his or her understanding of the role—that is, the limited knowledge of the role acquired by the child from observing persons in the roles. During "play" the responses the child directs toward itself from the role assumed is based on whatever the child has been able to learn through glimpses of the role, and usually this is limited information.

While the rudiments of self seem to be present during the play stage, no unified conception of the self is formed. The reason for this is due to the "discrete" and "unorganized" role-taking which occurs during this stage. The child can only assume one role at a time during this period and moves from one role to another in rapid succession. Meltzer states that the child forms a number of separate and discrete objects of itself, depending on the roles in which it acts toward itself (p. 19). What can be stressed, however, is that during the play stage, the child *learns* social roles and thus becomes prepared to enter the *game stage* of self-development.

The game stage rounds out the development of the self. Its main feature is that *the individual develops role-taking abilities to the point where several roles can be assumed simultaneously.* Likening this stage to an organized game, Mead notes that playing in an organized game requires one to be ready to assume the roles of everyone involved, especially if the roles are related to ones own. Being a successful leader in a small group, for example, involves taking the roles of all persons within that group simultaneously at some time or another and constructing responses to the members on the basis of the role-assumption of other members within the group. "The other assumed in this instance is an organization of the attitudes of those within the group." (Mead, p. 154) It is a composite abstracted out of the concrete roles of particular persons (Meltzer, p. 19). The leader, then, views himself or herself from this generalized standpoint, as well as viewing aspects of group understandings and activities from the generalized other standpoint. In a real sense, then, effective leaders of groups are greatly influenced by a social process deriving from individual members and manifested in the form of the generalized other, since much group leadership involves taking the attitude of the generalized other. While this social process is derived from individual members, the leader can form a unified conception of self from the abstract generalized sets of definitions and expectations and thus behave toward self and others in organized and consistent ways.

Mind as Process   If it were not centuries old, many might believe that the often-heard comment, "the person did not use his or her mind," comes directly from George Herbert Mead's conception of *mind*. For Mead, mind was not some fixed entity or structure within the head responsible for all human behavior. Rather, he conceived of mind as "process," manifested only when the individual carried on an internal conversation of significant gestures. In order to capture the conception of mind as Mead seems to have intended, a brief discussion of the social nature of *environment* and *objects* is necessary. "The social environment is endowed with meanings in terms of the process of social activity: it is an organization of objective relations which arises in relation to a group of organisms engaged in such activity, in processes of social experiences and behavior." (Mead, p. 130)

Mead has suggested that the human being is in a sense responsible for his or her environment (p. 130). This responsibility emerges because of the social nature of individuals' environments, which consist of *objects* and activities which center around these *objects*. Objects are anything in the environment which one refers to, and are not intrinsically meaningful but a result of the meaning that the object has for the individual. Thus, while others play crucial roles in determining an individual's social environment, the individual also has a role to play.

The importance of the above definitions of *environment* and *objects* for "minded" behavior as conceived by Mead becomes apparent when the role of mind in behavior directed toward objects is explored. Meltzer has suggested that mind temporarily inhibits behavior and involves imagining possible lines of action and/or previsioning the future through delaying, organizing and selecting a response to the stimuli of the environment (p. 20). This results in the deliberate control and organization of responses—results of *mind* as process in humans. The following example shows the mind in process and its relations to *environment* and *objects*.

A prostitute for one man may be a female from whom to buy sex; for another the prostitute could be a female to be avoided at all costs; and for another man, the prostitute may be his potential breadwinner. The meaning of the prostitute (object) to these three men will vary with the variations in their preparations for action toward her. Now this does not mean that these three men walk around with sets of organized behavior with which to respond to women recognized as prostitutes. They do, however, experience how other men respond to prostitutes. With this experience and an ability to interpret and define social situations, meaning for the prostitute emerges. Once meaning occurs, the three men organize their actions, map out plans of action, and decide whether to act. This means that behavior is not of a stimulus-response variety but rather of a stimulus-organization-response nature. It is within "organization" that mind manifests itself. The man, for instance, for whom prostitutes mean potential breadwinners, does not automatically react to a prostitute as a potential breadwinner. Instead, he delays his action by selectively perceiving certain aspects of her activities, inspecting them, organizing and selecting an appropriate response through an internal conversation with himself—all *minded behavior*—and then directs action toward her, which is constructed, organized and controlled.

The Social Nature of the Act   Let us briefly continue the line of thought developed in the example of the prostitute. Does recognition of a woman as a prostitute through role-taking, self-indication and an internal rehearsal of possible lines of action commensurate with the man's original intent of acting toward the prostitute result in action toward her? Not necessarily, according to Mead, since the human act has both overt and covert aspects. While an individual's action might be initially based on impulse, motivated as a result of defining the goal of an act (Meltzer, p. 23), in completing the act, constant adjustments to the defining actions of others are made and used to define the *goal* of the action to be directed. This illuminates the importance of previous acts in completing the total act as well as the role of *mind* in the social act. The individual builds *acts* through self-indication, self-interpretation, self-definition and so on; and puts together a pattern of action (Blumer, 1969, p. 64).

   If the prostitute is already a breadwinner for some other man, then despite the initial impulse of our hypothetical man to secure her as his breadwinner, she may display symbols dictating a kind of organized, directed and constructed act completely different from the one originally intended. His resultant act will reflect the defining nature of the actions of the prostitute for his goals. As Meltzer has suggested, the act from a Meadian point of view must be viewed as "the total process involved in human activity," which involves constructing and organizing behavior as well as imagining possible lines of action and defining the goals of action. These features of an act are evident in his four stages which comprise a completed act: impulse, perception, manipulation and consummation.[1]

   Certainly, much more could be said about Mead's influence on the development of symbolic interactionism. The preceding ideas, however, constitute the most important elements of his contributions and have

---

1. Meltzer interprets Mead's "impulse" as organisms experiencing disturbance of equilibrium. He further states that the presence of "impulses" in humans leads to nothing more than random, unorganized activity. It is the defining actions of others that channel behavior leading to the organization and construction of activity all of which involves perception, manipulation and consummation (Meltzer, p. 23).

had a profound effect on the development of the symbolic interaction perspective in social psychology.

MODERN SYMBOLIC INTERACTIONISM

Symbolic interactionism as we know it today is characterized by several varieties. Most scholars would attribute these "varieties" to diverse interpretations of Mead's posthumously published works. Because of this it is impossible to present a unified conception of the perspective. Instead, the perspective must be discussed in terms of schools, varieties and branches (Meltzer; Adler and Adler; Stryker, 1980) although Charon recently (1979) made a creditable attempt at integration. For purposes of this introduction to modern symbolic interactionism, two main types of the perspective are discussed, as well as several offshoots from these branches. The main types proposed in this volume are *processual symbolic interactionism* and *structural symbolic interactionism*. Processual symbolic interactionism will refer to those branches that focus on some major aspect of the nature of interaction as process. Structural symbolic interactionism is the label given those branches of symbolic interactionism which emphasize the constraining and/or setting influence of social structure (for example, roles, definitions of the situation, statuses, etc.) on social interaction.

Processual Symbolic Interactionism

Herbert Blumer The major proponent of processual symbolic interactionism has been Herbert Blumer. A student of Mead, Blumer is recognized as having coined the term "symbolic interactionism"—in what he called an "offhanded way" (Blumer, 1937)—and is generally recognized as the leader of the Chicago school of symbolic interactionism. Blumer has enjoyed an illustrious career in sociology, as reflected by his numerous influential articles in academic journals, in volumes edited by other scholars, and his own books, especially *Symbolic Interactionism: Perspectives and Methods*. According to Blumer, the first chapter in this work is an attempt to develop relatively explicit statements about the theoretical and methodological position of symbolic interactionism. While the perspective is similar to Meadian thought differences exist, because Blumerian symbolic interactionism attempts to deal with subject-matter and issues that were vague in Mead's work and in the works of other early contributors. Processual symbolic interactionism as developed by Blumer perhaps can be best introduced by discussing three general assumptions which he feels underlie the perspective. The assumptions are as follows:

> persons act toward objects (physical, social and abstract) on the basis of the meanings that the objects have for them; the meanings of objects for persons arises out of the social interaction that one has with one's fellows; and, the meanings given to objects are handled in and modified through, an interpretation process used by persons in dealing with objects which are encountered (Blumer 1969, p. 2).

It should be apparent that these assumptions are based in part on Mead's ideas. In fact, the first two assumptions are taken directly from *Mind, Self and Society*. The third, while implied by Mead, is a creation of Blumer. These assumptions are discussed below.

Persons act toward objects on the basis of the meanings that the objects have for them. The first assumption reemphasizes Mead's idea that human behavior is not a result of psychological states such as predetermined tendencies to act (attitudes), conscious or unconscious motives, personality sets or the like. Similarly, human action is not caused by factors often stressed by sociologists, including status demands, social roles, social norms, social values and so forth. Rather, human action is seen as a function of how the individual defines objects and organizes action toward objects. Using a previous example, because a man is looking for a prostitute does not adequately explain why he behaves toward some women as though they were prostitutes. A more plausible explanation for his behavior toward a particular woman begins with a meaning that the woman had for the man. The meaning would not be brought to the social situation by the man but would emerge during social interaction between the two. Behaviors exhibited by the woman which could aid the man in defining her as a prostitute might include suggestive body movements and speech. Once the man defined the woman as a prostitute, he would begin to map out his plan of action to be directed toward her which would include an internal conversation with himself during which he "role-takes" and tries out alternative courses of action.

The meanings of objects for persons arise out of the social interaction that one has with ones' fellows. The second assumption assumes that meanings of objects for individuals grow out of the way others react to them with respect to objects. Thus, meaning is not inherent in objects nor is the meaning of objects something to be found in the mind of an individual; instead, meaning is lodged in social interaction. For example, in our society, persons behave toward and define as prostitutes women who display certain behaviors. Because of the way that others have reacted (or do react), the man, through interaction with the woman, comes to define her as a prostitute. This means that the prostitute is a social creation constructed by persons in social interaction. In fact, in other societies and situations, women who display the same bodily movements and who use the same language as our hypothetical prostitute may not be defined as prostitutes. This is possible because persons interacting with these women do not experience behavior from others as a direct result of their interaction with women who use these gestures or language. Another example may drive the point home even further. Following a similar line of reasoning, races in the United States may be seen as social creations. This becomes obvious when one realizes that supposedly objective physiological criteria for racial classification are often disregarded in actual practice. Numerous persons with curly hair, broad noses, thick lips and brown skin are defined "white." Likewise, thousands of persons with straight hair, keen noses, thin lips and fair skin are defined "black." Is there any doubt that the meanings ascribed to persons in both physiologically-discrepant categories are social in origin? Since there appears to be no other source of the meanings it is plausible that they emerge from social interaction.

These meanings are handled in, and modified through, an interpretive process used by the person in dealing with the things he encounters. The third assumption of Blumer's symbolic interactionism is that the individual uses derived meanings of objects to engage in self-interaction. Contrary to some perspectives, the symbolic interaction point of view is that when the individual uses meanings he or she does more than simply apply the meaning derived from social interaction. The person uses meanings in his or her behavior indicating to himself or herself internally the objects that have meanings. Moreover, the meanings derived from social interaction undergo some modification in light of the situation in which the individual finds himself or herself and the direction of his or her action. Modification in this sense is seen as interpretation—a process which is formative and which uses meanings to guide human action. Returning briefly to the man in search of a prostitute, interpretation can be seen as a crucial factor. If he attends a neighborhood gathering which includes many of his close male and female friends and one of the women begins to display the same behavior as our prostitute, he is less likely to think of this female as a prostitute than if she were in a public bar and doing the same thing.

While the man may go so far as to indicate to himself that the behavior of the woman is unusual, the fact that she is a friend and at a social party is likely to result in a redefinition of her behavior as harmless flirtation. Just as interesting is the fact that in planning his course of action the man is likely to construct a plan that is much more appropriate to a response to "harmless flirtation" than to the gestures of a prostitute (even though he may be searching for one), and the behavior displayed by his friend may be no different from what he would find in a woman offering herself for money.

Blumer's assertion that meanings are handled and modified through an interpretive process involving self-reflectivity implies that human action is planned and rational behavior rather than mindless responses to stimuli. Following this line of thought Blumer also suggests that because of social norms and shared meanings, and through situational negotiation, persons continually fit together and guide each others acts. This makes possible joint action and group behavior but does not mean static behavior because renegotiation, re-alignments of action and new exposures are all sources of dynamism in social interaction.

Processual symbolic interactionism did not end with the contributions of W. I. Thomas, Charles Horton Cooley and George H. Mead, nor with the contributions of Herbert Blumer. Scholars too numerous to mention in this general chapter have made significant contributions which have served to refine and modify many of the concepts presently used.

An Elaboration of the Concept "Self": Erving Goffman   One such concept (some might even call it an *area* of processual symbolic interactionism) is "self." Given the importance of the "self" concept in processual symbolic interactionism, any treatment of the perspective should recognize significant contributions to its development. A set of contributions that have had a major influence on the development of the self concept has been developed by Erving Goffman. In a series of books and articles beginning with *Presentation of Self in Everyday Life,* Goffman has shown the dynamic character of the self—a process considered by many prior to his contributions to be a structure. In contrast, Goffman defined the self as social process, communicating, receiving and interpreting information about social actors (Fontana, 1980, p. 64). Some might hesitate to call Goffman a symbolic interactionist, but few would debate the point that he has been influenced by symbolic interactionism, and his view is that the locus of the self is other people's judgments. This other-oriented view did not however prevent him from developing a conception of the self which stressed individual's attempts to free themselves from others' definitions.

Goffman's early work emphasized what came to be known as the *dramaturgical perspective*. He defines this perspective in *The Presentation of Self in Everyday Life* as follows:

> The perspective employed in this report is that of the theatrical performance; the principles derived are dramaturgical ones. I shall consider the way in which the individual presents himself and his activity to others, the ways in which he guides and controls the impressions they form of him, and the kinds of things he may and may not do while sustaining his performance before them (p. xi).

Recognizing that components of the social structure are often thought to constrain human behavior, Goffman uses the dramaturgical perspective to focus on the *process* by which persons present themselves to others, thereby hiding their true selves. This focus becomes even more apparent in *Behavior in Public Places,* where he presents the "sincerity-cynicism" continuum which characterizes self-presentation throughout our lives. Every performance or any one performance can be located somewhere on the continuum, and the location represents the degree to which the performance reflects the self and/or the mask, the facade behind which the naked self hides. "Belief in performance," as an intervening variable, is a salient factor which also varies and as a result, varies our conceptions of ourselves as we "perform" in the social world. In other words, the self presented in public places can be "masked" to the point where it reflects very little of what we are really about or as a result of increases in behavior-belief congruence, the self presented may approach a "sincere performance."

For Goffman, persons in interaction put on performances consisting of a *front* characterized by setting, appearance and manner. In order to convey the desired impression, performers use *setting* which may include *location* of the interaction as well as physical objects in the environment (called props and referring to lighting and furniture); and front and back regions roughly equivalent to the on-stage scene and the back stage. *Appearance* (including clothing, hair style, facial expression and rank) and *manner* (referring to how one makes the presentation, such as meekly, aggressively, ashamedly) are also important during performance (Meltzer, Petras and Reynolds, pp. 48–9; Fontana, p. 66). Concepts such as *dramatic realization, discrepant roles* and *impression management* are keys, since the success of performance is a function of

how *significant* persons make the performance seem for others by skillful presentations and meeting others' expectations (dramatic realization); the fragile nature of human interaction means that it can be easily disrupted if discrepant elements exist (such as persons being out of
character in their roles or persons communicating out of character); and
the extent to which the enactment (performance) can be carried out
despite potentially disruptive features (Fontana, p. 67). Goffman's
dramaturgical metaphors, stressing the construction of social interaction, results in the production of a two-fold dynamic self. One aspect
of this self is inaccessible, *masked from* the world; and the other is
presented to the world for praise and approval.

In *Asylums,* Goffman looked behind the mask, to develop a view
of the personal self as manifested in the secondary adjustments persons
make to total institutions such as prisons, mental hospitals and the
military. Secondary adjustments are defined by Goffman as little acts of
rebellion or defiance which persons exhibit when they are stripped of
prior socialization, resocialized and publicly degraded. They represent a
kind of resistance to institutional control and thus contain the *personal
self.* That Goffman's views, emphases and conceptions of the self have
shifted over time is summarized very well by Fontana. She states:

> In *The Presentation of Self in Everyday Life,* Goffman im-
> plied that beneath the socially constructed self there was an
> ''inner'' self. His later works described the naked self that ex-
> ists behind the officially prescribed public self. In *Frame
> Analysis,* Goffman presents us with a much more desolate
> view of the self. After Goffman has peeled the layers of the
> onion which is the self, he finds no ''core'' inside it (p. 75).

Role-Person Merger: Ralph H. Turner   While his influence has not
been as pervasive as Blumer's or Goffman's, Ralph H. Turner's impact
on both processual symbolic interactionism and structural symbolic interactionism has been profound. As early as 1962 in an article entitled
''Role-taking: Process versus Conformity,'' Turner made a case for a
more processual view of the role-taking concept in symbolic interactionism which was represented by role theory. He offered several
criticisms of role theory—those contributing most to processual symbolic interactionism being that role theory seemed to have overemphasized structural influence on human behavior to the neglect of the
individual's own definitions of roles and performances of them; and,
that role theory had apparently shifted and accepted the anthropologist
Ralph Linton's emphasis on enacting the role prescribed rather than

Mead's point of "taking the role of the other." The latter emphasis suggests role-taking as a process of devising a performance on the basis of an "imputed other" role (Turner, pp. 22–23). In addition, because roles are rarely a neat set of rules or norms, persons often have to make explicit certain aspects of roles. This means creating and modifying as well as bringing the role to light—in a sense, making a social role. There is very little doubt that ideas such as these form the basis for Meltzer's famous distinction between the Iowa and Chicago Schools of symbolic interactionism which is practically synonymous with the processual-structural poles on the continuum proposed in this book.

Turner's recent views on the relationship between roles and persons (1978, pp. 1–23) touch upon behavior-belief congruence which results in what Goffman called "sincere performances" by persons. Concentrating on the identifying characteristics of role-person merger, Turner implies that Goffman's sincere performances constitute only one criterion of role-person mergers, the other two criteria being "playing a role" in inappropriate situations and a kind of ritualistic behavior in a Mertonian sense where alternative roles that may be more advantageous are eschewed in favor of a familiar role. Goffman's "sincere performances" can be interpreted to mean that roles played by persons are consistent with that aspect of the self hidden by "the mask." For Goffman, presentations of self often were cynical, in that aspects of the self were hidden under a mask. In contrast, Turner's view has been that persons construct their self-presentations (roles, performances, etc.) on the basis of their self-conceptions. This leads to an almost axiomatic conclusion that internal validation and external validation combine in some way to produce role-person merger and/or "sincere performances," perhaps in the sense that repeated external validation of roles positively alters internal validation (the successful anticipation of the behavior of relevant others which facilitates one's own role).

A final, but by no means exhaustive, contribution made by Ralph Turner to processual symbolic interactionism was made approximately fourteen years after the publication of Turner's article emphasizing the processual nature of human behavior and role-taking. In "The Real Self: From Institution to Impulse" Turner searches for the sources of the "real self." Real self is defined as the subjective cognitions individuals have of themselves (who and what am I). It should be recalled that early Goffman thought emphasized self being defined by others. Later shifts in Goffman's ideas emphasized the naked or real self as that which remains when individuals flee from institutional controls by secondary adjustments ("Minor, secret adaptations expressed in acts that defy the tightly structured role system. . ." [Fontana, p. 69]) Moreover, unlike Turner, Goffman stressed an aspect of self *presented* and an aspect *hidden* behind a mask or facade. In contrast, Turner apparently feels that the true self emerges in role-performances, since—as pointed out earlier—he feels that persons construct their performances on the basis of their self-conceptions. To return to his article; Turner suggests that the real self can be based in institution or impulse. When people to a great extent accept feelings, attitudes and actions anchored in institutions and manifested by institutional goal-oriented action as evidence of their real selves, the self is said to have an institutional focus. On the other hand, when people to a great degree perceive what Goffman calls "secondary adjustment," which includes outbursts, muttering, and institutionally controlled forms as expression of their true selves, then the self is said to have an impulse focus. Roughly paralleling the shifts in Goffman's emphasis on the self mentioned earlier, Turner posits the notion that during the last several decades in the United States, focus of self has shifted from an institutional focus to an impulse focus (Stryker, 1980, p. 113). Turner's shift seems to be more linear than Goffman's vacillating views of self-loci. The implications of the hypothesized shift for social structure promises to be an exciting and provocative line of investigation for years to come. Some of these implications are discussed later in this chapter under structural symbolic interactionism.

Social Construction of Behavior: Labelling Theory   Another set of contributions deriving from processual symbolic interactionism and contributing to it comes from a group of scholars who were greatly influenced by the work of Mead and Blumer—criminologists Frank Tannenbaum and Alfred Lindesmith, and the field research approach of the University of Chicago. Scholars such as Howard Becker, Erving Goffman, Thomas Scheff, Edwin Schur, Edwin Lemert and D. L. Rosenhan all at one time or another have had one thing in common and that is a contention that society produces the very behavior it seeks to prevent by defining certain behaviors as deviant. The name given these scholars and many others who endorse this point of view is *labelling theorists* or *societal reaction theorists*. More specifically, labelling theory is the idea that deviant behavior refers to the reification of socially constructed meanings which through a definable process are assigned a name. In other words, deviance is social and a deviant act is socially constructed by those who witness the act directly or indirectly. Erikson's contention that deviance is a property conferred upon certain forms of behavior; and Becker's notion that deviance refers not to the quality of an act committed but to the result of others enforcing certain rules and regulations to the actor, are both elaborations of Mead's conception of the *social object*.

We are reminded of Mead's analysis of social objects by Herbert Blumer:

1. The nature of an object is constructed by the meaning it has for the person or persons for whom it is an object.
2. The meaning is not intrinsic to the object but derives from how the person is initially prepared to act toward it.
3. All objects are social products in that they are formed and transformed by the defining process that takes place in social interaction.
4. People are prepared to act toward objects on the basis of the meanings of the objects for them.
5. Just because an object is something that is designated, one can organize one's action toward it or decide whether or not to act toward it (Blumer, 1969, pp. 68–9).

Herein lies the basic features of the labelling perspective, some of which have been emphasized more than others by those seeking to understand the procedures by which acts come to be defined as "deviant" acts. For example, the thrust of much of the work of Erikson, Becker, and Scheff in the area has been on the construction of deviance, or the first point listed above. Lemert, Goffman, and others, concentrating on the fourth and fifth points, emphasize an aspect of the labelling perspective which stresses the self as object. Apparently aware of the contention that the individual can become an object unto itself, they imply that through an internal conversation of significant gestures (minding behavior) and symbolic interaction with others, where labelling occurs as a result of viewing oneself from the generalized other viewpoint, the self as an "external social object" is redefined as it takes on new meaning and the individual becomes prepared to act toward it in different ways (based on the meaning acquired through self-interaction with the generalized other). These points seem to be major features of concepts such as primary deviance, secondary deviance and stigma, all of which refer to the extent to which an individual redefines the self. A final point to be made is that not only do persons who engage in secondary deviance come to *believe* that the labels assigned them are what they really are, but they *are* what they really *are*, because meanings of objects are social and thus arise out of social interaction.

The contribution here is obvious. By concentrating on the transformation of self-conceptions Lemert and Goffman broaden our understanding of the "self as object." In general, labelling theory has had a great impact on the study of deviance although it has not been without its critics. Much of the criticism is beyond the scope of what is intended here. However, several of the criticisms as they relate to processual symbolic interactionism are discussed in a later section of this chapter.

The Nature of the Interpretive Process   Much has been said thus far about self-reflexivity, definition of the situation, internal conversation of significant gestures and the interpretation process. It is doubtful, however, if one at this point could processually describe the latter concept. In order to do so, there would have to be a heavy reliance on fixed and stable meanings which if used to describe interaction with others and with oneself negates the dynamics of the interpretive process. If fixed and stable meanings are posited when describing how order and consistency occur, do we really have an understanding of how they occur? An answer to this question, based on another variant of processual symbolic interactionism, ethnomethodology would have to be No! Adherents of this perspective such as Harold Garfinkel and Aaron Cicourel, among others, would be unconvinced that exploring sharedness and intelligibility like this gives much information about the nature of the interpretive process. In other words, the dynamics of the interpretive process can be gleaned only through demonstrating how individuals achieve order and sharedness.

Harold Garfinkel seeks an answer to the "how" of ordering and sharedness in persons' activities in everyday life. He believes that these activities are synonymous with *how* the individual orders or makes everyday life *accountable*. In his collection of essays entitled *Studies in Ethnomethodology* Garfinkel states:

> The following studies seek to treat practical activities, practical circumstances, and practical sociological reasoning as topics of empirical study, and by paying to the most commonplace activities of daily life the attention usually accorded extraordinary events, seek to learn about them as phenomena in their own right. Their central recommendation is that the activities whereby members produce and manage settings of organized everyday affairs are identical with members' procedures for making these settings "account-able." The "reflexive," or incarnate character of accounting practices and accounts make up the crux of that recommendation (p. 11).

Accounts are the *rationales individuals use to obtain understandings of their activities in socially acceptable terms*. This means that persons "create both a setting and their understanding of that setting" (Freeman, 1980, p. 142). Even if the accounts are false (as when people lie), "how one lies, in terms of the abilities one must draw on to lie, differs little from how one understands" (Freeman, p. 144). Still, how do we come to know what we know?

Cicourel has developed a set of interpretive procedures which are thought to provide at least a partial answer to the above question (1970, 1972). He suggests that interpretation and interpretive procedures are *not* synonymous. Interpretive procedures are interwoven with the social and cultural setting which combine to produce the interpretation. Thus, interpretation is not a function of interpretive procedures alone but rather it is some function of these procedures *and* the social and cultural setting at a very general ordering level.

The interpretive procedures specified by Cicourel are (1) the reciprocity perspective, (2) the *et cetera* assumption, and (3) normal forms. The reciprocity perspective involves the assumption by a person in interaction that he or she and others would have the same experiences in the setting if they could exchange places; and that personal differences in assigning meaning can be disregarded in favor of believing in a common world (Fontana, 1980, p. 146). The et cetera assumption refers to persons in social interaction completing one another's utterances to enhance comprehensiveness in terms of what they assume is commonly known. As Fontana has suggested, both of the above assumptions contribute to the presumption of social consensus in the face of interaction which all too often appears vague and meaningless. A third interpretive procedure discussed by Cicourel is "normal forms." Normal forms refer to talk and appearance deemed acceptable (appropriate) and desirable in that they are used to delineate and specify their experiences. Those forms no doubt influence what persons experience, *how* they achieve interpretation and then how they construct their social worlds.

Admittedly, few of the processual symbolic interactionists discussed earlier in this chapter have expressed interest in the interpretive process as have ethnomethodologists. It seems, though, that ethnomethodological contributions could play a major role in refining a key concept in the perspective which in great part remains incomplete without further inquiry along such lines.

The Perspective as a Continuum   As will be seen in the next section, not all scholars who label themselves symbolic interactionists subscribe to what has been discussed about symbolic interactionism thus far. This is because some symbolic interactionists feel that the constraining effects of social structure should enjoy a more prominent position in the perspective than the foregoing consideration suggests. Within the continuum proposed, such scholars are closer to the category of structural symbolic interactionists, although their work may contain features of processual symbolic interactionism. At this point it is necessary to point out that the categories "structural symbolic interactionism" and "processual symbolic interactionism" are ideal in the sense that a continuum should be visualized where they are at opposite ends. Additionally, it is doubtful that any one branch of symbolic interactionism or any one scholar is purely processual or structural. Most works and scholars fall somewhere on the continuum rather than precisely at one of the opposite poles. Figure 3.1 illustrates this point.

Basic Theoretical Statements in Processual Symbolic Interactionism
Much work which could be placed close to the processual pole in symbolic interactionism appears not to be processual because of diverse concerns, esoteric concepts and different points of departure. The lack of integration is a difficult one and still awaits presentation. However, Manis and Meltzer have offered a broad outline of "the major substantive and methodological elements" characterizing symbolic interactionism which would appear to be acceptable to many within the processual branch of symbolic interactionism (1978, pp. 5–9). The discussion below is based heavily on their contributions and concludes our consideration of processual symbolic interactionism.

   1. *"Distinctively human behavior and interaction are carried on through the medium of symbols and their meanings"* This statement is referred to as the central idea in symbolic interactionism. It refers to the assumption that humans in social interaction do not typically respond to each other on a stimulus-response basis but rather respond to each other and other stimuli on the basis of symbolic meanings. These meanings are not inherent in the objects themselves but rather are the result of social interaction. Individuals act on the basis of interpretation of objects and thus the meaning objects have for them.

   2. *"The individual becomes humanized through interaction with others."* The individual is not born human. This means that he or she is not born capable of human action. Rather, it is through social association that humanization occurs. The individual gradually becomes capable of carrying on a conversation of significant gestures, using symbols and becoming an object unto itself. Interaction with others facilitates empathetic understanding; minded behavior, and self reflexivity—all uniquely human qualities.

   3. *"Human society is most usefully conceived as consisting of people in interaction."* Eschewing the reification of society, this proposition emphasizes the processual nature of human society. It further implies that social structure is constructed, maintained and modified by persons in social interaction rather than being autonomous and/or self-regulating.

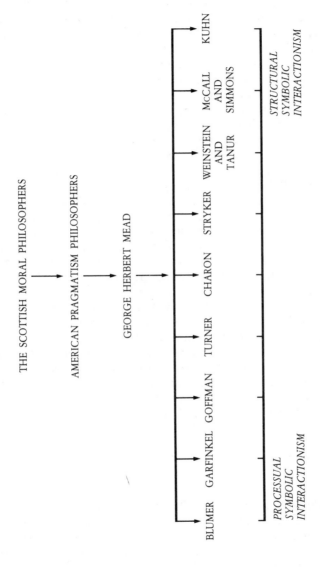

Figure 3.1
Illustrative figure of processual-structural continuum

101

4. *"Human beings are active in shaping their own behavior."* Numerous other perspectives in social psychology along with some varieties of symbolic interactionism assume a rather deterministic view of human behavior. In contrast, the above proposition suggests a more indeterministic view of human behavior in the sense that the individual participates in the construction of behavior. He or she does not "play" social roles, respond to stimuli, conform to societal norms. Rather, the individual selects stimuli, interprets stimuli, chooses between alternative courses of action, and the like.

5. *"Consciousness, or thinking, involves interaction with oneself."* The ability of individuals to engage in an internal conversation is assumed to be distinctively human and means that the individual can become an object unto oneself and make indications to oneself. The interaction that one carries on with others is duplicated with oneself and labelled minded behavior or thinking.

6. *"Human beings construct their behavior during the course of execution."* This proposition refers to the emergent nature of human behavior. Human behavior is not seen as a product of past experience, pre-established meanings, etc. Instead behavior is thought to be a function of interaction within an individual which in part is characterized by interpretations, outlining and rejecting choices of plans of actions.

7. *"An understanding of human conduct requires study of the actors' covert behavior."* Since human behavior is processual, symbolic interaction includes both observable and unobservable activity. Therefore, measures utilized to study human behavior from a symbolic interaction point of view must be able to assess actors' meanings in order to explain their conduct. This means that sympathetic introspection must be part and parcel of procedures used to study human conduct.

Let us now direct our attention to the right end of the symbolic interactionism continuum—structural symbolic interactionism.

Structural Symbolic Interactionism

Kuhn's Symbolic Interactionism   Manford H. Kuhn can be called the chief architect of structural symbolic interactionism. He was introduced to symbolic interactionism while a student of Kimball Young at the University of Wisconsin. After teaching at the University of Wisconsin, Whittier College and Mount Holyoke College, Kuhn launched his teaching career at the State University of Iowa in 1946 where he began to build what Meltzer and Petras refer to as the Iowa School of Symbolic Interactionism. Kuhn's point of departure (in collaboration with that of

Hickman) seems to be based on several Meadian assumptions: (1) that objects do not have intrinsic meaning but rather derive their meanings through social definitions; (2) that individuals behave toward objects in terms of their meanings; and (3) that the individual is not simply passive, automatically responding to group assigned meanings of objects (Hickman and Kuhn, pp. 25–26).

While these assumptions place Kuhn clearly within the symbolic interaction perspective, his substantive interest and methodological predilections distinguish his work from processual symbolic interactionism. First of all, Kuhn defines the self in *structural* terms. He sees the self as a structure of attitudes derived from the individual's internalized statuses and roles. It "consists of the individual's attitudes (plans of action) toward his own mind and body—as an organization of attitudes which are, in effect, the internalization of the individual's role recipes" (Hickman and Kuhn, pp. 38–43). Kuhn further views the self as a product of social interaction and as a framework within which social interaction occurs. By this he means that individuals' conceptions of themselves are derived from what others convey to them about themselves during social interaction in which they take roles and assume statuses. In addition, self-conception facilitates defining social situations, and in a sense establishes guidelines for social interaction. As Stryker suggests, Kuhn's view of the self is that it is a stable set of meanings that one attaches to oneself as an object (Stryker, 1980, p. 102).

Kuhn's distinctive operational definition of the self, which has given impetus to more structured views of the term, derives from his conception of attitudes as verbal statements and his theoretical definition of the self as "the individual's attitudes toward his own mind and body viewed as an object" (Hickman and Kuhn, p. 43). The two definitions combine to produce a definition of the self as a product of the verbal statements individuals make about themselves derived from their "orientational others." Orientational others refers to others toward whom the individual is emotionally and psychologically committed; those who are responsible for the basic concepts and categories used by the individual; those who constitute role-partners in meaningful social roles, thereby providing meaning of self; and, those who through intercommunication are sources of sustainment or change in self-conceptions (Kuhn, 1964, pp. 5–21).

In addition to this outline for operationalizing the self, Kuhn also makes a distinction between the self as a social object and other social objects. The self is always with the individual as he or she moves from situation to situation. Because of this omnipresence, the self serves as the basis upon which other attitudes are formed in various situations. As an illustration, as I move from a professor–student situation to a father–child situation to a lover relationship, my self-conception in-fluences plans of action I direct toward each of my role partners and other social objects in each situation. The self, then, emerges out of social interaction with others and also shapes and/or constrains interaction with others. It does so by defining situations and other objects in social interaction.

A final feature of the self from Kuhn's viewpoint concerns the extent to which it is anchored in the society and the implications of societal anchorage or nonanchorage. Kuhn and McPartland devised two categories to use in content analyzing responses to their now famous Twenty Statements Test (1954, pp. 68–76). The response categories were *consensual reference* and *subconsensual references*. They felt that these "content categories distinguish between statements (about the self) which refer to groups and classes when limits and conditions of membership are matters of common knowledge, i.e. *consensual;* and those which refer to groups, classes, attributes, traits or any other matters which would require interpretation by the respondent to be precise or to place his relation to other people, i.e. *subconsensual.*" It is assumed, for example, that terms like "black person," "white person," "Democrat" and "Republican" have shared meanings in society and can be distinguished from others like "racist," "chauvinist," "sensitive" and "overbearing," all of which are thought to be without positional reference and to require interpretation by the respondent before he or she can be classified. Tucker points out that these categories focus on the meaning of social objects in terms of behavior taken with regard to them and that *consensually* identified statements presumably will yield shared responses from most others. As a result of this shared meaning, others also can be expected to behave toward the self-defined consensual person in a similar manner in a variety of situations. This is so because such persons are thought to have interacted in numerous diverse situations, and are therefore effectively anchored in the main culture. The opposite is true for those who define themselves in a sub-consensual fashion. Finally, Stryker alludes to Kuhn's recognition of the variable salience of self-attitudes (which is a crucial variable in his own symbolic interaction framework) and the necessity for going beyond subjective identification (Stryker, 1980, p. 103). Kuhn and McPartland suggest other areas of social investigation to enhance symbolic interactionism as a perspective. These areas include a person's roles, preferences, role expectations, self-evaluations, patterns of reference group selection, etc. (68–76).

From the foregoing discussion, it should be apparent that Manford Kuhn has had a great impact on structural symbolic interactionism. This influence can be seen to some extent in some of Turner's concerns

and to an even greater extent in the works of McCall and Simmons, Stryker, and others, as we shall see.

Self, Roles and Social Interaction   An increasingly popular view of the role of self in structural symbolic interaction is that individuals strive to be certain kinds of people and thus maximize their reinforcements and profits from others. In "Meanings, Purposes and Structural Resources in Social Interaction," Eugene Weinstein and Judith Tanur provide a rationale for this growing emphasis, which closely resembles assumptions in behaviorism and social exchange formulations. They believe that the "assumption of purposiveness is a universal feature of all theoretical schemes for social action. From Aristotle to Schutz, from Homans to Parsons, from needs to values, some form of hedonic assumption is necessary to render social activity as sensible." Unlike perspectives such as modern behaviorism and social exchange, this view of structural symbolic interactionism places great emphasis on linking the self with roles, statuses, social types and/or categories. Additionally, there is also an emphasis on the individual's mapping out plans of action to be a particular kind of person. Interspersed with this is a dramaturgical element which stresses the self as character performed, as a performer and as an audience (McCall and Simmons, 1978). The first aspect of self implies that a distinctive set of statuses, values, motives, mannerisms and the like characterize a person. The second aspect of self means that the self is active, performing, etc., and the third aspect recognizes the self as an internal audience which appraises its performances based on internalized standards from significant others.

The self, then, according to this view of structural symbolic interaction, is a structure consisting of self-knowledge and self-feelings and, in general, numerous conceptions of self. This latter component is axiomatic, since self-conceptions are derived from role performances in numerous roles and situations. In other words, the individual is seen as having multiple conceptions of self or "role identities" which all together make up the self. Role identities are the character and role constructed by the individual as an occupant of a particular social position (Stryker, 1980, p. 120). They act as a variety of things, including a basis for self appraisal, defining social situations, objects and others. Because role identities are personal, social and idealized, the character and role devised are usually at variance with reality. When this occurs, it becomes necessary to legitimate self-conceptions by obtaining social role support from role performances. Such performances are devised to persuade others of an individual's claim to a role identity. Since performances always result in some discrepancy between one's identity and impressions from others, techniques such as selective interaction, selective perception and altercasting are used to achieve social support for role identities. Two other aspects of role identity are important in the sense that they have implication for social activity: prominence and salience of role identities. *Prominence* refers to the degree to which individual views of self (identities) are deemed important by the individual and have been supported by others. Implicit in prominence is an individual's commitment to and investment in an identity. *Salience* of role identities has three basic ingredients: (1) the extent to which a particular identity is in need of legitimation; (2) the extent to which a person needs or desires the gratifications attached to and resulting from a particular role performance; and (3) whether the individual perceives that the role identity can be profitably enacted in the situation. Role assumption in social interaction, then, is some function of prominence, salience and the audience of a performance (Stryker, 1980, p. 122).

Self-expectations also are crucial to salience in the sense that self-conceptions are intimately related. These idealized standards that persons set for themselves are met only rarely and threaten legitimation, calling forth techniques designed to close the gap between reality (active performance) and idealized image. When such techniques fail, attempts at altering the salience of role identities may be made. If *all* such attempts fail, feelings of self-unworthiness are likely to occur. This does not always happen because usually the individual has close ties with some primary group or in group which supports him or her by providing legitimation or role identities. Also, as Stryker points out, persons learn to circumvent threats to role identities through avoidance of certain performances, situations and persons.

Role Performance, Identity Salience and Social Interaction   It should be obvious that the discussion so far has been very much related to Kuhn's views on symbolic interactionism. Another related view has been developed by Stryker and is highly representative of structural symbolic interactionism.

The thrust of Stryker's "symbolic interactionist theory" is toward an explanation of social interaction. More specifically, he is interested in role performance as a consequence of the joint or singular effects of society and self. Recognizing and apparently influenced by many of Cooley's and Mead's ideas as well as those of Kuhn (the meaning of social objects and the limiting effect of meanings are examples), Turner (the concept of role making), McCall and Simmons and Burke (identity saliences), Stryker presents a version of symbolic interactionism which incorporates elements of role theory and deals with "the reciprocal impact of social person and social structure (1980, p. 52).

Before considering Stryker's "partial theory" a review of some

basic premises upon which it is based seems appropriate. These basic premises constitute what Stryker has referred to as a theoretical framework designed to enable the theorist to move from the level of the person to social structure and back. In his article "Identity Salience and Role Performance: The Relevance of Symbolic Interaction Theory for Family Research" Stryker constructs a framework based on Mead, Kuhn, Turner, and his own reflections on the nature of symbolic interactionism. The framework is as follows:

1. Behavior is dependent upon a named or classified world. The names or class terms attached to aspects of the environment, both physical and social, carry meaning in the form of shared behavioral expectations that grow out of social interaction. From interaction with others, one learns how to classify objects one comes into contact with and in that process one also learns how one is expected to behave with reference to those objects.

2. Among the class terms learned in interaction are the symbols that are used to designate "positions," which are the relatively stable, morphological components of social structure. These positions carry the shared behavioral expectations that are conventionally labelled "roles."

3. Persons who act in the context of organized patterns of behavior, i.e., in the context of social structure, name one another in the sense of recognizing one another as occupants of positions. When they name one another they invoke expectations with regard to each other's behavior.

4. Persons acting in the context of organized behavior apply names to themselves as well. These reflexively applied positional designations, which become part of the "self," create internalized expectations with regard to their own behavior.

5. When entering interactive situations, persons define the situation by applying names to it, to the other participants in the interaction, to themselves, and to particular features within the situation, and use the resulting definition to organize their own behavior accordingly.

6. Social behavior is not, however, determined by these definitions, though early definitions may constrain the possibilities for alternative definitions to emerge from interaction. Behavior is the product of a role-making process, initiated by expectations invoked in the process of defining

situations, but developing through a tentative, sometimes extremely subtle probing interchange among actors that can reshape the form and the content of the interaction.

7. The degree to which roles are "made" rather than simply "played" as well as the constituent elements entering the construction of roles, will depend on the larger social structures in which interactive situations are embedded. Some structures are "open," others relatively "closed" with respect to novelty in roles and in role enactments or performances. All structures impose some limits on the kinds of definitions that may be called into play and thus limit the possibilities for interaction.

8. To the degree that roles are made rather than only played as given, changes can occur in the character of definitions, in the names and class terms those definitions use, and in the possibilities for interaction; and such changes can in turn lead to changes in the larger social structures within which interactions take place.[2]

Following the above presentation, Stryker goes on to elaborate each of the statements, and in addition considers what he deems to be major concepts such as the social person, role, self, role-taking, socialization, social structure, role conflict and role strain, as based on work by Gregory Stone, Eugene Weinstein, Dennis Wrong, William J. Goode, and Robert K. Merton, among others. It is in his elaboration of self that several concepts important to theoretical formulation emerge— "identity salience," "commitment" and "self-esteem." "Identity salience" is defined as "the probability of invoking an identity." In other words, it means the importance to a person of placement as a social object by others in the same terms as a person places and announces him or her self. The concept is similar to McCall and Simmon's "prominence." "Commitment" refers to the extent that one's relationships to specified sets of persons depend on being a particular kind of person, in accepting certain positions and rules (Stryker, 1980, p. 61). With respect to identity salience, an identity hierarchy is assumed. This means that the individual, having perhaps numerous identities, orders the identities, in the sense that some identities are more likely than others to come forth in social situations. Again, in my example, if I have the identities Professor, Father and Lover, they are arranged hier-

---

2. From Sheldon Stryker, "Identity Salience and Role Performance," *Journal of Marriage and the Family* 30 (November 1968). Copyrighted 1968 by the National Council on Family Relations. Reprinted by permission.

archically, and one is more likely than the others to come forth in any particular situation. This results from the proposition that the higher the identity in the salience hierarchy, the more likely that the identity will be invoked in a given situation. Stryker recognizes that some situations do not elicit several identities because of what he terms structural isolation, which occurs when a situation is relatively unrelated to other situations. But when there is a relatively high degree of structural overlap between situations, several identities are likely to be called forth in any one of the situations. Of course, not all of the identities called up will be contradictory or conflicting, but if they *are* then their positions in the identity salience hierarchy determines, in part, the role performed and thus the behavior displayed. Therefore, the linkage between society and self is specified to some extent by introducing the concept identity salience. Further specification is made when commitment is added to conceptualize aspects of social structure linked to self.

If an individual values his or her relationships to specified others, and these relationships are contingent upon accepting certain kinds of positions and roles (being a certain type of person) then he or she is committed to some degree. "Commitment" to being a certain kind of person is some function of the importance of maintaining ties to a set of others. This means, in turn, invoking a certain identity in order to maintain ties to others.

Several dimensions characterize commitment. They are "the number of others to whom one relates through occupancy of a given position; the importance of others to whom one relates through occupancy of a given role; and, the number of distinctive kinds of activities attached to a particular linkage to another or others" (Stryker, 1980, p. 81).

"Self-esteem" is the third aspect of self felt to be crucial in the society–self linkages. It is seen as an intervening variable interpreting the relationship between identity structure and role performance. Through role-taking and socialization, two processes whereby persons learn their location and others' expectations, and become incorporated into organized patterns of interaction, individuals develop identities based on societal definitions. Because of this, a reasonable assumption is that persons seek identity validation and/or confirmation by behaving in ways that are identity-validating and/or identity-confirming. Stryker feels that a second assumption is warranted, stating simply that "persons like to think well of themselves, thus interweaving self-esteem with behavior in accordance with a salient identity." (Stryker, 1980, p. 64). Given this linkage it becomes axiomatic that when identity is defined in terms that reflect the norms and values of society or some segment of it, conforming behavior simultaneously produces self-esteem.

Using these three concepts and their elaboration, as well as other assumptions, Stryker presents a set of related hypotheses which purportedly offer a partial explanation of interaction as a function of society and self. The hypotheses are as follows:

1. The greater the commitment premised on an identity, the higher that identity will be in the salience hierarchy.
2. The greater the commitment premised on an identity and the more positive the evaluation of that identity, the higher the identity will be in the salience hierarchy.
3. The more a given network of commitment is premised on a particular identity as against other identities which may enter that network of commitment, the higher that identity will be in the salience hierarchy.
4. The more congruent the role expectations of those to whom one is committed by virtue of a given identity, the higher that identity will be in the salience hierarchy.
5. The larger the number of persons included in a network of commitment premised on a given identity for whom that identity is high in their own salience hierarchies, the higher that identity will be in the salience hierarchy.
6. The higher an identity in the salience hierarchy, the greater the probability of role performances being consistent with the role expectations attached to that identity.
7. The higher an identity in the salience hierarchy, the greater the probability that a person will perceive a given situation as an opportunity to perform in terms of that identity.
8. The higher an identity in the salience hierarchy, the greater the probability that a person will actively seek out opportunities to perform in terms of that identity.
9. The greater the commitment, the higher the identity salience, the greater impact the quality of role performance will have on self-esteem.
10. The greater the commitment, the higher the identity salience, the higher the probability that role performance will reflect institutionalized values and norms.
11. External events cutting existing commitments will increase the probability of adoption of novel identities.
12. The more that perceived consequences of a projected identity change are in the direction of reinforcing valued commitments, the less the resistance to change (pp. 83–4).

ISSUES AND DEBATES IN SYMBOLIC INTERACTIONISM

The Methodological Debate

A major debate in symbolic interactionism has probably become apparent, and that is the process vs. structure issue, seen by many as the Chicago School vs. the Iowa School, or, Blumerian symbolic interactionism vs. Kuhnian symbolic interactionism. Meltzer, Petras and Reynolds argue that the basic distinction between what are called here processual symbolic interactionism and structural symbolic interactionism is *methodological* in nature, centering on the opposition between humanistic and positivistic approaches to social investigation. They specify three related points of departure: "(1) the relative merits of phenomenological and operational approaches; (2) the appropriate techniques of observation; and (3) the nature of the concepts best suited for the analysis of human behavior" (p. 42). Processual symbolic interactionists stress the importance of taking the role of those being studied. This means engaging in sympathetic introspection in order to know something about the subject's world. When one is able to experience the subject's world as the subject experiences it, a meaningful analysis can presumably be made of his or her behavior. Such an approach has implications for the kinds of analyses which can be attempted and the kind of concepts which can be constructed. Herbert Blumer, in a classic article written in 1954, emphasizes the need for sociologists to direct attention toward the development of what he calls "sensitizing concepts." Blumer and other processual symbolic interactionists have continued to feel that given the nature of the individual and his or her relationship to the environment (social reality) attempts should be made to develop concepts which suggest "directions in which to look" at social phenomena.

Structural symbolic interactionists, in varying degrees, reject the idea that one can get "inside" other people and observe their interpretive processes in action. The self is viewed in more structural terms, which allows the social investigator to operationalize attributes of the self. Since human conduct is seen by structural symbolic interactionists as ultimately related to self-attributes, for most structural symbolic interactionists the investigation of social interaction implies using more positivistic techniques—constructing variables, constructing propositions and testing propositions without attempting empathy with those being studied. In summary, structural symbolic interactionists, taking their cues from Kuhn, feel that social psychology advances best through the development and utilization of stricter operational procedures.

The Theoretical Debate

The theoretical debate between structural and processual symbolic interactionists centers around several issues including: (1) the degree to which an individual's behavior is "free"; (2) conception of the nature of the self; and (3) the extent to which nonsymbolic interaction plays a role in human behavior. Meltzer and Petras discussed these issues nearly a decade ago and they still seem to be among the more crucial concerns of scholars working within the perspective (pp. 43–57).

An underlying assumption of processual symbolic interactionism is that the individual in social interaction with others does not merely act, but rather he or she *constructs social action*. While the individual certainly may have some idea of social roles that he or she as well as others are to perform, it is not the case that these role definitions determine the behavior that takes place. Rather, the individual copes with and defines a given situation, trying to define the action of others and to develop his or her own course of action. In contrast, structural symbolic interactionism implies that an individual's behavior is determined by self-definition, and the role definitions of others. Thus, if it is known how an individual defines him or her self, mother and father or friendship group, it is possible to predict the individual's behavior in some situations. Given this view of the source of human conduct (which is basically that behavior is a function of social definitions), the second theoretical difference between the two perspectives can be discussed.

Many structural symbolic interactionists conceive of the self as an organization of attitudes—an entity, a structure. Viewed thus, the self consists solely of definitions by others of the individual's identity. Processual symbolic interactionists view the self as process. For them, the self is the interplay between impulses (the "I") and internalized definitions (the "Me"). Thus, when individuals are performing social roles, from the structural perspective they are "role-taking" while from the processual perspective they are "making" social roles.

Another theoretical distinction between the two branches of symbolic interactionism is that of the "level of interaction" emphasized in studying the individual in his or her social environment. Processual symbolic interactionists have stressed symbolic interaction but also have recognized that individuals engage in nonsymbolic interaction. On the other hand, while structural symbolic interactionists have placed much emphasis on the "Me" aspect of the self, little, if any, attention has been directed to nonsymbolic interaction. This does not seem likely to change given the relatively recent suggestion by Stryker that it may be possible to conceive of the "I" as the playing-off of various "identities" (which may include memories of former Me's) against one another, thus obviating the need to conceive the "I" as impulse. This is an interesting point because the "I" is a source of creativity for the self and therefore is of crucial importance for processual symbolic interactionists. If the "I" can be conceived of as based on social definitions, then there is little reason to be concerned with nonsymbolic interaction.

The Huber–Blumer Debate

Another debate in symbolic interactionism encompasses a variety of issues ranging from theoretical and methodological to ideological. It appeared in 1973 in one of the most interesting series of articles and comments ever to be published in the *American Sociological Review,* consisting of an exchange between Joan Huber, Herbert Blumer and several adherents of symbolic interactionism. I think it is important to refer to it in a book of this kind because too often students are presented with facts as though a complete consensus existed among experts about the subject matter. This is rarely so in social psychology, or in any of the other social sciences, as the following discussion reflects.

In April 1973, the *American Sociological Review* published an article by Joan Huber entitled "Symbolic Interactionism as a Pragmatic Perspective: The Bias of Emergent Theory." While much of what Huber had to say is beyond the scope of this text, she does refer to several problems in symbolic interactionism which should be of interest to the beginning student:

1. Symbolic interactionists (and specifically Blumer) do not offer an explanation for the way in which scientists can seek to study social reality with "blank minds."
2. There is no evidence to show that symbolic interactionists more closely follow their position in research than those of different social psychological persuasions.
3. There is a contradiction in Blumer's idea about the research process.
4. Few rules exist in symbolic interactionism (of the emergent theory variety) indicating how one moves from observations to theory.
5. There is no way to distinguish the findings of sociologists from the findings of anyone else.

On the criticism that no explanation is given for the implied assumption that scientists approach social reality with "blank minds," Huber states her case in the following way. She notes that because research design, replication, hypothesis testing and operationalizing concepts lie outside the domain of symbolic interactionism, researchers using the perspective supposedly enter into scientific inquiry with "blank minds." The implicit question is whether it is possible to enter into research in this manner. In other words, while symbolic interactionists might make the claim to open-mindedness, there may well lie hidden certain biases which would be apparent if they spelled out in advance their research expectations.

Another criticism offered by Huber involves the contradiction between Blumer's statement that the symbolic interactionist begins his or her research with a "prior picture," an unavoidable prerequisite for study, and his emphatic warning that symbolic interactionists must not enter into research with preconceived ideas.

Noting Blumer's criticism of social theory, Huber presents Blumer's preference for sensitizing concepts rather than definitive ones, pointing out reporting and analytical probing. From Huber's perspective, this means that theory is seen as emerging from direct observation with little specification of the rules of logic to be used (p. 280). The first rules or guidelines that are provided (according to Huber) are inadequate since the only solution seems to be that well-informed observers should be used. But who are well-informed observers? The problem, Huber notes, becomes particularly acute when observers disagree with each other over the nature of some social reality. The difficulty of the problem is clear because a question must be raised about which observer's views should be thought of as the correct ones and which should be discarded. Huber's response to her own question is that ultimately the answer may lie in power processes—the more powerful the observer, the greater the likelihood that his or her views are heard and are used as the "correct views."

While Huber had much more to say, the above ideas probably are the most important ones for us to consider. Let us now turn to the reaction which these ideas generated.

In a rather emotional response, Blumer attempts to defend his views on symbolic interactionism, as well as those of Mead. His defense, somewhat abbreviated here, consists of the following:

1. An accusation that Huber espouses the view that "shaping" the scientific problem always preceded empirical observation.
2. A direct attack on the validity of the Huber contention that he endorsed beginning research with a blank mind.
3. A rebuttal of the idea that symbolic interactionists cannot test their assumptions.
4. A recommendation suggesting joint confrontation among

other unspecified means for solving the problem of a conflict between observers.

5. An attack on Huber's conscientiousness as an observer for
her contention that power plays a role in determining
which observer views are thought by investigators to be
empirical.

Replying in turn to Blumer, Huber makes a distinction between
"thinking about" problems along with other theoretical activities and
"theory." She states that the real issue is whether scientific knowledge
can be produced without some kind of logical framework, and goes
on to inquire about the "different type of logic" Blumer says is necessary, but never identifies, in social psychological research. Exploring
Blumer's idea that symbolic interaction research should be tailored by
scrutiny, Huber asks a penetrating question: How do researchers know
when they have scrutinized hard enough? Hammering on this theme as
well as other ideas appearing in her initial paper, Huber simply rejects
Blumer's comments—reiterating that the symbolic interactionist approach does not offer rules for deciding whose picture of reality is most
meaningful nor does the approach guarantee that persons using it will
scrutinize the reality any better than any one else.

Huber is taken to task in a subsequent issue of the *American
Sociological Review* by Raymond Schmitt and jointly by Gregory Stone,
David Maines, Harry Farberman, Gladys Stone and Norman Denzin. A
careful reading of their comments shows that they more or less attack
Huber on technical aspects of reference citations, interpretation of
isolated concepts and her assertion that the power variable may be an
important factor in symbolic interaction research. In a rather summary
fashion, Huber dismisses these criticisms.

The "Consciousness" Debate

A criticism often directed toward symbolic interactionism is that it overemphasizes consciousness in social interaction. Weinstein and Tanur
are convinced that people can have purposes of which they are unaware, and engage in social behavior in an effort to fulfill these purposes.
If the emphasis on consciousness led only to an argument over the efficacy of including or excluding the unconscious, a scholar's negation
of one or the other would bring closure (temporarily) to the argument. Instead, the overemphasis on consciousness is alleged to have implications for the kinds of methodological analyses deemed appropriate
for use within symbolic interactionism.

Many symbolic interactionists seem to endorse the idea that because the content of consciousness is qualitative, it cannot be quantified. Others believe that the content of consciousness can be quantified because the exterior expression of consciousness can be coded, classified, counted and collapsed. They state:

> the sensitizing orientation of symbolic interactionism can lead to work that is prospective, quantitative and oriented to explanation rather than only retrospective, qualitative and oriented toward understanding. This can be accomplished by using insights gained by taking a phenomenological stance and casting them, self-consciously and explicitly, into a framework of measurement rather than description (Weinstein and Tanur, 1976, p. 106).

The debate seems to hinge on the willingness of scholars to accept exterior expressions of the content of consciousness as reliable indicators of consciousness. Those who are unwilling to do so will no doubt continue to emphasize the construction of rich but vague descriptions of the contents of people's consciousness, while those less reluctant to do so will likely become increasingly quantitatively oriented in their analyses.

Is Social Structure Reified or Destroyed?

Processual symbolic interactionists have long alluded to the tendency of some scholars to construct and reify social structures, and then to use them to explain social interaction. A counterargument, of course, is that symbolic interactionists (especially processual ones) tend to focus their study on events interior to an episode of social interaction, thereby neglecting possible connections between episodes of interaction. Believing that episodes of interaction are interrelated and based on history, the more structurally oriented scholar feels that structures and patterns are destroyed when studies are so narrowly focused and ahistorical.

McPhail and Rexroat vs. Blumer

Clark McPhail and Cynthia Rexroat reported in a recent article that divergent lines of theory and methodology exist between George H. Mead's social behaviorism and Herbert Blumer's symbolic interactionism! Undaunted by the charges of heresy that were sure to follow, McPhail and Rexroat extensively explored Mead's writings on scientific inquiry (which appeared mostly in psychology and philosophy journals and lecture notes) as well as Blumer's numerous publications related to symbolic interactionism. They conclude that Mead's social behaviorism is amenable to behavioristic investigation *including* experimentation, and that there are fundamental differences between the epistemologies and ontological assumptions of Mead's social behaviorism and Blumer's symbolic interactionism.

Blumer's response to these contentions (1980) began a debate that is likely to continue for some time to come—if not between the principals, certainly between their protégés. He identifies three main aspects of McPhail's and Rexroat's argument: (1) differences between ontological assumptions in symbolic interactionism and those in social behaviorism; (2) differences between Blumer's and Mead's methodological schemes; and (3) McPhail's and Rexroat's presentation of examples of research which allegedly represent Mead's methodological stance.

On the first point, Blumer denies that ontological differences exist between his view of reality and Mead's. He states what he feels are the basic tenets of Mead's pragmatism, which implies both "opposition to the idealist position" *and* "opposition to the realist position." In essence, Blumer contends that Mead's position is that there is a real world which may or may not be perceived by persons or which may be perceived inaccurately. Furthermore, this real world is not immutable but subject to change, as persons construct their perceptions of it. Thus, to McPhail's and Rexroat's charges of vacillation and "waffling" (p. 457), and that his conception of reality is contrary to Mead's, Blumer responds that *his position is Mead's position.* He denies that he views reality as fixed and eternal in contrast to Mead's changeable reality, and takes McPhail and Rexroat to task for suggesting that his view of reality is solipsistic instead of socially shared. Blumer offers as evidence of this "misrepresentation" of his views a portion of his discussion in *Symbolic Interactionism* dealing with exploration (1969, pp. 39–41) and the statement that a careful reading of his contributions indicate that social objects are formed through the process of social interaction (1969, pp. 10–12).

On McPhail and Rexroat's contention that differences exist between Blumer's views and Mead's views on methodological perspectives, Blumer claims that no differences exist between his antecedents of scientific inquiry and those of Mead. He claims that McPhail and Rexroat succeed only in labelling him "erratic," and obviously this is a questionable criterion for "differences." Closely related to the antecedents of scientific inquiry issue is another one, the initiation of scientific inquiry. McPhail and Rexroat claim that there are differences between the two scholars on this issue. In response, Blumer reiterates the necessity of exploration in scientific inquiry, which is to acquaint the investigator with unfamiliar spheres of life, facilitating empirically grounded researcher perception. On the second phase of scientific inquiry, inspection, Blumer contends that his account of inspection means (in contrast to McPhail and Rexroat's interpretation) that the investigator *could* describe the problem, the ideas that guide his or her inquiry, the sources of data, the mode of inquiry, the nature of the data and the interpretation of the data in a manner conducive to replication. In his defense, Blumer refers to several studies as examples of his idea of naturalistic investigations using exploration and inspection. Included among these mentioned are Frederick Thrasher's *The Gang* and Louis Wirth's *The Ghetto.*

Blumer goes on to reject the suggestion that his treatment of "hypothesis" is different from Mead's in that it is a theoretical inductive empiricism. He also rejects several other allegations of differences including the idea that Mead did not think of observation as recording the natural ongoing character of things; that Blumer rejected certain traditional means of validating relationships between analytical components which were required by Mead; and that "hypotheses" (used by Mead) and "discoveries" (used by Blumer) were juxtaposed with each other. Finally, Blumer states that the two lines of study proposed by McPhail and Rexroat as representative of Mead's methodological approach are untenable and constitute distortions of Meadian thought.

In a stinging reply to Blumer's rebuttal, McPhail and Rexroat exhort interested scholars to decide between Mead *ex cathedra* Blumer or *ex libris* Mead (pp. 420–430). They point out that of twenty-eight attributions of position, opinion and thought to Mead in Blumer's rebuttal, he documents less than one-third. McPhail and Rexroat reiterate their claim that Blumer's writings reflect a realist position by noting his description of naturalistic methodology and his "repeated" designations of the natural makeup of human behavior. They state further that these kinds of designations attribute the meanings or characteristics to the behavior rather than to responses the investigator makes to the behavior. The critics go on to quote Mead as saying that the meanings of a behavior are the responses made to it and, they conclude, not the "discovery of a natural makeup." Corroboration between investigators coestablishes presence and meaning of behavior. These convergent responses are said to be basic units of analysis and since Blumer does not seem to accept this line of thought, according to McPhail and Rexroat, he separates himself from Mead and other pragmatists.

McPhail and Rexroat cite excerpts from Blumer's "What is Wrong With Social Theory?", *Symbolic Interactionism: Perspective and Method* and "The Problem of the Concept in Social Psychology" which they feel reaffirm their contention that he has been "erratic" on the issue of the role of antecedent theory in scientific inquiry. They point out that Mead has favorable things to say about experimental studies and observations in lieu of introspection and conclude that Mead does discuss procedures for the study of human behavior (in contrast to Blumer's contention that he did not). McPhail and Rexroat dismiss Blumer's claim that they have misconstrued Mead to serve their own purpose, which allegedly is the promotion of a special mode of inquiry. They also find unacceptable Blumer's rejection of the studies they present as representative of Mead's "taking the attitude of the other." In short, McPhail and Rexroat hold firm to their position that fundamental differences exist between Mead's social behaviorism and Blumer's symbolic interactionism. It is too early to speculate about the meaning of this debate for symbolic interactionism. Generally, it seems that symbolic interactionism, in the long run, will benefit from this exchange of lively discussion.

ASSESSMENT

Any assessment of symbolic interactionism will be inadequate unless it recognizes that there are numerous varieties of the perspective. A unitary assessment is inappropriate. For example, it is at present impossible to say whether symbolic interactionism is less suitable for quantitative analyses, that it is too structural or too processual, that it is ahistorical and so on. Because certain varieties of symbolic interactionism incorporate these corrective elements, in varying degrees, in their formulation, global criticisms are inadequate for the broad perspective. A particular brand of symbolic interactionism may indeed concentrate heavily on the social structure, attributing too much influence to roles, statuses, values and the like in social interaction, but this is not true for all of symbolic interactionism. Studies like Delph's *The Silent Community* and Douglas' *The Nude Beach* are symbolic interaction-type investigations, the former about how men construct sexual intimacy with each other undeterred by convention, identities, etc.; and the latter about sexual feelings and signs and, in general, the foundation of individual and social life. These studies are not open to the structural bias criticism. On the other hand, frameworks developed and underway by Stryker, Weinstein, McCall, Simmons and others foreordain the elimination of the so-called *structural* bias in symbolic interactionism by emphasizing the limiting effects of structure on social interaction.

If there is one global criticism aside from issues and debates within the perspective which can be directed toward symbolic interactionism, it may be one that often is directed toward social psychology in general, and that is lack of theoretical and methodological integration. This criticism, though, may be premature in light of demands being made for methodological integration (Weinstein and Tanur) and theoretical synthesis (Stryker, 1980).

CONCLUSIONS

The development of symbolic interactionism into the kind of perspective explored in this volume is attributed to scholars such as George H. Mead, Charles H. Cooley, W. I. Thomas, Herbert Blumer, Manford Kuhn, and others. They in turn were indebted to the Scottish moral philosophers and the American pragmatism philosophers. George H. Mead's contributions were particularly significant to the development of symbolic interactionism. Concentrating on such concepts as "mind," "self," "society," "objects," "social act," "social environment," and many others, Mead outlined a broad (sometimes vague and ambiguous) scheme for use in studying the relationships between the individual and the social environment. Others (most notably, Herbert Blumer and Manford Kuhn) drew upon Mead's ideas and expanded and elaborated his position. Blumer became the major proponent of processual symbolic interactionism, emphasizing Mead's views on the processual nature of social interaction, self and other key concepts. Kuhn, and those whom he influenced, developed a more structural view of symbolic interactionism based in part on Mead's ideas and extensions of the ideas.

Many issues in symbolic interactionism remain unresolved because of divergencies between the processual and structural approaches which involve differences in theoretical and methodological orientations. In addition, offshoots from the branches contribute even more to problematic areas in the perspective. Perhaps this should be expected in a relatively young discipline—one that is still developing and just beginning to seek synthesis and integration. One thing that seems certain regarding symbolic interactionism is that it makes an exciting contribution, and useful perspective for understanding interaction.

BIBLIOGRAPHY

Adler, Peter and Patricia A. Adler. "Symbolic Interactionism," in Jack D. Douglas, Patricia A. Adler, Peter Adler, Andrea Fontana, C. Robert Freeman and Joseph A. Kotarba, eds. *Introduction to the Sociologies of Everyday Life.* Allyn and Bacon, 1980.

Baldwin, James M. *Mental Development in the Child and the Race.* New York: Macmillan, 1906.

Becker, Howard S. *Outsiders.* New York: Free Press, 1963.

Blumer, Herbert. "The Problem of the Concept in Social Psychology," *American Journal of Sociology* 45 (1940), pp. 707–719.

――. "What Is Wrong With Social Theory?" *American Sociological Review* 19 (1954).

――. In Emerson P. Schmidt, *Man and Society.* New York: Prentice-Hall 1937.

――. *Symbolic Interactionism: Perspectives and Methods.* Englewood Cliffs, N.J.: Prentice-Hall, 1969.

――. "Comment on Symbolic Interactionism as a Pragmatic Perspective: The Bias of Emergent Theory," *American Sociological Review* 38 (1973), pp. 797–798.

――. "Mead and Blumer: The Convergent Methodological Perspectives of Social Behaviorism and Symbolic Interactionism," *American Sociological Review* 44 (1980), pp. 409–19.

Bryson, Gladys. *Man and Society: The Scottish Inquiry of the Eighteenth Century.* Princeton, N.J.: Princeton University Press, 1945.

Charon, Joel M. *Symbolic Interactionism.* Englewood Cliffs, N.J.: Prentice-Hall 1979.

Cicourel, Aaron. "The Acquisition of Social Structure: Toward a Developmental Sociology of Language and Meaning," in Jack Douglas, ed. *Understanding Everyday Life.* Chicago: Aldine, 1970.

――. "Basic and Normative Role in the Negotiation of Status and Role," in David Sudnow, ed. *Studies in Social Interaction,* New York: Free Press, 1972.

Cooley, Charles Horton. *Human Nature and the Social Order.* New York: Charles Scribner's Sons, 1902.

Delph, Edward William. *The Silent Community.* Beverly Hills, Ca.: Sage Publications, 1978.

Douglas, Jack D., Paul K. Rasmussen and Carol Ann Flanagan. *The Nude Beach.* Beverly Hills, Ca.: Sage Publications, 1977.

Erikson, Kai T. "Notes on the Sociology of Deviance," *Social Problems* 9 (1962).

Fontana, Andrea. "The Mask and Beyond: The Enigmatic Sociology of Erving Goffman," in Jack Douglas, Patricia A. Adler, Peter Adler, Andrea Fontana, C. Robert Freeman and Joseph A. Kotarba, eds. *Introduction to the Sociologies of Everyday Life.* Boston: Allyn and Bacon, 1980.

Freeman, C. Robert. "Phenomenological Sociology and Ethnomethodology," in Jack Douglas, Patricia A. Adler, Peter Adler, Andrea Fontana, C.

Robert Freeman and Joseph A. Kotarba, eds. *Introduction to the Sociologies of Everyday Life*. Boston: Allyn and Bacon, 1980.

Garfinkel, Harold. *Studies in Ethnomethodology*. Englewood Cliffs, N.J.: Prentice-Hall, 1967.

Goffman, Erving. *The Presentation of Self in Everyday Life*. New York: Anchor, 1959.

——. *Asylums*. New York: Anchor, 1961.

——. *Behavior in Public Places*. New York: Free Press, 1963.

Hickman, C. Addison and Manford H. Kuhn. *Individuals, Groups and Economic Behavior*. New York: Dryden Press, 1956.

Huber, Joan. "Symbolic Interactionism as a Pragmatic Perspective: The Bias of Emergent Theory," *American Sociological Review* 38 (April 1973), pp. 274–284.

——. "Reply to Blumer: But, Who Will Scrutinize the Scrutinizers?," *American Sociological Review* 38 (December 1973), pp. 798–800.

James, William. *Principles of Psychology*. New York: Henry Holt, 1890.

Kuhn, Manford. "Major Trends in Symbolic Interaction Theory in the Past Twenty-Five Years," *Sociological Quarterly* 5 (Winter 1964), pp. 61–84.

Kuhn, Manford and Thomas S. McPartland. "An Empirical Investigation of Self-Attitudes," *American Sociological Review* 19 (February 1954).

Lemert, Edwin. "Beyond Mead: The Societal Reaction to Deviance," *Social Problems* 21, no. 4 (April 1974), pp. 457–468.

Manis, Jerome G. and Bernard Meltzer. *Symbolic Interaction: A Reader in Social Psychology*. Boston: Allyn and Bacon, 1972.

——. *Symbolic Interaction: A Reader in Social Psychology*, 3rd ed. Boston: Allyn and Bacon, 1978.

McCall, George J. and J. S. Simmons. *Identities and Interactions*. New York: Free Press, 1978.

McPhail, Clark and Cynthia Rexroat. "Mead vs Blumer: The Divergent Methodological Perspectives of Social Behaviorism and Symbolic Interactionism," *American Sociological Review* 44 (1979), pp. 449–467.

——. "Ex Cathedra Blumer or Ex Libris Mead?" *American Sociological Review* 45 (1980), pp. 420–430.

Mead, George H. *Mind, Self and Society*. Chicago: University of Chicago Press, 1934.

Meltzer, Bernard N. "Mead's Social Psychology," in Jerome G. Manis and Bernard Meltzer, eds., *Symbolic Interaction: A Reader in Social Psychology*. Boston: Allyn and Bacon, 1978.

Meltzer, Bernard N. and John W. Petras. "The Chicago and Iowa Schools of Symbolic Interactionism," In J. G. Manis and B. N. Meltzer, *Symbolic Interaction: A Reader in Social Psychology*, 2nd ed. Boston: Allyn and Bacon, 1972, pp. 43–57.

Meltzer, Bernard N., John W. Petras and Larry T. Reynolds. *Symbolic Interactionism; Genesis, Varieties and Criticism*. London: Routledge and Kegan Paul, 1975.

Morris, Charles W., ed. *Mind, Self and Society*. Chicago: University of Chicago Press, 1934.

Rose, Arnold. *Human Behavior and Social Process*. Boston: Houghton Mifflin, 1962.

Scheff, Thomas. *Being Mentally Ill: A Sociological Theory*. Chicago: Aldine, 1966.

Schmitt, Raymond L. "S. I. and Emergent Theory: A Reexamination," *American Sociological Review* 39, (1974) pp. 453–456.

Stone, Greogory P., D. R. Maines, H. A. Farberman, G. I. Stone and N. K. Denzin. "On Methodology and Craftsmanship in the Criticism of Sociological Perspectives," *American Sociological Review* 39, (1974) pp. 456–462.

Stryker, Sheldon. "Identity Salience and Role Performance: The Relevance of Symbolic Interaction Theory for Family Research," *Journal of Marriage and the Family* 30 (November 1968), pp. 558–564.

——. *Symbolic Interactionism: A Social Structural Version*. Menlo Park, Ca.: Benjamin/Cummings, 1980.

Thrasher, Frederick. *The Gang*. Chicago: University of Chicago Press, 1927.

Tucker, Charles W. "Some Methodological Problems of Kuhn's Self Theory," *Sociological Quarterly* 7, no. 3, (Summer 1966), pp. 345–358.

Turner, Ralph H. "Role Taking: Process Versus Conformity," in Arnold M. Rose, ed. *Human Behavior and Social Process*. Boston: Houghton Mifflin, 1962.

——. "The Real Self: From Institution to Impulse," *American Journal of Sociology* 81 (March 1976), pp. 989–1016.

——. "The Role and the Person," *The American Journal of Sociology* 84 (July 1978), pp. 1–23.

Weinstein, Eugene A. and Judith M. Tanur. "Meanings, Purposes and Structural Resources in Social Interaction," *Cornell Journal of Social Relations* 11, no. 1, (Spring 1976), pp. 105–110.

Wirth, Louis. *The Ghetto*. Chicago: University of Chicago Press, 1928.

BEHAVIORAL SOCIAL PSYCHOLOGY

4

Behavioral social psychology is one of the most controversial perspectives in the social sciences. The controversy stems from its *methodological emphasis*, its *theoretical standpoint*, and certain *ethical concerns* surrounding its use. Methodologically, behavioral social psychology subscribes to an attitude of *operationism*, an attitude that became especially pronounced in the late 1920s with the tremendous growth of behaviorism in American psychology. Operationism's basic dictum is that a concept is nothing more nor less than the procedures used to measure the concept. The "self," for example, from a behavioral point of view, is nothing more than the results of the Twenty Statements Test (see the discussion of Manford H. Kuhn in Chapter 3). The self may be more than the test, but that "more" cannot be observed, measured, and/or manipulated under controlled conditions, so it must be discarded. It is of little use to science and thus has no place in behavioral social psychology which is concerned with prediction and control.

Theoretically, behavioral social psychology is often thought to be atheoretical and/or descriptive even though there is a great deal of theory in the perspective. Even B. F. Skinner's work, on which much of the modern perspective is based, is not totally descriptive. Also, proponents of associationism and hedonism have played major *theoretical* roles in behavioral social psychology by integrating their principles with analyses of experimental results, much to the chagrin of some and the delight of others.

The ethical issue raised by behavioral social psychology is simply whether social scientists have a right to use behavioral principles with human subjects. Of course behavioral social psychologists are not the only social scientists today whose work is closely scrutinized by governmental agencies, university officials and laymen. Behavioral scientists in general are being asked to justify their efforts to predict and control human behavior through experimental manipulation of human subjects.

The polemical nature of behavioral social psychology does not end here. There are charges of tautologies in the interpretations of results, logical gaps in the perspective and so on. However, such controversy can be seen as an indication of continual development of the perspective. In fact, the 1970s proved to be very important for behavioral theory and research in what has been called *sociological social psychology*. We must be mindful of the fact, though, that this could not have occurred without earlier development in the behavioral perspective. Let us turn to some earlier direct and indirect influences on behaviorism.

ANTECEDENTS OF BEHAVIORIST THOUGHT

The Influence of Greek Naturalism, French Materialism and Animal Psychology

Behaviorism as we know it today has numerous antecedents. Lundin has pointed to Greek naturalism, singling out Aristotle as perhaps the first "behaviorist" since he considered sensation, mind and movement of the body to be acts *of* the body and not separate *from* the body (p. 157). Moreover, Aristotle and other Greek naturalists emphasized objective, observable phenomena—a premise that enjoyed a prominent position in Watsonian behaviorism. French materialism as characterized by the work of Julian da la Mettrie (1709–1751), Pierre Cabanis (1757–1805) and Auguste Comte (1798–1857), among others, also is said to have influenced the emergence of behaviorism. Mettrie's hedonism and his feeling that the mind could be interpreted from a physical standpoint; Cabanis' definition of the mind as physiological functions; and Comte's rejection of introspection while advancing objective, observable knowledge, all are thought to have contributed to the perspective discussed in this chapter.

Another field which contributed to behaviorism, especially in the way of experimentation is animal psychology. George J. Romanes (1848–1884) set the stage for studying animal behavior along with C. Lloyd Morgan (1852–1936), another pioneer in animal studies, whose observations were conducted partly in naturalistic settings and partly under controlled laboratory conditions. Lundin refers to Morgan's most remembered contribution as an application of the law of parsimony, stating that "we must not interpret an action as demonstrating a higher psychical process if it could be interpreted as the outcome of one that stood lower in the psychological scale" (animals have habits rather than intelligence) (Lundin, p. 159).

Pavlovian conditioning, association and functionalism also directly and indirectly influenced behaviorism. The significance of the influences should become apparent in subsequent sections. Let us begin with E. L. Thorndike from the school of associationism.

The Influence of Thorndike's Associationism

Most social psychologists of sociological or psychological persuasion recognize Edward L. Thorndike's psychological associationism as extremely important to the development of behaviorism. He lived from 1874–1949, and is said to have developed one of the first organized theories of learning. His most significant contribution to behaviorism was in the area of reinforcement. But, unlike Ivan Pavlov who felt that *recency* and *frequency* were the underlying factors in stimulus-response connections, Thorndike posited reinforcement as the basis for such connections.

Thorndike, though a contemporary of Pavlov, worked independently of him, with no knowledge of Pavlovian conditioning. In fact, his work preceded Pavlov's by three years according to Pavlov himself (Pavlov, 1928, pp. 39–40). Thorndike's studies covered a span of over fifty years during which time he conducted innumerable animal experiments involving maze learning, and contributed to the fields of mental study, educational psychology and behaviorism. It is the latter contribution that we are concerned with here.

Thorndike was an initiator and adherent of *trial and error learning*. Perhaps due to the influence of the philosophical pragmatist William James (whom Thorndike studied under at Harvard), Thorndike's conclusions from early animal experiments were tinged with philosophical pragmatism (see Chapter 3). He observed that cats emitted correct responses to open the door of puzzle boxes in order to get food (such as flipping switches, pulling ropes, etc.), only after making a number of incorrect responses (such as clawing, biting and aimlessly moving about). Once the correct response was made, the time it took the cats to free themselves on subsequent occasions diminished (a measure of learning). This occurred, according to Thorndike, through a gradual and random process whereby correct responses became "stamped in" and incorrect ones fell into disuse. The *law of exercise* developed by Thorndike involving the strengthening of stimulus-response connections through use and the weakening of others through disuse could explain a part of this learning:

> Any response to a situation will, other things being equal, be more strongly connected with the situation in proportion to the number of times it has been connected (used?) with that situation and to the average vigor and duration of the connection (Thorndike, 1911, p. 244).

Along with the law of exercise, Thorndike developed the *law of effect* which became vital to, though controversial in, behaviorism, and rounded out his framework of learning:

> of several responses made to the same situation, those which are accompanied or closely followed by satisfaction to the animal will, other things being equal, be more firmly connected with the situation, so that, when it recurs they will be more likely to recur; those which are accompanied or closely followed by discomfort to the animal will, other things being equal, have their connections with that situation weakened, so that when its recurs, they will be less likely to recur. The greater the satisfaction or discomfort, the greater the strengthening or weakening of the bond (p. 244).

The source of the controversy lay in such concepts as "satisfying state of affairs," "annoying state of affairs," "discomfort," and the like, which were defined somewhat behavioristically:

> By a satisfying state of affairs is meant one which the animal does nothing to avoid, often does things which maintain or renew it. By an annoying state of affairs is meant one which the animal does nothing to preserve, often doing things which put an end to it (p. 245).

Nevertheless, Thorndike's inclusion of the *law of effect* proved to be an insight because later he had to alter the *law of exercise* following experiments with chickens and his discovery that the law of effect was a necessary accompaniment of the law of exercise—mere repetition was inadequate for stimulus-response (S-R) connection bonding without satisfying consequences. The law of effect, too, was modified by Thorndike in 1932, when experimental results indicated that reinforcement did indeed strengthen S-R connections but that punishment did not necessarily weaken them. Further experimentation produced findings related to *generalization.* Reinforcing consequences "acted not only to strengthen the S-R connections to which they belonged but also to adjacent connections both before and after the rewarded connections" (Lundin, p. 140). The degree of the effect on surrounding connections of a rewarded connection was a function of their distance from the rewarded connection.

To say that Thorndike's work generated disapproval is an understatement. John B. Watson, joined by other behaviorists such as Edwin Guthrie, accused Thorndike of being subjective (in concepts such as satisfaction, annoyance, etc.) and teleological (in talking of behavior as a function of its consequences). In spite of this, B. F. Skinner resurrected the law of effect in 1938 enhancing its credibility in his *principle of reinforcement.* Skinner, careful to omit the subjective terms used by Thorndike, contended that positive reinforcement increased the *probability* of a response recurrence. Observing the recurrence was enough for Skinner to support Thorndike's idea that indeed behavior *was* determined by its consequences.

The Influence of the Russian Scholars

John B. Watson's disdain for the study of states of consciousness was predated by two Russian scholars, Ivan Pavlov (1848–1936) and V. M. Bekhterev (1887–1927). Bekhterev studied conditioning independently of the better-known Pavlov, examining what he called associative reflexes through the study of motor responses (Watson, 1971, p. 424). A physiologist, he felt that such responses as the knee jerk when the patellar tendon is tapped and the withdrawal of a hand when it touches a hot object, were reflexes involving no mental process. Expressing this in *Objective Psychology* (1907), he further stated that many complex forms of human behavior could be explained in a similar manner, including thinking, which was seen as some function of speech musculature devoid of subjective processes (Watson, 1971, p. 424).

Ivan Pavlov, also a physiologist and an associate of Bekhterev, contributed greatly to behaviorism. Beginning his study of conditioned reflexes during the period 1900–1901, Pavlov explored a phenomenon that he had noticed prior to 1900 in his work on the function of saliva in digestion. He had observed that his experimental dogs salivated *prior* to meat being given them, when they saw the food, or even when they heard footsteps of the attendant. The reflex of salivation occurred when stimuli that had been *associated* with the natural stimulus occurred, once the two had been paired together.

Pavlov was somewhat intrigued by his observations but wondered whether he should pursue them because of their "psychic" nature. Watson reports that many leading physiologists actually discouraged Pavlov from pursuing a line of work they felt would inevitably lead him to psychic concerns. Finally though, Pavlov resolved to go on with his investigations, insuring the physiological nature of his study "by maintaining the role of the external observer with no consideration of introspective findings" (Watson, 1971, p. 420). It is said that he always remained aloof from psychology believing it to be doomed and never even allowing psychological terminology to be used in his laboratory.

Pavlov's contributions to behaviorism in psychology were many, even though he would have been uncomfortable with the credit. He himself gave a great deal of recognition for his investigation to Ivan Sechenor, who claimed that all psychological processes had a physiological genesis, and that psychical processes were reflexes which could be learned and unlearned. Let us turn to Pavlov's contributions to what is now called *classical conditioning* and the concepts he elaborated through experimentation and interpretation: conditioned response, unconditioned response, conditioned stimulus, unconditioned stimulus, extinction, spontaneous recovery, generalization, discrimination, reinforcement, and experimental neurosis.

As reported in *Conditioned Reflexes* (1927) and *Lectures on Conditioned Reflexes* (1928), he termed the attendant's footsteps, the dog's dish and other stimuli which would elicit salivation including lights, buzzers and a metronome's clicking sounds *conditioned stimuli* (CS). The salivating response was called a *conditioned response* (CR). The actual food for the dog became an *unconditioned stimulus* (US) and the natural salivation to food was called an *unconditioned response* (UR). Both types of responses, conditioned and unconditioned, were thought to be physiologically based. Pavlov also manipulated the conditioned stimulus presenting it without the natural stimulus (food) and observed that over a period of time the conditioned response tended to *extinguish*. However, if the conditioned stimulus were presented after a period of time had elapsed, the dogs once again salivated. This was termed *spontaneous recovery* meaning that complete extinction had not occurred.

Introducing the term *reinforcement*, Pavlov discovered that he could present the dogs food with a specific tone of the metronome and not with other tones (selective reinforcement) and salivation would occur to the former and not the latter. In other words he could develop *discrimination* in the dogs. The principle of generalization was also established by Pavlov, whereby one particular rate or beat of the metronome established the conditioned response and then beating rates of lesser magnitude were also observed to elicit the response, indicating the stimulus had generalized to other stimuli similar to the original.

Experimental neuroses and *higher-order conditioning* were two further results produced by the Pavlovian experiments. Pavlov found in his experiments on discrimination that dogs pushed beyond their limits of discrimination would begin to engage in erratic behavior such as barking, wrestling with their harnesses, floundering about, etc. indicating that experimental manipulation had produced neurotic behavior.

A final result to be mentioned is Pavlov's findings on higher-order conditioning. He discovered that a conditioned stimulus could be paired with another neutral stimulus and the latter would then be able to elicit the conditioned response (dog salivation). This was called second-order conditioning. Third order conditioning was also possible as Pavlov found, but he concluded that is was not possible to go beyond this (Watson, 1971, p. 423).

THE FOUNDING OF BEHAVIORISM

Watsonian Behaviorism

As with any perspective in social psychology, behaviorism owes its development to many scholars. Some of these stand out above others. John Broadus Watson (1878–1958) is considered by many to be the founder of behaviorism.

Watson studied biology, physiology and psychology at the University of Chicago under Jacques Loeb, H. H. Donaldson and James R. Angell. He received his Ph.D. in 1903 under the direction of Angell and Donaldson using neurological and psychological techniques to complete his dissertation entitled "Animal Education: The Psychical Development of the White Rat." Following a brief teaching stint at

Chicago, in 1908 Watson assumed the directorship of the psychological laboratory at Johns Hopkins University, where he remained until 1920, the year he left the academic world following a scandalous divorce. He then entered the advertising firm of J. Walter Thompson in New York where he continued to contribute to psychology until around 1930 (Lundin, pp. 163–164).

In Chapter 3 Watsonian behaviorism was discussed as a way of viewing behavior, and as a way of using behavior to explain individual experience from an external standpoint. This two-fold view of behaviorism derives from the "Behaviorist's Manifesto" proposed by Watson in 1912 in a series of lectures at Columbia University and published in 1913 in the *Psychological Review* of which he was the editor. Watson states:

> Psychology as the behaviorist views it is a purely objective experimental branch of natural science. Its theoretical goal is the prediction and control of behavior. Introspection forms no essential part of the methods, nor is the scientific value of its data dependent upon the readiness with which they lend themselves to interpretation in terms of consciousness. The behaviorist, in his efforts to get a unitary scheme of animal response, recognizes no dividing line between man and brute. The behavior of man, with all its refinements and complexity, forms only a part of behaviorism's total scheme of investigation (1913, p. 158).

Ignoring introspection and promoting an objective science stressing observation (experimental or naturalistic), testing and reporting, Watson's psychology is heavily deterministic. Moving from the position that heredity influenced human behavior, Watson rejects the existence of instincts in humans and emphasizes behavior as a function of environment. For Watson, human behavior is not a result of the individual's free will. Individuals *do not* construct, produce or determine behavior. Human behavior is a function of environment. Consider the following statement:

> Give me a dozen healthy infants, well-formed, and my own specified world to bring them up in and I'll guarantee to take any one at random and train him to become any type of specialist I might select—doctor, lawyer, artist, merchant-chief and yes, even beggar man and thief, regardless of his talents, penchants, tendencies, abilities, vocations and race of his ancestors. (1930, p. 82)

Watson's psychology is appropriately labelled stimulus-response psychology. Stimuli produce either overt or covert responses. The only difference between the two types of responses from Watson's point of view is that overt responses (walking, talking etc.) are easily observed, while covert responses are subtle, like glandular secretion, thinking (talking to oneself), and feelings (bodily reactions), which *can* be observed but only with the right sophisticated techniques. Presumably these techniques can detect small mouth, lip and tongue movements, thus obviating the need to conceptualize thinking in nonobservable terms. Important here is the fact that even covert responses remain on the *observable* level, and this is a crucial condition in Watson's system of psychology. The concept "stimulus" for Watson refers to objects in the environment or change in the *tissues* of the organism due to some physiological condition (1919, p. 10). This change can be due to deprivation, which for Watson does not result in the organism *wanting* the stimulus but rather creates some modification in the structure of the organism producing some response.

While some behaviorists assume some intervening mediating influence between stimulus and response, Watson does *not* endorse such influence feeling it to be too subjective. Concepts like mind and consciousness were first deemed beyond the realm of psychology and later "nonexistent" in Watson's scheme (Watson and McDougall, p. 26). His conception of learning, for example, ignores "mind" aspects such as memory, relegating the latter to skill and/or verbal habit and performance. Learning is based on the Pavlovian laws of recency and frequency, thus becoming little more than conditioned responses. This should not be surprising since in Watson's view of things emotion, memory, thinking, personality, and so on can all be conceptualized in terms of bodily (and therefore observable) reactions.

Watson has been lauded for his role in the development of modern behaviorism, and his insistence upon the lawful nature of behavior and an objective study of human behavior which would enhance predictability and control. Lundin, however, criticizes the extreme environmentalism that characterizes Watson's work, which virtually ignores the limiting effects of hereditary factors, and his failure to include Thorndike's law of effect which would have refined his theory of learning.

Other Early Behaviorists

Other early behaviorists were the associationist Edwin R. Guthrie (1886–1959), Albert P. Weiss (1879–1931) and Karl Lashley (1890–1958). Guthrie's guiding principle for behaviorism was *contiguity*. For him, behavior modification is a function of the contiguity of stimuli and responses. Learning occurs on a one-trial basis. If a response is elicited by a stimulus once, then a stimulus-response association has been made. Rejecting recency, frequency and reinforcement as key variables in conditioning, Guthrie contends that the criterion of learning is *movement*. Movement is defined as a pattern of molar and glandular responses or actions. In contrast, acts, which Guthrie feels are often used as criteria of learning are "series of movements that bring about end results" (Schultz, p. 224). Single movements are learned after one trial, but learning a total act (a constellation of movements) usually requires repetition.

Basing much of his work in physiology, Karl Lashley conducted brain experiments, removing parts of animals' brains in an effort to assess the effect on behavior retention and performance. Because it had been assumed that different parts of the brain were linked with the retention and performance of learned responses, results indicating that animals could learn just as well, though more slowly, with one part of the cortex as with another part were surprising. His findings challenged the primacy of the reflex arc as an elemental unit of behavior, suggesting that the brain played a more active role in learning.

Albert P. Weiss was another scholar who contributed to early behaviorism, mainly through his fervor for the perspective. An early death prevented him from fully developing the program of research on child development he had outlined (Schultz, p. 215). During his relatively brief career at Ohio State University he maintained that behavior, because of its biological basis, could be reduced to physical-chemical entities (Schultz, p. 215). Recognizing that humans were social beings, he incorporated the social into his reductionist system and introduced the term "biosocial." The socialization process was the basic unit of cognition for Weiss which he felt should be approached from both a physiological and a social standpoint within a natural science framework.

THE EMERGENCE OF MODERN BEHAVIORISM

Skinner's Behaviorism

Informed scholars would agree, with few exceptions, that Burrhus F. Skinner (1904–) has been the most important influence in the emergence of behaviorism as a viable modern-day perspective. Educated at Hamilton College (A.B. degree in English) and Harvard University (M.A. and Ph.D. degrees in psychology in 1930 and 1931), Skinner has held positions at Michigan University, the University of Minnesota, Indiana University (where he was chairperson of psychology from 1945–1948) and Harvard University.

Skinner's contributions to modern behaviorism are so pervasive that it is almost impossible to speak of any aspect of behavioral social psychology without mentioning his name. While he has been accused of being concerned with only limited aspects of behavior, in truth Skinner's system has dealt with a broad range of behavior from "bits" of behavior in a learning situation to macro behavior characterizing a culture, indeed the world. This is evidenced by his major publications including *The Behavior of Organisms* (1938), *Walden II* (1948), *Science and Human Behavior* (1953), *Verbal Behavior* (1957), *Schedules of Reinforcement* (1957, with C. B. Ferster), *The Technology of Teaching* (1968), *Beyond Freedom and Dignity* (1971) and *About Behaviorism* (1974). He began his illustrious career with a molecular approach to animal behavior, emphasizing and developing learning principles and using the "Skinner box" to study limited movement and bar-pressing behavior in rats. *Beyond Freedom and Dignity* showed that Skinner had moved far away from such limited concerns about animal behavior to include a variety of human individual and social endeavors. Remaining a genetic environmentalist, Skinner has interpreted and redefined many ideas of freedom and dignity according to behavioristic psychological principles, and has suggested positive reinforcement as an alternative to aversive environmental control in society.

When Skinner began his career, he opted for an inductive strategy of theorizing which many have labelled atheoretical. This does not mean that Skinner's concepts, principles and in general his contribution overall emerged from original observations. He has borrowed and incorporated concepts and principles, implicitly and explicitly, in his system of behavior from Watson, Thorndike and Pavlov (Skinner, 1938, p. 61). Following Pavlov's classical conditioning and the dictates of the theoretical goal of behaviorism as expressed in Watson's "behaviorist manifesto," Skinner recognized *type S* conditioning as an appropriate kind of learning. He labelled it *respondent conditioning*. However, Skinner departed from many early behaviorists when he suggested that a good deal of behavior was *not* of the stimulus-response variety but rather, of an *operant* nature. That is, some behavior was felt by Skinner not to have an observed antecedent (stimulus) but instead occurred, operated on the environment and consequently affected the probability of its occurrence on future occasions. This class of behavior was termed operant. At this point Skinner reintroduces in altered form Thorndike's law of effect. "If the occurrence of an operant is followed by the presentation of a reinforcing stimulus, the strength is increased'' (Skinner, 1938). He does not address the question of why a reinforcer is a reinforcer, and thus avoids the subjectivism characteristic of Thorndike's law and other behaviorists' formulations. It should be pointed out that Skinner's emphasis on simply observing and measuring functional relationships between responses and reinforcing consequences is not adequate for many scholars opposed to his behaviorism.

As mentioned earlier, Skinner's contributions to modern behaviorism are vast and far-reaching. Concepts such as positive and negative reinforcers, extinction, schedules of reinforcement, discrimination, secondary reinforcement, aversive conditioning, and differentiation are vital in his system. Discussion of these concepts is omitted here because they are treated in detail later in this chapter. One should recognize, however, that Skinner's influence on their development has been enormous. Like many early behaviorists, he has insisted upon defining his concepts and accounting for human behavior in completely observable terms. To those who would define drives, emotions, motivations, desires, and other concepts thought to be responsible for human behavior in terms of internal processes, Skinner offers a challenge of defining them operationally and in terms of observable events.

Skinner's system, as outlined in *The Technology of Teaching*, has been widely used in the areas of teaching and behavior modification (eliminating undesirable behavior and shaping desirable behavior in autistic children, the mentally ill and others displaying deviant behavior). The popularity of *Walden II*, in which he discusses a utopian ''behavioral'' society and of *Beyond Freedom and Dignity*, where he offers a technology of behavior to solve societal probelms, attest to his widespread appeal. Skinner's influence seems to have increased throughout his career, and it may very well be the case that its peak has not been reached, in spite of the alleged decline in behaviorism. Let us turn to some other contributors to modern behaviorism before outlining the perspective which owes so much to Burrhus F. Skinner.

Hullian Behaviorism

Clark Leonard Hull (1884–1952) is recognized as one of the most brilliant psychologists of all time. Schultz states:

> First and foremost a behaviorist, Hull has achieved a highly respected position in contemporary psychology. Perhaps no previous psychologist has been so consistently and keenly de-

voted to the problems inherent in scientific nature (1969, p. 225).

Citing Wolman's contention that few had Hull's great mastery of mathematics and formal logic, Schultz traces the beginning of Hull's career at the University of Wisconsin in 1918 (when he received his Ph.D. there) to Yale University, where he assumed a research professorship in 1929. While at Wisconsin, Hull studied and published in the area of hypnosis and suggestibility. At Yale, however, he concentrated on behaviorism. Using the hypothetico-deductive method (a type of theorizing referred to in Chapter 2 as *explicitly structured theorizing,* involving constructing postulates and deriving experimentally testable propositions), Hull developed a theoretical formulation of human behavior (*Principles of Behavior*).

Hull's point of departure in his theoretical framework is the assumption that human behavior is a function of continuous interaction between the organism and its environment within the limiting conditions of the organism's *biological adaptation* to its *particular environment.* It is within the latter part of this statement that the germ of Hull's most important, albeit controversial, contribution to behaviorism lies.

Taking something of a functionalist theoretical approach while remaining behavioristic, Hull feels that biological adaptation facilitates the organism's survival. Implicit in Hull's framework is the assumption that the organism has a need for survival that is manifested by its behavior whenever its survival is threatened. Such behavior, for Hull, represents a need for something to reduce the need. Thus his theoretical framework is one of *motivation.* Needs produce motivation, which in turn produces behavior. In other words, threatened survival of the organism produces biological needs (called drives by Hull) and ensuing behavior designed to reduce the need (drive) and thus insure the survival of the organism. The intensity of the behavior is thought to be an indicator of the *strength of the drive.*

Drives are primarily of two types. *Primary drives* are associated with the biological needs of the organism and linked directly with its survival, while *secondary drives* are previously neutral stimuli in the environment associated with primary drive reduction which assume need reduction characteristics (elicit responses similar to those elicited by the primary drives). It should be remembered that primary drives for Hull are those that arise from the organism's *tissue need* and they are biological and not social. The ''social'' enters with secondary drives, but only on the basis of primary drives. Abstinence from sexual intercourse, for example, might activate sexually oriented behavior designed to achieve sexual coitus. (Deprivation is also thought to be an indicator of the strength of drives, albeit imperfect.) Thus physiological changes produce a need for sex (a primary drive). If proper setting is associated with physiological changes, then proper setting will also become capable of eliciting a need for sex and accompanying behavior. In addition, if sexually oriented behavior (for example, foreplay) often results in a decrease in the intensity of bodily tissue need (as occurs when there is foreplay to the point of orgasm), then foreplay can become in Hull's frame of reference *secondary reinforcement*.

A final note on Hull's behaviorism is his explanation of stimulus-response connections which goes beyond conditioning and includes a modified version of Thorndike's law of effect. Substituting "satisfying state of affairs" with "reduction of a primary drive," Hull says that strengthened stimulus-response connections (learning) cannot be explained solely by the Pavlovian principles of recency and frequency but must be related to reinforcement—if a stimulus-response relationship is followed by a reduction in need, then on subsequent occasions, the probability is high that the same stimulus will evoke the same response (1943, pp. 386–387).

Needless to say, Hull's behaviorism has met enormous resistance, especially from those who have followed scholars (like J. R. Kantor and B. F. Skinner) who have foregone any attempts to attribute human behavior to internal states. Hull's influence can be seen in some modern behavioristic interpretations of findings and in some theoretical formulations (for example, Albert Bandura's *Social Learning Theory*).

Let us turn now to a behavioral framework used often in sociological social psychology within the past two decades.

BEHAVIORISM IN SOCIOLOGICAL SOCIAL PSYCHOLOGY

Prior to the 1970s it was rare to find sociological social psychologists using behaviorism in their theoretical formulations and research investigations. Many of these scholars felt that behaviorism was too static, or were reluctant to ignore "internal processes" in human behavior. Still others failed to distinguish between *early* behaviorism and *modern* behaviorism. Kurt Back, in reviewing Robert Burgess and Donald Bushell's *Behavioral Sociology*, implied that nothing new or profound had been added to sociology or social psychology with its publication.

His criticism of the book, however, seemed directed toward classical conditioning rather than modern behaviorism.

Criticisms such as the above levied at the emerging behavioral group in sociological social psychology in the 1960s probably would have ended the modest "movement" if it had not been for two important factors: the popularity among a handful of sociological social psychologists of several behavioral publications, and the persistence of a small but informed group of sociological social psychologists.

Child Development: A Systematic and Empirical Theory, by Sidney Bijou and Donald Baer, was published in 1961. In 1963, Arthur K. Staats and Carolyn Staats published *Complex Human Behavior: A Systematic Extension of Learning Principle.* Both books appealed to sociological social psychologists because of the clear and concise manner in which behaviorism was presented, and because of their strong emphasis on the application of behaviorism to everyday topics and concerns. These two books are discussed in greater detail later. "Are Operant Principles Tautological?" and "A Differential Association— Reinforcement Theory of Criminal Behavior," articles published jointly by two young scholars, Robert Burgess from Washington University and Donald Akers from the University of Kentucky (both began their professional careers at the University of Washington just as Robert E. L. Faris, the symbolic interactionist, was retiring) also had an impact on the sociological world. The former article appeared in *The Psychological Record* which is not read widely by sociologists, but the latter appeared in *Social Problems,* whose audience is primarily sociologists.

By the time *Behavioral Sociology* was published, a sprinkling of articles published by sociological social psychologists, several of whom were students of Burgess', began to appear in psychological and sociological journals. Also during the latter 1960s Richard Emerson, the exchange theorist, and Robert Leik, the methodologist (both colleagues of Burgess') began to show some interest in behaviorism. Emerson's "Operant Theory and Social Exchange" was published in Burgess and Bushell's volume.

Another sociologist interested in behaviorism during this time, as evidenced by the publication of one of his major works *Society and Economic Growth: A Behavioral Perspective of Social Change* was John H. Kunkel, who has continued to express interest in behaviorism. He published "A Behavioral Model of Man: Propositions and Implications" (with Richard Nagasawa, who attended the University of Washington during Burgess' tenure there) in 1973, followed by *Behavior, Social Problems and Change* in 1975. Attention will now be directed to the substantive relevance for behaviorism of the aforementioned publications and scholars.

By no means all the sociological social psychological publications of relevance to modern behaviorism are included here, nor can all the sociological social psychologists interested in behaviorism be mentioned. However, it is intended that the publications and scholars mentioned are representative of their respective categories during the emergence of modern behaviorism in sociological social psychology from the middle 1960s through the early 1970s.

In the eighty-six pages of their *Child Development: A Systematic and Empirical Theory,* Bijou and Baer accomplished what often takes authors many more pages to present—a clear and concise presentation of modern behaviorism. One of the main features of the book is especially relevant to those who see behaviorism as a unitary system from its founding. This is their discussion of the distinction between "respondent" behavior and "operant" behavior. Skinner had posited the distinction over two decades earlier, but somehow it had never been grasped by many opposed to behaviorism in sociological social psychology. Nearly half of the volume is devoted to operant behavior, discussing key principles and concepts and applying them to daily social interaction.

The final chapter of Bijou and Baer's book is devoted to a discussion of "complex human behavior," involving intricate interaction between respondents which are controlled by preceding stimuli and operants which are controlled by their consequences. "Emotional behavior" and "self control" are used as examples of these types of complex behaviors. According to Bijou and Baer, emotional behavior is respondent in nature, controlled by *eliciting* stimuli which often prove to be *reinforcing* as well. They state: "Emotional responses, then, are respondent responses to particular kinds of eliciting stimulation: usually to stimulation made up of reinforcing stimuli, positive or negative, being presented or removed, or the beginning of extinction" (p. 74).

"Self-control" is also thought to involve operants and respondents, in that certain operant behaviors manipulate eliciting stimuli that in turn affect respondent behavior. Again there is an emphasis on the interaction between operants and respondents in order to explain complex human behavior. A unique feature of this approach is that Bijou and Baer add a dynamic element of child development, using a behavioral perspective. They conceptualize the child as an interrelated cluster of responses and stimuli with the environment and the child having a reciprocal effect on each other (pp. 14–16). They do this and yet retain the dictum that a behavioral approach concentrates on observable rather than "inner" processes. Given this accomplishment there should be little wonder that at least some sociological social psychologists began to look at modern behaviorism closely.

Complex Human Behavior is another book which caught the attention of sociological social psychologists, because of its unencumbered explanation of modern behaviorism and its vivid application of behavioral principles to everyday topics and concerns. Responding to the criticism that there was a dearth of behavioral experiments concerned with relevant complex human behavior, Arthur and Carolyn Staats defend the failure of many experimentalists to extend their efforts to more complex phenomena. They contend that analyses of simple situations are prerequisites to determining "the principles relating environmental variables to behavioral variables" (p. 6).

Once such prerequisites had been fulfilled it is then possible to extend behavioral methods and products to life occurrences. The Staats conclude that the time has come, and this is the value of their book. In a manner similar to Bijou and Baer, they offer "behavioral" alternatives to explanations of social psychological phenomena thought by many to be beyond the realm of modern behaviorism. Social interaction and human motivation, they suggest, can be accounted for without using "inner factors," and by emphasizing the roles of discriminative stimuli and reinforcing stimuli. They feel it is also appropriate to interpret other concepts like "personality," "self," and "attitudes" from a behavioral standpoint. For example, in their discussion of "self" they state:

> According to this usage, the term has been defined as the "attitudes" and "feelings" of the individual about himself. Customarily, psychologists who have used this term in this manner infer that there are inner processes which determine what the individual will say about himself. These inner processes might at various times be called "feelings," "perceptions," "evaluations," and so on.
>
> However, such internal processes are not observed. Rather, the observations from which such internal processes are inferred generally include largely the verbal statements of the individual, particularly that verbal behavior which is descriptive of himself and his actions. Considered in this manner, it would be appropriate to use *self* only as a descriptive term, to stand for the verbal behavior the individual emits concerning himself, not as an explanatory term standing for some inner psychic agent (pp. 260-1).

Alternative explanations of traditional social psychological concepts such as the above undoubtedly intrigued sociological social psychologists who had never seriously considered behaviorism as a perspective which could be used in social psychological explanation. *Complex Human Behavior* calls attention to the possibility of using such behavioral principles and therein lies its contribution to behavioral social psychology.

Two other publications mentioned earlier were important for behaviorism's continual emergence in sociological social psychology in the mid-1960s. It is true that George Homans had set the stage some years earlier in several articles and books including *Social Behavior: Its Elementary Forms*. However his brand of behaviorism seems either to have been largely ignored, or to have been converted into the Social Exchange Perspective. In a prologue to Burgess and Bushell's book, Homans continues to advance a case for behaviorism:

> The reason why I think it necessary to make this brief and obvious statement about the nature of explanation, and therefore of theory, is that the principles of behavioral psychology are the general propositions we use, whether implicitly or explicitly, in explaining all social phenomena. That is their primary relevance to the social sciences. This view is certainly not generally accepted, and the failure to accept it depends on a trained incapacity to recognize the part played by psychological propositions in social theory (p. 4).

But the year was 1966 and behaviorism was not visible in sociological social psychology despite Homans' prominence in the field. Part of the reason for this may have been his apparent acceptance without alteration of psychological principles which some felt were necessary to avoid circular thought. "Are Operant Principles Tautological?" was an article written in response to charges of tautology in behaviorism (especially from sociological social psychologists). Burgess and Akers' argument is that propositions in operant behavior often do little more than restate definitions. Their purpose is to "order" operant principles into an integrated set of nontautological statements of general and derived propositions (Burgess and Akers, 1966, p. 305). To a very great extent Burgess and Akers succeed in making explicit principles of modern behaviorism which had remained implicit in Skinner-influenced expositions of the perspective. As a result, a formulation emerges which minimizes tautological (circular) reasoning and therefore appeals to many just beginning to explore the perspective.

The authors' second article, "A Differential Association-Reinforcement Theory of Criminal Behavior" shows how nontautological operant principles can be used to provide a behavioral explanation of socialization into criminal behavior. Burgess and Akers reformulate

Sutherland's "differential-association" theory of criminal behavior. They begin by reformulating a major statement in the theory that "criminal behavior is learned." Burgess and Akers suggest that "criminal behavior is learned according to the principle of operant conditioning" and construct seven operant-based propositions from nine of Sutherland's key statements in differential association theory.

With the publication of this article, behaviorism made a bid for respectability among sociologists. Other articles, such as a "Communication Network: An Experimental Reevaluation" by Robert Burgess, and Richard Emerson's "Operant Psychology and Social Exchange" also enhanced the credibility of behaviorism in sociology and in sociological social psychology.

MODERN BEHAVIORISM FRAMEWORK IN SOCIOLOGICAL SOCIAL PSYCHOLOGY

In the following section a set of concepts and principles of modern behaviorism is presented. Most of the framework is derived from Skinnerian behaviorism and the contributions of modern behaviorists within both sociological social psychology and psychological social psychology. Excluded from the presentation is J. R. Kantor's "interbehaviorism," Albert Bandura's "modification of behaviorism" and Bijou and Baer's "behavior analysis." These systems are discussed following the modern behaviorism framework since their departure is rather significant. For now let us consider some basic concepts and principles of modern behaviorism as used by some scholars in sociological social psychology within the last two decades.

Basic Concepts in Modern Behaviorism

Operant   The concept "operant" is basic to modern behaviorism. In fact, it helps to distinguish modern behaviorism from the older stimulus-response versions of behaviorism. An operant is defined as *a behavior (response) emitted by a person which produces change in his or her environment.* This may be a wink, a smile, a growl, a verbal remark and even, in some instances, silence. While these examples are all different, they have in common one element, the production of change in one's environment. A wink may result in an invitation to join another person in some social exchange. A smile can mean that one person is making a friendly overture toward another. A growl can cause aggressive behaviors to be directed toward the source. A verbal remark may call forth another from another person. In the case of silence, depending on the situation, it can be taken as a rebuff, agreement, or fear—all of which may alter a person's environment.

Respondent   A concept often confused with "operant" is "respondent." Respondents are distinguished from operants in that they are responses made by organisms which *follow* some kind of stimulation. An object moves toward the eye and the eye closes. A physician taps a patient's knee and the knee jerks. A person is shown a slice of cake and begins to salivate. These are examples of respondent behavior. A major difference between operants and respondents lies in both behaviors' relationship to stimuli. Operants are controlled by their consequences (stimuli which follow their occurrences) while respondents are controlled by stimuli which *precede their occurrences*. As illustration, when a child asks a parent for a glass of water and receives it, "asking" is an operant which has "operated" on the child's environment, thereby causing it to change (receiving a glass of water). In contrast, a respondent occurs when a pediatrician taps the child's knee and the child's leg jerks. The tapping of the knee is the stimulus for the leg to move and, as in this example, precedes movement of the leg (the response). Bijou and Baer make the following statement about respondent behavior:

> Respondents are not controlled by their consequences; stimulation which follows them is not liable to affect them. For example, reduction in size of the pupil of the eye is a respondent. This response is elicited by presenting a bright light to the open-eyed organism, and the contracting response invariably follows. You may stand in front of a mirror with a flashlight and observe the changes in size of your own pupils. If you try it, try also to prevent the response as you turn the flashlight to shine in your eye: "will yourself" not to contract your pupil. You will fail to prevent the response. Similarly, someone might stand beside you and offer you $100 if you will *not* contract your pupil as the light is shined in. You will still fail to prevent the response when the eliciting stimulus is applied. Again, someone might tell you that he will give you $100 if you *will* contract the pupil of your eye. Unless you can arrange for an eliciting stimulus of a light to flash in your eye,

you will fail to win the $100. Respondents, therefore, are simply functions of the particular kinds of stimulation which precede them, not functions of stimulations which follow them (1961, p. 26).

Implicit in the above statement is the idea that the relationship between stimuli and responses is practically automatic in those occurrences of respondent behavior. Thus, respondent behavior appears to be involuntary, and operant behavior is voluntary behavior. Much of modern behaviorism is concerned with the latter type of behavior.

Stimulus   Another concept which is important in modern behaviorism is "stimulus." Stimulus refers to *events, consequences and/or changes in a person's environment.* These events, consequences and/or changes may be divided into five broad categories: positive reinforcers, neutral events, positive punishers and negative punishers. Events, consequences and/or changes in a person's environment caused by some operant and which increases the operant's occurrence are called *positive reinforcers.* When the parent gives the child water following the child's request, asking for water in the future should increase in frequency. Water, then, is a positive reinforcer increasing the frequency of "asking" behavior. Other examples of positive reinforcers may be milk (for babies), candy (for toddlers), parental approval (for preadolescents), the esteem of peers (for the teenager) and monetary reward from an employer (for adults) (Bijou and Baer, 1961, pp. 33–4).

Negative reinforcers are stimuli which may remove, avoid or terminate certain other stimuli and thereby cause an operant to increase in frequency of occurrence. The major difference between these stimuli and positive reinforcers lies in the processes of positive reinforcement and negative reinforcement. Positive reinforcement involves some additive to the person's environment which results in an increase in the probability of an operant's occurrence (for example, the child receives water). On the other hand, negative reinforcement is a process whereby the frequency of an operant's occurrence is increased because of environmental change which is characterized by the subtraction of something from the environment. For instance, walking away from a person who is verbally abusing one may be negatively reinforcing in that walking away removes the abuser from one's environment and increases the likelihood of "walking away from abuse" behavior in the future.

A third category of stimuli is termed *neutral.* These are events, and consequences, which follow some operant and have no effect on the probability of that operant's future occurrence. While these stimuli are discussed in the literature rather extensively, it is difficult to imagine their existence to any great degree in everyday social interactions. For example, if one person directs action toward another, the other person, in an effort to provide neutral stimuli, may ignore the action and/or pretend that the action never happened. Such a response, presumably, would be designed to neither increase nor decrease the frequency of the directed action. Realistically, is is highly doubtful that the desired result would be obtained. By the time most persons reach their teenage years, they are so socialized in social interaction strategies that efforts to present neutral consequences are almost futile. The individual has matured to the point of being able to pick up even the most subtle cues, and to attribute meaning to a variety of behavior.

Because social life is not always characterized by operant occurrences which result in positive and/or negative reinforcement, or neutral consequences, it is important to consider two other classes of stimuli: *positive punishers* and *negative punishers*. The sociologist Robert L. Burgess, perhaps more than any other person in modern behaviorism, has been responsible for emphasizing these two stimulus categories. According to Burgess, positive punishers are those events, consequences and/or changes in the person's environment which, when presented following an operant's occurrence, result in a decrease in the operant's occurrence. A perfect example of the process of positive punishment is seen in the situation where an employee who has established a pattern of tardiness is finally called into his or her employer's office. The scene may be as follows: the employer delivers a reprimand to the employee, and from that day on the employee reports to work on time. The employer has delivered positive punishment since the reprimand has resulted in a decrease in the employee's tardiness behavior. The positive punisher, in this case, is the employer's reprimand. With positive punishment, as with positive reinforcement, something is *added* to the environment. In this case, the reprimand is the addition and the decrease in the operant's occurrence characterizes the consequence as punishment—thus, the process, positive punishment.

The effect of negative punishment is the same as positive punishment in that it results in a decrease in an operant's occurrence. It is different from positive punishment in that the operant's decrease in frequency is due to the *removal of stimuli in the person's environment*. In many instances the stimuli that are removed are positive reinforcers. Using the same example of the tardy worker, an employer may decide upon a negative punishment strategem for correcting the employee's behavior. Such a strategy might be to withhold a portion of the employee's paycheck (assuming that the paycheck is a positive reinforcer for the employee's behavior). If withholding a portion of the paycheck results in an alteration of the behavior, then negative punishment has occurred. A more definitive statement of the nature of negative punishment is given by Burgess and Bushell. They refer to negative punishment as *those changes, consequences, alternatives, etc. in the person's environment which remove other stimuli and thereby cause an operant to decrease in its frequency of occurrence* (p. 30).

Contingencies of Reinforcement   The term "contingencies of reinforcement" refers to conditions under which changes, events or consequences occur in a person's environment following his or her operant acts according to certain patterns. Often such conditions and patterns are referred to as "schedules of reinforcement" (Burgess and Bushell). There are two basic types of reinforcement schedules with contingencies of reinforcement: continuous and intermittent.

When reinforcement *immediately follows each response or operant emitted by an organism,* a continuous reinforcement schedule is in effect. If, for example, a child receives praise from his or her parents after each instance of polite verbal behavior, a continuous reinforcement schedule is being used by the parents to shape polite verbal behavior in their child. While continuous schedules have been used widely in laboratory experiments, they rarely exist in everyday social situations, primarily because of the extensive monitoring of behavior required when such a schedule is used. Intermittent schedules seem to be more characteristic of the reinforcement contingencies applied to behavior in real life. These are characterized by *reinforcement following some operant emissions but not others.* Burgess and Bushell refer to the impossibility of reinforcing every response emitted by an individual. Note that even if one attempted to teach a young child a particular social skill (for example, saying "thank you"), it is improbable that there would be a 1:1 ratio between the instances of reinforcement and the instances of the operant ("thank you"). A ratio of this kind could be obtained, perhaps, only if the "teacher" had absolute control over the child and, additionally, could perceive accurately all of the child's operant emissions. Since this is rarely the case in everyday life, it seems fair to say that most socialization as well as social interaction situations are based on intermittent schedules of reinforcement at best.

A brief review of the literature will show a variety of intermittent schedules. All of these, however, are derived from two types: interval and ratio schedules. Interval schedules are based on the *time* between instances of reinforcement. They are constructed so that the first response after a certain amount of time has elapsed is reinforced. The time period between reinforcement can be *fixed* (as when the first response is reinforced after each five minute time period has passed) or *variable* (where on an average of each five minute time period the first response is reinforced) (the first response is reinforced after the fifth minute and the sixth minute but then not until the eleventh and twentieth minutes or the first response reinforced. The former type of interval schedule is called *fixed interval* (FI) and the latter type is referred to as *variable interval* (VI) since the time period between reinforcement varies around some mean time period (in the above example, the mean time period is five minutes).

Ratio schedules are based on the number of responses between reinforcement. They are constructed so that reinforcement follows some *n*th response. In the case of *fixed ratio schedules* (FR), reinforcement follows every *n*th response (after every fourth response for example). In *variable ratio* (VR) reinforcement schedules, reinforcement is delivered following some average response (for example, reinforcement may be given after the third, eleventh and twelfth response in a fifteen response-reinforcement frame, thus reinforcement follows on an average every fifth response).

Differential Reinforcement   One of the most important principles related to behavioral social psychology is "differential reinforcement." The importance of this principle can be seen if one uses the behavioral perspective to explain learning a language, norm formation in a group and decision-making, as well as hosts of other individual and group behaviors in everyday life. Differential reinforcement occurs in those social situations where persons choose to follow one line of action rather than another although either alternative leads to the same outcome. Following this line of thought, why, given that a child can behave politely and receive attention from his or her parents, or throw temper tantrums and also receive attention from the parents, are temper tantrums exhibited more frequently? Certainly, in order to adequately understand a specific case it is necessary to have some insight into the nature of the specific parent-child interaction. One may be able to obtain a general understanding of the case by using a particular social psychological perspective to explore certain known elements. This is a common procedure. For example, some social psychologists would attribute the greater frequency of temper tantrums in the child to personality traits, while others would say that socialization is responsible for behavioral differences—that is, the child learned to respond in such a manner. The exact nature of the learning process may or may not be outlined in such explanations. In contrast, a behavioral explanation of the differential frequency of polite behavior and temper tantrums exhibited by the child would be much more specific and might entail analyzing the case in terms of the principle of differential reinforcement.

The principle of *differential reinforcement* suggests that if there are a number of different operants which will produce a particular reinforcer, the operant which produces the reinforcer in the greatest amount, frequency and probability is the operant most likely to occur (Burgess and Akers, 1966). Differential reinforcement involves strengthening some behaviors while extinguishing others. The person who seeks admission into a social group often experiences differential reinforcement of his or her behaviors as he or she begins to exhibit new behaviors and discard old ones. Often ethnic and racial minority group members in a culture feel the need to adapt, and manifest behaviors much like those of the culture's majority group members. A reason why this need is felt is the fact that dominant behaviors in a culture are linked with the culture's reinforcement system. Thus, behaviors deemed appropriate in a culture are more likely than others to be reinforced by the culture. Employment in many occupations in our society is dependent upon the potential employee's articulation of standard American speech. If an ethnic or racial minority group member hopes to obtain employment, in many instances he or she has to discard ethnic and / or racial minority patterns of articulation and adopt standard speech since the latter has a greater probability of being reinforced. A less complicated example of differential reinforcement is seen as a young child learns to verbalize a word. A child may emit a sound which only vaguely resembles the word to be learned (for example, wa for water). This sound may initially be reinforced by the child's caretakers. Gradually though, the caretakers may to begin to selectively reinforce those sounds most closely resembling the word water. Through this process, the child finally comes to say "water."

Discriminative Stimulus   The social world is extremely complex, so much so that there are a variety of stimuli impinging upon the individual as he or she interacts in daily life. Also, individuals repond to their environments in a variety of ways, producing certain consequences in their environments. Because of this complexity, it is sometimes difficult to pinpoint the exact nature of the response-stimulus-response sequence in a given instance of social interaction. Some social responses emitted by persons almost appear to be stimulus-response based. That is, stimuli appear to elicit the responses. Yet operants are not elicited by stimuli (Bijou and Baer, 1961, p. 49). Nevertheless, most of us have experienced social situations at one time or another which appear to be best characterized by a stimulus-response model. The child who suddenly screams when a person possessing certain physical characteristics appears; the romantic feeling which sweeps over certain people in a room with a companion when the lights are dimmed and soft music plays; the rage expressed by some females when males act in condescending ways toward them—all these are hypothetical situations with a common theme. On the surface there appears to be something in each situation which calls out a particular response. In fact there would seem to be little, if any, difference between what happens in these hypothetical situations and respondent behavior which is stimulus-response based. This means that some stimulus seems to be eliciting some response in the same manner that the leg gives a jerk when tapped, or the eye closes when an object moves too near. While we admit that all the answers are not known, at the present time most authorities agree that operant behavioral emissions go through a process somewhat different from respondent behavioral emissions.

Respondent behavioral emissions, for the most part, involve stimulus-response sequences. Operant behavioral emissions, which on the surface may resemble respondent behavior, involve the process of "stimulus discrimination," whereby an operant is emitted by the individual only in the presence of certain stimuli. Another way of saying this is that certain stimuli mark the occasion for operant emissions. In such instances, the presence of stimuli may set the occasion for the occurrence of an operant because in the past when such stimuli were present, changes and/or alterations in the person's environment have increased the likelihood that the operant would be emitted. This kind of operant is known in behavioral circles as a "discriminated operant," because it is under the control of a preceding discriminated stimulus (Bijou and Baer, 1961, p. 49) and the person emitting it is thought to be discriminating.

The stimuli marking or signalling the occasion for the emission of an operant and in whose presence the strength of an operant is increased are referred to as SD^s. Not all such stimuli are associated with an increase in the strength of operants. Some stimuli linked to the process of stimulus discrimination can decrease the probability of an operant's occurrences. This type of stimulus is referred to as an S-Delta. Consider the following example: often when a child is left with a babysitter, the child emits certain behaviors associated directly with the parents' absence from the home. However, upon the parents' return it is likely that the behaviors emitted during their absence decrease in frequency or cease altogether. Thus, the parents' presence serves as a discriminative stimulus (S-Delta) which decreases the probability of certain behavioral emissions.

Stimulus Generalization   Stimulus generalization occurs when a stimulus (or stimuli), because of repeated associations with reinforcement, becomes a reinforcer and/or a discriminative stimulus; and other stimuli also take on reinforcing and/or discrimination stimulus properties because of similarity to the former reinforcer and/or discriminative stimulus (Bijou and Baer, 1961, p. 51; Burgess and Akers, 1966). Stimulus generalization is part-and-parcel of everyday social interaction, but perhaps is in evidence most when babies are learning to respond to sights and sounds. This is because stimulus generalization is, in a sense, a failure to discriminate (Bijou and Baer, 1961, p. 51). As stated earlier, a stimulus can come to mark the occasion for the occurrence of a response (stimulus discrimination) as when mother or father's arrival home is the occasion for a scream of glee which is then followed by hugs, kisses and other signs of affection from the parent (all which serve to strengthen "arrival home" as an SD for the scream). If a child emits the same gleeful noise when other males and females resembling the parents enter the home, then stimulus generalization is operating. When a six-month old's often-repeated emissions of this kind are not followed by the reinforcer by mother or father when they enter the house, the child gradually learns to discriminate between the parents' arrival home and other persons' entrances. The discriminative process is completed when only mother or father's entrance sets the occasion for the gleeful yell.

Ironically, stimulus generalization can also be seen in consistently discriminating behaviors exhibited toward members of ethnic or racial groups when a majority group member treats "all blacks alike" or "all Italians alike" or "all Poles alike." Sometimes it is with great embarrassment that majority group members realize that the appearance of a member of these groups should not set the occasion for the occurrence of a particular response. (The condescending verbal mimicking behavior often exhibited by well-meaning whites upon meeting a black for the first time is an excellent example of stimulus generalization and of a failure to invoke stimulus discrimination). On the other hand, some whites (also well-intentioned) have made terrible mistakes by discriminating too finely. For instance, not recognizing that the comment "You are so different from other blacks" is in no way complimentary and is, in fact, insulting, has cut short a number of budding interracial friendships.

Response Generalization and Response Differentiation   Stimulus discrimination and stimulus generalization are linked to two other basic concepts in behavioral social psychology. These concepts are response generalization and response differentiation. Persons learn to make fine distinctions between similar classes of responses because of selective reinforcement. Moreover, these responses (operants) usually come to have a high probability of occurrence in some stimulus situations but not in others (stimulus discrimination). However, strengthening one response *within* a class of responses may have the effect of strengthening other responses within that class of responses. A person who is successful in robbing banks by physical force may in actuality increase the use of physical force and other types of behavior associated with physical force in future robberies. Much of what may seem to be novel and seemingly unreinforced behaviors emitted by a person, may in fact be behaviors that are functions of a process of response generalization.

Response differentiation also is intimately related to *stimulus generalization, stimulus discrimination,* and in addition, *differential* reinforcement. It occurs when the duration and intensity of a response is altered by reinforcement. This alteration appears to be highly probable under conditions of stimulus discrimination and/or differential reinforcement. A person may exhibit a variety of flirtatious behaviors toward members of the opposite sex, including winking an eye. If winking of an eye results in the desired reaction from others more frequently than alternative flirtatious behaviors, then not only is it likely that the probability of winking an eye will be altered but also the intensity and duration for eye-winking behavior in certain situations will be strengthened.

Extinction   Extinction is the process whereby an operant returns to its operant level. Extinction involves nonreinforcement of an operant's occurrence. Additionally, it should also involve nonpunishment of an operant's occurrence, since the object of the extinction process should be to return the operant to the operant level rather than below it (the extreme being total removal of the operant from the person's operant repertoire). This means, basically, that extinction ultimately depends upon neutral stimuli following an operant's occurrence (i.e., neither reinforcement or punishment) at some point in the extinction process. The major problem here and with the concept as stated previously is the difficulty in finding neutral stimuli in social interaction situations.

While we have dealt with a number of key concepts in the behavioral perspective, *all* of the concepts have not been discussed. This is a virtual impossibility in a volume of this type. However, a thorough grasp of the concepts presented here should greatly facilitate an introductory understanding of behavioral social psychology.

Assumptions Underlying Modern Behaviorism

1. Human Organisms are Dynamic in Social Interaction   The assumption that human organisms in social interaction are dynamic is basic to an understanding of behavioral social psychology in sociology. Unless a response is emitted by an individual and operates on the environment, explanations related to the establishment of behavior are relegated to a "modelling" formulation. Moreover, maintenance of responses during the early stages of "shaping" is impossible to explain without the underlying assumption of human behavior dynamism. Indeed, it might be pointed out that one major difference between Watsonian behaviorism and present-day behavioral social psychology is that the former type of behaviorism implies that stimuli occurred prior to responses. Modern behavioral social psychology, in contrast, assumes that responses are antecedent to stimuli. This may not seem to be a major concern; however, both distinctive conceptions have implications for the nature of man. Watsonian behaviorism implies that humans are inert and only moved to action when stimuli impinge on them. In contrast, modern behaviorism suggests that persons are dynamic. This in turn means that humans do not sit idly by waiting upon stimuli. Instead, they act, and in time their actions produce consequences in the social world. These consequences have implications for the recurrence of the acts.

2. Operants Produce Stimulus Events   All operants have the potential to produce stimulus events that alter their future occurrence (Burgess and Akers, 1966, p. 309). This is an important assumption in behavioral social psychology because it helps to provide the basis for the distinction between stimulus-response psychology and modern behaviorism. Along with the first assumption (that human organisms are active), the case is bolstered that social actions emitted by humans may act on the environment producing positive, negative or neutral consequences which either increase, decrease or have no effect on the future occurrence of the social action. Without this assumption, not only would it be difficult to explain the "shaping" of behavior, but it would be practically impossible to talk about the maintenance of behavior or decreases in behavior occurrences (at least from a behavioral perspective).

3. Reinforcement Functions to Maintain an Active Repertoire of Behavior   It has been stated that the maintenance of an active repertoire of behavior is one of the primary functions of reinforcement. The assumption is related directly to the likelihood that an acquired response will continue to be emitted under appropriate stimulus conditions. While the assumption seems plausible enough, another even more salient question arises. Why should a person, under certain conditions, emit a particular response? From modern behaviorism there seems to be no answer other than the idea that reinforcement has increased the probability of an operant's occurrence. Perhaps this is so, but many contend that we still need to know why the operant's response has increased in frequency. Unfortunately, discussions in the literature about the consequences operating on the environment do not give a satisfactory answer although Bijou contends that functional relationships do answer adequately the question of "why" (1979, p. 5). This problem is discussed later in this chapter.

Most behaviorists feel that operant principles are violated when "desire for a reinforcer" is used to explain the occurrence of some behavior. Yet Skinner himself acknowledges that most reinforcers seem to be related to biological processes important to the organism's survival. If this is true, then secondary or conditioned reinforcers could be reinforcing for social responses because of the unique (or not so unique) relationship to primary reinforcers such as food, water, sex, etc. One must hasten to add that this is *not* an assumption of modern behaviorism, nor is it likely to be in the near future. Nevertheless it *is* provocative.

4. Recurrence of an Activity under Similar Circumstances   In Kunkel and Nagasawa's "A Behavioral Model of Man: Propositions and Implications," a major assumption of behavioral social psychology is advanced as follows: *If an activity is followed by a reinforcer it is likely to recur in similar circumstances* (p. 534). Now there is very little difference between this assumption and statements made by Skinner and others. However, Kunkel and Nagasawa's intent in presenting this assumption is not to construct new or different postulates, but rather, to examine the literature in an effort to discover postulates basic to the behavioral perspective. Their effort is creditable and to a certain extent, unique. The uniqueness of their effort becomes apparent when one realizes that Kunkel and Nagasawa, in a very simple and ingenious move, construct a proposition that enables us to see the effects of the reinforcement principle, the derived principle of stimulus generalization, and the law of stimulus discrimination. Stating precisely what they mean by "reinforcer" (material objects, symbols, behaviors of others, etc.), the authors avoid the circular reasoning said to be characteristic of many behaviorists (Lerner, p. 275) by defining the concept in terms other than probability. Nevertheless, they too fail to address the question of why a reinforcer which follows an activity increases the occurrence of the activity, other than to say that it does. Moreover, it is not clear that they subscribe to a "survival of the organism" model.

Kunkel and Nagasawa's uncomplicated postulate, which merits inclusion here, suggests not only that stimuli generalize but also that stimuli present in a situation may signal an activity's occurrence (the law of stimulus discrimination).

5. Deprivation   A fifth assumption may be stated as follows: If a person is deprived of some items, these items tend to be reinforcers; if a person is not deprived of some items, they do not tend to be reinforcers. Quoted verbatim from Kunkel and Nagasawa, assumption five seems to be essential to behaviorism, primarily because more often than not reinforcement principles do not operate effectively unless deprivation of some kind is present in the human organism. Bijou and Baer offer an alternative principle which modifies the above. They state that "the reinforcing property of many (not all) stimuli depends on their supply or availability to the individual over an extended period." (1978, pp. 26–27).

What seems to be implied by the Kunkel-Nagasawa assumption is some kind of modified law of effect and/or Hull-Kunkel-Nagasawa principle. Bijou and Baer's principle clearly is different if reviewed in context. The question which arises in Kunkel and Nagasawa's model is why is deprivation an important ingredient of a reinforcer? Many modern behaviorists would ignore the question, especially as it applied to their experimental results. Yet, why do Mithaug and Burgess conclude their study:

> probably the most effective way to establish and maintain social cooperation, in general, is to provide positive reinforcement to each of the members contingent upon the cooperative act as well as some form of individual feedback for appropriate individual responses.

Why is individual reinforcement effective in shaping up cooperative behavior? Skinner (1966) suggests that the answer certainly does not lie in the concepts of drives or needs but rather in contingencies of reinforcement. Skinner's feeling is that society arranges contingencies of reinforcement in archaic ways, making great use of aversive control (punishment) rather than positive reinforcement. Moreover, because we use reinforcers to satisfy "needs" we fail to use them to fulfill man's nature. Skinner contends that "men are happy in an environment in which active, productive, and creative behavior is reinforced in effective ways'' (1966, p. 166). Is perceived happiness the key to why a reinforcer is a reinforcer regardless of whether we concentrate on reinforcers or contingencies of reinforcement? Whether the drive is learned or biological does not seem to be the issue here. The issue is related to whether man's (woman's) behavior is, as Hull suggested, purposive. The model accepted by at least some behaviorists in the late 1960s and early 1970s seems to suggest this as a possibility, at least implicitly. Of course Skinner cannot be included among the latter and makes this clear in *About Behaviorism.*

6. Modelling and Learning   Another behavioral assumption posited in sociological social psychology is related to ''modelling''. This refers to a learning process whereby some person (or persons) emit responses that have been learned by observing others' activities and the consequences of those activities. Continued emission of the behavior, according to this line of thought, is dependent upon whether the person ''trying-out'' the observed behavior is rewarded (Kunkel and Nagasawa, p. 534). Quoting Kunkel and Nagasawa, the sixth assumption underlying modern behaviorism is: If an activity is learned through modelling, then the observer is likely to repeat it in similar circumstances (provided the model's behavior was reinforced).

The sixth assumption, aside from broadening the scope of the behavioral perspective, is especially significant for sociologically oriented behaviorists.

Many of these scholars, along with others have long argued that much of what we learn does not occur through response-stimulus-response patterning but rather, through vicarious experiences in our day-to-day activities. Certainly this is important when one realizes that in most societies numerous norms and values must be learned. Additionally, it is virtually impossible for all of this learning to occur through direct response-stimulus-response learning. On the subject of modelling, Albert Bandura (who has done extensive theorizing and research on the subject), states that observing others' outcomes helps one define the nature and effectiveness of directly experienced reinforcers by providing a standard for evaluating the consequences of one's behavior as beneficial, equitable and fair. Bandura's rationale for modelling then has a cognitive element conspiciously absent in many behavioristic formulations but somewhat compatible with sociological social psychology. More will be said about Bandura's modifications in the next section.

We see then that some of the behaviorism with which many sociological social psychologists became familar in the late 1960s and early 1970s seem to have an underlying ''purposive'' influence as in Bandura's formulation and the social exchange perspective discussed in the next chapter. For the most part, however, the behaviorism to which the handful of sociologists began to give some attention was Skinner-influenced behaviorism. It was a behaviorism characterized, in large part, by the avoidance of mentalistic constructs. The "inner life" of the individual was felt to be beyond objective study, and therefore ignored in research studies. For many scholars of different social psychological persuasions, this "empty organism" approach to the study of human behavior was inadequate and numerous criticisms were directed toward modern behaviorism.

Aside from those criticisms directed toward the older stimulus-response psychology, others emerged about modern behaviorism. From those inclined toward cognitive social psychology came the charge that cognitive processes could not be explained because behaviorism ignored states of mind, conscious feelings, and so on. Symbolic interactionists were just as concerned because many of their major concepts, like self and generalized other, seemed to be ignored by behaviorists. Furthermore, "individual creativity," "uniqueness" and "nature of man" were thought to be overlooked. Others felt that behavioral experiments lacked external validity. Findings in the laboratory could not be duplicated in the real world. These are but a few of the charges levied at modern behaviorism. Skinner enumerates twenty such criticisms in *About Behaviorism* (pp. 4–5). Behaviorists like Skinner and Bijou have countered that present-day behaviorism is misunderstood on these points as well as many others, because of the sensitivity of the field, confusion over the meanings of concepts and a dearth of knowledge of behavior analysis outside the field. This may be so, but it is also true that behaviorism has evolved into a different kind of perspective than the one outlined earlier. It appears to be a kind of behaviorism which attempts to restore balance to a perspective which once dealt exclusively with external antecedent events (as a response to those who devoted attention solely to internal factors). Skinner refers to many features of the emerging variety of behaviorism as "radical behaviorism." Bijou and Baer's label "behavior analysis" is the one used in this volume to distinguish the newer variety. Let us examine briefly some of its philosophical underpinnings.

Behavior analysis seems to be couched in (1) environmental determinism with broad latitudes to include continuous interaction between the organism (genetic endowment included) and its environment including others; (2) an evolutionary principle which suggests basically that behavior occurs because appropriate mechanisms have been selected in the course of evolution; (3) an emphasis on objective observation; and (4) analyses of interactions and explanations are functional.

Distinguishing features of behavior analysis are the increased emphasis on the role of environment as it affects the organism before and after it responds, an emphasis on the genetic endowment of the organism, and the point that a susceptibility to reinforcement is due to its survival value and not to any associated feelings (Skinner, 1974). Given these underpinnings of behavior analysis, let us explore further some features of the perspective.

BEHAVIOR ANALYSIS

A framework of behavior analysis based on B. F. Skinner's behaviorism and J. R. Kantor's interbehaviorism has been developed by Sidney Bijou and Donald Baer (1978). They define their analysis as one of human psychological development which involves "progressive changes in interaction between the behavior of individuals and the events in their environment (p. 2). They state that theirs is a "natural science" approach which deals with observable events, and that therefore their theoretical statements are "generalized propositions about *observable* interactions between the environment and behavior" (p. 6). This particular point of view eschews the inclusion of nonobservable hypothetical constructs as causes of behavior and instead embraces the idea that human behavior is some function of species characteristics, biological maturation and human organism—environment interaction. As far as behavior analysis in social psychology is concerned, the point of departure would be the latter—the analyses of human behavior in interaction with the environment.

Bijou and Baer place human behavior (response) in two broad categories, respondent and operant, basically defined as they are earlier in this chapter and as they themselves defined them in their earlier presentation of behavior analysis (1961). Expanding the meaning of response to include the concept "response class," they point out that responses made by individuals are always different from one time to the next. This means that responses come in classes or collections. Response class refers to "those varied forms of response that accomplish the same function" (1978, p. 20). Some members of a response class are similar while others are quite different, but one condition must be met if they are to make up a response class and that is that their effects on the environment are the same or they respond to the same event in the environment.

Persons are not only considered as sources of respondents and operant responses, but also as sources of stimuli. An individual, in part,

tion. In any case, the system of modern behavior analysis does not consider a stimulus condition, antecedent or consequent to a response, to be the cause of a response; a stimulus condition is viewed as one of the events in a multiplex field. Here one seeks not the cause of behavior but the past interactions that have led to changes in relationships among stimuli, setting factors, and responses that constitute the situation under study. (p. 5).

A final word about the presentation of aspects of behavior analysis in this chapter. While some might object to generalizing the perspective to all humans (Lerner, p. 272) this seems clearly valid in view of Bijou and Baer's expressed basic concern, "the understanding of all such interactions of human behavior and environment" (Bijou and Baer, 1978, p. 4).

SOCIAL LEARNING THEORY AND BEHAVIOR ANALYSIS

Behavior analysis is frequently associated with social learning theory although the two systems are quite different, as Bijou points out (1979, p. 11). It is true that the two perspectives have some of the same ancestors and use similar concepts and principles. Yet there are crucial and significant differences which carry them down different paths. A brief sketch of some key ideas in social learning theory should show how the two perspectives differ. The discussion of social learning theory to follow is based on the work of one of the most well known social learning theorists, Albert Bandura. Bandura's theoretical book *Social Learning Theory* is probably the clearest and most concise statement about social learning theory today, and is used as the basis for this discussion.

Some Elements of Social Learning Theory

Social learning theory emphasizes two kinds of learning: learning by response consequences and learning through modelling. Let us explore each of these kinds of learning.

Learning by Response Consequences   This mode of learning, said to be the more rudimentary of the two, refers to the development and maintenance of behavior through operant conditioning procedures. Persons in daily social interaction produce behaviors, and some of these behaviors are reinforced, others seem to have no effects, and still others are punished. The reinforced behaviors, called successful by Bandura (p. 17), are selected and others, called ineffectual, are discarded. The selection and discarding of behaviors is thus a function of differential reinforcement and involves an *awareness* on the part of persons that some of their behaviors have positive consequences and others do not. This awareness is the *cognitive element* involved in learning. Thus, unlike modern behaviorism, behavior analysis, radical behaviorism and other variations of behaviorism, responses are not strengthened automatically by their consequences.

According to Bandura, several functions are associated with response consequences. They have *informative functions, motivational functions* and *reinforcing functions.* The informative function is information gained by persons from observing various outcomes of the effects of their action. Through such observations they develop hypotheses about the appropriateness of responses in social settings. If the hypotheses are correct, persons' performances are successful; if the hypotheses are incorrect, ineffective performances are likely to occur. This process selectively reinforces and selects cognitions which are related directly to behavior.

The *motivational function* of response consequences is also important for behavior. Because individuals can think about past experiences they can also anticipate the consequences of their responses. From previous experiences they build expectations about the benefits which can be derived from certain actions therefore converting future consequences into current motivators of behavior (Bandura, p. 18). This means that much behavior is under the control of anticipatory consequences.

If cognitive and motivational elements are crucial aspects of learning by response consequences what, then, is the role of the reinforcing function (thought to be automatic) in behavioral analysis? Bandura, supported by many other learning theorists, questions the automatic response strengthening ability of reinforcement. He chooses, instead, to emphasize the informative and motivational functions of reinforcement and suggests that it is perhaps more accurate to conceive of reinforcement as the regulation of behavior. In addition, whether or not reinforcement creates new behavior or regulates what may have been learned through observation is felt to be difficult to determine.

Learning through Modelling   Bandura feels that most social learning occurs observationally, through modelling. This means that most persons observe others and then form ideas about performing behaviors which later serve as guidelines (information) for their own performances (behavior). Several processes are involved and include *attentional processes, retention processes, motor reproduction processes* and *motivational processes.*

In order to learn by observation persons must attend to and perceive accurately significant features of the modelled behavior (Bandura, p. 24). Selective attention and selective (and accurate) perception are crucial aspects of learning by observation. What are some of the processes affecting determinants of attention? *Associational patterns, characteristics of the model* and *the form in which the model is presented* all affect attention. Behavior observation is linked with patterns of association. One has the opportunity to observe the behavior of those close around and does not have this opportunity when individuals are not a part of his or her association pattern. Some models' behaviors also are of great *functional* value for the observer and this affects attention just as their interpersonal characteristics such as their charm, warmth, beauty, intelligence and the like. The *form* in which the model is presented also can be so intrinsically rewarding that it holds attention (for example, television, movies, etc.) (pp. 24–25). Finally, the nature of the modelled behavior (for example, salience, complexity), observers' capacities to process information, and their perceptual sets (past experiences and situational requirements) affect attention and perception.

Retention of behaviors that have been modelled is thought to be a key process in observational learning, which relies mainly upon an imagined system and a verbal system (Bandura, p. 25). The imaginal system is operative in observational learning when certain sensations cause persons to perceive external events when they are physically absent. Repeated exposure to and close association between events often enable persons to experience images of events in such a manner. The verbal system's role in observational learning is thought to be salient because most of the cognitive processes regulating behavior are verbal rather than visual and because the system speeds up human observational learning and retention. The verbal system involves verbal coding (symbolic codes) of modelled behavior, which enables behavior to be acquired, retained and later reproduced in the form of information to guide the observer's behavior. Other factors affecting retention include enactment of the modelled behavior, mental rehearsal and developmental stage of the observer.

MOTOR REPRODUCTION PROCESSES   Modelling also involves converting symbolic representation into behavior enactment. In reproducing the behavior of a model one's responses must be organized spatially and temporally according to the model's patterns of behavior. Firstly, there is response selection and organization at the cognitive level followed by enactment at the behavioral level. If response selection and organization indicate a high availability of component skills, then behavioral enactment is possible—low availability requires prior cognitive development. Corrective adjustments of initial efforts at the behavioral level (usually characterized by incongruence between symbolic representation and behavioral enactment) serve to increase the accuracy of matching behavior. The source of these adjustments is performance feedback, usually from others.

MOTIVATIONAL PROCESSES   Learning through modelling also is influenced by motivational processes. Persons more frequently adopt modelled behavior which they feel results in rewarding outcomes rather than behavior resulting in outcomes unrewarded or punished. Moreover, since persons evaluate the outcome of their own behavior, they are more likely to enact those behaviors which result in self-satisfaction rather than self-dissatisfaction. Bandura feels, in sum, that learning through modelling and the creation of matching behavior is a complex process. Further discussions of the process is beyond the scope of this book; however, the complexity of the modelling process is seen in Bandura's statement that:

> . . . the failure of an observer to match the behavior of a model may result from any of the following: not observing the relevant activities, inadequately coding modelled events for memory representation, failing to retain what was learned, physical inability to perform, or experiencing insufficient incentives. (p. 29).

Certainly the foregoing paragraphs do not constitute comprehensive coverage of the perspective by Bandura and those who follow his lines of theory and research. Discussions on cognitive control, antecedent determinants, consequent determinants and reciprocal determinism would be necessary to approach comprehensive presentation but would be superfluous, I believe, for the behavioral considerations in this book. Bandura's comments on the origins of behavior are endorsed by many social learning theorists:

. . . The capacity to use symbols provides humans with a powerful means of dealing with their environment. Through verbal and imagined symbols people process and preserve experiences in representational forms that serve as guides for future behavior. The capability for intentional action is rooted in symbolic activity. Images of desirable futures foster courses of action designed to lead toward more distant goals. Through the medium of symbols people can solve problems without having to enact all the various alternative solutions; and they can foresee the probable consequences of different actions and alter their behavior accordingly. Without symbolizing powers, humans would be incapable of reflective thought. A theory of human behavior therefore cannot afford to neglect symbolic activities. (p. 13).

Differences between Social Learning Theory and Behavior Analysis

Behavior analysis and social learning theory differ in major ways. Behavior analysis, in focusing on aspects of the continuous interaction between the environment and the organism which is observable, does not attribute behavior to antecedent feelings and states of mind. Such cognitive elements are felt to be hypothetical constructs which bring investigation to an end by inhibiting more ''precise analyses of the roles of the environment'' (Skinner, 1974, p. 18). Social learning theory as espoused by Bandura and others posits intervening and/or conditional cognitive influences between antecedent inducements and response consequences. Conditionally, cognitive factors affect behavior by partly determining the observation and perceptions by external events. Moreover it is felt that much human behavior is included and sustained in the absence of compelling immediate external stimulation (Bandura, p. 161).

Behavior analysis also dismisses any attempt to attribute behavior to motivation in the Hullian sense. Persons are not thought to engage in a behavior in order to get some reward or because they expect some benefit. In this sense behavior analysis is not purposive—it is not a homing device (Skinner, 1974, p. 56). It *is* purposive when motives and purposes are felt to be the effects of reinforcements. They do not direct behavior but they may be conditions produced by reinforcement. Giving a child an affectionate hug when she or he has been polite in church does not mean that the child is polite in order to receive the hug. Such polite behavior, according to behavior analysis, would be due to reinforcement contingencies operating during the time of politeness.

Social learning theorists, in contrast, contend that a person's ability to symbolically represent future consequences can be a source of motivation. Moreover, goal-setting and self-regulated reinforcement, both cognitively based and involving the individual committing him or her self to explicit goals and developing standards by which he or she evaluates own performances, may serve as motivators of behavior. Because people evaluate their own behavior and because goals specify the conditional requirements for positive self-evaluation, when there is congruence between self-satisfaction and goal attainment, goal-oriented behavior is an incentive for action.

Social learning theory also questions the automatic shaping ability of reinforcers and the idea that reinforcement *strengthens* response. Experiments on the relationship between awareness of reinforcement indicate that there is some question, because of lack of evidence, as to whether behavior is affected when reinforcement consequences are unknown (Bandura, pp. 19–21. Those cited by Bandura include Spielberger and DeNike, 1966; Dulany, 1968; and, Kennedy, 1970, 1971.) In addition Bandura suggests that the concept "response strengthening" should be discarded since once some responses are acquired they cannot be strengthened any further. "Regulating behavior by its consequences" is offered as an alternative to "reinforcement of behavior by its consequences." Behavior analysis takes the position (and this is a basic assumption underlying the perspective) that social reinforcers are reinforcing to persons because those whose behaviors are reinforced by them have survived through on evolutionary process and transmitted this susceptibility to the species (Skinner, 1974, p. 47). Regarding reinforcement and response strength social learning theory seems to acknowledge only the *rate* of occurrence of a response while behavior analysis considers *rate magnitude* (vigor and/or effort put forth) and *latency* (the promptness with which it occurs with reference to a stimulus as indicators of the strength of a response) (Bijou and Baer, 1978, p. 49).

Obviously there are numerous other distinctions which can be made between present-day social learning theory and behavior analysis. As advances are made in both perspectives some of these differences may diminish, but for the time being, it suffices to say that behavior analysis is not a learning theory; it is a self-sufficient system (Bijou, p. 4).

AN EVALUATION OF BEHAVIORAL
SOCIAL PSYCHOLOGY

Behaviorism in psychology has a relatively long history. Its presence in social psychology is much shorter, although Deutsch and Krauss included behaviorism as a perspective in their *Theories in Social Psychology* under the label "The Reinforcement Theorists." They pay particular attention to the learning theories of Miller and Dollard and Bandura and Walters, to the Yale Communication Research Program on the effects of diverse kinds of communication on attitude change led by Carl Hovland, to the exchange ideas of Thibaut and Kelley and George Homans (to be discussed in the next chapter), and to the work of B. F. Skinner. Behaviorism in social psychology during this time appeared to be a cornucopia of theories and research developed by scholars of varying philosophical, theoretical and research persuasions. This is not to imply that all is unity in behavioral social psychology today; as we have seen, this is not the case. However, there is generally agreement on the philosophy underlying behaviorism, the nature of its general theory, the research methodology and the procedures for relating basic research to applied research and for practical application (Bijou, p. 4).

As a perspective "behavior analysis" seems to have evolved from early behaviorism, modern behaviorism and interbehaviorism, and presently is the dominant variety of behaviorism of relevance to social psychology. It has been influenced greatly by Kantor's "interbehaviorism" which concentrates on the interactions of organisms and stimulus objects, and by Skinner's "radical behaviorism" which attempts explanations of behavior from a balanced "external-internal antecedent event" point of view. In presenting a more comprehensive discussion of behavior analysis than they did in 1961, Bijou and Baer state:

> It should be apparent that this analysis of human development cannot in any way be considered the same as the behavior theory of John B. Watson (1930) who defined stimuli and responses only in terms of their behavior. Nor can this analysis be identified with the learning theory of Robert R. Sears (1947, 1951) or the social learning theory of Bandura and Walters (1963) and Bandura (1977) because they include nonobservable hypothetical concepts modelled after the work of Hull (1943). But this formulation can readily be identified with the philosophy of science and behavior theory of B. F. Skinner and J. R. Kantor (1978, p. 33).

Despite recent statements on behavior analysis, numerous criticisms have been directed toward the perspective. Some of these criticisms are considered below.

Lerner points out what may be called *circular reasoning* related to the function of reinforcemnt and the cause of behavior (p. 275). He states:

> Here we see another instance of overgeneralization as well as of circular reasoning. To rephrase some of Bower's earlier arguments: What does reinforcement do? It increases the probability of behavior occurrence. When a behavior increases in probability of occurrence, what causes this? Reinforcement!

If the above is true about reinforcement, then the function of reinforcment is to increase the probability of behavior and the reason why behavior increases is because it is reinforced. In contrast, "a susceptibility to reinforcement is due to its survival value." "Behavior occurs because appropriate mechanisms have been selected in the course of evolution" (Skinner, 1974, p. 47). Thus, when a behavior increases in probability of occurrence, the cause of that increase is related to evolutionary principles. A more focused criticism of the perspective, then, is the relative underdevelopment of research directed toward the susceptibility of humans toward different kinds of social reinforcers and the value of those reinforcers for survival.

Behaviorism as we know it today is also accused of neglecting the fact that humans think, attend to or disregard their environments, solve problems, describe phenomena and in general are characterized by "higher mental processes." Skinner suggests that whatever these activities might be called they are still behaviors, and potentially observable ones at that. Behavior analysis does not reject these behaviors but it does reject the notion that they are in some inaccessible place to be used to explain behavior. From his point of view, which reflects that held by most behavior analysts, mentalistic explanations explain very little if anything (Skinner, p. 224).

Behavior analysis also is criticized for failing to "explain" research findings. Bijou has suggested that this criticism is often directed toward a failure of behavior analysts to include in their interpretation (especially of child development) developmental stages of hypothetical entities such as cognitive structure or psychosexual phases. Behavior analysis *is* nonmentalistic in the sense that it insists upon aspects of its system dealing with observable behavior. It does not ignore feelings, cognitive structures and the like; it merely points out that they may be collateral products emanating from observable conditions producing behavior.

Another criticism directed toward behavior analysis is that the human organism is conceptualized as passive. Like many others, this criticism seems to be directed toward classical behaviorism rather than modern behaviorism or behavior analysis. In 1969, Skinner implied that the behavioral perspective no longer viewed the organism and environment as separate but rather focused on the interrelations among them. This is spelled out with more clarity in Bijou and Baer (1978) and Bijou (1979). In discussing child development, Bijou states:

> In this kind of thorough-going interactional system, a child influences the course of his or her own development in at least two ways: (a) to each interaction, the child contributes the responses and the internal stimuli, the characteristics of which are determined by his or her genetic and personal histories; and (b) as the child develops, he or she responds more and more to specific stimuli and setting factors that are brought about by his or her own behavior, as in self-management. (p. 7).

Finally, behavior analysis is thought to be incapable of analyzing complex interactions. Bijou considers this criticism to be one of the more serious and insists that the perspective is expanding its domain to include complex interaction. Expansion and elaboration of theoretical formulations, experimental demonstration of functional relationships, novel concepts and principles are all being incorporated into behavior analysis. Continued advancement of this kind, believes Bijou, will enable a relatively new perspective to demonstrate its logical, operational, empirical and pragmatic adequacy in analyzing complex interactions.

Unlike Lerner, who feels that behavior analysis offers a simple formula for understanding human behavior and development (p. 276), behavior analysis is posited here as a complex and developing perspective. Bijou and Baer's concentrations (and others) on stimulus and response functions and classes, reciprocal interaction between the organism and the environment and complex interaction dictate a complex approach to the study of human behavior. Much of the difficulty arises from the fact that adherents of behavior analysis are unwilling to alter behaviorism to include inner determinants of behavior nor are they willing to use behavior analysis to explain only simple interaction—they ask only that the perspective be given further opportunity to demonstrate its full potential.

Part of this demonstration, I believe, will be determined by one aspect of behavior analysis which remains neglected, and that is the "survival values" of social reinforcers and social behaviors. Explorations into these phenomena may further support behavior analysis as a vital and valuable perspective in social psychology and lay to rest once and for all charges of tautological reasoning.

CONCLUSION

Beginning with the Greek naturalists and extending to the behavior analysts, behaviorism has undergone numerous major modifications and alterations. Even so, the perspective today is commonly misunderstood (Hamblin and Kunkel, p. 64). Many people believe that behavioral social psychologists remain principally interested in animal behavior, classical conditioning and in general, in stimulus-response psychology. Obviously this is not so, as we have seen. Yet even when the theoretical framework used and the subject-matter of interest to behavioral social psychologists are comprehended, much controversy surrounds behaviorism. Criticisms of it abound, ranging from allegations that it ignores mental states to its "indifference to the warmth and richness of human life" (Skinner, 1974, pp. 4–5). Statements by behaviorists claiming that the allegations are not altogether true seem to fall on deaf ears.

A major problem contributing to the controversies surrounding behaviorism is referred to by Skinner in *About Behaviorism:*

> Unfortunately, very little is known about this analysis outside the field. Its most active investigators, and there are hundreds of them, seldom make any effort to explain themselves to nonspecialists (p. 8).

Another problem confronting behaviorism in social psychology is the fear by many that social psychology is becoming psychologized (see Chapter 1). This may not be a meaningful problem for psychological social psychologists but it is a sensitive issue for social psychologists whose parent discipline is sociology, where the major social psychological perspective has been and remains symbolic interactionism. In fact, it has been such a problem that relatively few "behavior analyses" have been made by sociological social psychologists. Instead, often they have borrowed behavior analysis principles only to convert them later into *social exchange* statements or to attempt explanations interspersing behaviorism with some mentalistic and/or purposive explanatory scheme. No denigration of such efforts is intended; however, it is incumbent upon such scholars to state clearly their attempts at synthesis in order to avoid the confusion and misconceptions that often are the consequences of such presentations.

The latter remarks do not mean that behavior analyses must be strictly *psychological;* indeed, they have not been for some time. It does mean, however, that those employing the perspective must be aware of the underlying philosophy and general theoretical framework. Furthermore, deviation from the philosophy and theory underlying behaviorism should be made known in the same manner as some related systems. Social learning theory, as we have seen, is such a system, as is the topic of our next chapter, social exchange. Both are related to but differ in important ways from behavioral social psychology—a perspective which, though difficult for many social psychologists to espouse is, nevertheless, a vital theoretical and research system in contemporary social psychology.

BIBLIOGRAPHY

Back, Kurt W. "Review Essay of *Behavioral Sociology: The Experimental Analysis of Social Process,*" *American Sociological Review* 35, no. 6 (December 1970), pp. 1098–1100.

Bandura, Albert. *Social Learning Theory.* Englewood Cliffs, N. J.: Prentice-Hall, 1977.

Bijou, Sidney W. "Some Clarifications on the Meaning of a Behavior Analysis of Child Development," *The Psychological Record* 29 (1979), pp. 3–13.

Bijou, Sidney W. and Donald M. Baer. *Child Development: A Systematic and Empirical Theory,* vol. 1. Englewood Cliffs, N. J.: Prentice-Hall, 1961.

——. *Behavior Analysis of Child Development.* Englewood Cliffs, N. J.: Prentice-Hall, 1978.

Burgess, Robert L. "Communication Networks: An Experimental Reevaluation," *Journal of Experimental Social Psychology* (1968), pp. 324–337.

Burgess, Robert L. and Ronald L. Akers. "A Differential Association—Reinforcement Theory of Criminal Behavior," *Social Problems* 14 (Fall 1966), pp. 128–147.

———. "Are Operant Principles Tautological?" *The Psychological Record* 16 (1966), pp. 305–312.

Burgess, Robert L. and Donald Bushell, eds. *Behavioral Sociology: The Experimental Analysis of Social Process.* New York: Columbia University Press, 1969.

Deutsch, Morton and Robert M. Krauss. *Theories in Social Psychology.* New York: Basic Books, 1965.

Dulany, D.E. "Awareness, Rules, and Propositional Control: A Confrontation with S–R Behavior Theory," in T.R. Dixon and D.L. Horton, eds. *Verbal Behavior and General Behavior Theory.* Englewood Cliffs: Prentice-Hall, 1968.

Emerson, Richard. "Operant Psychology and Exchange Theory" in Burgess and Bushell, eds., *Behavioral Sociology: The Experimental Analysis of Social Process.* New York: Columbia University Press, 1969.

Ferster, C. B. and B. F. Skinner. *Schedules of Reinforcement.* New York: Appleton-Century-Crofts, 1957.

Hamblin, Robert L. and John H. Kunkel. *Behavioral Theory in Sociology.* New Brunswick, N. J.: Transactions Books, 1977.

Homans, George C. *Social Behavior: Its Elementary Forms.* New York: Harcourt, Brace and World, 1961.

Hull, Clark L. *Principles of Behavior.* New York: Appleton-Century-Crofts, 1943.

Kantor, J. R. *Interbehavioral Psychology.* Granville, Oh.: Principia Press, 1959.

Kennedy, T. D. "Verbal Conditioning Without Awareness: The Use of Programmed Reinforcement and Recurring Assessment of Awareness," *Journal of Experimental Psychology* 84 (1970), pp. 484–494.

———. "Reinforcement Frequency, Task Characteristics and Interval of Awareness Assessment as Factors in Verbal Conditioning Without Awareness," *Journal of Experimental Psychology* 88 (1971), pp. 103–112.

Kunkel, John H. *Society and Economic Growth: A Behavioral Perspective of Social Change.* New York: Oxford University Press, 1970.

———. *Behavior, Social Problems: A Social Learning Approach.* Englewood Cliffs, N.J.: Prentice-Hall, 1975.

Kunkel, John H. and Richard Nagasawa. "A Behavioral Model of Man: Propositions and Implications," *American Sociological Review* 38 (1973), pp. 530–543.

Lerner, Richard M. *Concepts and Theories of Human Development.* Reading, Ma: Addison-Wesley, 1976.

Lundin, Robert. *Theories and Systems of Psychology,* 2nd ed. Lexington, Ma: D. C. Heath, 1979.

Mithaug, Dennis E. and Robert L. Burgess. "The Effects of Different Reinforcement Contingencies in the Development of Social Cooperation," *Journal of Experimental Child Psychology* 5 (1968), pp. 441–454.

Pavlov, Ivan P. *Conditioned Reflexes.* London: Oxford University Press, 1927.

———. *Lectures on Conditioned Reflexes.* New York: International Press, 1928.

Schultz, Duane P. *A History of Modern Psychology.* New York: Academic Press, 1969.

Skinner, B. F. *The Behavior of Organisms: An Experimental Analysis.* New York: Appleton-Centruy-Crofts, 1938.

———. *Walden II.* New York: Macmillan, 1948.

———. *Science and Human Behavior.* New York: Macmillan, 1953.

———. *Verbal Behavior.* New York: Appleton-Century-Crofts, 1957.

———. "Contingencies of Reinforcement in the Design of A Culture," *Behavioral Science* 11 (1966), pp. 159–166.

———. *The Technology of Teaching.* New York: Appleton-Century-Crofts, 1968.

———. *Beyond Freedom and Dignity.* New York: Knopf, 1971.

———. *About Behaviorism.* New York: Knopf, 1974.

Spielberger, C. D. and L. D. DeNike. "Descriptive Behaviorism versus Cognitive Theory in Verbal Operant Conditioning," *Psychological Review* 73 (1966), pp. 306–326.

Staats, Arthur W. and Carolyn K. Staats. *Complex Human Behavior: A Systematic Extension of Learning Principle.* New York: Holt, Rinehart and Winston, 1963.

Thorndike, Edward L. *Animal Intelligence.* New York: Macmillan, 1911.

Watson, John B. "Psychology as the Behaviorist Views It," *Psychological Review* 20 (1913), pp. 158–177.

———. *Psychology From the Standpoint of a Behaviorist.* Philadelphia: Lippincott, 1919.

———. *Behaviorism,* rev. ed. New York: Norton, 1930.

Watson, John B. and William McDougall. *The Battle of Behaviorism.* New York: Norton, 1929.

Watson, Robert L. *The Great Psychologists.* Philadelphia: Lippincott, 1971.

THE
SOCIAL
EXCHANGE
PERSPECTIVE

5

No less controversial than the perspective discussed in the preceding chapter is that of social exchange. In fact social exchange is included in some discussions of behaviorism (Hamblin and Kunkel, 1977). While it is true that behaviorism is an ancestor of social exchange, the position taken here is that it is sufficiently distinct to warrant a discussion in its own right. In addition to psychological generalizations, the social exchange perspective was also founded on "various economic analogies" (Kunkel and Hamblin, p. 14). Therefore, economics also shares parental responsibility for social exchange, along with psychology and sociology.

The development of the social exchange perspective and the direction of that development have been influenced by the contributions of numerous scholars. Some of the early contributors were John Thibaut, Harold Kelley, Richard Emerson, Peter Blau and of course the founder of the perspective, George Casper Homans. Gibbs has stated that this theory about elementary social behavior stems from a unique synthesis of various key notions in experimental psychology, economics, and sociology (Gibbs, p. 27). The impact of the synthesis has been felt in disciplines like sociology, anthropology, economics, political science and of course social psychology. In social psychology, exchange theory has played a catalytic role in theory and research in such areas as interpersonal bargaining, equity, the distribution of rewards, conformity and self-presentation (Gergen, 1977, p. 91). Johnson has said about social exchange that it "also serves well in its role as organizer of experience and as social sensitizer; it is especially useful in pointing out relationships among highly diverse phenomena" (p. 110). As a "theory," social exchange as originally formulated would fall into our classification of a sensitizing theory that forms in direct relationship to emergent properties of the phenomena under investigation. Now this does not mean that more structured variations of social exchange have not been developed; indeed they have (Emerson, 1972 a and b; Heath; Maris). What it does mean is that five main propositions, stemming from and "abstractly expressing" empirical uniformities, formed the underlying basis of social exchange as set forth by George C. Homans in 1961. The fact that Homans' conceptualization differed in significant ways from behaviorism (upon which much of social exchange was based) may very well attest to the "processual" development of social exchange and thus warrant inclusion in the sensitizing "theory" category. Moreover, that social exchange is "purposive" and modern behaviorism and/or behavior analysis lacks the purposive element is a major point being made here, which will be returned to later.

The parallel is striking: What John B. Watson did in 1913 for behaviorism, George C. Homans did in 1958 for social exchange. Homans wrote what many might call "the social exchange manifesto." Portions of Homans' article, in which social exchange is proposed as an explanatory system for social interactions, are presented below.

> As I survey small group research today, I feel that apart form just helping on with it, three sorts of things need to be done. The first is to show the relation between the results of experimental work done under laboratory conditions and the results of quasi-anthropological field research on what those of us who do it are pleased to call real-life groups in industry and elsewhere . . . The second job is to pull together in some set of general propositions the actual results from the laboratory and from the field, of work on small groups—proposition that attest, sum up, to an approximation, what happens in elementary social behavior, even though we might not be able to explain why the propositions take the form they do . . . The third job is to begin to show how the propositions that empirically hold good in small groups may be derived from some set of still more general propositions . . . I have come to think that all three of these jobs would be furthered by our

adopting the view that interaction between persons is an exchange of goods, material and nonmaterial (Homans, 1958, p. 597).

Homans was not alone in his contention that social exchange is a viable perspective to use in analyzing social interaction. John Thibaut and Harold Kelley obviously had been thinking along similar lines, as their book *The Social Psychology of Groups* indicated when published the following year (1959). Homans, however, was the architect, and he continued his design in 1961. Let us consider Homans and other early proponents of the social exchange perspective, noting the fact at the same time that the perspective has not yet reached its thirtieth birthday.

THE FOUNDING OF SOCIAL EXCHANGE

George C. Homans

"To consider social behavior as an exchange of goods may clarify the relations among four bodies of theory: Behavioral psychology, economics, propositions about the dynamics of influence, and propositions about the structure of small groups" (Homans, 1958, p. 607).

George C. Homans began his article in honor of Georg Simmel, "Social Behavior as Exchange," with the above statement, and it has led to the development of a distinctive theoretical perspective in the "sociobehavioral sciences," in particular in sociology and sociological social psychology. As stated earlier, the "manifesto" was Homans' corrective response to three problems plaguing small group research at that time. Beginning his exchange paradigm with a link to behavioral psychology, Homans proposed adoption of the view that social interaction was "an exchange of goods, material and nonmaterial based on behavioral psychological principles." In an exploratory manner, Homans loosely applies his paradigm to the social influence process, group processes, group stability and group differentiation. He concludes his landmark article with an application of his paradigm to Blau's findings in *The Dynamics of Bureaucracy* in an effort to show that group stability and structural differentiation are some function of the social exchange process involving rewards and costs. Homans makes a final pitch for social exchange with the following statement:

In our unguarded moments we sociologists find words like "reward" and "cost" slipping into what we say. Human nature will break in upon even our most elaborate theories. But we seldom let it have its way with us and follow up systematically what these words imply. Of all our many "approaches" to social behavior, the one that sees it as an economy is the most neglected, and yet it is the one we use every moment of our lives . . . (p. 606).

With the above, the social exchange perspective was underway. What *The Human Group, The Dynamics of Bureaucracy,* and other research had implied was now explicit.

Homans' initial statement on social exchange was followed by a more formal one: *Social Behavior: Its Elementary Forms.* In discussing the kind of behavior that he was concerned with, Homans stated that (1) the behavior must be social—it must be rewarded or punished by the behavior of others; (2) a particular person acting in some way toward an other must be rewarded or punished by that other and not by a third party; and (3) the behavior must be actual behavior and not a norm of behavior. He labelled the behavior *elementary social behavior* and said it was characterized by face-to-face contact, mutual and direct influence and "actual" behavior. The study of such behavior, Homans felt, depended on observations of such face-to-face contacts because of the difficulties confronting the researcher who attempts to study large numbers of persons at one time. The subject matter, however, remains elementary social behavior.

Homans' "exchange theory" as outlined in *Social Behavior: Its Elementary Forms* has been said to owe much to the Skinnerian tradition despite the fact that its major aim was to explain why *social* life proceeds as it does (Gergen, 1969, p. 102). He formulated five main propositions, from which he demonstrated that propositions concerning findings presented in *The Human Group* could be deduced (Johnson, p. 56). The propositions are as follows:

1. If in the past the occurrence of a particular stimulus situation has been the occasion on which a man's activity has been rewarded, then the more similar the present stimulus situation is to the past one, the more likely he is to emit the activity, or some similar activity, now.

2. The more often within a given period of time a man's activity rewards the activity of another, the more often the other will emit the activity.

3. The more valuable to a man a unit of the activity another gives him, the more often he will emit activity rewarded by the activity of the other.

4. The more often a man has in the recent past received a rewarding activity from another, the less valuable any further unit of that activity becomes to him.

5. The more to a man's disadvantage the rule of distributive justice fails of realization, the more likely he is to display the emotional behavior we call anger.

Propositions 1 through 4 are vulgarized versions of several operant principles and/or concepts discussed in the preceding chapter—namely stimulus generalization, positive reinforcement, selective reinforcement and satiation. Proposition 1, for example, is similar to but differs significantly from stimulus generalization in that the concept "reward" is used instead of "reinforced." While some social and behavioral scientists (for example, Kunkel and Nagasawa, 1973) fail to distinguish between the two concepts, a distinction is warranted. "Reward" ordinarily implies pleasure, while "reinforced" technically refers (as we saw in the last chapter) to the increased probability of a behavior's occurrence. The idea of "pleasure" and/or motivation is deliberately omitted from the concepts "reinforcement," "reinforcer," and "reinforced." Homans, then, in his first proposition departs significantly from Skinnerian behaviorism by implying pleasure and/or motivation with his usage of the concept reward.

Proposition 2 also implies a departure from Skinnerian behaviorism with the inclusion of the concept "reward." The more often (within a period of time) an individual receives rewards for some behavior, the more often the individual will produce the behavior. Producing the behavior is linked with receiving a reward. Such an interpretation is plausible because Homans is unlikely to state that the greater the increase in the probability of a person's activity the more likely the person is to perform the activity. If this is correct, then Homans' proposition basically states that "if a person emits some activity (operant) and is rewarded, then this increases the likelihood that the activity will recur." In operant terms, "if a person emits an operant which is rewarded, then reinforcement will occur." No proposition in Skinnerian behaviorism takes this particular form, but this interpretation appears to be part and parcel of Homans' social exchange proposition as well as others, as we shall see.

Proposition 3 also suggests that value of the reward is inextricably interwoven with the probability of a behavior's occurrence. Homans' idea is that valuable rewards selectively reinforce activities. Those activities, producing the rewards are, quite simply, more often emitted. Bandura would suggest as stated in Chapter 4 that "awareness" is responsible, and Homans', too, seems to imply this in proposition 3.

That Homans' propositions are more closely related to a motivation-based behaviorism than Skinnerian behaviorism can be seen again in proposition 4. If reward and reinforcement were synonymous terms in Homans' formulation, and were Skinnerian in nature, proposition 4 would read like this: "The more often a man (woman) has in the recent past received an activity which increases the likelihood of an activity's occurrence the less valuable any further unit of that activity became to him." Homans does not intend this! This is apparent as he goes on to state the following about proposition 3: "and therefore, by proposition 3, the less often he will emit the activity that *gets him* (her) that reward" (1961, p. 55). The latter statement is explicitly motivational, and therefore distinct from Skinnerian behaviorism.

Homans also used behavioral terminology to provide a rationale for proposition 5. Again, however, the behaviorism is *not* of the Skinner variety. It does, though, seem to be related to Hull's secondary reinforcement, especially when Homans discusses a pigeon's displayed contentment, anger, etc. when grain is used as a reward under cetain reinforcement contingencies (1961, pp. 72–73). Heath has stated that this is not directly borrowed either from behavioral social psychology or from economics. He points out, correctly, that there are two main aspects of the *distributive justice* proportion: (1) the claim that violation of persons' expectations produces anger; and (2) in exchange relations, the rule of distributive justice specifies reward expectations for persons (Heath). With respect to the latter, Homans feels that while persons ordinarily do not figure out whether there is proportionality between their investments and profits (rewards minus costs), they do compare their investments and profits with the investments and profits of others. Thus, "if one man is 'better' than another in his investments, he should also be 'better' than the other in the value of the contribution he makes and in the reward he gets for it" (Homans, 1961, p. 245). If in fact the comparison is negative for the individual, anger results (the second component of the distributive justice proposition). Elements of behaviorism are implicit in the proposition in that positive and negative comparisons with others are proposed as reinforcing and punishing respectively.

Homans' basic propositions constitute the core of his proposal for social exchange interpretations of human behavior. Other concepts such as rewards, costs, values, sentiments, etc., elaborated later in this chapter, also were influenced by Homans. As Johnson has pointed out,

Homans' introduction of behaviorism (more Hullian than Skinnerian) also involved invoking a concept of exchange that, unlike the operant perspective, produced widespread approval among sociological social psychologists (p. 56). But, as pointed out earlier, Homans was not alone in his convictions. Two other social psychologists also made an impact on social exchange, approximately one year after its founding.

John W. Thibaut and Harold H. Kelley

In 1959, two social psychologists, John W. Thibaut and Harold H. Kelley (both were students of the field theorist Kurt Lewin) published *The Social Psychology of Groups*. While their contribution was not labelled social exchange, it is clearly within the domain of the Homans-inspired perspective. Chadwick-Jones (p. 2) has stated that their contribution has important characteristics in common with Homans' 1961 and 1974 books, and with Blau's 1964 book. All four volumes express a major interest in "the interdependence of relationships between persons and in the actual process of social behavior" (Chadwick-Jones, p. 2). The interdependency of social interaction was seen simultaneously as the problem areas for research *and* the unit of study. Thibaut and Kelley are concerned with how person *A* affects person *B's* behavior, and how person *B* affects person *A's* behavior. The implication here, of course, is that analysis of social interaction must be from the position of both *A* and *B*. This emphasis on the *mutual interdependency of persons* led to a basic concern with dyadic relationships in *The Social Psychology of Groups*, and a secondary concern (though no less significant for the social exchange perspective) showing how dyadic conceptualization could be extended to larger social groups.

Using the pay-off matrix to illustrate social exchange principles, Thibaut and Kelley investigated numerous issues related to group process. The most important ones for the emerging social exchange perspectives seem to have been related to the two-fold question: why do some persons choose to remain in a relationship where the services being provided seem relatively meager compared with (1) what has been experienced in the past in other relationships; and (2) what the person knows about other relationships? It would seem that remaining in such a relationship should violate behaviorist ideas implicit in social exchange. In other words, when certain behavior is not reinforced then its rate of emission should diminish. Recognizing Homans' contention that a long time may pass before it stops altogether, is this the explanation to be given for continued dyadic relationships (person-other relationships) even when *outcomes* are perceived as insufficient by one or both persons (rewards minus costs = outcome)? Insufficient outcomes should be nonreinforcing or punishing while sufficient ones should be reinforcing.

Thibaut and Kelley, responding to the above questions, further distinguish the social exchange perspective from Skinnerian behaviorism by introducing the cognitive variable "actor expectations." They suggest that outcome value in a social relationship must always be measured in terms of actor expectation. This means that the value of a particular relationship to one or both of the actors involved will be some function, in part of (1) the actor's judgment of the relationship in terms of his or her past experiences in this relationship and/or what he or she knows about other similar relationships (comparison level); and (2) the actor's evaluation of the present relationship in light of what appears to be available alternatives to the current relationship (comparison level for alternatives) (Thibaut and Kelley, p. 81). Thibaut and Kelley distinguish between *attraction* and *dependence* in social relationships. For them, the level of outcomes received relative to comparison level defines actor *attraction* in a particular relationship, while *dependence* refers to outcomes received relative to the comparison level for alternatives.

Interestingly, Thibaut and Kelley's distinction between *attraction* and *dependence* was obscured later by Emerson. Emerson's contributions are discussed later, but briefly, in this case, he merged the two with his discussion of the two elements characterizing dependence—motivational investment and available alternatives. While some may be tempted to quarrel with this, Chadwick-Jones (p. 45) has pointed out that *"comparison level* gives an assessment of the relationship itself, how far it is satisfying to the individual, while *comparison level for alternatives* "involves the lowest level of outcomes acceptable in the face of available alternatives." Chadwick-Jones goes on to note that the rewards sought depend on the individual's needs, and a person's evaluation of his or her outcomes is a function of comparing the outcomes with what he or she feels is deserved. Thus outcomes are expected to be proportional to investment. When they are, the individual is satisfied; when they are not, the individual is dissatisfied. Degrees of satisfaction or dissatisfaction are therefore related to attraction (Emerson's goal mediation), while comparison level for alternatives and, therefore, *dependence* is related to Emerson's available alternatives. It seems, then, that Emerson *combines* Thibaut and Kelley's attraction and dependence to form the concept "dependence."

Returning now to Thibaut and Kelley's contribution to early social exchange, they underscore the fact that persons may elect to remain in relationships even when there is a low level of attraction simply because alternatives to such a relationship are perceived (a cognitive element) as nonexistent or inadequate. They go on to construct pay-off matrix diagrams concentrating basically on the comparison level for alternatives variable. Theoretically, their analyses have given us insight into the different kinds of control (and obversely, dependence) individuals may have over each other.

There are three basic types of control, according to Thibaut and Kelley: contact control, fate control and behavior control. *Contact control* occurs where person *A*'s presence is very important for person *B*, in the sense that person *B* receives highly positive outcomes when *A* is around. Now, in this situation, person *A* cannot affect any particular responses that person *B* makes. In fact, *B* appears to enjoy his or her own responses regardless of what *A* does in some situations, and does not really need *A* in other situations. Some may feel that such a relationship occurs only rarely; however, one needs only to be reminded of situations where adults in trouble feel the need to be around parents, older adult relations or siblings during moments of stress and crisis.

Fate control refers to a type of control where *A* may vary his or her behavior and not affect his or her own outcome but affect the outcome of *B* regardless of *B*'s action. This kind of control is to be distinguished from *behavior control*, where *A* can vary his or her behavior and make it desirable for *B* to vary his or hers. Thus, in the latter situation, *B*'s outcome is a function of both *A*'s *and* his or her behavior choices, while in the former situation *B*'s outcome is solely dependent upon *A*'s behavior choice. Figure 5.1 illustrates these two types of control.

Thibaut and Kelley spend a good deal of time discussing the theoretical implications of their types of control, introducing the notion of fate control, conversion, counterpower—all beyond the scope of this discussion. What is necessary at this point is to return to several assumptions which appear to underlie their efforts. The first concerns the relative importance of comparison level and comparison level alternative. Thibaut and Kelley seem to imply that the latter is most important for determining whether or not a person remains in a relationship.

Defining *outcomes* as rewards, payoffs, reinforcement, and utilities and rewards as pleasures, satisfaction, etc., Thibaut and Kelley imply that satisfactory outcomes are those that constitute rewards which reduce drives or fulfill needs (Chadwick-Jones, p. 49). With the latter Hullian assumption, Thibaut and Kelley's line of thought can be illustrated as shown in Table 5.1.

If we follow Thibaut and Kelley's lead, in instances 1 and 3 *A* remains in the relationship, while in instances 2 and 4 *A* leaves the relationship. On the other hand, instance 2 may very well be exemplified by those marriages in which one spouse experiences satisfactory interaction with the other, above that experienced previously and above that

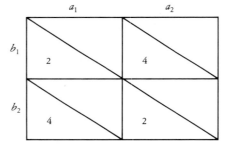

Figure 5.1
Fate control and behavior control

observed in other marriages; and yet the same spouse may have an alternative available which could result in outcomes more satisfying than what is presently being received. Given all of these factors, the spouse may choose to remain in the relationship, hoping that the situation will change, in spite of the fact that the reward-cost outcome presently being received is lower than what *could* be received if he or she left the relationship. Interestingly, this appears to characterize what Merton has called the "ritualistic" type of adaptation (pp. 149–153).[1]

Instance 3, where outcomes are below the comparison level but above the comparison level alternative, implies that an individual may stay in a relationship that is not satisfying simply because no better

1. Merton contends that this mode of adaptation is used by individuals who reject cultural goals but accept institutionalized means for obtaining the goals. In contrast, the innovator accepts the cultural goals but rejects the institutionalized means for achieving these goals.

FOR A		PREDICTIONS FOR A
1. OUTCOMES ABOVE COMPARISON LEVEL	OUTCOMES ABOVE COMPARISON LEVEL ALTERNATIVE	SATISFIED, REMAINS IN RELATIONSHIP
2. OUTCOMES ABOVE COMPARISON LEVEL	OUTCOMES BELOW COMPARISON LEVEL ALTERNATIVE	SATISFIED, BUT LEAVES RELATIONSHIP
3. OUTCOMES BELOW COMPARISON LEVEL	OUTCOMES ABOVE COMPARISON LEVEL ALTERNATIVE	DISSATISFIED, BUT REMAINS IN RELATIONSHIP
4. OUTCOMES BELOW COMPARISON LEVEL	OUTCOMES BELOW COMPARISON LEVEL ALTERNATIVE	DISSATISFIED, LEAVES RELATIONSHIP

Table 5.1
Outcomes in a dyadic relationship

alternative is available (Burgess and Nielsen). It is possible, however, that the person may elect to leave the relationship in the style of Merton's "innovator" since the person knows that more positive outcomes are possible even though better alternatives may not be presently perceived—"searching" behavior characterizes this instance.

Robert Burgess and Joyce C. Nielsen report experimental findings from their study of structural determinants of exchange relations which support certain theoretical assertions made by Thibaut and Kelley. More specifically the Burgess and Nielsen study provides empirical evidence supporting the idea that if a person values an exchange relationship and if he or she does not have a more attractive alternative for mediating goals, the person may remain in the exchange relationship *even if he or she is at a power disadvantage.*

Unexpectedly, however, Burgess and Nielsen's findings also support the idea that persons may *remain* in a relationship even when there *are* attractive alternatives. The condition under which this occurs is when the person who has a power advantage experiences alternatives becoming gradually more attractive and simply reduces his/her contributions to the weaker actor to a point of equity, but not to the point of disrupting the exchange relationship. This may be interpreted to mean that as a person becomes more powerful in a relationship he or she begins to interact at a less costly level. Therefore, there may be little need to leave the relationship in spite of the fact that the relationship may be at some level below the comparison level for alternatives. At the same time, because of decreased costs for the powerful actor, outcome may be above the comparison level.

Seemingly, Burgess and Nielsen's findings may be used to support at least one of the contentions made earlier about the Thibaut and Kelley assertions. Admittedly, some may question whether any variable in the Burgess and Nielsen experiments approximated Thibaut and Kelley's "comparison level." This is due to Thibaut and Kelley's concern with enduring relationships.

Another assumption made by Thibaut and Kelley is their assigning the comparison level a value of zero in their matrix analyses. This means that when outcomes are below the comparison level, they are seen as costly (dissatisfying). Those outcomes that fall at the value of zero are neutral (neither satisfying nor dissatisfying), and outcomes above the comparison level are relatively satisfying. The assignment of values to different outcomes is also made against the *comparison level for alternative* criterion in a similar manner, which introduces a kind of complexity beyond the scope of this introductory treatment. A final point, however, can be made. Because Thibaut and Kelley are concerned with enduring relationships, some recognition that comparison levels change should have been a focal point of the analysis. Put another way, if outcomes consistently meet only the value zero in a relationship, it is indeed possible that subjective neutrality will diminish and cost will emerge as a result. Moreover, because comparison levels may tend to rise with subsequent outcomes which exceed the zero value, any analysis must be dynamic since this will affect the general problem of outcome control in an enduring relationship. Thus, while person *A* may exercise behavior control over person *B* by giving response *A-1*, over a period of time, *B's* comparison levels may rise to the point that response *A-1* will no longer be sufficient to control *B's* behavior and may, in fact, be perceived by *B* as costly.

Social Exchange and Power-Dependence Relationships: Richard Emerson

In 1962, four years following Homans' founding of social exchange, Richard Emerson invoked social exchange principles to explain power tactics (Johnson, p. 57). His article "Power-Dependence Relations" proved to be a major contribution to social exchange in its early years.

Later contributions to social exchange have been made by Emerson, and will be discussed in a later section. For now, attention is devoted to Emerson's first contribution.

Emerson proposed the existence of an underlying tendency toward balance in social association because of the instability inherent in imbalanced relationships. This equilibrium model was based on the idea that imbalance encourages the use of power which sets *balancing mechanisms* into operation. A major postulate set forth by Emerson suggests that *the power* of one actor over another in a dyadic relationship is equal to the *dependence* of the latter actor on the former actor (the power of actor A over actor B is equal to the *dependence* of actor B on actor A). Dependence is seen as consisting of two elements: "motivational investments" and "availability of alternatives." Generally, if a person is dependent on another in a relationship, he or she has some interest in maintaining the relationship because of services being provided and limited alternatives for goal mediation.

Though not explicit, the concepts "reward" and "cost" underlie Emerson's early contribution. Power in a dyadic relationship is ultimately determined by the reward value of services provided one person by another and the availability of alternative reward sources. The reward value of services received by a person is felt by Emerson to relate directly to his or her motivational investment as well as to the availability of alternatives for goal mediation. In this sense, Emerson's model is a "purposive" one. If alternatives are available for goal mediation outside of a particular exchange relationship this directly affects one's motivational investment in the relationship and thus dependence on others. Yet it must be remembered that the powerful person also has some motivational interest, however meager in a relationship. In this sense, the powerful person expects to receive some reward although he or she is characterized by a high availability of alternative reward sources (this, in part, defines "powerful"). Since in social exchange a person's rewards and costs are crucial, Emerson seems to feel that stability is dependent on both parties receiving approximately equal amounts of rewards (and costs). If not, then balancing mechanisms go into effect.

A social relationship is seen as imbalanced when one person has a power advantage over another, meaning that one person is less motivationally involved in the relationship and has other alternatives available for goal mediation. The basis of this imbalance obviously is unequal rewards and costs incurred by parties in the relationship. According to Emerson, when this happens, certain balancing operations go into effect to restore the relationship to its natural state, which is "balance." Four alternatives are thought to be available to the dependent person in such a relationship: (1) a decrease in motivational involvement in the relationship by the dependent party; (2) an increase in motivational investment by the powerful actor (this can be induced by the dependent actor); (3) an increase in available alternatives for mediating goals; and (4) a decrease in available alternatives for mediating goals experienced by the powerful actor (this decrease in alternatives also can be manipulated by the dependent party).

Peter M. Blau's Social Exchange

The second major volume devoted to the social exchange perspective was published in 1964. Written by Peter M. Blau it was entitled *Exchange and Power in Social Life*. Reminding us of Homans' suggestion that processes of social association can be conceptualized as an exchange of activity, tangible or intangible and more or less rewarding or costly, between at least two persons, Blau states that social exchange is omnipresent and can be observed in all kinds of social relations once one is conceptually sensitized to the framework (p. 88). For Blau, social exchange is directed toward behavior which meets two specifications: (1) behavior which is "oriented toward ends that can be achieved only through interaction with other persons;" and (2) behavior which seeks to adapt means to further the achievement of these ends (p. 5). While these two specifications may seem to be rigorous in the sense that they make the perspective somewhat esoteric, dealing only with specialized instances of social behavior, Blau feels that much behavior still fell under the rubric of social exchange (p. 5).

He covers a variety of topics, including social integration, social support, social power, social expectation, legitimation, organization, complex structures and substructures and dialectical forces in social association. The range of his discussion can be seen in several major propositions constructed and proposed. Heath, and Lindesmith, Strauss and Denzin (1975) have presented a set of assumptions which represents the chief conclusions reached by Blau.

1. The desire for social reward leads men to enter into exchange relationships with one another.
2. Reciprocal social exchanges create trust and social bonds between men.
3. Unilateral services create power and status differences.
4. Power differences make organization possible.
5. The fair exercise of power evokes social approval and the unfair exercise of power evokes social disapproval.

6. If subordinates collectively agree that their superior exercises power generously, they will legitimate his power.
7. Legitimate power is required for stable organization.
8. If subordinates collectively experience unfair exercise of power, an opposition movement will develop.

While some similarities exist between this set of propositions and the one to be discussed next, there are some major differences. These differences occur because Blau's first chapter sets the theme for an analysis of social exchange, and the propositions that follow mostly are taken from this chapter. Not only do they subsume the ones listed above, but they extend beyond them. Let us now consider the propositions.

1. Most human pleasures have their roots in social life. This statement is a basic assumption underlying Blau's social exchange formulation. As Blau himself states, "whether we think of love, power, professional recognition, competitive sports, etc. gratifications experienced by individuals are contingent on the actions of others." This assumption sets the tone for an analysis of social life but does not depart significantly from assumptions in other perspectives.

Given that most human pleasures have their roots in social life and that rewards and costs are very much a part of the social interaction process, it is almost axiomatic that "individuals associate with each other because they all profit from their association" (Blau, p. 15). This means, in effect, that not only does "desire for social rewards" lead men into exchange relationships, but that profits reaped by all concerned (though not necessarily equal profits) enhance the likelihood that such a relationship will continue. This is by no means a simple statement since, as Blau notes, what is rewarding to one person may be displeasing or costly to another. Moreover, what is rewarding at one time may be costly at another. Important to remember, though, is that profit (reward minus cost) is not only a motivating force behind social associations but also a maintaining force in social associations. As the next proposition states, this motivating and maintaining force surrounds such feelings as social attraction and desires for various kinds of rewards.

2. Social attraction induces persons to establish social associations without encouragement from others and to expand the scope of such associations. While the desire for social rewards may lead persons into social exchange relationships, the establishment and the expansion of the scope of such relationships are a function of social attraction. To put it another way, not only must there be a desire for social rewards, but there must also be an expectation that such an association will result in rewards. Once the association has been formed, maintenance of the relationship is dependent, in part, upon continuation of the expectation. For example, a student may wish to interact socially with another but not initiate interaction until he or she feels that the initial step will be rewarded. If the initial step is rewarded and a relationship is formed, continuation and expansion of the relationship is dependent in part upon fulfillment of mutual expectations held by both parties.

To give another example, a traditional housewife might begin to feel that she no longer wants to be a part of morning neighborhood coffee klatches, neighborhood block parties, car pools and the like. Instead, she may decide that she wants a different kind of fulfillment in her life—one that involves associating with women who have professional careers *outside* of the house. Initial contact with such women may be a function of the desire for this different kind of social reward (motivating force). If this initial contact proves to be as rewarding as it was perceived, future interaction (from the housewife's position) will be not only a motivating force behind the interaction but also will function to *maintain* and expand the level and amount of interaction between the housewife and her new associates. Needless to say, in order to get a complete picture of this social interaction process, one must examine it from *both* the housewife's position *and* her new associates' positions in terms of rewards, costs and profits.

One final note can be made concerning expansion of the scope of social associations of the type in the above example. There are numerous instances where housewives have found their new associations so rewarding that they have relinquished their domestic duties and opted instead for work careers of their own.

3. Profits experienced from primitive psychological processes such as those underlying social attraction lead to processes of social exchange. In addition to expectations, it is the mutual profits experienced from social associations that prompt humans to continue social associations. Once reciprocity has been established, we have social exchange. Now, it is not as necessary for the reciprocity in rendering services to be in kind as it is for it to be in degree. More important, what happens if profit is experienced by only one of the parties in a two-party association? Blau contends that if the party experiencing the profit "needs" the profit (or has a high motivational investment in maintaining it), there are several available alternatives; (1) the party may force others to provide the service; (2) the party may obtain needed services elsewhere; (3) the party may find ways to do without the service; (4) the party may provide needed services to others; and (5) the party may provide more *valuable* rewards to others. It is the fifth alternative which leads to status-giving and the fourth proposition.

4. Exchange processes give rise to differentiation of power. This is a more encompassing proposition than a similar one stated by Heath and listed earlier (Heath's proposition 3). The proposition here implies that unilateral services can result in power differences only if social exchange has been established—perhaps by rewarding others initially by expressions of gratitude for services provided (Blau, p. 21). The reason why exchange processes give rise to power differences is the independence of one of the parties in the exchange and the dependence of the other. Yet unless the dependent party views the subservience positively, power differences may not emerge. In other words, the dependent party must feel that his or her subservience is justified and that the independent party is not exploiting him or her. If the opposite is true, Emerson's power-balancing mechanisms may go into effect, or at a minimum, there will be some disapproval (overt or covert) by the dependent party.

It must be remembered that power is a calculated reward given by dependents in order to extract benefits from independents. Therefore, for social exchange, in a very real sense, power is granted by dependents as long as they feel obligated to parties benefiting them. Powerful parties, in turn, maintain their power only as long as they are perceived to *provide* needed services to others while simultaneously *not* demanding services as valuable or more valuable. This means that if power is to emerge and be maintained, powerful parties must be cautious about extracting needed services from dependents.

5. In cases of three or more persons in a social exchange relationship with an independent party, collective approval of the independent party's power leads to the legitimation of that power. Collective approval of power is manifested by positive communication between subordinates in a social exchange relationship, while legitimation is manifested by group pressures and collective feelings of obligations to comply with the independent party's demands. Blau suggests that there are fundamental differences between the dynamics of power in a collective situation and the power of one individual over another (p. 23). He feels the significance of approval or disapproval of the superior is much weaker in a one-to-one relationship. On the other hand, collective situations have implications for social structure. The latter statement is acceptable, but the former is questionable since the *intensity of the relationship* is, seemingly, ignored as a salient intervening variable. It would seem that if the exchange relationship is relatively intense, disapproval resulting in withdrawal or threatened withdrawal may be even more costly for the superior party despite its so-called independence. Admittedly, this is an empirical question—although it is interesting how often spouses who seem to hold superior positions find themselves considerably more dependent when the "weaker" spouse decides that he or she has had enough and either threatens or begins to withdraw from the relationship.

6. Collective disapproval of power engenders opposition. The rationale for this proposition as given by Blau is based on communication between persons who feel exploited by unfair demands. The notion is rather simple. Persons who experience "exploitation" as a result of unjustified demands made by powerful others will presumably communicate these feelings to others who share them as well as anger, frustration and aggression. When such communication takes place between subordinates, there is a great probability that a desire for retaliation against the exploiter will emerge. Interestingly, Blau suggests that this wish for retaliation seems to be dictated by nature. The translation of a "wish" for retaliation into actual opposition appears to be some function of the social support exploited persons give each other. This is due to discussion among the exploited about common grievances, and shared feelings of hostility which "reinforce their aggressive opposition against those in power." Thus, "collective" disapproval of power involves social support, communication, feelings of hostility and reinforcement. All of these ingredients are deemed necessary for the "shared discontent" which results in opposition. Such opposition can be manifested in ideology and/or social movements against existing "power" objects.

7. Differentiation of power in a collective situation evokes contrasting forces—legitimating processes which foster organization, and countervailing forces which deny legitimacy thereby promoting opposition. We have seen that when unilateral services are provided by a superior party in groups of three persons or more, and the recipients choose to subordinate themselves to the superior party, differentiation of power occurs. Collective approval and collective disapproval of power result in legitimation and opposition respectively. Blau feels that in many instances *both* legitimation and opposition are evoked simultaneously by differentiation of power. Because legitimating processes lead to the organization of those with similar interests, and countervailing forces inhibit legitimacy, the scope of the collectivity expands to include even more groups. Expansion of the scope of the collectivity, however, does not prevent the emergence of conflict and opposition. These are factors which may "recurrently redivide collectivities and stimulate reorganization" within the collectivity.

8. Value consensus serves as a mediating link for social transactions between individuals and groups without an direct contact. This proposition is difficult to derive from any basic assumptions in social exchange. In fact, we know of no social exchange postulates which would imply such a derivation. Yet the proposition is very important to the perspective. The salience can be seen in the expectation of reciprocity in initial social associations between individuals and groups. Unless a particular set of values holds, namely, returning a service if one is provided, then feelings of obligations can hardly be expected to occur. Without such feelings of obligations, it seems that social exchange would rarely occur. Moreover it has been pointed out that value consensus may very well serve the same function for social structures as do processes like personal attraction and social approval in small groups, in terms of precipitating social exchange transactions.

9. *Processes of social attraction or hostility create integrative bonds between associates.* Blau has stated that ''the greater the attraction of individuals to one another and to the group as a whole, particularly if their intrinsic attraction to the association generated common identification, the more cohesive is the group'' (p. 33). In order for voluntary groups to form among individuals, it is necessary for social attraction to occur and for integrative bonds to develop.

Many groups have emerged because persons have the opportunity to interact or circumstances provide the opportunity to associate. When initial interaction occurs, many persons become increasingly attracted to each other. Once attraction emerges there is a tendency for persons to expect impending associations to be rewarding, and to find social acceptance among those toward whom they may be attracted. As a result, those who aspire to social acceptance may attempt to impress others with certain qualities which they hope will be rewarding. Should other attempts be successful, integrative bonds are likely to develop. The reason why this is likely to occur is the mutual advantage of the association. Now these advantages may be of either an intrinsic or extrinsic nature. Blau suggests that intrinsic rewards include personal attraction and social acceptance, while extrinsic advantages include such rewards as social and instrumental services. The former type of reward is intrinsic to the association while the latter type is externally based. If the advantages are intrinsic, reciprocity may serve to reaffirm and sustain the association itself as an indicator of commitment. If the advantage is extrinsic, it is the mutual benefit *from* the association and mutual dependence *upon* the benefit that may result in favorable comparisons. If the comparisons are favorable, this may create ties of cohesion between those interacting.

Social exchange as conceived by Blau is explicitly purposive and more clearly imbued with Hull's behavioral principles than Homans' social exchange. For example, Blau states:

> social rewards owe their significance to the psychological processes of secondary reinforcement. The primary gratifications

of human beings are originally contingent on, and become associated with, certain actions of others in their environment such as the mother's nurturing or the father's approval. These and related actions of other human beings become, in due course, intrinsic social rewards that act as secondary reinforcers for the individual's behavior . . . these secondary reinforcers stimulate him to look for challenges he can meet . . . (p. 42).

For Blau then, as with Hull, it seems that the social enters in on the basis of primary drives (see Chapter 4).

Also, though not developed formally, Blau places more emphasis on cognitive elements in social exchange with his discussion of social expectations. This is seen in the following statement:

The satisfactions human beings experience in their social associations depend on the expectations they bring to them as well as on the actual benefits they receive in them . . . .The fact that an individual derives outstanding rewards from associating with others increases his attraction to them, his dependence on them, and, in the long run, his level of expectation concerning what constitutes satisfactory social relations (p. 143).

Blau emphasizes more the similarities and differences between social exchange and economic exchange and recognizes the idea that "unspecified obligations" and "trust" distinguish the two types. Finally, it is Blau's hypothesis that economic exchange is impersonal and focused exclusively on specific extrinsic benefits. Social exchange, in contrast, is thought to direct attention to the intrinsic significance of social associations.

Homans' Attempt to "Bring Men Back In"

Homans took the opportunity to further the cause of the social exchange perspective in his presidential address to the annual meeting of the American Sociological Association in September 1964. He delivered a stinging criticism of structural-functionalism explanatory schemes, later printed under the title "Bringing Men Back In." He indicated, among other things, that the functionalist school had never produced a functional theory that was an explanation (Homans, 1964, p. 818). He acknowledged that norms, the interrelation of roles and institutions, emphasis on consequences rather than causes of institutions and societal equilibrium all were legitimate concerns. He felt, however, that they were *empirical interests* and not *general theory*. He stated:

> The only inescapable office of theory is to explain. The theory of evolution is an explanation why and how evolution occurs. To look for the consequences of institutions, to show the interrelationships of institutions is not the same thing as explaining why the interrelationships are what they are. The question is a practical and not a philosophical one—not whether it is legitimate to take the role as the fundamental unit, nor whether institutions are really real, but whether the theoretical program of functionalism has in fact led to explanations of social phenomena, including the findings of functional analysis itself. Nor is the question whether functionalism might not do so, but whether it had done so as of today. I think it has not (p. 811).

For Homans, a theory assumes the form of a deductive system. This means that it contains lower-order and higher-order propositions and the lower-order ones followed logically from the higher-order ones. Within this system it is important to define properties and categories but that is not enough. *Definitions of properties, propositions stating relationships between properties,* and *the formation of a deductive system using the propositions* constituted a theory for Homans (p. 812).

Emphasizing the explanatory function of theory, Homans contends that when functionalists attempted to construct theory their efforts always result in general propositions that are psychological (about the behavior of men). In a sketchy reformulation of sociologist Neil Smelser's explanation of social changes in the British cotton industry between 1770 and 1840, Homans attempts to show how the explanations offered by Smelser are, in fact, explanations of men's behavior rather than one of roles, functions, and in gerneral, the conditions of society. Homans states:

> What I do claim is that, no matter what we say our theories are, when we seriously try to explain social phenomena by constructing even the veriest sketches of deductive systems, we find ourselves in fact, and whether we admit it or not, using what I have called psychological explanations, I need hardly add that our actual explanations are our actual theories (p. 817).

A major point is that there is little need to draw lines of distinction between the personal and the social since they are identical and make up the social system. He suggests as proof of this that the same set of general propositions can be used to explain the phenomena of both personality and society. Needless to say, the set of general propositions is about the *behavior of men and not societies* (p. 818). We hardly need to remind ourselves that at least some of these general propositions are contained in *Social Behavior: Its Elementary Forms* (1961).

Secord and Backman's Application of Social Exchange Principles

The emerging social exchange perspective received another boost toward legitimation in 1964 when Paul F. Secord and Carl W. Backman's first edition of the popular textbook *Social Psychology* devoted a great deal of attention to exchange theory explanations of social phenomena. Findings related to interpersonal attraction including sociometric choices, opportunity to interact, friendship formation, etc. are couched within a social exchange framework and explanations offered. The social exchange perspective, Secord and Backman contend, succeeds in integrating and making sense out of a wide variety of data on interpersonal attraction.

Some examples of explanations of findings said to be facilitated by the social exchange perspective relate to links between similarity and interpersonal attraction. Many studies report that friends seem to be similar in terms of socioeconomic background, age, race, religion, etc. Secord and Backman feel that an explanation for this might lie in two social exchange processes. First, they suggest, many of the above similarities are related to frequency of interaction through the social structure; and second, similar background characteristics are associated with similar values (p. 256). Regarding the first social exchange process, persons similar in terms of age, class in college, socioeconomic background and so forth, have greater opportunity to interact and therefore should be expected to interact more. Moreover, they can also provide rewards to each other by consensual validation at a relatively low cost. With respect to the second social exchange process, attraction between persons similar in abilities and personal traits may be some function of the mutual rewards received from engaging in an activity as a result of the similarity. Such rewards obviously are not forthcoming if one engages in interaction with those not possessing the same abilities or traits. Playing tennis or bridge and engaging in discussion on social psychology are examples of social interaction between similar persons that often results in mutual rewards—ones which are contingent on similarity between participants. In both instances, social interaction is analyzed by looking at the implications of similarity between persons in terms of rewards and costs.

Secord and Backman also show how a number of other empirical findings can be interpreted within a social exchange framework. Some of the findings and their interpretations include:

1. Those who are located close to each other are more likely to interact *because of the low cost of initiating such interactions.*

2. When two people interact continuously, each becomes able to predict the behavior of the other, and predictability *leads to attraction by reducing the costs of interaction and increasing the level of rewards exchanged.*

3. Continued interaction with those who are physically close *costs less in time and effort than interaction with those more distant. Thus, profit with those physically closer is higher.*

4. As persons interact they exchange information and this increases the degree to which they are similar and contribute further to attraction.

5. Persons receiving many sociometric voices have characteristics *that have considerable reward value to an appreciable number of group members at low cost for the members* (p. 257).

Secord and Backman also present a process analysis of friendship formation which includes several sequential events and stages leading to the development of friendship. This process analysis is best described in their own words:

The formation of a dyad may be summarized in terms of exchange theory as follows. When a group of strangers meet, each person samples interaction with various other persons and estimates the profit entailed in various alternative interactions. Generally he commits himself to the interactions yielding the highest profit. In a dyad he engages in a process of bargaining, by means of which he elicits rewards from the other person in exchange for his own rewarding behavior toward the person. Bargaining is characterized by an attempt to obtain maximum cost. In part, the process may include some misrepresentation of one's own resources in order to encourage rewarding responses from the other person. As a whole, bargaining tends toward maximizing the rewards and minimizing the costs of both members of the dyad. As a relation develops, a stage called commitment is arrived at. In this stage, the process of sampling and estimating interactions with alternative persons is minimized or stopped altogether, and the members of the dyad focus on their interaction with each other. An end stage may be reached when the relation becomes institutionalized, as in engagement or marriage (p. 261).

The merit of Secord and Backman's contributions to social exchange lies in the dissemination of exchange theory principles. For the first time, social exchange theory explanations of everyday social psychological topics had been given in a text with wide appeal to students and teachers alike. Undoubtedly, their inclusion of social exchange in an introductory textbook made the perspective even more visible to potential scholars of and contributors to the field of social psychology.

Criticism During the Founding Period of Social Exchange

The period 1958 to 1965 is defined here as the founding period of social exchange. Following this period numerous contributions were made to the perspective, many resulting from critiques of Homans' *Social Behavior: Its Elementary Forms* by James A. Davis and Kenneth E. Boulding. Davis, a sociologist, acknowledged the "sensitizing" contribution of Homans' work. He speaks of the "ring of truth" that the volume had and the idea that it told us "about people" (Davis, pp. 455–456). He also refers to the unifying function of social exchange in that sociology and psychology are merged. Because of this, the volume represents "a greater step forward in unifying the behavioral sciences than many a book with that avowed purpose" (p. 456).

Davis does, however, have some reservations about social exchange theory as explicated in Homans' volume. He is not convinced that Homans' verbal reasoning enables adequate conclusions to be drawn from premises. Davis also feels that concepts such as "cost," "investments," "profit," and "distributive justice," have no empirical interpretation. Instead, such concepts are facets of a data classification system (p. 458). Davis later refers to this system as a conceptual framework rather than as a theory, since there are no propositions about specific variables thus no predictions about specific empirical events (p. 458).

Kenneth Boulding's criticism of Homans' volume seems to be based on the fact that Homans does not include an explicit recognition of the economic model of exchange involving indifference curves, bargaining paths, contract curves, etc. He suggests that Homans also fails to recognize other systems as legitimate forms of human intercourse (Boulding, p. 460). Such systems, according to Boulding, might include threat systems, love systems and others which he felt were different from pure exchange.

Both Davis and Boulding contributed greatly to the development of social exchange. Davis' comments may well have spurred Homans' "theory" in the direction it has taken, and Boulding's comments undoubtedly suggested directions the emerging perspective could take.

Another critique, entitled "Homans in the Skinner Box," was written by Morton Deutsch. Deutsch begins his critique of Homans' *Social Behavior: Its Elementary Forms* with a summary of its central ideas. Following the summary Deutsch launches the first of several criticisms on the logical adequacy of Homans' formulation. He notes that Homans implies that the nominal concept "value of an activity" suggests that the value of a unit of an activity can be compared with the values of units of other activities. This means the existence of a single dimension to which the values of different experiences can be compared, for example, "getting a B + on an exam," "being kissed by one's sweetheart," "being served a cold glass of beer," (Deutsch, p. 161). Deutsch does not consider that such a "common currency" exists.

Additionally, Deutsch does not agree that Homans could operationalize the value of measuring "the frequency of acts emitted after an act has been reinforced by rewarding a person with a given value" (p. 161). Homans does not attempt to determine how values are acquired or what determines the value of an act (p. 161). Because Homans does not provide nominal and operational definitions of reinforcement, Deutsch feels that Homans is in the position of stating that a value is that which is valued. Among other criticisms, Deutsch also chides Homans for neglecting the effects of different contingencies of reinforcement, inconsistencies in the meanings of his nominal concepts such as reward, the inability to explain novel responses and an "egocentric view of men as interested in what their behavior gets them" (p. 162).

Deutsch has not been alone in his criticisms of Homans' social exchange and many points raised by him have been restated by others since that time. Chadwick-Jones states (p. 214) that some criticism of

Homans' distributive justice discussion is a restatement of Deutsch's criticism of the concept value discussed above.

SOCIAL EXCHANGE FOLLOWING THE FOUNDING PERIOD

Kenneth Gergen's Behavioral Exchange

Little more than a decade after its founding, Kenneth Gergen's book on social exchange appeared. *The Psychology of Behavior Exchange* is important for three main reasons: (1) it explicitly couches the social exchange perspective in a motivational framework; (2) it integrates a wide variety of findings; and (3) it has had tremendous implications for theory in social psychology.

Gergen begins what he calls "the process of developing a theory of human interaction" by discussing five criteria for a theoretical formulation. These five criteria are (1) predictive capability, (2) linkage with observables, (3) extent of data base, (4) heuristic value and (5) parsimony. Realizing that the theorist often has to compromise in the theory building process, Gergen then begins his process by couching social exchange in a motivational framework.

Gergen questions the efficacy of Skinnerian behaviorism in the social exchange perspective. He terms it "hedonism turned inside out" (1969, p. 12). Gergen acknowledges that Skinnerian behaviorism's reliance on real world facts and the perspective's parsimony makes it a powerful perspective. For example, he points out that the concept "reinforcement" is especially problematic in that it does not lend itself to "advance specification." He notes that its definition emphasizing change in the probability of a behavior's occurrence signals reinforcement only after it has occurred. This means that the concept has little predictive power, saying only that what has occurred in the past will recur under similar conditions. Gergen also questions Skinner's concept of "explanation" as the isolation of systematic relationships between environment and behavior. He rejects Skinner's idea that the "why" of functional relationships is not important because it means that explanations are of little heuristic value since they lead to no further investigation.

On a different topic, Gergen contends that the pleasure–pain dichotomy is too abstract to make differential predictions. This means that the scheme allows only speculation after the fact. But, what is the alternative? If Skinner's position is fraught with difficulties, and hedonism is too abstract, is there any way out? Gergen's alternative suggests that we go into the organism and develop a more differentiated view of the pleasure–pain dichotomy. It must be remembered, according to Gergen, that there are various types of pleasures and aversions (p. 14). This view places Gergen clearly outside Skinner's position and very much into the Hullian framework. Gergen states:

> If we do not restrict ourselves to a literal translation of "pleasure and pain," the result can take the form of a set of needs or drives, each having slightly different physiological underpinnings, and each being satisfied by specific types of reinforcement. Investigations stemming from such a theory would ultimately indicate the relative strengths of these drives in relationship to each other over time.

According to Gergen, such a procedure is justified because of (1) the *strength* of hedonism, (2) the alteration of reinforcement to the point when it can be identified *a priori* and (3) the fact that various types of reinforcements and punishments can be hypothesized, given the procedure. Finally, on the motivational basis for social exchange, Gergen contends that concepts like "reward," "cathected," "punishment," and "cost" are "too loaded." He suggests as an alternative the neutral concepts "satisfaction" and "dissatisfaction" (p. 17).

To summarize, if the motivational basis for social exchange had been obscured in the founding of social exchange and subsequent writings, Gergen places the perspective clearly within a motivational framework. He even states that the learned basis of motivation is the ultimate dependence upon native reinforcers that the organism seeks.

In his efforts to develop a theory of human interaction, Gergen turns to the issue of a satisfier that does not produce satisfaction. In other words, at this point the *value* of a satisfier comes under close scrutiny. Gergen points out that cultural and subcultural norms play roles. Such factors as satiation and deprivation are also important. Other factors, such as whether the organism is in a chronic state of need approval, also are felt to influence satisfaction as an indicator of social motive. Gergen covers a wide variety of topics including interdependency, accommodation, interpersonal bargaining reciprocity, etc. In his coverage he is well aware of the fact that he introduces a number of assumptions that are not part and parcel of social exchange. His admission of these turns out to be a major difference between social exchange *then* and *now*. Gergen admits that he introduced into social exchange

(1) data exchange and retrieval, (2) comparison process, and (3) logical processes.

Gergen's last major contribution is in the area of theory. In *The Psychology of Behavior Exchange* he questions a common assumption that underlies not only social exchange but other perspectives, dealing with human interaction. This assumption is that knowledge is cumulative and that it accumulates in the same way as it does in the physical sciences. This means that the facts are stable, and the more facts the greater the power of theory. Only if these assumptions are valid can viable theory be developed. Otherwise, according to Gergen, the study of human behavior would be historical. He concludes that this is what psychological theories are, noting how they impinge on society and how this affects behavior subsequently. Such theories become *information* that individuals take into account in determining their behavior and in a sense negate prediction and control.

Social Exchange and Operant Theory

Richard Emerson's contributions to the social exchange perspective continued after the founding period. His "Operant Psychology and Exchange Theory," published in Burgess and Bushell's *Behavioral Sociology,* had as its stated aims: (1) to show how exchange theory can incorporate and use operant principles; and (2) to show how exchange theory is different from or added something to modern behaviorism.

Emerson says that operant principles should be used as valuable building blocks in theorizing about social phenomena, along with social exchange principles. He contends that operant explanations of social phenomena often seem to involve little more than direct translation of sociological concepts into operant concepts, with loss in explanatory power since the latter tells us something about men and women but very little about organized society (1969, p. 382). In order to avoid such "empty" theorizing, Emerson suggests the following strategy: (1) a reduction in the generality of operant principles through the introduction of new concepts containing social structured attributes; (2) focusing attention upon the above-mentioned added attributes, meaning that organized society is not taken as a given condition; and (3) conceptualizing the operant principles used with care and not stating them in some vulgarized form which may obscure relations between operant principles.

In his discussion of the direction social exchange can take, Emerson's concern is with social structure and structural change, with a focus on *social power* (p. 386). Identifying the core of operant psychology as the concepts operant, discrimination, stimulus, and reinforcing stimulus, Emerson says that since they are defined in terms of each other, they form a single, inseparable conceptual unit which describes a longitudinal organism—environment interaction relation (p. 387). Based on this description an exchange relation is defined as a special case of the conceptual unit where the behavior of an organism, in addition to being an operant, is also a reinforcer for another party—thus, exchange becomes reciprocal reinforcement. This leads to a focus on the domain of social exchange as an analysis of the social relation rather than the person in the unit. If this strategy is followed, declares Emerson, new principles of social structure and social change should emerge which provide fuller explanations of sociological social psychological phenomena. In order to illustrate his point, Emerson suggests that the relevance of operant psychology for sociology is first and foremost, social power. Noting that most contributors to the social exchange perspective have focused on social power at one time or another, Emerson says that simply acknowledging that operant psychology might tell us something about social power is not enough. One should also be knowledgeable about restrictions on the *use* of social power, since in numerous instances such restrictions will be social structurally based.

Following this line of reasoning, while parents often *do* have control over their children's reinforcement contingencies, various kinds of expected behavior may not be forthcoming. While the reasons may be numerous, and may include the possibility that parents are inept at effectively managing schedules of reinforcement, two other reasons deserve consideration: (1) the child has control over certain reinforcement contingencies for the parents which may restrict parents' power (the principle of reciprocity): and (2) agencies external to the parent-child relationship also control the parents' behavior. Thus what we see here is a complex arrangement of exchange relations between people. While it is *not* possible to explain these complex arrangements using the operant perspective alone, it *does* seem possible to explain them if there is some synthesis of the operant and social exchange perspective.

Emerson also expands his original power-dependence relation formulation by his specification of the conditions under which one or more power balancing operations are likely to go into effect in exchange relationships characterized by power-dependence imbalances. He suggests that "a wide variety of conditions can operate to slow or accelerate the process (of balancing) or to determine the specific path which balancing processes take" (pp. 391–392). They include: (1) cognitive states or knowledge on the part of the participants; (2) situationally determined paths of action open to the disadvantaged party; and, (3) the objective opportunity structure of alternatives which may involve one's location in the structure.

Emerson also discusses the difference between ''simple'' and ''productive'' exchanges, the former being defined as a type of exchange where the behavior of two or more persons is independently reinforcing for the persons involved regardless of the action of each. Exchanges of services when these services are needed illustrates ''simple exchange.'' The latter type of exchange (called productive exchange) connotes a relationship where persons find the joint activity rewarding. Each person's behavior is not automatically rewarding for others, but rather it is the joint action that is rewarding (as when people play bridge, tennis, etc.).

To summarize, Emerson's discussion of social exchange and operant theory has four major points. The first relates to the contention that *operant, discrimination, stimulus* and *reinforcer* constitute a single conceptual unit which when applied to social interaction enables the exchange theorist to avoid tautological pitfalls. Secondly, Emerson suggests that strength of a reinforcer and the relationship between variable schedules of reinforcement and strength determined *value* as a variable in the *dependence* concept. Value is seen as an inverse function of alternatives over time (p. 404). Thirdly, Emerson proposes the idea that the contingency of a reinforcer upon a discriminative stimulus provides the basis for the exchange concept ''alternative'' as a factor in dependence. A fourth feature of Emerson's discussion is that the contingency of reinforcers upon behavior leads to an emphasis on social power, and the reciprocal nature of such a contingency provides the basis for distinguishing between simple exchanges and productive ones. He also says that a distinction between the two types of exchange provides the basis for the study of networks versus groups and organizations as different forms of social structure. In addition, the introduction of power balancing mechanisms is thought to enable the production of structural changes. Finally, suggesting longitudinal experimentation and/or experimental case study as methods of investigation for the social exchange-operant framework, Emerson feels that pursuing social exchange along the lines explicated in his article would *raise* and *answer* new psychological questions (p. 404).

Social Exchange: From Theory to Perspective

It has been suggested in this chapter that Homans' *Social Behavior: Its Elementary Forms* is more appropriately identified as an expansion of his founding of the social exchange perspective than it is as a ''social theory.'' Nonetheless, Homans' work has often been evaluated as theory. A notable attempt made in 1970 by Ronald Maris is a case in point. Maris' ''The Logical Adequacy of Homans' Social Theory'' is predicated on the assumption that if the logical adequacy of Homans' contributions could be shown, then four major rewards would be reaped: (1) it would integrate many disparate and unrelated propositions; (2) it would offer a system to reject and thus make the accumulation of knowledge possible by giving form and substance to Homans' propositions; (3) it would offer a systematic theory to be used in discovering empirical association which might otherwise be overlooked; and (4) it would further encourage social scientists to move from description to explanation (pp. 1069–1070).

With a qualified ''yes'' to the question of whether Homans' theory is logically adequate, Maris sets out to demonstrate the theory's logical adequacy by presenting his reformulation. This begins with a ''search'' for Homans' postulates, definitions and theorems. Maris identifies five postulates, all of which are listed in this chapter. He then directs his search toward the theorems, and decides quickly that Homans has not deduced propositions through the manipulation of postulates in accordance with rules of inference (p. 1075). This recognition results in Maris devising his own rules of logic to construct arguments, to establish relationships between (suggested) propositions in the theory and to discover new empirical relationships. His efforts result in a presentation of forty theorem candidates—twenty-three of which mentioned by Homans and seventeen that were not (p. 1069).

Maris' efforts to evaluate the logical adequacy of Homans' theory have been criticized by many including Don Gray, Robert Price, Stephen Turner and more recently, Jack Gibbs. Criticisms of Maris range from Turner's concern at Maris' inclusion of divergent techniques of inferences drawn from a variety of logical systems, to Price's feeling that deductive rules of logic from Homans' theory might well have to account for *time*. More recent comments by Gibbs on Maris' attempt to assess the logical adequacy of Homans theory indicate that Maris' effort was futile (Gibbs, p. 31). This results from three steps that were conspicuously absent in Homans' original formulation: (1) explicit identification of postulates and related definition; (2) a statement of theorems; and, (3) a stipulation of the rules of logic employed.

The position taken here is that while Maris' reformulation of Homans' social theory may have been fraught with difficulties his task may have been made even more difficult by the fact that he was attempting to evaluate the logical adequacy of a *perspective* rather than a *theory*. In fact, criticisms of Maris' effort attest in part to this possibility. The stated difficulties with Maris is that he introduces concepts not appearing in the postulates, devises his own rules of logic, includes several strong assumptions and devises his own theorems. What more can one ask of a fruitful *perspective* in social psychology?

Homans' Revised Social Exchange

Homans begins the revised edition of *Social Behavior: It's Elementary Forms* with a discussion of what is meant by elementary forms of social behavior. His concern is with the general features of behavior and the behavior that appears among persons whether or not it is due to conscious or unconscious organization (Homans, 1974, pp. 3-4). Homans' concern with the general features of behavior relates to the process of *behaving,* that is, the process by which individuals come to abide by or do not come to abide by norms dictating certain action. His focus is on the behavior that appears among persons related to persons organizing in a group, ranking and assigning themselves, both deliberately and unwittingly, to their own positions as a result of social interaction. As in the first edition, Homans says that some behaviors are elements of larger social units and occur in small groups. Studying these behaviors, according to Homans (particulars of more general behavior), enables a close-up view of fundamental behavior.

There are three changes in Homans' general propositions. First of all, he begins his discussion of propositions with what was proposition 2 in his earlier edition. He terms it the "success" proposition, and adds qualifiers to what is known in behavioral social psychology as the *continuous reinforcement schedule*. Homans is aware of the potential conflict between his first proposition and *intermittent schedules of reinforcement* but suggests that the latter schedules do "not render invalid the success proposition itself because it holds good over a wide range of behavior" (p. 18). Secondly, Homan's propositions in the revised edition are less cumbersome in terms of terminology and tend toward gender neutrality on occasions. He often substitutes "person" for "man" or "men." A third change in propositions is the substitution of the aggression-approval proposition for the distributive justice proposition. The aggression-approval proposition is divided into two parts: one called the frustration-aggression hypothesis, the other called the approval hypothesis. Succinctly, Homans' revised propositions take the following forms.

1. For all actions taken by persons, the more often a particular action is rewarded, the more likely the person is to perform that action.

2. If in the past the occurrence of a particular stimulus, or set of stimuli, has been the occasion on which a person's action has been rewarded, then the more similar the present stimuli are to the past ones the more likely the person is to perform the action, or similar action, now.

3. The more valuable to a person is the result of his action, the more likely he is to perform the action.

4. The more often in the recent past a person has received a particular reward, the less valuable any further unit of that reward becomes for him.

5a. When a person's action does not result in the reward expected, or results in unexpected punishment, he or she will be angry, more likely to perform aggressive behavior, and the results of such behavior become more valuable to him or her.

5b. When a person's action receives expected reward, especially a greater reward than expected, or does not receive expected punishment, he or she will be pleased, will become more likely to perform approving behavior, and the results of such behavior become more valuable to him or her (Homans, pp. 16–39).

Another significant revision in the 1974 edition is Homans' recognition that imitation and modelling have roles in social behavior. He feels that the tendency to imitate others is inherited; however, he contends that eventually the action performed must bring reward if it is to persist. When rewarded, the person will not only repeat the action but also tend to adopt the action as a generalized form of behavior (p. 24). In addition, given the success proposition, Homans recognizes too that persons also learn certain behaviors vicariously, that is, from observing others receive rewards for performing certain actions. If, when an occasion presents itself, an individual performs the action and is rewarded, he or she is likely to repeat the action. The initial stimulus to the action of concern is the observed success of the model (p. 25). The remainder of Homans' 1974 volume follows closely the earlier 1961 edition.

Thus it appears that Homans continued his efforts to contribute to the development of what Gibbs has referred to as the most distinctive theoretical perspective in contemporary sociology (including social psychology) (p. 27). Undoubtedly those who were disenchanted with his original volume were even more disappointed with his revised edition since theorizing was no more formed in the revised edition than it was in the original edition. The theory of elementary social behavior remained then, a *perspective* in 1974.

Concepts in Social Exchange

John Kunkel and Richard Nagasawa have stated that the core of social exchange is Homans' five theorems derived from four axioms based largely on elementary economics and Skinner's paradigm of animal studies (1973, p. 531). These four axioms are as follows:

1. The more fully an animal has been deprived of a positive reinforcer, the more often it emits an activity so reinforced; the more fully it has been satisfied, the less often it does so.
2. The more often an activity is reinforced, the more often the animal emits it; the more often an activity is punished, the less often the animal emits it.
3. The withdrawal of a positive reinforcer releases the emotional behavior we call aggression, the presentation of a positive reinforcer may release, besides the reinforced activity, some degree of positive emotional behavior.
4. Any increase in the frequency of a particular activity entails by that very fact a decrease in the frequency of an alternative activity. (Homans, 1961, pp. 28–29).

They contend further that the theorems (discussed earlier in this chapter) have become so identified with modern-day social behaviorism that learning theory and exchange theory are almost regarded as one (p. 531). Bijou (1979) later denied that behaviorism and learning theory are synonymous perspectives, and rightly so. Learning theory has been influenced greatly by Albert Bandura, and his insistence that much human learning occurs through modelling and vicarious experience rather than direct experience. In a more recent explication of learning theory, Bandura (1977) even expanded his consideration of the importance of cognitive structure in behavior. Behaviorists like Skinner, Bijou, Baer and others mentioned in chapter 4 would hardly accept the contention that cognitive structures exist in the minds of persons prior to behavior.

Some may consider the distinctions between behaviorism and learning theory as they relate to social exchange nit-picking. Hamblin and Kunkel claim that the approaches are not necessarily contradictory since Skinner does not *deny* internal processes. This is despite the fact that much of Skinner's *About Behaviorism* reveals striking differences between him and Bandura, Homans and many other social exchange adherents. Meeker, for example, in an often-cited article, states that an exchange orientation is used to develop a theory of social exchange decision-making defining values as "the evaluation and cognitive structures that are premises of behavioral decision-making" (p. 486). Skinner would hardly accept this statement and Homans may be unlikely to reject it. Therein lies the difference between social exchange as developed by Homans and the many others who have followed him, and behaviorism as developed by Skinner and his followers.

Whether deliberately or not, differences between social exchange and modern behaviorism have been obscured by many contributors to social exchange. Richard Emerson has been an exception, as substantiated by his interpretation of the notion that social exchange is founded upon behavioral principles. For Emerson this means, in part, that "exchange theory is different from or adds something to behaviorism" (Emerson, 1969, p. 380). Why differences between the perspectives have not been emphasized more remains a mystery. A cursory glance at some of the key concepts in social exchange shows that there are glaring differences between the perspectives. Let us turn our attention to some of these concepts, which have been chosen because they were present at the founding and have appeared repeatedly following the founding of the perspective. As the concepts are discussed their counterparts (or the absence of them) in behaviorism will occasionally be mentioned to show how major portions of structural aspects of the two perspectives differ.

In the second (1974) edition of *Social Psychology,* Secord and Backman propose four concepts basic to the social exchange perspective: (1) reward, (2) cost, (3) outcome, and (4) comparison level. To this group of concepts two others are added, (5) activity, and (6) sentiments.

Reward   If not couched within the social exchange perspective, and if influenced heavily by Skinnerian behaviorism, this concept can be quite ambiguous. In part, it is unclear whether reward has a counterpart in behaviorism. Some would undoubtedly point to "reinforcer" as a similar concept. Stolte and Emerson seem willing to do so when they conceive of an exchange relation as "an interactive relation between two parties (persons or organized groups) based upon reciprocal reinforcement " (1977, p. 119). This alone does not point to their willingness to interchange the concepts reinforcers and reward. However, a further statement lessens any doubts: "The behaviors that one party performs in the relation is assumed to be *valued by* and *rewarding to* the other party'' (p. 119, emphasis mine). It seems clear, then, that reinforcement and reward are one and the same for these authors.

It is important to remind ourselves at this juncture that Skinnerian behaviorists conceive of reinforcement as a probability-based concept totally unrelated to reward, which implies pleasure and/or gratification (see Chapter 4). But this is the social exchange perspective, and it is quite legitimate to link value and gratification inextricably to *reward*. During the founding period, reward was defined as ''any activity by one person that contributes to the gratification of another person's need . . . '' (Homans, 1961). Relatively recent concerns with extending social exchange beyond elementary social behavior would dictate substituting ''party'' for ''person,'' but the nature of the definition remains unchanged.

Cost   Another social exchange concept which is basic in social exchange formulations is cost. Like reward, cost has had an ambiguous history in social exchange where Skinnerian behaviorism has been emphasized and the concept punishment used as a synonym. Punishment is a consequence which decreases the probability of a response occurrence (see Chapter 4) in Skinnerian paradigm. In social exchange, cost has been referred to as ''any activity by one person which frustrates or blocks the gratification of another person's needs'' (Homans, 1961). An alteration in the definition of cost similar to the one stated for reward is necessary if extension beyond elementary social behavior is made. As reward is linked with pleasure, satisfaction and benefit (Gergen, 1969, p. 36), cost is linked with frustration, dissatisfaction and pain.

Outcome   In social exchange, outcome has been extremely difficult to conceptualize. Often referred to as *rewards minus costs*, the outcome in social exchange is said to yield a *profit* if rewards exceed costs and a *loss* of costs exceed rewards. The problem with conceptualizing outcome in this manner is that rewards and costs are worked out arithmetically (Gergen, 1969, p. 36). Given the fact that a unit of behavior may provide multiple rewards and that costs may vary over time and situations, finding rewards and costs arithmetically is highly suspect. Outcome defined as the difference between rewards and costs may not, then, be justifiable. In a similar vein to Deutsch (1964, p. 162), Gergen has stated that even if rewards and costs are quantifiable, they may not be additive. This means that one unit of reward may not cancel out one unit of cost. Gergen suggests explaining sources of rewards and costs to increase our understanding of outcomes. Sources of outcomes include those produced intrinsically and extrinsically. Intrinsically produced outcomes depend on what the person does, and extrinsic outcomes depend on the behavior of other(s) (Gergen, 1969, pp. 37–38). Implied in the distinction between sources of rewards and costs is the notion that intrinsically produced outcomes may be more valuable than extrinsic ones.

It should be obvious that much work remains to be done on the concept outcome. Rewards, costs and, ultimately, outcome are the result of person perception which varies between persons, within persons, and over situations and time periods.

Comparison Level   Secord and Backman suggest that "comparison levels" for persons in social exchange may be based on at least four factors: (1) past experiences in a particular relationship; (2) past experiences in comparable relationships; (3) individual judgments of what outcomes others similar to oneself are receiving; and (4) individual perceptions of outcomes available in alternative relationships. The concept "comparison level" refers to some *minimum level of expectation for social exchange outcomes.* According to the above line of thought, if two persons are engaged in conversation (an instance of social exchange), there are some minimum outcome expectations from the conversation. Certainly this expectation level will vary from person to person because of individual differences with respect to perceptions of rewards and costs (Upshaw). This means also that comparison level as an exchange concept faces similar difficulties in conceptualization and operationalization as does outcome. The companion concept, comparison level for alternative (CLALT), is discussed elsewhere in this chapter. Its relationship to comparison level and thus its importance as a concept in the social exchange perspective has probably become obvious by this time.

Activity   According to Homans, activity refers to "a kind of behavior" (1961, p. 32). It is a descriptive term which remains static while its properties vary (Homans suggests "value" and "frequency" as properties of *activities* which vary in amount). It is in this discussion of activity that Homans makes his case for diminishing the traditional distinction between goods and services—an important stage in the construction of a social exchange perspective. Alluding to the tendency for persons to play down the *act* of transferring physical objects transferred (goods), Homans suggests that the act and the goods both are rewards and/or costs and may be measured in value and quantity. The economic theme in social exchange becomes more pronounced at this point. Properties of activities have been included in exchange discussions by numerous scholars including Kuhn, Emerson (1969), and Stolte and Emerson. The importance of properties of *activities* to further development of social exchange signals continuing efforts in this direction.

Sentiments   Sentiments refer to a special class of activities (verbal and symbolic) that the members of a community say are signs of the attitudes and feelings persons take toward each other (Homans, 1961) —social approval, social acceptance, respect, hostility, power, etc. As Blau points out, these activities can also be used in social exchange, although not all can be used in a "bartering" manner. Social approval and respect, for example, if they are to be significant in social interaction, must be given spontaneously, or at least must appear so. "These evaluations of a person or his/her attributes reward him/her only if he or she has reason to assume that they are *not* primarily motivated by the explicit intention to reward . . . " (Blau, p. 99). Sentiments are important in social exchange in that they are social variables which are proposed to take on "exchange" qualities similar to economic variables. A listing of these variables is almost impossible but a grasp of the scope of the list of such variables can be seen if one reviews the vast number of "sentiments" used in social exchange investigations.

At this point, there should be little doubt that within social exchange there are concepts which are quite distinct from concepts in behavioral social psychology. Concepts in social exchange may be founded on behavioral social psychology but differences between the two sets of concepts are significant, and obscuring the differences serves only to confuse an understanding of both perspectives—their similarities and their differences.

SOCIAL EXCHANGE: CONTEMPORARY DIRECTIONS

Since the beginning of social exchange numerous topics have been explored by scholars interested in applying the perspective to social psychological phenomena. No two topics, however, have been as central to social exchange as *power* and *equity* (Cook and Emerson, p. 722). Power was recognized during the founding period as a potentially fruitful topic, as evidenced by its appearance in the title of one of the perspective's most popular books, *Exchange and Power in Social Life* (Blau). *Equity* began its rise as an important topic in social exchange with Adams' "Inequity in Social Exchange" (1965); it reached a crucial period of development in 1973 with Walster, Berscheid and Walster's "New Directions in Equity Research;" and has become even more prominent since 1975, the year in which *The Journal of Social Issues* devoted an entire volume (31, no. 3) to "justice." Volume 9 of *Advances in Experimental Social Psychology* (1976), edited by Leonard Berkowitz and Elaine Walster was also devoted to equity theory. Contributions to the formulation have continued since. Adams and Freedman's comment that the annual growth rate of publications on equity theory was an "exponentially increasing one showing no signs of symoting" (p. 43) seems appropriate into the 1980s. Leading the way has been Gerald S. Leventhal's "What Should be Done with Equity Theory?" which is discussed later in this section. For the present, however, let us consider the "basic" equity theory framework proposed by Walster, Berscheid and Walster, following which criticisms of the basic framework and extensions of the framework are presented.

Elaine Walster, Ellen Berscheid and G. William Walster contributed their article "New Directions in Equity Research" to the *Journal of Personality and Social Psychology*. The article had a four-fold purpose: (1) to introduce and explicate a general theory of equity; (2) to summarize research on equity up to 1973; (3) to show how equity theory is related to other major social psychological theories; and (4) to imply how equity theory can be used to explore everyday social problems. The article has had far reaching implications for the social exchange perspective in general and for Homans' original distributive justice proposition more specifically, as we shall see.

The Equity Theory Formulation

Equity theory assumes that "man is selfish" (Walster, Berscheid and Walster, p. 2). With this general postulate as a point of departure, the authors suggest four propositions which can be used to explain how humans distribute rewards, resources and punishment. The propositions are as follows:

1. Individuals will try to maximize their outcomes (where outcomes equal rewards minus costs).
2a. Groups can maximize collective reward by evolving accepted systems for "equitably" apportioning rewards and costs among members. Thus members will evolve such systems of equity and will attempt to induce members to accept and adhere to these systems.

2b. Groups will generally reward members who treat others equitably and generally punish members who treat others inequitably.

3. When individuals find themselves participating in inequitable relationships, they become distressed. The more inequitable the relationship, the more distress individuals feel.

4. Individuals who discover they are in an inequitable relationship attempt to eliminate their distress by restoring equity. The greater the inequity that exists, the more distress they feel, and the harder they try to restore equity (pp. 151–154).

Inputs and *outcomes* are major nominal concepts in the theoretical formulation and are defined respectively as "what a person perceives as his contribution to the exchange for which he expects a just return" and "the individuals 'receipts' from a relationship . . . the sum of the rewards he obtains from the relationship (positive consequences) minus the cost he incurs (negative consequences)" (Walster and Walster, pp. 22–23).

In stating their first proposition that persons will attempt maximization of their outcomes, Walster, Berscheid and Walster point out that groups make compromises to avoid the disruption that would likely follow if persons continually attempted maximization of their outcomes. These compromises are worked out by making it *profitable* for group members to engage in equitable behavior and *costly* for them to behave inequitably. However, a corollary to proposition 1 is presented which states that persons *do* behave inequitably when they come to perceive that such behavior maximizes outcomes. One of two reasons generally accompanies such inequitable behavior: "First, an individual should behave inequitably whenever he is confident that in a given instance he can maximize his outcomes by doing so; second, it is to the individual's long-range benefit to behave inequitably now and then" (p. 5). The second reason involves "testing limits" to determine whether or not negative sanctions against inequity are in operation. Regardless of the reason though, because persons often reap punishment when they *behave* inequitably *and* when they *acquiesce* to inequity (by deprivation and/or ridicule from peers) socialization experiences quickly result in associating inequity with punishment (p. 6). Because of this socialization and resultant association, participation in inequitable relationships results in the participants feeling distressful. These feelings of distress increase with increasing degrees of inequity in the relationship. Such distress leads to attempts on the part of participants to reduce the distress through equity restoration. It should be pointed out here, however, that Walster, Berscheid and Walster report that *victims'* efforts at equity restoration often eliminate *exploiters'* needs to restore equity.

Returning to the elimination of distress, participants are said to attempt equity restoration through (1) "actually" restoring equity by altering own or others' outcomes or inputs; or (2) "psychologically" restoring equity through perceptual distortion of own or others' inputs or outcomes. In summary, groups attempt to insure individual maximization of outcomes by evolving equitable systems of apportioning resources. In addition, through vicarious socialization techniques, groups socialize their members to engage in equitable behavior by rewarding equitable behavior and punishing inequitable behavior. Persons who experience this kind of socialization are likely to feel distress when they participate in inequitable relationships as either exploiters *or* victims. These feelings of distress will lead to attempts at distress reduction through "actual" restoration of equity or "psychological" restoration of equity.

Application of the Formulation   In applying their theory, Walster, Berscheid and Walster explore the relevance of the formulation for *exploitative relationships, helping relationships* and *intimate relationships.* We will first look at their application of equity theory to exploitative relationships, their most lengthy discussion of application.

The authors state that when exploitation occurs, the exploiter feels distress which may arise from two sources: fear of retaliation and threatened self-esteem—both being rooted in the socialization process. Based on early socialization which punishes persons for participation in inequitable relationships, persons come to feel distressed when they behave inequitably toward others. This feeling (*retaliation distress*) may be manifested in a fear of punishment of the victim, his or her sympathizers, legal agencies or even God (p. 8). In addition, a second kind of distress may be generated which is labelled *self-concept distress* and refers to the discomfort persons feel when they violate their own internalized "standards of fairness" and experience conflict with their own self-expectations.

Exploiters in inequitable relationships can reduce distress through "actual" equity restoration by *victim compensation* (increasing their inputs or by allowing victims in the relationships to lower inputs); in addition, exploiters may also restore equity through *self-deprivation* (lowering their own outcomes or increasing their inputs). The latter technique for equity restoration does not appear, however, to be a popular one for exploiters to use, based on exploitation literature.

Exploiters can also restore equity (from their point of view) to inequitable relationships via restoration of *psychological equity*. In such instances the exploiter convinces him or her self that the victims' relative outcomes are *just,* or he or she minimizes his or her own outcome. These techniques are characterized by distortions of reality and include *derogation of the victim* (she or he deserved it), *minimization of victim suffering* (oh, I didn't hurt him or her) and *denial of responsibility for the act* (I did nothing, it just happened or someone else did it).

Thus far we have considered equity restoration techniques employed by the exploiter. Victims, too, attempt to restore equity to inequitable relationships since they also experience distress in such relationships. In fact, Walster, Berscheid and Walster derive a proposition which states "a participant will be more distressed by inequity when he is a victim than when he is a harmdoer" (p. 24). They suggest that the victim loses in every way in an inequitable relationship. Based on literature available at that time, they conclude that victims attempt equity restoration through *demands for compensation, retaliation,* and *justification* of the inequity (distortion of reality—psychological equity). The latter usually occurs when the victim is relatively weak and can only acknowledge the exploitation and his or her weakness ("I love her anyway") or justify the exploitation ("I had it coming"). The authors cite Lerner and Matthew's 1967 conclusion that victims often find it less upsetting to restore psychological equity than to admit their defenselessness.

Equity Theory and Helping Relations   Comparing participants in helping relationships with victims and exploiters in exploitative relationships, Walster, Berscheid and Walster state that helping relationships may be viewed from an equity theory point of view where the helper's role is seen as being similar to the victim's role and the recipient's role is seen as being similar to the exploiter's role. Assuming that initially the helper and the recipient are in an equitable relationship, once the roles are defined as above, the helper is in an *unprofitable inequitable relationship* and the recipient is in a *profitable inequitable relationship*. Based on what has been said earlier about inequitable relationships, we would expect these participants to experience discomfort and also to attempt "actual" or "psychological" equity restoration. In addition, the authors report two determinants of participant responses in helping situations: *intentionality* and *ability to repay* (p. 26). Apparently *intentional inequity* produces strong distress and results in strong desires to repay on the part of the recipient. In other words, when the helper intentionally provides help to the recipient, this activates a stronger distress to repay than when the help is given inadvertently. *Ability to repay* also affects participants in helping situations. If the recipient cannot repay, he or she is more likely to use "psychological equity" restoration techniques than to attempt "actual" equity restoration.

Equity Theory and Intimate Relations In a final application of their theoretical formulation, Walster, Berscheid and Walster conclude that individual's romantic involvements are influenced by equity consideration (p. 32). However, because persons tend to become involved with others of "equal" social standing, and because there is "a constant upward bias in one's choices," romantic choices seem to be a compromise between accepting what the individual realizes he or she deserves and the constant demand for the ideal person (p. 33). The authors report that findings are mixed regarding equity theory and romantic choices but do seem to be influenced, in part, by equity considerations.

Criticisms and Extensions of Equity Theory

This theoretical formulation sitmulated a great deal of debate regarding equity notions in general. In the introduction to the *Journal of Social Issues* volume devoted to issues related to justice, including equity, Melvin Lerner states that the articles in it "enable one to examine the assumptions social observers have employed to understand the role which justice plays in human endeavors" (Lerner, 1975, p. 1). Based on reactions to the articles and the influence that they have had on the course of social exchange theory and research, 1975 seems to have been an important year for social exchange in general, and for equity theory in particular. Some of the major issues raised in the volume are discussed here because they have tremendously influenced the social exchange perspective.

Elaine Walster and G. William Walster begin their article "Equity and Social Justice" with a review of the formulation proposed by Walster, Berscheid and Walster in 1973. Following this they discuss the equality-proportionality controversy and then the relationship between power and equity. They state as the aim of their essay the presentation of a framework for understanding theoretical and research developments in the area of social justice.

How are rewards to be distributed? What is fair and what is unfair? How do people come to define fairness? These are all questions related to social justice, and according to Walster and Walster there are two major lines of thought on the issues. These lines of thought are *equal justice* and *distribution justice*. "In the case of equal justice, rewards are distributed equally among men . . . . In the case of distribution justice, rewards are distributed in proportion to merit" (p. 24). Reviewing the literature, Walster and Walster specify several variables which they feel affected apportionment of resources. Time constraints, communication costs, potential benefits and significance for future decisions are all thought to affect whether resources are allocated equally or proportionately in social interaction. The need for rapid decisions seems to be closely associated with equal division of resources, as does costly negotiations, small benefits and one-time-only situations (p. 28).

In a different but related vein, Walster and Walster also consider whether it is necessary to distinguish between equality and proportionality as different forms of justice (pp. 28–29). They contend that since input relevance determines outcomes, no distinction need be made. With respect to equality, humanity is the relevant input, and since all persons possess equal amounts of humanity, the rewards should be divided equally. The inputs vary when proportionality has been studied as a form of justice, including many forms which may be considered legitimate (need, intelligence, beauty, etc.) and thus persons who possess different amounts of these inputs are rewarded differentially. The same theoretical framework (equity theory) Walster and Walster contend, is operational in both situations.

Finally, the authors present what they term a scenario to explain decision-making regarding whether equality or proportionality prevails in a society or community. The scenario is as follows:

1. In a society, members have a vested interest in evolving some system for allocating the community's social and material goods.
2. Every member also has a vested interest in persuading others that the inputs he happens to possess are relevant and important ones and that he thus is entitled to maximum reward.
3. The more powerful an individual (or coalition of individuals) is, the more successful it will be in (a) capturing the lion's share of community goods and (b) persuading others to acknowledge the equitability of the unbalanced allocation.
4. Over time, the powerful persons who control community resources will evolve a social philosophy to buttress their right to monopolize community goods; and, over time, the entire community will come to accept this justification of the status quo.

5. So long as society's distribution of power remains the
   same, members will accept the existing standard of equity;
   if marked shifts in the distribution of power occur, however, the emerging groups will be motivated to push for a
   new, more profitable, definition of equity (p. 30).

With respect to the equality-equity controversy, Sampson approaches the argument somewhat differently. He says that equity principles must be placed within their proper perspective. Beginning with a
brief history of the concept of equality, Sampson notes the eighteenth
century with its emphasis on fundamental uniformity of the physical
sciences, the emergent French middle class, the early Stoic idea of man's
equality and the Christian view of equality all fostered *equality* as a
form of justice. With the rise of Social Darwinism in the late nineteenth
century equity returned, with its emphasis on open competition, investments, strength, skill and talent. This meant that inequality could
be justified on the basis of inequality of merit (Sampson, 1975, p. 50).

Sampson argues that "equity is *not* natural, inevitable, or even
functionally necessary to solving societal and interpersonal issues of
distribution" and contends that "equality is a viable alternative" (p.
61). The preference for equity as a mode of distribution is a function of
Western historical and cultural patterns, especially the socialization process which grooms persons to play active roles within a capitalistic economic system. Sampson suggests four factors which influence whether
persons follow an equity or equality principle. These are (1) the
person's interaction goals, (2) the persons' basic orientations (competition or cooperation), (3) situated identity (our behavior used by others
to form impressions and lodge us in situations), and (4) sex-role
socialization.

Sampson's "On Justice as Equality" contains the following:

By nature man is not an equity theorist; that equity theory
may apply broadly today in a particular social and historical
context is a piece of datum of contemporary social history (p.
49).

The article concludes:

As long as all we can give away to others is an equity principle
of human relations, without placing it into its proper context
and outlining ways for achieving alternatives, as social psychologists we are thereby reinforcing dominant cultural trends

which, in my view, work to thwart solutions to those very problems which many of us have proclaimed to be of vital importance (p. 61).

Morton Deutsch also offers some observations on questions of social justice. He feels that the focus on equity is too limited in that it is only *one* of several possible principles of distributive justice. He recognizes that the focus is a natural one in a society dominated by economic values, but believes that justice is basically concerned with individuals and societal well-being, and that the natural values of justice foster effective social cooperation to promote individual well-being (1975, p. 140). This means that external circumstances confronting the individual and the group determine the distribution values which should operate. Such values might mean, for instance, distributing rewards according to need, proportionality, and equality depending on the circumstances. These conditions may be hypothesized as follows:

In cooperative relations in which economic productivity is a primary goal, equity rather than equality or need will be the dominant principle of distributive justice.

In cooperative relations in which the fostering or maintenance of enjoyable social relations is the common goal, equality will be the dominant principle of distributive justice.

In cooperative relations in which the fostering of personal development and personal welfare is the common goal, need will be the dominant principle of distributive justice (p. 143).

Since a group is likely to have more than one orientation Deutsch hypothesizes that one orientation rather than another will be likely to predominate. He states:

In conclusion, I would like to reiterate the thesis of this paper. Given the nature of Western society, whose characteristics predispose it to have an economic orientation, it has been natural for social psychologists to focus on equity as the central principle of distributive justice.

J. Stacy Adams and Sara Freedman express four major concerns in their critique of equity theory. First of all, they find that the nature or quality of equity "distress" had not been empirically determined. Secondly, there is a paucity of research on the instrumental uses of inequity. Thirdly, they contend that equity theorists and researchers have not explored the dynamic aspects of inequity reduction. The fourth and final concern relates to the nonquantification of inequity.

Regarding the first concern, Adams and Freedman suggest that "distress" in equity theory is a hypothetical construct not adequately operationalized. It is their feeling that determining the existence and quality of distress would be a contribution to core aspects of the theory. Moreover, anger and guilt are only two of a much broader range of distress experiences. In addition, they suggest that accompanying each form of distress is a different distribution of equity-restoring responses (p. 45).

The second concern stated by Adams and Freedman focuses on the *instrumental functions* of inequity, which had been largely ignored by researchers and theorists. One such function involves the notion that inequity may *inform an advantaged participant in the relationship that inequity is occurring.* The basic idea is that the advantaged party in an inequitable relationship may not be aware of the inequity. Inequity can also be used for personal gain, in the sense that *a person can deliberately create obligations,* thus causing others to perceive that his or her inputs are smaller than another's, or that that person's costs are greater. Adams and Freedman also point out that inequity can be used by one of the participants *to show displeasure in an exchange relationship to end the relationship.*

A third concern is that *equity researchers have ignored the interactive nature of inequitable relationships and therefore the dynamic aspects of inequity resolution.* To begin with, individuals' perceptions of their inputs and outcomes may be different. Thus "the logical implication that the partner of a person suffering disadvantageous inequity necessarily experiences advantageous inequity has no psychological validity" (p. 49). On the other hand, both persons, because of the weights they give to inputs and outcomes, may perceive disadvantageous inequity. Still, assuming that the participants in an exchange relationship experience advantageous and disadvantageous inequity and that "distress" moves them to seek equity resolution, they may *not* seek compatible means of reducing inequity. Joint equity requires coordination, and without it new forms of inequity may arise, thus signifying that achieving equity in an exchange relationship may be extremely difficult—not a simple task, as implied by the foregoing equity formulation.

Adams and Freedman's fourth concern is the operational inadequacy of the concept "inequity." It is their feeling that while equity researchers often had experimentally induced inequity through manipulations of a single objective outcome or input, they had never manipulated total, net outcomes or total inputs (p. 52). The former type of manipulation, according to Adams and Freedman, had the unfortunate effect of resulting in great amounts of unexplained variance in dependent variables. This means that manipulating single inputs and outcomes seems inadequate for explaining inequity. One explanation offered is that manipulation of an outcome and/or input has variable effects on the inequity experienced by subjects. Subjects may perceive numerous outcomes; in addition, an outcome perceived by one person may be evaluated by another as an input. It goes without saying, then, that manipulation of single outcomes may produce variable net outcomes among subjects (p. 53). A final point made by Adams and Freedman is that due to subject perception variability on outcomes and inputs the magnitude and maybe even the quality of inequity experienced by subjects are variable. The result is a common tendency by researchers to treat the variability as error variance when in actuality it is the very nature of equity theory.

Also related to the operational adequacy of equity theory concepts is Adams and Freedman's contention that there is a need to establish a unit of measurement common to both inputs and outcomes. Such a unit of measurement should measure "equally well a person's own inputs and outcomes and his perceptions of a comparison person's inputs and outcomes" (p. 53). The important point here is that inputs and outcomes would be identified by subjects and not experimenters.

Finally, on the topic of quantification of inequity, the authors point out the level of measurement which traditionally had been used to measure inequity had generally been below the interval level. Since such measurement had resulted in a loss of information which seriously hampers prediction, Adams and Freedman state that equity theorists should develop parametric measures of inequity. They conclude that the operational weaknesses in equity theory render the formulation inadequate for practical application. This is so, they state, in spite of the formulation's relevance for understanding a wide array of social exchange relationships between persons, groups, organizations and institutions.

Gergen, Greenberg and Willis have stated that Adams and Freedman may be too optimistic in assuming that the measurement problem in equity theory can be solved through methodological refinements which allow the determination of how inputs and outcome combined result in experimental inequity (p. 97). They feel that such problems can be solved only through broadly based combined methodological and conceptual analyses.

In 1976 Gerald S. Leventhal, following prolific research into the allocation phenomenon (Adams and Freedman list fifteen mostly coauthored Leventhal contributions between 1969 and 1973[2]), published "The Distribution of Rewards and Resources in Groups and Organizations." In what was to become a major reference source for allocation ideas, Leventhal makes the following statement about equity theory:

> The equity model identifies important psychological processes and causal variables that must be taken into account in the study of allocation behavior. However, by itself the model provides too limited a framework for a comprehensive analysis of allocation behavior (p. 94).

Apparently agreeing with such scholars as Deutsch and Sampson that equity theory offers too limited a framework, Leventhal proposes other normative rules which also determine allocation behavior. Stating that the equity rule is *one* factor determining allocation of resources, Leventhal recognizes other rules such as *need, equal distribution, adhering to commitments* and *reciprocity*.

Leventhal initiates his theoretical treatment of allocation behavior by defining *allocation norm*. According to Leventhal it can be defined as "a social rule which specifies criteria that define certain distributions of rewards and resources as fair and just" (p. 94). He contends that in given situations several allocation norms often exist simultaneously. The existence of several allocation norms at the same time frequently leads to different allocation decisions being made simultaneously and the arousal of incompatible response tendencies. When the latter occurs compromise responses partially satisfying requirements of all allocation decisions involved must be made. In addition, the social system facilitates the differential emergence of allocation norms. Sampson, for example, intimated the possibility that present day cultural patterns in the United States favor the equity norm of allocation. In other words roles and practices prevailing at a particular time in a culture or society may facilitate the allocation of resources according to some norms and not others. In such instances *conformity pressures* and *modelling processes* influence allocators' decisions to follow certain socially approved norms of allocation.

Pursuing the basis for the influence of allocation norms on alloca-

---

2. Three papers were read at Psychological Association meetings (Honolulu in 1972, Atlanta in 1972 and Montreal in 1973); eight articles published in the *Journal of Personality and Social Psychology;* and one each in *Journal of Experimental Social Psychology, Child Development, Journal of Applied Social Psychology* and *Psychonomic Science* (Adams and Freedman, pp. 75–78).

tion decisions, Leventhal posits the idea that the *pattern of benefits derived from following certain norms of allocation over others* (instrumental value) is probably a key factor in allocation decisions. This belief leads Leventhal to consider the instrumental values of particular allocation norms. With respect to the equity norm, high productivity is thought to be directly related to distribution on the basis of merit. Leventhal hypothesizes the following ways in which equity norms are related to high performance:

1. Equitable allocations ensure that recipients whose behavior is most useful have greatest access to essential resources;
2. Equitable allocations reinforce those recipients whose behavior is most useful and beneficial;
3. Equitable allocations deliver law reinforcement to recipients whose behavior is least useful; and,
4. Equitable allocations demonstrate to recipients they can increase their rewards by working harder and improving their performance (p. 96).

The effects of equity allocation are not all positive, however, and this is pointed out in Leventhal's review of the literature of the countereffects of equity norms. Counterproduction effects include the effects of disruptions in groups when *cooperation* and *interdependence* facilitates group goal accomplishment; the fact that an equity norm may produce resentment in poor performers who receive relatively lower rewards; emergent tension; and antagonism among group members. All of the aforementioned are indicators of the counterproductive effects of equity allocation of resources.

On the question of why allocators distribute rewards equitably these major reasons seem likely: (1) the desire to conform to established rules; and (2) the belief that high productivity is thereby fostered. Reasons for believing that equitable reward distribution fosters high productivity include: (1) equity allocation provides essential resources to those who use more of them in their roles as better and/or more effective performers; (2) equitable allocation of rewards are attractive to high contributors who will be more likely to remain with the group while poor performers probably will drop out (group membership rejection rationale); (3) equity allocation of rewards allows evaluations of recipients' performance relative to others (member comparison rationale). This may involve the construction of categories of performers on the part of the allocator who may evaluate and reward recipients on the basis of allocator expectancies which may vary for different types of recipients. And (4) equity allocation allows allocators to overreward recipients to maximize production. Leventhal cites numerous studies indicating that perhaps as a result of the norm of reciprocity (and maybe other equity and/or exchange processes) the use of short-term overrewarding could stimulate improved performance among poor performers. Long-term use, however, is thought to remove incentive for improved performance among poor performers as well as provoking dissatisfaction among high performers.

Leventhal explores another important issue which emerges in all allocation situations—*potential for conflict*. Returning to Walster, Berscheid and Walster's first proposition, implying that persons try to maximize their rewards and that social comparison processes are operative, Leventhal notes that recipient satisfaction and/or dissatisfaction may be a thorny issue in any allocation system. This raises the question of possible conflictual interaction between the recipient and others, including the allocator. Methods of preventing such conflicts, according to Leventhal, include changing the distribution of rewards, and secrecy about reward distribution. Those recipients who are most likely to respond antagonistically may be given higher rewards; the allocator may keep secret how rewards are distributed to recipients, and, the higher rewarded recipients may not disclose their rewards to recipients who receive low rewards.

In his discussion of the *equality norm*, Leventhal notes that rules of equality are likely to influence the allocation decision when such rules are *deemed appropriate to follow in social settings and when the allocator desires certain types of benefits such as solidarity and harmony among group members* (instrumental value). In reality it appears that both equity and equality norms frequently affect an allocator's decisions regarding reward distribution (p. 114). When such instances occur, compromise allocation responses are made characterized by a move toward equality but never the complete attainment of equality. Dependent upon the allocator's primary goal (for example, maximizing productivity or minimizing antagonism and maintaining solidarity in a group), either the equality norm or the equity norm is weakened as manifested in the allocation response. Sometimes, however, both norms dictate the same allocation response as when recipients have similar task inputs or when there is vague information about task inputs (p. 115). Regardless of the norm used, however, recipients' satisfaction with rules of distribution are often manipulated by a secret alteration of the perceived basis of the decision, by justification of the decision and enhancement of the value of the reward.

Finally, Leventhal considers three other norms of allocation: *adhering to commitments, the reciprocity norm* and *norms affecting respon-*

siveness to needs (pp. 121–126). Adhering to commitments implies that allocators often honor prior commitments to recipients; the norm of reciprocity suggests past contributions to the allocator may be the basis for reward distribution; and need norms have been suggested by many who have noted that rewards sometimes are distributed in accordance with recipient needs. Problems often arise with respect to the latter norm because of discrepancies between the allocator's perception of the needs of the recipient and the recipient's perception of own needs. Degrees of harm and/or propriety of the need of the recipient often influence the allocation decision when the above discrepencies in allocator and recipient perceptions of need occur.

In a recent theoretical exposition, Leventhal (whose contributions to the reward distribution literature cannot be overemphasized) proposes a *justice judgment model* incorporating *equity theory* into a larger theoretical framework. Leventhal contends that three major problems plague equity theory: (1) equity theory proposes a unidimensional conception of fairness rather than a multidimensional one; (2) equity theory neglects the procedures that generate the final reward distribution; and (3) equity theory seems to overemphasize the importance of fairness in social relationships (p. 28). We have already discussed Leventhal's and others' disagreement with the unidimensional approach to equity theory and their contentions that there are numerous forms of justice in addition to merit. In addition, Leventhal has referred to the ambiguity surrounding the concept "equity." Contrasting equity theory researchers' relatively narrow definitions of equity (justice based on merit) with Webster's definition ("a free and reasonable conformity to accepted standards of natural right, law and justice without prejudice, favoritism, or fraud and without rigor entailing under hardship"), Leventhal introduced the terms "fairness" and "justice" (in Webster's general sense) as substitutes for the concept equity. *Contribution rule* was used "to refer to equity in the narrow sense of justice that is based on a matching of rewards to contributions" (p. 29). The term *distribution fairness* was introduced to refer to "judgments of fair distribution, irrespective of whether the criterion of justice is based on needs, equality, contributions or a combination of these factors" (p. 29).

Other major nominal concepts in Leventhal's model include *justice rule,* defined as "an individual's belief that a distribution of outcomes or procedure for distributing outcomes is fair and appropriate when it satisfies certain criteria" (p. 30). Two categories of justice rules are *distribution rules,* which are "the individual's belief that is fair and appropriate when rewards, punishments, or resources are distributed in accordance with certain criteria"; and *procedural rules* which define "an individual's belief that allocative procedures which satisfy certain criteria are fair and appropriate" (p. 30).

The justice judgment model suggested by Leventhal assumes that persons apply distribution rules selectively and use different rules from time to time. Moreover, the model assumes that evaluation of fairness is characterized by sequential stages. The stages are *weighting* where decisions are made regarding the distribution rules to use; *preliminary estimation* where individuals estimate the amounts and types of outcomes recipients deserve according to each of the distribution rules to be used; *rule combination* which involves the individual reaching a final judgment on the recipient's deservingness based on a combination of the preliminary estimate; and, *outcome evaluation* which is the final stage, where the fairness of the recipient's outcomes is determined.

Leventhal contends that three new directions for research on fairness are pointed to by the justice-judgment model. The directions are (1) studies of factors determining relative weights of distribution rules, (2) studies of the attribution processes used by persons to estimate distribution rule deservingness, and (3) studies which analyze the role of distribution rules.

One of the developments in studies of allocation discussed by Leventhal is the perception of *procedural fairness*. According to this line of thought, equity theory has generally ignored the regulatory procedures guiding allocative processes. Leventhal states that an individual's perceptions of fairness of procedural components of the social system regulating allocation of resources are important determinants of perceived fairness (p. 35). Using an incident of resource allocation, Leventhal attempts to show that individual cognitive maps of events precede reward distribution and evaluation. Components of the cognitive maps are (1) selection of decision-makers, (2) establishment of ground rules related to informing potential recipients of available rewards and how they may be obtained, (3) information-gathering (for evaluating potential recipients), (4) procedures defining the final decision process by which rewards and punishments are netted out, (5) appeal systems which allow recipients to vent grievances, (6) safeguards against unethical conduct by allocators and (7) procedures for instituting change in the mechanisms that regulate resource distribution. At any point in time any one of the above components of the individual's cognitive map "may become the focus of a judgment process that evaluates the fairness of that procedure" (p. 39).

When justice rules are used by the individual to evaluate the fairness of allocative procedures they are referred to as *procedural rules*. Leventhal identifies six: (1) *consistency rule* which basically states that allocative procedures apply consistently from one person to another; (2)

bias-suppression rule which negates self-interest and narrow preconceived ideas; (3) *accuracy rule* which means that the information and opinions on which allocations are made should be relatively free of error; (4) *correctability rule* which refers to opportunities to rectify mistakes in decisions through modifications or reversal of decisions; (5) *representativeness rule* meaning that the allocative process must reflect concerns, values, etc. of important subgroups in the allocation population; and (6) *ethicability rule* signifying that procedures for allocation are consistent with individual's moral and ethical values.

Leventhal has stated that equity theory overemphasizes perceived fairness as a behavior determinant. He feels that there are other equally important determinants of social behavior. Because of this concern, an exploration of factors that cause concern about fairness, and the relative potency of concerns about fairness are explored. Leventhal argues that *social role, importance of other goals, probability of violation* and *monolithic versus pluralistic social systems* all affect the level of concern about fairness. Persons occupying social roles which emphasize fairness (judges, sports umpires, etc.) may, while role-playing, express concern about fairness. Once such individuals no longer occupy certain roles, however, their concern for fairness may lessen. If other goals are considered to be of greater importance than fairness, a person's concerns about fairness may be lessened. This often happens when behavior control of another person is desired. Also, if there is suspicion of violation of justice rules this may increase concern about fairness of distribution of allocation procedures. Finally, if a system is uniform and imposes consistent, nonchanging distribution and procedural rules, little attention will be devoted to fairness. This tends to be the case in monolithic systems, and is the opposite in pluralist systems. Leventhal summarizes by saying that there is little available evidence to support the notion that the concern for fairness is the primary motivator of behavior.

FURTHER DEVELOPMENTS IN SOCIAL EXCHANGE

In the middle 1970s, several influential scholars (for example Homans, Walster and Walster, Lerner) suggested that the power-equity linkage in social exchange had been given too little attention by those theorizing and conducting research within the perspective. In 1978, the power-equity linkage was examined by Karen S. Cook and Richard M. Emerson in their article "Power, Equity and Commitment in Exchange

Networks.'' They propose that exchange theory brings power and justice, equity and other normative constraints upon exploitation into a single analytic framework when power is viewed as the capacity to exploit (p. 721).

One hundred and twelve subjects (fifty-six males and fifty-six females) were randomly assigned to same-sex four-persons networks in a factorial design described by Cook and Emerson as containing two balanced between-subject variables and two within-subject variables with trials nested in equity. The experiment involved subject bargaining, power manipulation and equity manipulation.

The results obtained from the experiment suggested the following conclusions according to Cook and Emerson: (1) power is a social structural variable, more specifically, an attribute of position in a network structure; (2) there are normative constraints on the use of power in networks; (3) emergent commitments impede the use of power in exchange networks; and (4) under conditions of unequal power, females form stronger commitments.

Cook and Emerson also offered an hypothesis about commitment which they hoped would lead to further research on the topic: *Commitment formation varies inversely with risk-taking behavior in exchange situations involving uncertain outcomes* (p. 738).

A final point about Cook and Emerson's work is that their report that the norm of equity is activated through subject awareness of distribution of resources across exchange networks was cited by Tallman and Tallman (1979, p. 220) as supporting the idea that opportunity to interact affects distribution rules. The Tallmans feel that it affects equity rules, but it remains unclear whether equity refers to proportionality or equality for Cook and Emerson (Cook and Emerson, pp. 727–728). The latters' interpretation of findings in the literature suggesting that women might be more concerned about equity than men (p. 728) heightens the ambiguity, especially in light of Sampson's and Deutsch's interpretations of similar findings, suggesting that females tend toward equality and males toward equity.

In the preceding discussion it was stated that Cook and Emerson found that there were normative constraints on the use of power in exchange networks. How these normative constraints emerge is not discussed, and the Tallmans feel that a concern with norm emergence is a legitimate area for social exchange theorists and researchers. They explore the interesting issues of development and change in social values and norms related to distribution (1979). Their first task is to examine how social structure influences *choices of courses of action* which result in satisfaction (humans are assumed to be satisfaction seekers). Also, according to Tallman and Tallman, individuals have to make choices between potentially satisfying goods because of the scarcity of desired benefits. In addition, those elements within the structure which influence the formation of values and norms of distributive justice are examined.

On social structure and value formation, the authors defined value as "a preferential ordering that is relatively stable over time" (p. 218). They exclude from the concept value momentary fluctuation reflecting physical and/or psychological reactions to deprivation and satiation. Believing that the basis for valuing some goods over others lies in the types of goods, Tallman and Tallman adopt Emerson's concept of *exchange domain* for their analysis. Exchange domain, according to Emerson, refers to that subset of goods which are viewed by actors as equally capable of satisfying specific needs; thus, each good within the domain is substituted for the other. Drawing upon the principle of marginal utility, the Tallmans propose that the *value* of an exchange domain varies directly with the perceived utility of the domain's goods. Utility, they contend further, is determined by the goods' *satisfying potential.* Satisfying potential is determined by the goods' potential to please or satisfy if owned or possessed and the goods' availability to the actor. It follows, then, that the more scarce a domain is, the more highly it is *valued.* Valuing a domain will result in a willingness to give up resources for it to some point after which value declines. Finally, the authors believe that a domain will be valued not only because an actor perceives that it is scarce to him or her but also because of the domain's perceived scarcity within the social structure.

The Tallmans' discussion of "social structure and norm formation" also provided some interesting insights. They offer the proposition that social structures have an unequal distribution of valued goods; and, based on observations by Heath, and Cook and Emerson, they claim that those who control greater amounts of the goods have a bargaining advantage for two reasons: they can withhold their resources longer and get satisfactory rates of exchange; and, they can be more competitive because they can offer more of their resources for a desired good. There are intervening factors, however, since persons in a network must be mutually dependent to some extent lest the network cease to exist. This means that there is a need for cooperation among network members. Such a need leads to coalition formation. Citing support from Ofshe and Ofshe (1970a, 1970b), Tallman and Tallman point out that persons seek to form coalitions with those they believe can best facilitate their payoffs (p. 220). Thus, actors in weak positions seek equal payoffs and those in strong positions seek *proportional payoffs.* The authors contend, however, that adherence to a particular norm of distribution also may be influenced by "one's perception of available opportunities to form coalitions" (p. 220).

Extending their theoretical framework to a discussion of "norms of distributive justice and solidarity," the Tallmans refer to a situation characterized by unequal resources where actor A controls resources desired by a number of other actors (Bs). It is to the Bs' advantages in such a situation to form a coalition since A can offer inducements for compliance to any one of the Bs. If Bs have the opportunity to interact, the coalition formed should be based on the distribution of equality. Such a coalition should continue because of the necessity for cooperation among the Bs. If, on the other hand, Bs compete with each other for A's resources, distrust and suspicion may emerge among Bs. This can be minimized through the formation of norms which make defections from the coalition costly thereby strengthening the norms of cooperation. When a third class of actor (Cs) is introduced who offers different resources, this may weaken the coalition of Bs because all negotiation and coalitions must include the third class. The norm of equality which derives from coalitions among weak actors is less likely to predominate because As and Cs are likely to seek payoffs proportional with their resources (p. 222). The Tallmans predict:

> that the greater the complexity in the division of labor within a social structure, the more likely the prevailing norms of distributive justice for relevant exchange domains will be based on the principle of proportionality.

The Tallmans conclude their article with an application of the theoretical framework to Mexico and the United States, with favorable results.

Helping Behavior and Social Exchange

On a final, but by no means exhaustive, consideration of contemporary directions in social exchange, helping behavior is often couched within the social exchange perspective. Specifically, helping behavior is to be found within resource-theory frameworks. Edna Foa and Uriel Foa have been at the forefront of investigations into resource-theory phenomena (1974). Defining resources as "Anything transacted in an interpersonal situation . . . any item, concrete or symbolic, which can become the object of exchange among people," altruistic behavior for Foa and Foa, clearly can be placed within the social exchange perspective (Foa and

Foa, 1980, p. 78). The resource provided by the helper may be services or goods. In return the helper receives (from those helped) expressions of gratitude, admiration (from those helped as well as others) and even goods and services.

Other work in helping behavior has suggested that it frequently takes on the quality of a secondary reinforcer meaning that altruism itself becomes self-rewarding for individuals (Weiss et al., 1971). This means that while *some* helping behavior may be a function of the opportunity to obtain reciprocal and / or external rewards, due to socialization effects (involving the pairing of altruistic behavior with external rewards) other helping behavior may come to have self-gratifying effects and occurs without the expectation of material or social reward (Kenrick Baumann and Cialdini, p. 754).

SOCIAL EXCHANGE IN RETROSPECT AND IN THE FUTURE

The Ambiguity of Basic Assumptions Underlying Social Exchange

In an emerging perspective scholars with different topical interests often disagree over its underlying basic assumptions. The social exchange perspective, not yet thirty years old, is an example, for scholars working within it seem to have divergent thoughts concerning the perspective's basic assumptions. Some place social exchange partly within Skinnerian behaviorism. Others reflect little of Skinnerian behaviorism. My position in this chapter is that Skinner and most of his followers would hardly subscribe to the motivational elements characterizing most social exchange contributions. Many social exchange theorists freely borrow concepts from Skinnerian behaviorism, yet seemingly fail to realize that Skinnerian assumptions *should accompany the concept unless it is explicitly stated that the assumptions have been dismissed or altered.* This would serve to explicitly differentiate between the Skinnerian framework and those being presented.

Cognitive and motivational elements have frequently been introduced into social exchange formulations and research when theorists and researchers have contended that their formulations are couched in Skinnerian behviorism terms. While I have no quarrel with altering behavioral concepts and principles to fit social exchange (Homans did this in his original formulation), such alterations should be stated, so as to minimize concept and principle ambiguity and inconsistency. If Skinnerian behaviorism and its underlying assumptions are part and parcel of social exchange, then social exchange formulations should reflect the asumptions as well as the concepts. This has not been the case thus far in the development of the perspective and one can only speculate about the amount of conceptual ambiguity which has resulted.

Social Exchange as Need Reduction or Drive Reduction Psychology

Another criticism of social exchange which may or may not be legitimate is that its reliance on reward and punishment *reflects a variation of need and drive reduction psychology*. First of all, Skinnerian behaviorism is not based on need and drive reduction psychology, as we have seen. Therefore, if the social exchange perspective is based on Skinnerian behaviorism, the criticism is unfounded. If the perspective is motivation-oriented this need not mean that physiologically based internal drives and tension-states determine human behavior. Social exchange ideas advanced by Deutsch (1975), Sampson, Cook and Emerson and others refer to the importance of socialization effects related to sex role differences on exchange processes. Perhaps further advances in social exchange linking social exchange concepts and principles to other socialization effects and principles will clarify the motivation orientation of the social exchange perspective.

Social Exchange: Simple or Complex?

Lindesmith, Strauss and Denzin suggested in 1977 that social exchange was too simplistic to take into account the full range of interaction that occurs among persons. While their contribution might have been valid for social exchange during the first two or three years of its existence as an emerging perspective in social psychology, many informed scholars would take issue with such a contention today. Contributions discussed in this chapter as well as numerous others not included attest to the complexity of the perspective. Jasso's "A New Theory of Distributive Justice," which attempts to understand the sentiment of justice by describing how individual choice with respect to valuation of goods, aggregate formation and sense of fairness combines with actual good distribution and intercorrelations of good distribution, is a case in point. The literature is replete with similar examples reflecting the complexity of the social exchange perspective.

The Social Structural Bias in Social Exchange

"Because social behavior consists of events and not of structure, our explanation of the behavior, like explanation of physical events, must be considered in terms of processes or sequences of interconnected processes" (Lindesmith, Strauss and Denzin, 1975, p. 270). Aside from the obvious fact that "sequences of interconnected processes could possibly be interpreted as social structure," (p. 270), these authors also state that there is an enormous range of behavior which can be accounted for only in terms of social structure. If this seems confusing, it is because it is, in fact, confusing. On the one hand, social exchange is criticized because it tends to deal with social structural explanations of social behavior. Yet it is admitted that much behavior can be explained only in terms of social structure. The question apparent at this juncture is, what are we to believe about the criticism of social exchange that it is *too social structurally* oriented? Not too much should be made of this criticism. In contrast, Secord and Backman in their discussion of various social exchange findings, state that much of the focus of the perspective is "on the relations between individuals rather than on the individuals themselves, and on *process* rather than on structural aspects of a relation" (p. 233).

What appears to be the problem here is a failure on the part of some critics to recognize that exchange contributions made by scholars like Cook, Emerson, Thibaut and Kelley, Burgess and Nielsen, Leventhal and many others, focus on *both* process *and* structure. To concentrate on one at a particular point in time does not negate the importance of the other. In fact, certain critics themselves adopt this strategy but nevertheless criticize social exchange theorists for doing precisely the same thing.

The Value Bias in Social Exchange

That a status quo existed in social exchange up to 1975 cannot be overlooked. In fact the value bias in social exchange was likened by Sampson to the Davis and Moore bias in social stratification. Walster and Walster (1975) contend that equity and equality are aspects of the same analytical framework. Notwithstanding, Sampson (1975) suggests that the predominance of equity within our particular socioeconomic framework has led many scholars to conceive of it as natural and inevitable. By the same token, deviation from equity, such as a preference for equality, is seen as unnatural. This argument, according to Sampson, is circular, culture bound, and inhibits scientific growth in a discipline. Furthermore, discussing alternative conceptions of solutions to human injustice may obscure the need for social exchange theorists to redirect efforts toward practical problems of everyday life (applied theory and research) rather than toward the needs of a theoretical model and/or basic research (p. 58). Deutsch echoes Sampson's concerns in his attempt to outline issues related to a broader conception of distributive justice than equity including both equality and need (1975, p. 149).

A perusal of the literature since Sampson and Deutsch indicates the value bias in social exchange. Since 1975 there has been some alteration in the course social exchange scholars have followed. Though not alone, Leventhal (1976, 1980) has led the way in theoretically extending aspects of social exchange in such a way so as to minimize the value bias. He has cast equity theory within a general allocation framework which includes other rules of allocation such as need, adhering to commitments, equality and so on. Such innovative extensions of social exchange can only serve to increase the integrative and pragmatic adequacies of this vital and exciting perspective in social psychology.

CONCLUSIONS

Some aspects of the social exchange perspective can be traced back to Aristotle. However, the overall system of social exchange as we know it had its beginnings in Homans' social exchange "manifesto" published in 1958. Homans, along with scholars such as John Thibaut, Harold Kelley, Peter Blau, Richard Emerson and others contributed to the development of the perspective during its founding years. Since the founding period, these same scholars along with others like Kenneth Gergen, Elaine Walster, G. William Walster, Karen Cook, Ronald Maris, Edward E. Sampson, Robert Burgess, Joyce Nielsen, Morton Deutsch and Melvin Lerner have altered, expanded and reformulated aspects of social exchange. The perspective has moved from a relatively simple reward-cost-outcome model with implicit assumptions of motivation to one whose complexity is substantiated by its emphases on indifference curves, negotiation, bargaining and extensions of exchange principles from dyadic relationships to macrostructures.

Early criticisms of social exchange on the grounds of its simplicity, its structural bias, and so on, are no longer valid. In their place new ones have emerged which must be given serious attention. Criticisms such as conceptual ambiguity, imprecise measurement, pragmatic inadequacy and so on, must be addressed by scholars in the field. There is little doubt that they will be, because social exchange has come a long way since its founding and present-day efforts indicate further refinements, extensions, and developments in the perspective.

BIBLIOGRAPHY

Adams, J. S. "Inequity in Social Exchange" in Leonard Berkowitz, *Advances in Experimental Psychology.* New York: Academic Press, 1965.

Adams, J. Stacy and Sara Freedman. "Equity Theory Revisited: Comments and Annotated Bibliography," in L. Berkowitz and W. Walster, eds. *Advances in Experimental Social Psychology* 9 (1976), pp. 43–90.

Bandura, Albert. *Principles of Behavior Modification.* New York: Holt, Rinehart, and Winston, 1969.

———. *Social Learning Theory.* Englewood Cliffs: Prentice-Hall, 1977.

Berkowitz, Leonard and Elaine Walster, eds. *Advances in Experimental Social Psychology* 9 (1976).

Bijou, Sidney W. "Some Clarifications on the Meaning of a Behavior Analysis of Child Development," *The Psychological Record* 29 (1979), pp. 3–13.

Blau, Peter M. *The Dynamics of Bureaucracy.* Chicago: University of Chicago Press, 1955.

———. *Exchange and Power in Social Life.* New York: John Wiley, 1964.

Boulding, Kenneth E. "An Economist's View of Homan's Social Behavior. Its Elementary Forms," *American Journal of Sociology* 67 (January 1962), pp. 458–461.

Burgess, Robert L. and Donald Bushell. *Behavioral Sociology: The Experimental Analysis of Social Process.* New York: Columbia University Press, 1969.

Burgess, Robert L. and Joyce M. Nielsen. "An Experimental Analysis of Some Structural Determinants of Equitable and Inequitable Exchange Relations," *American Sociological Review* 39 (June 1974), pp. 427–443.

Chadwick-Jones, John K. *Social Exchange Theory: Its Structure and Influence in Social Psychology.* New York: Academic Press, 1976.

Cook, Karen. "Expectations, Evaluations and Equity," *American Sociological Review* 40, (1975), pp. 372–388.

Cook, Karen and Richard M. Emerson. "Power, Equity, Commitment in Exchange Relations," *American Sociological Review* 43 (1978), pp. 721–739.

Davis, James A. "Review: Social Behavior," *American Journal of Sociology* 67 (January 1962), pp. 454–461.

Deutsch, Morton. "Homans in the Skinner Box," *Sociological Inquiry* 34 (Spring 1964), pp. 156–165.

——. "Equity, Equality, and Need: What Determines Which Value Will Be Used as the Basis of Distributive Justice," *Journal of Social Issues* 31 (November 1975), pp. 137–149.

Emerson, Richard M. "Power-Dependence Relations," *American Sociological Review* 27 (1962), pp. 31–41.

——. "Operant Psychology and Exchange Theory," in Robert Burgess and Donald Bushell, *Behavioral Sociology*. New York, Columbia University Press, 1969.

——. "Exchange Theory, Part 1: A Psychological Basis for Social Exchange," in J. Berger, M. Zelditch and B. Anderson, *Sociological Theories in Progress*. Boston: Houghton Mifflin, 1972.

Foa, Uriel G. and Edna B. Foa. *Societal Structures of the Mind*. Springfield, Ill.: Thomas Press, 1974.

Foa, Edna B. and Uriel G. Foa. "Resource Theory: Interpersonal Behavior as Exchange," in K. Gergen, M. Greenberg and R. Willis, eds. *Social Exchange: Advances in Theory and Research*. New York: Plenum Press, 1980.

Gergen, Kenneth J. *The Psychology of Behavior Exchange*. Reading, Ma.: Addison-Wesley, 1969.

——. "Social Exchange Theory in a World of Transient Fact," in R. Hamblin and J. Kunkel, *Behavioral Theory in Sociology*. New Brunswick, N. J.: Transaction Books, 1977.

Gergen, Kenneth J., Martin Greenberg and Richard Willis, eds. *Social Exchange: Advances in Theory and Research*. New York: Plenum Press, 1980.

Gibbs, Jack P. "Homans and the Methodology of Theory Construction," in R. Hamblin and J. Kunkel, *Behavioral Theory in Sociology*. New Brunswick, N.J.: Transaction Books, 1977.

Gray, Don. "Some Comments Concerning Maris on Logical Adequacy," *American Sociological Review* 36 (August 1971), pp. 706–709.

Hamblin, Robert L. and John H. Kunkel. *Behavioral Theory in Sociology*. New Brunswick, N.J.: Transaction Books, 1977.

Heath, Anthony J. "Review Article: Exchange Theory," *British Journal of Political Science* (January 1971), pp. 91–119.

Homans, George. *The Human Group*. New York: Harcourt, Brace, and World, 1950.

———. "Social Behavior as Exchange," *American Journal of Sociology* 63 (May 1958), pp. 597–606.

———. *Social Behavior: Its Elementary Forms.* New York: Harcourt, Brace, and World, 1961.

———. "Bringing Men Back In," *American Sociological Review* 31 (August 1964), pp. 809–818.

———. "The Sociological Relevance of Behaviorism," in Robert L. Burgess and Don Bushell, *Behavioral Sociology: The Experimental Analysis of Social Process.* New York: Columbia University Press, 1969.

———. *Social Behavior: Its Elementary Forms,* rev. ed. New York: Harcourt, Brace Jovanovich, 1974.

Jasso, Guillermina. "A New Theory of Distributive Justice," *American Sociological Review* 45 (February 1980), pp. 3–32.

Johnson, Weldon T. "Exchange in Perspective: The Promises of George C. Homans," in R. Hamblin and J. Kunkel, *Behavioral Theory in Sociology.* New York: Harcourt, Brace Jovanovich, 1977.

Kenrick, Douglas T., Donald Baumann and Robert B. Cialdini. "Step in the Socialization of Altruism as Hedonism: Effects of Negative Mood on Children's Generosity Under Public and Private Conditions," *Journal of Personality and Social Psychology* 5 (1979), pp. 747–753.

Kuhn, A. *The Study of Society: A Multidisciplinary Approach.* London: Tavistock, 1963.

Kunkel, John H. and Richard Nagasawa. "A Behavioral Model of Man: Propositions and Implications," *American Sociological Review* 38 (1973), pp. 540–543.

Lerner, Melvin J. "The Justice Motive in Social Behavior: Introduction," *Journal of Social Issues* 31 (1975), pp. 1–19.

Lerner, Melvin J. and G. Matthews. "Reactions to the Suffering of Others Under Conditions of Indirect Responsibility," *Journal of Personality and Social Psychology* 5 (1967), pp. 319–325.

Leventhal, Gerald S. "The Distribution of Rewards and Resources in Groups and Organizations," in L. Berkowitz and E. Walster, eds. *Advances in Experimental Social Psychology* 9 (1976), pp. 91–131.

———. "What Should Be Done With Equity Theory?" in K. Gergen, M. Greenberg and R. Willis, eds., *Social Exchange: Advances in Theory and Research.* New York: Plenum Press, 1980.

Lindesmith, Alfred R., Anselm L. Strauss, and Norman Denzin. *Social Psychology.* New York: Holt, Rinehart and Winston, 1975.

———. *Social Psychology,* 3rd ed. New York: Holt, Rinehart and Winston, 1977.

Maris, Ronald. "The Logical Adequacy of Homan's Social Theory," *American Sociological Review* 35 (December 1970), pp. 1069–1081.

Meeker, B. F. "Decision and Exchange," *American Sociological Review* 36 (June 1971), pp. 485–495.

Merton, Robert K. *Social Theory and Social Structure*. Glencoe: The Free Press, 1957.

Ofshe, R. and L. Ofshe. "Choice Behavior in Coalition Games," *Behavioral Science* 15, (1970b), pp. 337–349.

Ofshe, L. and R. Ofshe. *Utility and Choice in Social Interaction*. Englewood Cliffs: Prentice-Hall, 1970a.

Prince, Robert. "On Maris and the Logic of Time," *American Sociological Review* 36 (August 1971), pp. 711–713.

Sampson, Edward E. "On Justice as Equality," *Journal of Social Issues* 31 (1975), pp. 45–64.

Secord, Paul F. and Carl W. Backman. *Social Psychology*. New York: McGraw-Hill, 1964.

———. *Social Psychology*, 2nd ed. New York: McGraw-Hill, 1974.

Skinner, B. F. *About Behaviorism*. New York: Knopf, 1974.

Stolte, John F. and Richard M. Emerson. "Structural Inequality: Position and Power in Network Structures," in R. Hamblin and J. Kunkel, *Behavioral Theory in Sociology*. New Brunswick, N.J.: Transaction Books, 1977.

Tallman, Irving and Marilyn Ihinger-Tallman. "Values, Distributive Justice and Social Change," *American Sociological Review* 44 (April 1979), pp. 216–235.

Thibaut, John W. and Harold H. Kelly. *The Social Psychology of Groups*. New York: John Wiley, 1959.

Turner, Stephen. "The Logical Adequacy of 'The Logical Adequacy of Homan's Social Theory,'" *American Sociological Review* 36 (August 1971), pp. 709–711.

Upshaw, H. "Comparison Level as a Function of Reward-Cost Orientation," *Journal of Personality* 35 (1967), pp. 290–296.

Walster, Elaine, and G. W. Walster. "Equity and Social Justice," *Journal of Social Issues* 31 (1975), pp. 21–41.

Walster, Elaine, E. Berscheid and G. W. Walster. "New Directions in Equity Research," *Journal of Personality and Social Psychology* 25 (1973), pp. 151–176.

Weiss, R. F., W. Buchanan, L. Alstatt and J. P. Lombardo. "Altruism is Rewarding," *Science* 171 (1971), pp. 1262–1263.

THE
GESTALT
PERSPECTIVE

6

In their popular textbook, *Theories in Social Psychology,* Morton Deutsch and Robert Krauss posit two basic assumptions underlying gestalt social psychology. They are (1) perception is organized and (2) the organization is as good as stimulus conditions permit (Deutsch and Krauss, p. 16). Viewed in this manner, gestalt social psychology is conceptualized as being concerned chiefly with perception. Lundin has echoed this contention but recognizes that the gestalt perspective's emphasis on perception was an early contribution which later was extended to include the fields of learning, thinking, and memory. To this list of emphases others can be added, most notably attribution theory, which is discussed later in this chapter. For now, let us turn to some antecedents of the gestalt perspective.

BEFORE THE GESTALT PERSPECTIVE

As with the social exchange perspective, gestalt social psychology has many early contributors. Some of the more important ones frequently mentioned are Immanuel Kant, John Stuart Mill, Franz Brentano, Carl

Stumpf, Ernest Mach and Christian von Ehrenfels (Lundin, pp. 222–223). Because of Mach's and von Ehrenfels' direct influences on the development of the gestalt perspective, a brief discussion of their contributions follow.

Ernest Mach, as early as 1886, and Christian von Ehrenfels in 1890, had both spoken of *time and space forms* and demonstrated the *principle of transposition*—all major concepts in the gestalt perspective. Time and space forms were added to the summation of sensations which were thought to be the basis for all science. The principle of transposition was said to be exemplified by a melody retaining its structural recognition even though its keys and notes are changing. In a similar manner a circle was said to retain its structure regardless of size or color. Red, blue or green, large, medium, or small, a circle, in structure, is a circle.

Both Mach and Ehrenfels were members of the Austrian gestalt school and limited their study to perceptual organization. They, along with other members of the school, assumed that *perception was some function of processes operating within the central nervous system to combine numerous separate sensations into a meaningful whole (experience)*. Some feel that it was this conception of perception and the relatively narrow range of study in Austrian gestalt psychology that led to the gradual decline of the Austrian gestalt school and the emergence of the German gestalt perspective, hereafter called the "gestalt perspective."

THE FOUNDING OF THE GESTALT PERSPECTIVE

The gestalt perspective was founded on the postulate that *sensation and perception are indistinguishable*. This means that meaningful (organized) experiences occur automatically as a result of the functioning of the sensory areas of the brain (Neel, p. 273). Therefore, the idea of individual sensation being combined into a meaningful whole was rejected by adherents of the gestalt movement which started at Frankfort and Berlin and expanded to the United States. The person most responsible for the movement was Max Wertheimer (1880–1943), although Wolfgang Kohler (1887–1967) and Kurt Koffka (1886–1941) have been labelled cofounders of the German gestalt movement because of their roles as subjects in Wertheimer's initial experiment (Lundin, p. 222).

Max Wertheimer as the Founder

Wertheimer's initial observation, one that spearheaded the gestalt perspective, supported what was to become a central idea in the perspective, that perception of the world and actual occurrences in the world may not be coterminous. The experimental results were called the *phi phenomenon*.

Using a tachistoscope to present a succession of visual stimuli for varying lengths of time, Wertheimer conducted a landmark experiment. This involved alternate presentation of two vertical lines on the right and left side of the face of the tachistoscope (Lundin, p. 223). The finding was startling: variations in the interval of time between presentations of the alternative stimuli caused variations in what was perceived by the subjects. "If the interval of time between exposures was as long as one second Wertheimer's subjects saw first one still line on the right." Decreasing the interval of time between exposures, Wertheimer found that his subjects perceived movement from position to position. "At one-fifteenth of a second, the subjects saw not two lines but a single line appearing to move across the screen from left to right" (Lundin, p. 223). Shorter intervals produced no movements as perceived by the subjects.

Lundin has reported that several explanations had previously been suggested to the illusion of apparent movement. One explanation was that movement of the eyes accounted for the illusion, but this had to be rejected when the experiment was varied to include presentation of "a vertical line followed by horizontal lines both at the right and left of the middle vertical" (Lundin, p. 223). This variation produced movement in both directions—left and right simultaneously. Thus, the phi phenomenon was born, and so was the gestalt perspective when Wertheimer interpreted his findings. The experiments were published in 1912.

Gestalt Psychology as Protest

When a novel perspective emerges on the academic scene it is usually the result of multiple factors and influences. Some of these are positive and contributory; others are negative and represent disenchantment with existing or newly emerging perspectives. The latter factors are also contributory in the sense that they, too, help to define the parameters of the emerging perspective which in this case is the gestalt perspective. Some of these factors are discussed below.

The Gestaltists' Disenchantment with Introspection   Kohler states in *Gestalt Psychology* that sudden interests in irregular phenomena often spawn new eras in science and that these irregularities often become essential topics of scientific investigations. He goes on to say that introspection inhibits scientific revolution because it discards particularly interesting observations (Kohler, p. 67). More specifically, introspection is seen as a procedure used to separate acquired knowledge from pure or raw sensations. That is, the procedure focuses only on actual sensations. The introspectionist contends that books, desks, dogs, etc. cannot be observed since these items suggest knowledge about certain classes of objects to which they belong, the use of these objects and so forth. From the introspective point of view, "pure seeing" had nothing to do with such knowledge (p. 69).

The introspectionist, according to Kohler, separates all of these acquired meanings from the *seen* material which consists of simple sensations. The sensations are the basic units of cognition which should be of concern. Interestingly, however, this means that objects do not exist among sensory data since objects exist only when sensory data have become thoroughly imbued with meaning. If the introspectionist is correct, "direct experience" consists only of "feeling" sensations. Yet, what criteria are used to determine which experiences are genuine sensory facts and which experiences are to be discarded?

All past learning is effective in present situations only to the degree to which past learning can be recalled. According to the introspectionist point of view, learning often results in a kind of illusion, in a deception about the nature of given physical conditions. Learning creates constancies which are absent except in our perceptions. Demonstrations involving experiments of observations through holes in a screen show pure sensory facts. Yet what happens is that constancies are destroyed by introspection. The precise factors which would otherwise cause recall are excluded in experiments of this kind. To illustrate this point; it is indeed possible that one would not be able to perceive a picture of oneself if one viewed a one-inch portion of one's body through a hole in a screen! Perhaps it should be mentioned at this point that there very well may be a difference between pure sensory experience (unlearned) and phases of experience which are products of learning. The important thing here, however, is that millions of people never transform the objects of their environments into true sensations. Therefore, the pragmatism of transformation is questionable. It seems instead that persons react to objects on the *basis of the meanings that objects have for them.*

While gestalt psychologists were not enamored with introspection because of these reasons, they were not very enthusiastic with another emerging perspective of that era either—behaviorism. Gestaltists did agree with behaviorists, however, on a number of points of criticism about introspection.

They felt that introspection lacked the methodological virtue of the observer outside the system being observed (Kohler, p. 11). Being outside of the system under investigation was deemed important, in order not to create artificial relationships which were simply a result of the investigation itself. As Kohler puts it, introspection and its objects were felt by behaviorists to be facts within the same system and the chances that the former leaves the latter undisturbed are exceedingly small. Quite obviously this criticism is directed toward the question of whether it is possible for social scientists to be objective in their research if they are immersed in the phenomena under investigation. For instance, can black social psychologists engage in objective studies of race relations? Is it possible for women social psychologists to objectively study social psychological effects of the women's movement if they endorse the women's movement?

A second criticism levied by behaviorists and endorsed by gestaltists is the kind faced by present-day symbolic interactionists, ethnomethodologists and phenomenologists. The criticism was that a common science is impossible if everyone has his or her own direct experience with no commonalities. Introspection seems to be subjectivity in an extreme form since it is implicitly assumed that one is forever excluded from the direct experience of others (Kohler, p. 14). This means that no matter how hard a researcher attempts to study some social psychological phenomenon through introspection, he or she will end up with subjective views of the phenomenon.

The third criticism of introspection made by behaviorists was that *introspection is closely connected with a philosophical bias.* They felt that "direct experience" appeared to be related to such terms as mind and soul—phenomena which could not be directly observed. If the phenomena could not be directly observed, it was questionable that they existed. In fact, many behaviorists saw introspection as a mere defense of unenlightenment (Kohler, p. 10).

Proponents of the gestalt perspective agreed with behaviorists' criticisms of introspection, but they did not agree with the alternative offered by behaviorism.

The Gestaltists' Disenchantment with Behaviorism   Several gestalt psychologists including Kohler, Koffka and Wertheimer contended that behaviorists failed to include a crucial variable, which intervened between stimuli and responses, simply because they could not find a scientific way to investigate the phenomenon (Neel, p. 274). The phenomenon in question was the organism's *perceptual organization.* Thus, while Watsonian behaviorists during that time were proposing an

S-R sequence, gestaltists posited an S-O-R sequence—stimuli-organ-ism's perceptual organization-response (determined by perception).

Behaviorists were also criticized for accepting Thorndike's concept of trial-and-error learning. Gestalt psychologists made this response: *errors do not occur accidentally, but rather are the result of the organism's perception of the field in which it operates.* This means that behavior is always appropriate to the perceived field. Thus a child, in attempting to learn a particular game, does so not through successive trial-and-error methods but because his or her perceptual organization facilitates "appropriate" responses. Gestaltists were convinced that learning was insight-based. Such phenomena as association, habit and recall were "not the facts by which the course of mental life was principally deter-mined (since) learning involved recognition of understandable relation-ships" (Kohler, p. 326).

From the gestalt point of view, Thorndike's concept of trial-and-error learning stated that learning occurred between pleasure and its sensory bias and involved experienced causal relations. As Kohler sug-gested, when one is thirsty one is inclined to think of a refreshing drink. Certainly recall plays a role in this process but the main question was thought to be whether *thinking* of the drink and the person's thirst were causally related (Kohler, p. 336).

THE STRUCTURE OF EARLY GESTALT THOUGHT

Max Wertheimer founded gestalt psychology in 1912 but Kurt Koffka and Wolfgang Kohler contributed immensely to its development dur-ing the formative years (Watson, p. 472). In this section, the basic con-cepts proposed by these scholars are considered, after which assump-tions underlying the gestalt perspective and their application to social psychological phenomena are discussed.

Basic Concepts in Early Gestalt Psychology

The very nature of the gestalt social psychological perspective makes it difficult to delineate basic concepts. This is due to the tautological characteristics of the perspective itself. For example, the concept "gestalt," as later discussed, signifies "form," "shape," "structure," and "organization" among other meanings. Additionally, there often appears to be little, if any, difference between "terms" and "propositions." An instance of this occurs in Wertheimer's and Koffka's definition of the concept "pragnanz." Wertheimer defined pragnanz as "organization in its most typical form and toward which structures tend" (Sahakian). But if gestalt means "organization," "form" and "structure," then pragnanz means *gestalt in its most* typical gestalt and toward which gestalt tends! Neglecting the obvious tautology for a moment, is the meaning of pragnanz a "nominal definition" or a "proposition" in gestalt social psychology? The question is difficult to answer and may be inappropriate if the intent of the gestalt founders was "holism." This means that the tautology may have been intentional, as suggested by the blurred lines of distinction between concepts, postulates and theorems. Early proponents of the gestalt perspective may have wanted us to view the perspective as "more than the sum of its parts." From their perspective this could only be accomplished if we view how the "whole" (perspective) affects the "parts" (concepts, postulates, etc.).

While this pedagogical approach may be appropriate from a gestalt point of view, it may not be desirable for those introduced to the gestalt perspective for the first time. Indeed, such an approach could be confusing and result in charges of lack of clarity, redundancy, tautology and "double-talk." For this reason, it is deemed desirable in this volume to break down the gestalt approach into its component parts. While undoubtedly something will be lost, since the perspective should be viewed as a gestalt, the advantage of comprehension offsets the loss.

The first concept to be discussed is gestalt. Gestalt refers to a *quality* that is present in a whole but not present in any component of the whole. Take five persons, for example, with specified role relationships: one adult male, one adult female and three children. Dependent upon how the collection of persons and their roles are arranged, we may have a family of five, or two broken families with children, two single adults and three children, etc. In other words, we may arrange the parts in different ways and get different wholes which possess different qualities (Woodworth). The concept of family is not implicit in any of the persons taken separately but only in the coherent functional whole. As Koffka suggested in the *Encyclopedia of the Social Sciences* (1931, p. 654), to understand this hypothetical family as well as the individuals within this family, we must use laws of behavior related to families rather than laws related to individuals.

Another concept important in the development of the gestalt perspective has been the term isomorphism. Isomorphism was defined by Kohler as *the thesis that our experience and the processes which underlie* these experiences have the same structure (p. 201). These processes underlying the experiences are cerebral process brain functions which tend toward organization in the same way as do our experiences. Thus events in our experiences are projected upon the brain. Such events are not reproduced point by point, but rather as a representative of the experiences, in the same way that a map is a representative of a geographical territory. This is obviously related to the proposition in gestalt psychology that "perception is organized"—in fact, the concept is similar to map-making. Perception is an indistinguishable aspect of sensation, and occurs as experiences first enter the nervous system (Neel, p. 281).

A third key concept in early gestalt psychology is pragnanz. It should be pointed out here that pragnanz will be treated as a *concept* in gestalt social psychology. It refers to *perception of a pattern of stimuli in such a way as to make the best pattern possible* (Neel, p. 279). This concept is explored in greater detail later in the section on propositions.

"Perceptual grouping" is a fourth concept in early gestalt thought, deemed of vital importance in the perspective. The term refers to *what will be seen as occurring (grouped) together or organized in the perceptual field.* From this concept, gestaltists posited the existence of numerous relationships related to perception, based on similarity, contiguity, proximity, common fate, group boundaries and good form among others. Some of these relationships are discussed in succeeding sections of this chapter.

The fifth concept discussed here is organization. While "gestalt" means "organization," it also seems to mean other things. Woodworth initially suggested two definitions of organization: "organization at a sensory level occurs whenever shapes and patterns are heard or seen, while organization at a higher level, more dependent on the use of past experiences, takes place when figures are named and objects recognized" (p. 127). He classified Wertheimer's factors of organization as peripheral factors, central factors and reinforcing factors. *Peripheral factors* included the organizing factors of proximity, continuity, similarity and closed figure; *central factors* originate in the individual and are imposed on the stimuli; and *reinforcing factors* include the factors of good figure and pregnance. Woodworth observes:

> If, while you are looking at a mass of dots and lines, some figure begins to emerge that is simple, symmetrical, like an object, or definite in any way, your natural reaction is to emphasize that figure and bring it out as fully as possible (p. 131).

There were, certainly, additional terms and concepts used in early gestalt psychology. However those mentioned here are the essential ones.

Assumptions and Propositions in Early Gestalt Psychology

As stated earlier, two basic assumptions listed by Deutsch and Krauss were (1) that perception is organized and (2) that the organization tends to be as good as the stimulus conditions permit. While the two notions undoubtedly are major ideas in gestalt social psychology, they can hardly be thought of as encompassing most of the ideas characterizing the gestalt system. In this section, an attempt is made to delineate additional key assumptions believed to be crucial underlying ideas. It should be mentioned, however, that careful reading of gestalt materials may reveal additional assumptions not included in the coverage here. Many of the assumptions listed and discussed below are paraphrasings of excerpts taken from Max Wertheimer's address before the Kant Society in Berlin in December 1924. Wertheimer's address is deemed important because during the speech he attempted to answer two very important questions: What is gestalt psychology? and What does gestalt psychology intend?

In answering these questions Wertheimer argued that in attempting to understand the essentials of living, we often move from the world of everyday events to the world of science hoping that in this world greater understanding will be gained, and yet, while "one may have learned a great deal, one is poorer than before" (Ellis, p. 1). Certainly there often has been a systematic collection of data, but just as often we have failed to include those phenomena directly related to living—that which is most vivid and real in living has eluded us. For example, what processes take place when the criminal suddenly "sees" the error of his or her ways? When you suddenly see the answer to a problem you have been working on? Wertheimer felt that while we may be told that the above experiences are intuitions, talents, judgments, creative fantasy and the like, these are little more than names for the experiences. They are not penetrating answers (Ellis, p. 1).

An essential element of the problem of providing penetrating answers to dilemmas of mental and social life seems to lie in the application of modern science to life in general, according to Wertheimer. In attempting to solve the problem, efforts range from distinguishing between sciences and life (there are regions of life inaccessible to science) to suggestions that the "scientific method" (with its procedures, fundamental assumptions and emphasis on exactness and precision) has no place in the study of mental life. Wertheimer suggested an examination of the fundamental assumptions of science. He was aware of the fact that there were threads of commonality which seemed to run throughout hosts of research investigations suggesting a specific direction for science and its methods; however, he also felt that science encompassed methodologies that perhaps were concealed by the dominant ones (Ellis, p. 2). In other words, the reason why we often fail to provide adequate answers to essential questions about life may be *the (traditional) techniques used in efforts to provide those answers.*

Wertheimer resolved that gestalt psychology would be dissatisfied with inadequate solutions to the dilemmas of life. For him gestalt psychology was dedicated to penetrating the problems associated with providing answers to the dilemmas of mental and social life "by examining the fundamental assumptions of science." This means, then, that the gestalt perspective is not only a theoretical framework but is also a research framework—not only an end but a means to an end.

Basic Assumptions in Early Gestalt Thought   The orientation of early gestalt psychology can be recognized throughout the previous discussion. The orientation departed significantly from scientific problem-solving in the European scientific tradition of the late nineteenth and early twentieth centuries, which emphasized (1) isolating elements within wholes, (2) discovering their locus, and (3) reassembling the isolated elements. Wertheimer and other early gestaltists ushered in an orientation which emphasized a holistic approach to scientific problem solving. Their alternative is best expressed as follows:

1. There exist in social and mental life "whole" phenomena.
2. The nature of these phenomena cannot be deduced from an examination of the elements in isolation from each other.
3. There are relations between elements in whole phenomena.
4. The relations between these elements are themselves a function of the intrinsic character of the whole.
5. Understanding the nature of the elements as well as the relations between elements is dependent upon their dynamic functional relationship to the whole.
6. Understanding any element of a whole is dependent upon understanding that element's dynamic function relative to the whole.

Wertheimer, Kohler and Koffka reflected this alternative to the traditional European scientific approach in their works and advancements of gestalt ideas. Moreover, additional assumptions emerged from their interpretations of numerous experimental findings. These additional assumptions are as follows:

7. Psychological structures constitute wholes.
8. Psychological structures tend toward organizations.
9. Psychological organization is as good as prevailing conditions allow.
10. There exists within the nervous system a field of forces which must be held in equilibrium.
11. There is spontaneous organized grouping in the sensory field determined by primary sensory organizations.
12. Behavior is governed by a field of interacting forces organized into dynamic patterns.

The first six assumptions relate directly to the mode of analysis used in gestalt psychology, while the latter six have something to say about the phenomena to be investigated. For example, assumption 7 could be considered a definition because it defines psychological structures as wholes. Yet, it is considered here as a *basic underlying assumption* because the German concept "gestalt" originally signified "form," "shape," "configuration." Wertheimer and his associates added the concepts "structure" and "whole." Certainly there is a difference between "form," "shape," "configuration," and "whole." Moreover, when "organization" is added as a characteristic of gestalt the meaning of gestalt again becomes propositional in nature. What this means simply is that inherent in the concept gestalt are crucial assumptions which form part of the basis for the gestalt perspective. The same is true for assumption 8. Organization seems to occur when "configurations have obtained maximum balance so that no further improvement would be obtained by any local change." (Sahakian, p. 205). Certainly "whole," "organization," "shape," "form," and "configuration," have different meanings, yet gestalt implies all four concepts (Neel, p. 204). Because of this ambiguity, many of the characteristics of gestalt are regarded as assumptions of gestalt. Wertheimer himself defined "organization" as "toward which structures tend" (Sahakian, p. 205). Deutsch and Krauss (pp. 15–16) imply that perception has certain properties as a system (structure?) and that perception is organized. Others such as Neel, Ellis and Sahakian have not mentioned the problem. Indeed, what has been suggested here as a problem may, in fact, be an example of gestalt psychology at its best if gestalt constitutes "whole," "form," "shape," "configuration," "structure," and "organization." This may mean that it becomes necessary to posit the basic assumption that gestalt (the whole) is *highly correlated with organization*. Perhaps this is what is meant by the statement that perception tends toward, rather than is, organization.

Assumption 9 is derived from Koffka's *Principles of Gestalt Psychology* (p. 110). Taking his cue from Wertheimer's *Law of Pragnanz*, Koffka implies that psychological organization tends toward good form and that good form is motivational in character. Because organization tends toward "good form," if conditions are favorable, then, psychological organization will be articulate, consistent and closed.

Assumption 10 suggests that the nervous system of the organism conforms to the same locus as the person's psychological experience. That is, there are fields of forces within the nervous system which must be held in equilibrium. These neural processes, which presumably conform to principles or organization, are presumed to be operating when "closed" perception takes place in a field where the original stimuli are imperfect or vague. Forces within the brain are thought to close the gap in the field caused by imperfect stimuli and result in "complete" perception.

The eleventh assumption inherent in gestalt social psychology is that there is spontaneous grouping in the sensory field caused by primary sensory organization. As will be recalled, the assumption of primary sensory organization distinguished the German and Austrian gestalt schools. While, according to the assumption of primary sensory organization, stimuli may be raw and unorganized as they initially project on the brain, the sensory organ automatically patterns them. This, of course, is due to the "organized character" of the neural processes within the brain.

The twelfth basic assumption underlying gestalt social psychology to be listed here is that behavior is governed by a field of interacting forces organized into dynamic patterns. These forces are thought to be of two types, *psychological* and *physical*. Psychological forces are basic units of analysis for social and behavioral scientists in that these forces have their genesis in the broad aspects of experience and behavior. But what is the nature of this field of interacting forces? The gestaltists felt that these interacting forces had two sources; response salience (the existing stimulus field) and response dispositions (representation of past experiences including "memories, desires, fantasies and plans for the future." It was the interaction, then, between response salience and response disposition forces that govern behavior.

Propositions in Early Gestalt Psychology   As a theoretical perspective, gestalt psychology was developed inductively. That is, the orientation emerged from interpretations of experiments on perceptual processes. It is of interest to note that prior to Wertheimer's initial experiments leading to the discovery of the phi phenomenon, he had shown how the association test could be used to discover a person's hidden knowledge; Koffka had conducted research on imagery and thought; and Kohler's work had been in the area of hearing (Woodworth, 1948, p. 121). While the three scholars had researched different sensory variables, they had in common a desire to understand and study the meaningful experiences of human beings. They also had in common a belief that the dynamics of behavior were more clearly revealed in direct experience than in external observations and in examining parts by beginning with wholes and working downward. To reiterate, these assumptions greatly influenced the basic assumptions of the gestalt perspective.

Because the gestalt perspective was developed primarily from the study of perceptual processes, most of the propositions listed and discussed here are related to perception but could apply to other experience and behavior. From Deutsch and Krauss, five major propositions about perception may be identified. They are as follows:

1. Perception is organized.
2. The organization tends to be as good as stimulus conditions permit.
3. If perceptions are organized, then some aspects of perception will remain constant despite a change in all of the elements being perceived as long as the interrelations among the elements remain the same.
4. If perceptions are organized, then the perception of any element will be influenced by the total field of which it is a part.
5. If perception is organized—this will be the interrelation of the entities being perceived rather than the entities themselves. (Deutsch and Krauss, pp. 16–17).

Regarding propositions 1 and 2, we immediately see that perception is viewed as structure and in holistic terms. If this is the case, then it is axiomatic that the first two perception propositions would be stated as aforementioned.

Proposition 3 is actually a version of Kohler's experiment developed in 1918. In what has been called a crucial experiment in gestalt social psychology, Kohler attempted to demonstrate that learning was a function of having gained insight into the relationship among stimuli rather than reinforcement of a particular response. Kohler's method of investigation was referred to as the *transposition experiment.*

By means of differential reinforcement, the subject in Kohler's experiment learned to discriminate between two shades of gray—one lighter than the other. Response to the darker shade of gray was reinforced with food while response to the lighter shade was not. As expected, the subject increased approach responses toward the darker shade of gray. Once discrimination was established, an even lighter shade of gray was introduced and the darker of the two previous shades of gray taken away. The subjects then approached the very same shade of gray they had previously been avoiding because it was not the darker shade. This presumably indicated that the subject had learned patterns of relationships among stimuli rather than specific responses to specified reinforced stimuli (Neel, p. 277). It should be apparent that proposition 3 is related to basic assumptions 2 through 4.

Propositions 4 and 5 are related directly to the fifth and sixth assumptions stated earlier and need no further explication.

Additional gestalt propositions related to perception have been discussed by Neel, Sahakian, Shaw and Costanzo, Ellis (1955) and Woodworth (1948). Some of these propositions are discussed below.

Proposition 6. *Perception is organized in such a way that certain aspects of the field will stand out as figures against the background formed by the rest of the field.* Neel reports that the gestaltists posited the figure-ground relationship as given. Her interpretation, however, is that figure was whatever was important at a given time. This interpretation seems reasonable if indeed perception tends toward organization (assumption 8). For example, if one is shown a picture of a college campus, it is quite likely that the spaces between the buildings (background) will not be noticed unless one is asked to judge the distance between the buildings. At this point, there may occur figure-ground reversal where the spaces between the buildings become salient (figure) instead of the buildings (which now become background). The ability of the human organism to organize in this fashion cannot be overemphasized. One has only to imagine the chaos in perception that would occur if the organism had to consider both figure and ground simultaneously without organization. Perhaps the result would be nonperception.

Proposition 7. *Items will be perceived together if they are similar in some way to each other.* This is related to the gestalt assumption of "spontaneous organized grouping" and "tendency toward organization." Thus, explanations often given for "grouping" males, females, whites, blacks, etc., may center around a "natural tendency" given an identification-oriented socialization about these aggregates of people.

Often, present-day explanations given for tendencies to "group" in this manner include feminist orientation, male chauvinism, black racism and white racism. Yet, it is entirely plausible that none of these appellations are appropriate since inherent in their meanings are intentional derogatory prejudgments. If the gestalt law of similarity holds, apologies should perhaps be extended.

Admittedly, such a view does not suggest why sex and race are seen as relevant characteristics for similarity to be based upon while other characteristics seem to be less relevant. It is the case, however, that more than a few persons in our society frequently "group" redheads, group blonde persons with blue eyes, group persons with full lips, etc. It is contended here that more characteristics than we ordinarily think about are used by persons to base similarity upon.

Proposition 8. *Perceptual grouping occurs if items are in proximity to each other.* The "grouping" assumption (assumption 11) is also apparent here. The old adages "you can tell a man by the company he keeps" and "birds of a feather flock together" are appropriate here. Aside from these, however, there is the difficulty that many have had understanding how persons of the same ethnic or racial background can cast aspersions on their own who reside in certain neighborhoods. For example, middle and upper class blacks and whites often can be overheard "grouping" all individuals in a certain section of a city despite the ethnic and racial mix of the section. The law of perceptual proximity would seem to be operating here.

Proposition 9. *Perception tends toward good form.* This proposition is known as *pragnanz* and also as the *law of good figure.* It is related directly to the tenth assumption listed earlier. "Good form" was defined by Wertheimer as the organization and patterning toward which structures maximal simplicity and balance. According to Sahakian (p. 205) good form is motivational, and this has implications not only for perception, but also for human behavior.

For example, the law of pragnanz has been interpreted to mean that one perceives a pattern in such a way as to make it the best pattern possible (Neel, 179). This certainly has implications for tendencies on the parts of individuals in human relationships to perceive their relationships as the *best* ones (for example, parent-child relationship, marital relationships, lover relationships, friendships), and maybe even act accordingly. That is, until they are shown in some way that their relationships are *not* the best.

Proposition 10. *Perceptions, thoughts, actions and memories tend toward closure.* The relationship between propositions 9 and 10 should be apparent. However, most writers have felt that the closure principle is important enough to warrant independent treatment. *Closure* is exemplified when we perceptually complete advertisement figures in newspapers—recognizing a "complete" male or female figure even though the figure depicted may be minus legs or parts of arms, etc. Closure in thinking and memory is thought to be manifested when stimuli are altered or remembered in ways in which *they were supposed to be* rather than in the way that *they actually appear*. With respect to closure of actions, Zeigarnik discovered in 1927 that when persons were interrupted prior to task completion they invariably would resume the task in preference to any other activity (Zeigarnik). In other words there is a tendency toward closure in behavior. A final proposition to be discussed relates to assumption 12 and concerns behavior. While this by no means exhausts the lower order principles of gestalt psychology—it does indicate the kinds of problems and issues that were thought to be important by early gestalt social psychologists.

Proposition 11. *Behavior is a function of the existing stimulus field.* As pointed out earlier, Koffka was convinced that the person operates within a psychophysical field and that the subject matter for the social and behavioral sciences is the person's perception of the existing field. The existing stimulus field consists of a person's *perception of the present field* and *representations of the past* such as memories, desires, fantasies, etc. It was the interaction between the past, present and future forces within the field that determined behavior.

Having considered some of the *basic tenets* in the gestalt perspective proposed by its founders, attention will now be directed to several additional contributions by them on social psychological topics.

OTHER FOUNDING CONTRIBUTIONS

Gestalt social psychology in America has focused heavily on perceptual processes. However, it is important to point out that the founding fathers considered their new approach much more general in the sense that it could be applied to a wide variety of phenomena. Koffka gives one of the more concise discussions of *socialization* from a gestalt perspective.

Socialization in Early Gestalt Psychology

Rejecting Thorndike's learning principles as well as other learning and behavioral theories of that era, Koffka attempted to develop a theory of *learning as process*. This attempt was made by asking the basic question "when in learning activities does learning take place?" In order to answer this question, Koffka chose cases where learning occurred without the intention to learn. Such cases, according to Koffka might include situations where animals run for food or to escape punishment; where humans improve their abilities to walk on slippery streets; where infants acquire a language; and, where adults learn the lesson of social experiences (p. 534). Koffka felt that repetition may have two functions; (1) it gives a number of opportunities for process A to occur (repetition has no effects on later performances unless process A occurs): and (2) once process A has occurred, each repetition will add to the aggregated trace system and thoroughly exert an influence on later performances. Succinctly then, learning involves three elements: (1) the arousal of a specific process; (2) the trace of this process; and (3) the effect of this trace on later processes (p. 541). For Koffka, learning is "the modification of an accomplishment in a certain direction" and consisted of creating traces of a particular kind, consolidating the traces and making them more and more available both in repetitive and in new situations.

Koffka contended that any activity might be called a learning activity if the organism does not return completely to its old state after a process has occurred in the organism's psychophysical field (p. 535). We know this to be the case, said Koffka, because the organism cannot return to its old state due to the fact that the process itself effects a permanent change—it leaves a trace. This means that even the first performance of an activity is a learning process in that behavior is modified and the organism changed. This change modifies later processes.

In his discussion of learning, Koffka criticized definitions of learning as *accomplishment*. For him, one may in fact learn *bad* habits as well as good ones. Moreover, repetition may or may not lead to improved performances (accomplishment). Improved performance is some function of the trace effect of practice. For example, practice, in and of itself, may result in no gain in typing ability for a child who plays with a typewriter before he or she can read or write. On the other hand, a child who can read and write may very well increase his or her typing ability through practice. What one sees here is that the processes producing the traces are different in the two activities *and* the accomplishments are different.

With respect to the latter case, Koffka would submit that typing as a process involves more than merely the action of pounding the keyboard; it involves hitting the keyboard in a mechanically stable way involving definite relationships between keys (totally absent in the former example). Thus, the traces from this process are left behind to influence later performance which causes the occurrence of a new process. According to Koffka:

Generally speaking, if an accomplishment X involves the aspects A, B, C. . ., then improvement can occur only in those aspects which were, in however low a degree, also represented in the process and were thereby left in the trace system. Since energy accomplishment is of this type, repetition can lead to improvement only to the extent to which the partial aspects are present in performers (pp. 537–538).

Group Formation in Early Gestalt Psychology

Early gestalt theorists conceived of two kinds of groups—sociological groups and psychological ones. Sociological groups designated any collection of individuals that had an existence in the sense in which a gestalt has existence. For Koffka, the term sociological group could be used interchangeably with the concept geographical group. In addition to a simple collection of persons, however, Koffka added the idea of gestalt.

According to the gestaltists, sociological groups have definite characteristics which are gestalt in nature. Koffka discussed two gestalt characteristics of sociological groups; (1) the strength of the gestalt, and (2) the composition of the group. The strength of the gestalt character of the group was defined in terms of *the degree of interdependence of the parts.* "The stronger the gestalt, the more will each of its parts depend on all the others, and the wider dependence affects every aspect of the parts" (p. 650). A second characteristic is related to the composition of the group. The sociological group is composed of individuals, and while the existence of individuals may be somewhat group-determined, it is not exclusively so. Social factors enter in, but Koffka was convinced that there remains an element that is *not* social. Individuals are different from each other apart from social influence and since the *individuals* making up the group *determine* the group's nature, there remains a nonsocial *element in groups.* In a very strong gestalt parts do not exist prior to wholes. In sociological groups, the members of groups are not completely determined by the group (individuals exist prior to groups) and thus, the sociological group is not the strongest gestalt type possible.

What happens when persons experience themselves as parts of groups as exemplified in the statement "we do this?" Here we are concerned with the existence of what Koffka calls the psychological group. The statement "we do this" means that each person does not do something for him or herself independently but that the activity is done jointly. The word "we" refers to a reality that is more than they + "I". What is the relationship? A sociological group is dependent upon a psychological group. The behaviors of persons in a sociological group depend upon the behaviors of others. "We" experiences are not the only experiences necessary for group formation but they are necessary. Mere presence of others will not lead to social behavior. Interestingly, the gestalt interpretation of group formation ends here.

Social Influence in Early Gestalt Psychology

From a gestalt perspective, social influence is a function of Wertheimer's main contention "that humans desire to think clearly and are able to do so" (Woodworth, p. 151). "There is a tendency to structural clarity, surveyability, to truth as against petty views" (p. 199). What this means is that an *element of motivation* is inherent in gestalt psychology although it was not brought to full fruition until Kurt Lewin's field theory. However Wertheimer's initial discussion of "good form," "organizations," etc., seems to be the basis for much of the literature on social influence, especially in those instances where the group exerts influence on the individual.

   While Koffka was not convinced that the individual was so completely interdependent with others, social psychologists like Arthur Cohen seem to be more certain of the interdependence—so certain in fact that he feels it almost automatic that influencing an individual would be greatly enhanced when a person's stable relationship with a group was disrupted. It seems that because the individual acts as a "group member" rather than in terms of his or her personal preferences implies that the group has a powerful influence over the individual. Because the group provides support for an individual's beliefs, attitudes and values, in order for the person to validate or make sense out of or have good form, group influence is significant. How will the individual in a group perceive the stimulus field? Does the group affect his or her judgment? What is the result of a need for the individual to root his or her perceptions is social reality? This social reality could be best exemplified when there is a validation of one's ideas, opinions, etc. It is at this point that attitude change explanations are proposed by gestaltists. The group, because of the high dependency of members on each other in terms of affection, emotion, and companionship, acts as a validating agent for the individual and gives the individual support for his or her social reality.

Attitude Formation and Change
in Early Gestalt Psychology

Attitude, as defined by Koffka, refers to actual forces that exist between the field and the ego (p. 395). It is "like an expectation of something more or less definite," for example, being curious, suspicious, etc. Koffka felt that the degree to which these attitudes reveal themselves in consciousness was variable. Nevertheless, attitudes were felt to influence the organism's organization of the environmental field in perception. Quite simply, the gestalt position is that attitudes can and do influence perception. They do so by emphasizing some of the contents of the field while suppressing others (Kohler, p. 169). Kohler has said:

> As a matter of sheer observation, I can by introspection, transform the white in the shadow and the black in full light into two similar groups. There can hardly be a more radical influence of attitude upon sensory experience than this transformation. (p. 117)

Attitude formation and change have not been major topics of investigation for gestaltists as they have been for field theorists. Nevertheless, attitude formation seemingly is some consequence of the individual's need to organize his or her perceptions. The precise processes inherent in attitude formation could be thought of as a function of group processes. In 1935 Sherif designed a classic experiment, asking the questions "How will the individual in a group perceive the stimulus field?" "Will the group affect his (her) judgments? and, will he (she) carry these effects over into a situation in which he or she subsequently faces the stimulus without others around him or her?" Sherif's techniques and findings are discussed in the next section.

CONTRIBUTORS TO THE GESTALT
PERSPECTIVE AFTER ITS FOUNDING

The founding of the German gestalt perspective led to hundreds of experiments and a considerable amount of theoretical work. With the migration of many gestalt psychologists to the United States due to the rise of Hitler (Koffka in 1927, Wertheimer in 1933, and Kohler in 1935), the perspective began to have a more pronounced impact on psychology as a discipline. American psychology was influenced by gestalt psychology despite its mixed reception in the United States. Watson has said that there were American psychologists of that era sympathetic to gestalt psychology but rarely did they become total adherents (p. 483). Some felt that it was little more than a theory of perception while others felt that the basic assumption that "mental life is organized" should be a testable proposition rather than a "given."

Despite these criticisms, as well as charges of empirical inadequacy, operational inadequacy, lack of experimental control and anti-quantification charges, gestalt theory influenced American psychology. Lundin feels that renewed interest in cognitive psychology, adherence to holistic analyses and emphases on organizing principles in psychology can all be attributed to the influence of the gestalt perspective. In this section, contributions to the gestalt perspective of several prominent scholars are discussed and the gestalt perspective's influence in social psychology should become even more apparent.

Muzafer Sherif

While the gestalt perspective has been linked historically with perception, it has influenced thinking on a variety of topics (Kanizsa, pp. 56–57). This is to be expected since one of its basic tenets is that psychological phenomena are organized and there are psychological phenomena apart from perception. The publication of Muzafer Sherif's *The Psychology of Social Norms* in 1936 is an example of the eclecticism of the gestalt approach. Sherif's volume (republished in 1963) emphasized, among other things, that individuals in social interaction become more than a collection of separate persons—they become an organized whole. Sherif stated: "the pattern of the social situation creates a psychological atmosphere that is not inherent in its discrete parts" (p. 83). Sherif's contention was that social norms emerge in ambiguous situations and have an "organizing effect" on individuals within those situations even after they have left the situations.

Using the autokinetic effect, which inhibits the localization of light because of the absence of a reference point (the effect is produced when a small beam of light is directed across a dark room), Sherif conducted experiments on norm formation. He tested subjects under isolated conditions and in pairs. The experiment was simple: subjects were taken into a room, seated at a small table and asked to judge the distance the small beam of light appeared to move in the completely dark room. Approximately one hundred judgments were given by each subject and expressed in inches and fractions of inches. Initially, there were wide ranges of variations in judgments. As more judgments were given, however, variability in judgments decreased. Subjects were also reported to have established varied ranges of judged movement. Gradually, however, subjects tended toward organization in their perceptions of light movement. When subjects were placed in two- or three-person groups, their previous personal ranges of movement were altered and there appeared gradual movement of all subjects toward a norm. When subjects experienced first the autokinetic effect in groups, norm convergence was found to be quicker and even retained when the subjects were later tested alone. Further experimenting, according to Sherif, revealed that confederate subjects (those asked to make all judgments within a particular range) influenced the judgments of naive subjects both when they were together and when the naive subject was alone. The tendency of groups toward organization and the tendency for individuals to be influenced by groups were demonstrated—both findings very much supportive of gestalt principles.

Solomon Asch

Deutsch and Krauss and Sahakian classify Solomon Asch as a member of the gestalt social psychology group. A cursory glance at his numerous works reveals a much more eclectic scholar, but Asch did contribute immensely to the development of the gestalt orientation in social psychology. Much of his research consisted of showing that *social experience is organized in the most coherent and meaningful way possible.* One of Asch's pioneering experiments was published in 1946 and explored the problem of how persons form impressions of personality. The experiment was relatively simple. It required over one thousand college students to write succinct descriptions of impressions they acquired from an experimenter reading a list of different characteristics of a hypothetical person. For example the list might read as follows: lethargic, insecure, warm, quiet, insincere, withdrawn. Asch reported that all of the subjects responded to instructions that they write brief descriptions of the "person" by forming a unified impression which was *complete and rounded.* The experiment was taken as support for the idea that cognitions, like perceptions, *tend toward organization.*

Asch followed this with another entitled "The Doctrine of Suggestion, Prestige and Imitation in Social Psychology." It also supported several gestalt principles, including the ideas that (1) psychological phenomena are organized forms, (2) organized forms are more than the sums of their parts and (3) parts of organized form are influenced by the whole. The implications of support for these gestalt principles were especially significant since behaviorism was offering an alternative explanation for interpersonal influence which was a basic concern in Asch's experiment.

Asch asked subjects to rank ten professions on the qualities "idealism," "character stability," "conscientiousness," "usefulness" and "intelligence." He provided subjects with one of two kinds of information. Some of the subjects were given information that several hundred other college students had ranked one of the professions (politics) high on all of the qualities. Others were informed that the same profession had been ranked low. Asch found that those subjects receiving the "high ranked profession information" ranked the profession highly; those receiving the "low ranked profession information" ranked the profession low. When Asch probed his subjects as to the kinds of professional roles they were using to evaluate the profession, subjects ranking the profession highly were using high level political roles and those who ranked the profession low were using lower level political roles. This signified to Asch that his subjects, rather than automatically conforming to a majority opinion, deliberated and formed a unified perception of the professionals being evaluated. Thus the "whole" affected the "part" in the gestalt tradition.

Another well-known Asch experiment related to gestalt principles was a series of experiments reported in the early and middle 1950s called "Effects of Group Pressure Upon the Modification and Distortion of Judgment." Asch systematically manipulated and controlled group pressure in an effort to observe the effect on individual judgment. The basic experiment involved assembling and seating around a table groups of seven to nine college students and giving them certain instructions regarding the experiment. Briefly, the instructions involved explaining to the students that their task was to discriminate between lengths of lines on pairs of white cards on a stimulus display in front of them. They were informed that on the left of the display there was a white card with a single line and on the right side of the display there was one with three lines of varying lengths. Subjects were told that one of the lines on the right was equal in length to the line on the left, and were then asked to judge which line on the right equalled the standard line on the left. They were told that there would be twelve comparisons and that they would be asked to give their judgments, which would be recorded, in turn.

The uniqueness of the experiment stemmed from the fact that in actuality all but one of the subjects in each of the groups were confederates. The basic experimental trials can be characterized in the following manner: on the first two trials, confederates gave "correct" responses; on the sixteen subsequent trials, confederates unanimously gave twelve "incorrect" responses and four "correct" responses. Conformity was measured on the twelve critical trials.

Asch found that of the total number of comparisons judged by the naive subjects, over one-third were incorrect—meaning that there was a tendency for naive subjects to conform to majority opinion. In contrast, subjects making comparisons alone (they constituted control subjects) rarely gave incorrect responses. There was great individual variation in the responses given by naive subjects ranging from those who gave responses completely independent of the majority to those who conformed on all trials. Those who gave responses contradictory to majority judgment, however, experienced inner conflict and had doubts about their own judgment. The impact of the "whole" on the members of the "whole" was apparent in this experiment, giving credence to a gestalt principle. Numerous variations on Asch's experiment have been conducted (one example is the study by Coleman, Blake and Moulton, 1958) specifying the role of situational factors in conformity with varying results. Nevertheless, Solomon Asch's initial investigation proved that gestalt principles could be demonstrated on social psychological phenomena other than perception.

George Katona

In the forward to George Katona's *Organizing and Memorizing,* Max Wertheimer wrote that Katona's contribution, which employed gestalt methods, should be of vital interest to the psychologist and educator. Katona, who acknowledged his indebtedness to Wertheimer, Kohler and Koffka as well as several unnamed professors and instructors at NYU, Brooklyn College, Newark University and the New School for Social Research, investigated the theory of learning using the gestalt approach.

Katona reports the results of his experiments on two processes of "learning by understanding" and "learning by memorization." Using two groups of college students and employing ordinary playing cards, the experiment involved a particular card trick which involved alternating red and black cards or placing one suit of cards on the table in order (ace, 2, 3, 4, etc.).

Katona concluded as a result of his experiments that learning by memorizing is different from learning by understanding, in that learning by understanding involves *the discovery of a principle* while learning by memory involves *simple repetition.* Katona suggests that learning by understanding involves essentially the same features as problem-solving in that both consist primarily of changing or organizing material (p. 53). Furthermore, learning by understanding "involves grouping a material so as to make an inner relationship apparent" (p. 54). Finally, Katona states that "remembering" was a reconstruction of organization processes.

In addition to the gestalt conclusions which supported gestalt principles, Katona also offers an answer to the question of why we retain certain events, situations, etc., in our memories. He feels that we retain *more* than facts or words. For him, retention is a function of reconstructing "whole-qualities representing a structure, a principle, an essence or combinations of principles, items and words." Stated another way, "we retain organized wholes rather than individual items" (p. 230).

Fritz Heider

A landmark contribution to social psychology was made in 1958 with the publication of *The Psychology of Interpersonal Relations* by Fritz Heider. Heider's contribution was heavily influenced by the gestalt approach of Wolfgang Kohler as he acknowledged in his special note of thanks to the gestaltist.

The chief focus of Heider's volume is perception. In fact, Sahakian states that Heider's book could have been entitled *The Psychology of Interpersonal Perception*. Admittedly perception is emphasized heavily, but another outstanding feature of the book is the defense offered for studying common-sense psychology. Common-sense psychology is seen as valuable for the scientific understanding of interpersonal relations in two ways: (1) it guides our behavior toward other people; and (2) it may contain "truths" despite its "unschooled and subjective" approach.

The first value of common-sense psychology can be elaborated further according to Heider, by noting the fact that in everyday life ideas are formulated about other people and about social situations. We interpret these people's actions and make predictions about their behaviors given certain circumstances. While we build up the psychology in an informal manner, this "naive" psychology gives us the principles necessary to construct an image of the social environment, and in addition, guides our reaction to the social environment. Heider states: "An explanation of this behavior, therefore must deal with common-sense psychology regardless of whether its assumptions and principles prove valid under scientific scrutiny" (1958, p. 5). For example, if an individual feels that his or her astrological sign determines his or her personality, then this belief has to be taken into account in explaining the person's behavior.

The second value of common-sense psychology is that "scientific psychology" can learn a great deal from "common-sense" psychology. Heider acknowledges the charge that scientists can find many contradictions in data produced by a common-sense psychological approach. However, he says that scientists should also acknowledge the numerous contradictory findings produced when "scientific" approaches have been used. Moreover, common-sense psychology is depicted as a fertile ground for fruitful concepts and hunches for hypotheses. Heider did feel, however, that the *ultimate evidence* on which we base our theories should be that gained by scientific methods.

Heider, himself, endorsed two rather related humanistic methods of investigation: word analysis and situation analysis. Using language as a conceptual tool, Heider believed that in our search for key concepts in interpersonal relations we had to begin with common-sense psychology as expressed by everyday language. "By careful analysis of language expression, we can attempt to arrive at concepts that will enable us to clarify the implicit relations among words referring to psychological phenomena " (1958, p. 10). His extended discussion and examples are thought-provoking but beyond the scope of this book. For now let us direct our attention to Heider's *POX* model, which contains a major contribution to this gestalt perspective.

Heider's POX Model   This model first appeared in a 1946 article entitled "Attitudes and Cognition Organization." He discussed the model further in *The Psychology of Interpersonal Relations*. Initially, Heider's model emphasized *sentiment relations* of a person toward another and toward an object belonging to him or her. Sentiment relations refer to a person's evaluation (positive or negative) of another or some object which included liking, approving, admiring, rejecting, disliking, condemning and so forth. When Heider elaborated the model in 1958, he expanded his discussion of *unit relations* as another type of relationship which exists between persons—a person's perception of another person and an object as elements. Elements in the system could be seen as *belonging together* (U) or as *not belonging together* (not U). *Unit relations* were felt by Heider to be vital in the POX model since the notion of "a balanced state" presupposes that elements are seen as belonging together. The basis for "togetherness" of the elements was thought to be the gestalt principles of similarity, proximity, common fate, etc.

A critical assumption in Heider's system is that *unit relations and sentiment relations tend toward a balanced state*. A balanced state exists when relations among elements fit together and tension is absent among the elements. An imbalanced state occurs in systems of two elements when one relation is positive and the other relation negative. In triadic systems (those with three elements such as P, O, and X), imbalance occurs when *one* relation is negative and the other positive. For example, if Person likes Other, and Other is perceived to like a particular social fraternity which Person dislikes, the system is *imbalanced*. The system would be balanced if Person liked the social fraternity, disliked Other, or perceived that Other disliked the social fraternity. Consider Figure 6.1, where pluses equal positive relations, minuses equal negative relations and arrows show direction. Example (h) may be a special case of imbalance if elements within the system are interconnected and not isolated from each other. Succinctly, an absence of negative relations and an even number of negative relations within the triadic system produce balanced states and one negative relation or any odd number of negative relations produce imbalance. Heider's model stimulated numerous other balance theory formulations all assuming tendencies toward balance in cognitive processes or as the original gestaltist would say, tendencies toward "good form."

Heider's influence has been felt in many diverse areas of social psychology. His greatest influence in present-day social psychology is in the area of "attribution theory" which is seen here as a derivative of gestalt psychology generally and a major thesis of Heider's work in particular. An important theme proposed by Heider is that people seek to develop orderly and coherent views of their environment. In the process, they are thought to build up a naive psychology where they look beneath surface behaviors of others. Persons were thought to look at others producing behaviors, at their motives and attitudes, and at the social context within which behaviors occurred.

Figure 6.1
Heider's balanced and unbalanced states

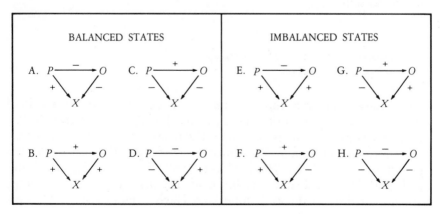

In the next section, other current topical interests in social psychology which have been influenced by the gestalt perspective are considered. One topic discussed and linked with others rather extensively is "attribution theory." Because it is the topical interest in contemporary social psychology most heavily influenced by the gestalt tradition, the final section in this chapter is devoted to some recent work in the area.

CONTEMPORARY VESTIGES OF THE GESTALT PERSPECTIVE

Contrary to some beliefs, the gestalt perspective remains an influence in social psychology today. Admittedly the influence is more diffuse than several decades ago but it persists, nevertheless. If the gestalt perspective has passed its prime as some feel (Lundin, p. 236), it is still a potent influence on numerous social psychological topics. Manifestations of the gestalt influence in present-day social psychology include the numerous holistic approaches to studying social psychological phenomena, the rejection by many scholars in social psychology of the traditional natural science approach to study of social life, and the acceptance by many of the necessity for taking the perspective of the actor into account in order to understand his or her psychological and social worlds. Perhaps the most specific influence of the gestalt perspective in social psychology is on the topic "attribution theory." Attribution theory, itself, is frequently linked with a variety of social psychological concerns. Some of these concerns, as well as the nature of attribution theory are discussed in this section.

Attribution Theory in the Gestalt Psychology Perspective

Some have suggested that attribution theory is derived from field theory, especially the work of Fritz Heider (Shaw and Costanzo). In this volume attribution theory is seen as a derivative of the gestalt perspective, since Heider's major contribution most frequently is categorized as gestalt in nature (Ellis; Henle; Neel, 1969; Sahakian). Edward Jones and Keith Davis and Harold Kelley made the first significant statements about "attribution theory." Jones and Davis' "From Acts to Disposition: The Attribution Process in Person Perception" (1965) and Harold Kelley's "Attribution Theory in Social Psychology" (1967) began a new era for the gestalt perspective in social psychology.

Jones and Davis' Attribution Theory   Relying heavily on Heider's *The Psychology of Interpersonal Relations,* Jones and Davis developed a theory of *inferring dispositions from overt acts.* The basic question they attempted to answer was whether inferences about the intentions of persons could be made from observations of their behaviors. Actually the question is extremely complex because persons often engage in deceptive behavior and *external* factors frequently affect persons' behavior. Jones and Davis felt that inferences about the intention of others were possible if the perceiver had knowledge of other's awareness of the consequences of his or her actions and if the perceiver felt that others had the ability to produce such action. The basic assumption is that "intentional significance" is a direct function of alternatives open to the actor. For example, in order for a student to be able to infer certain intentions underlying a professor's administration of an unannounced examination (behavior), he or she must be able to relate the professor's actions to other possible actions open to the professor, and to infer whether the consequences of giving an unannounced examination are anticipated by the professor. How does one determine intentional significance? How does one come to know the alternatives open to an actor? Jones and Davis' answer to these questions was to scrutinize the acts of others for *molar responses* made by persons which reflect choice. *Effects* were referred to as *discriminable changes in the environment produced by acts.*

Jones and Davis' major contention is that focusing on *noncommon effects* meant scrutinizing changes in the environment caused by actions (on the part of a person) for which the reason appears to be singular. If an individual produces some action and multiple reasons can be attached to it, then causal information to be gained from the action is minimal. On the other hand if an individual produces an act and seemingly only one reason for the act can be attached to it, then the act is causally informative. That is, the act may tell us a great deal about the producer. Accurate attributions also were thought to be some function of scrutinizing *unusual patterns of behavior*—those actions of an individual that depart significantly from the actions produced by most other persons and which tend to be low in social desirability. If certain actions produced by a person have *noncommon effects* and are *unusual* then we are likely to be able to propose an attribute-effect linkage for the act. In other words, "inferences concerning the traits of others about which we have a high degree of confidence" are likely to be made

(Baron and Byrne, p. 60). Such inferences are referred to as *correspondent inferences.*

Inferences about the intentions of others (going from acts to dispositions) are also affected by the genesis of individuals' behavior. In other words, whether or not a person's behavior stems from the person's internal factor(s) or external factors affect attribution of causality. Behaviors which are basically influenced by *external* forces cannot be used to infer motives and traits about persons. Therefore, a major preliminary step in attributing cause to individuals' traits is to determine the genesis of individuals' behavior—that is, does the behavior stem from internal or external causes?

Kelley's Attribution Theory Harold Kelley, defining attribution as the *process of perceiving the dispositional properties of entities in the environment,* was concerned chiefly with external attribution. The basic question Kelley attempts to answer is under what conditions will persons make attribution to the environment? In providing an answer to this question, Kelley clarifies a necessary first step in causal attribution and therefore in attempts to understand persons. Kelley argues that three factors are used by persons to make attributions to the environment: *distinctiveness, consistency,* and *consensus.* Distinctiveness refers to the extent to which there is similarity in a person's actions under different stimulus conditions. Consistency is the extent to which a person produces the same act at other times given certain stimulus conditions. Consensus, for Kelley, actually refers to the existence of social support for the action of an individual. Do others in the same situation respond similarly? Using these three factors, Kelley proposes that attribution to internal cause (and therefore, to the individual) is likely when there are conditions of high consistency, low consensus and low distinctiveness. Attribution to the environment (external attribution) is felt to be likely under conditions of high consistency, high consensus and high distinctiveness. Returning to our hypothetical professor who administers an unannounced examination: how is attribution determined? Suppose, for example that (1) he or she is known to have given unannounced exams in other courses; (2) that he or she is known to have given unannounced exams on other occasions in the course; and (3) that no other professor in the department administers unannounced examinations. In this case we have the conditions of *low* distinctiveness, *high* consistency and *low* consensus, and attribution is likely to be made to the professor (internal causes, for example, "He's a weirdo"). A different level of attribution is likely when the professor has administered unannounced exams in other courses, has administered unannounced exams in this particular class on other occasions and if other professors in the department who teach the course have administered unannounced exams. Given these conditions, the likelihood would be great, following Kelley's line of reasoning, that attribution would be made to the environment (for example, the particular kind of course, the type of students taking the course, departmental demands, and the like).

Biases in Attribution   A major concern of social psychologists devoting attention to attribution theory has been the sources of bias in attribution which may threaten accurate perceptions of one's own traits and motives underlying behavior as well as the motives, traits, and behaviors of others. Goldberg's finding that persons tend to perceive various traits as only partially accurate about themselves but as very accurate about others is instructive. His premise is that such a finding logically follows if persons tend to perceive their own behavior as stemming from external causes and the behaviors of others as being internally caused. The literature is replete with observations of the phenomenon (see for example, Monson and Snyder, and Eisen). It is referred to as the *actor-observer difference in attribution bias* and is thought to be some function of (1) focus of attention and/or (2) the availability of information among other possible causes. With respect to the first, differences in focus of attention exist between the two. Actors tend to focus on situational variables rather than on their own behaviors, while observers tend to concentrate on the behaviors of others rather than on situational variables. The diverse emphasis leads to two different attributions of behavior—one external and the other internal. A second explanation, the availability of information, uses a tendency on the part of observers toward *extrapolating response disposition* as an essential variable in making attributions. Since actors have little or no need to *assume* how they have behaved in the past or under different conditions because they have the information, their attributions will be based on readily available information. In contrast, observers generally have limited information about an actor's response disposition and usually base their attributions, in part, on *extrapolating response dispositions* of actors—assuming that the behavior exhibited at a present point in time is the same kind of behavior exhibited in the past. It should be pointed out, however, that an *availability of information* explanation alone may implicitly suggest that the actor's information is more accurate than observer's and perhaps, actor's attributions are more accurate. Caution would have to be exercised with such a singular explanation however since there is some evidence that actors shift toward internal atttributions and away from external attributions with the passage of time and hypothesized increasing vagueness of situational factors (Moore, Sherwood, Liu and Underwood, 1979).

Egoistic bias in attribution has been another concern of attribution theory researchers. This bias refers to the tendency of persons to attribute their positive outcomes to internal causes and their negative ones to external causes. This bias has been studied in one topical area, achievement, with some degree of frequency. Findings from several studies related to achievement and attribution theory are discussed below.

Achievement and Attribution Theory   Bernard Weiner, Irene Frieze, and Andy Kukla, among others have studied the relationship between attribution and achievement. Along with other colleagues, in 1972 they argued that high achievers attribute their success to ability and effort, and their failure to lack of effort. This pattern of attribution was thought to motivate persons to continue trying to achieve when they were successful and to try even harder when they were not successful. They also found that actors and observers tend to attribute success to internal factors and failure to external factors and internal factors equally. A rationale for this pattern of attribution was provided in 1978 by Bradley who contended that *maintenance of a positive self-image* may be an important variable to consider when examining the locus of central attribution. Persons motivated to maintain a positive self-image may be more likely to attribute success than failure to internal factors. This pattern would most likely preserve a positive self-image.

In 1976, Wortman proposed that the motive in humans for personal control was manifested by tendencies to attribute events to personally controllable causes. These tendencies, she argued, would become especially apparent when outcomes were *negative*. Wortman also felt that since internal factors such as effort or trying may vary in personal controllability, the latter was the most important variable to consider in attribution research. For Wortman, then, dimensions of causal attributions (Weiner et al., 1972; Weiner, 1974) such as internal or external control and stable vs. variable causal factors are secondary to *whether the actor feels able to manipulate factors causing outcome* (personally controllable outcomes).

As provocative as Wortman's views on attribution and achievement have been, her contention that the human motive for personal control leads to personal attribution for negative outcomes was not supported in a subsequent research effort. Wiley, Crittenden and Birg found that, perhaps because of the egoistical pattern of attribution, failure was seen ''as more external than success'' (p. 220). In fact, the hypothesis they proposed was supported. This stated:

The more favorable the outcome of an achievement-related event, the greater the tendency to attribute it to generally controllable as opposed to uncontrollable causes (p. 216).

Numerous other studies have documented the existence of an egoistic bias in causal attribution which enables the individual to maintain a positive self-image by taking responsibility for positive outcome and assuming less responsibility for negative outcome (Sicoly and Ross; Carver, DeGregorio and Gillis). Further investigation into the egoistic bias undoubtedly will continue. A major contribution of such investigations may well be an explication of particular lines of convergence between symbolic interactionism and the contemporary gestalt perspective. Two relatively recent contributions point in this direction and are discussed below.

Jean Geriot's Identity Construction Formulation   In 1977, Geriot presented a theoretical framework focusing on how perceivers construct identities of others. Identity was defined as "an integrated system of cognitions" with "no qualitative precedence" being "granted *a priori* to cognition relative to psychological characteristics over cognition about social attributes, or vice versa" (Geriot, p. 692). Geriot points out that identity construction had been viewed dichotomously in that distinctions commonly were made between social and personal identities in terms of the types of categories used. This implies differences in identity construction: social indentity had been claimed to be built up from social interaction between role participants and personal identity was thought to be an unfolding of personal dispositions. For Geriot, there is no organizing core around which identity is elaborated; instead, the problem addressed is "under which conditions certain categorizations are most likely to take place" (p. 692). Finally Geriot suggests that the theoretical framework presented could contribute to decreasing the gap between two theoretical positions emphasizing the central role of interpersonal attribution processes—the Heideran position and the interactionist position. Reviewing Jones and Davis' approach, which emphasizes separating the personal from the social sources of causality and linking individual dispositions and behavior, Geriot makes a theoretical case for the necessity of merging the personal and the social. Turner's approach (1956) failed to do this, according to Geriot because it basically emphasized person's tendencies to interpret others' actions as indicating role-performance. Geriot's hope, then, is to present a theoretical scheme for the identity construction process sufficiently broad enough to encompass various inferential activities. Geriot conceptualized the major problem in the following manner:

> The problem that the framework addresses is not what the perceiver is or is not able to infer about the other's personality but, rather, under which conditions the perceiver in-situation comes to view the others as a performance of role(s) or as a person endowed with distinctive personality characteristics which explain action (p. 697).

Geriot's formulation is couched within the "stranger" context because of the recognition that early stages of categorization influence later stages. Additionally, the formulation assumes that *a perceiver's perspective varies in time and across situations* leading to another assumption that *construction of other's identity at any given time is either as performer or as person.* The basic assumption underlying the framework according to Geriot is:

> It is assumed that P may initiate his construction of O's identity by following either one of two inferential paths which form or initial branching which refers to 'differential cues selected and used by P to make inferences' (p. 698).

Two types of categorizing are possible following Geriot's formulation. Others can be perceived initially qua performers when their behaviors are viewed within the context of an imputed role. This would imply that Other's behavior is viewed holistically (as a gestalt, in terms of the whole scene) with all of its role relationships. In order for Other's behavior to be perceived in this manner, it is necessary for Person to recognize and/or to construct Other's role. In addition, Person must also have the role in his or her repertoire in order to be able to interpret Other's actions as manifestations of the role. Other's role must also invoke role-attribution in the perceiver. Role-expectations play a crucial part because role-performance is evaluated accordingly. Dependent on both role-expectations and role-evaluation is role appropriate personal characteristics because the latter are attributed. The self implied in the stranger role may be imputed to the stranger or the stranger may be seen as playing a character whose qualities emerge during performances. Whether the performance is perceived as one in good faith, sincere, insincere, without awareness, played without or with great degrees of role distance, Person must perceive Other as enacting a role. If not, then Other will be viewed as "person." This means that *perceiver will attribute other's observed behavior to psychological causes internal to other.* If, however, Other's behavior seems to be *caused* by external forces, perceiver cannot construct the stranger's identity if he or she is viewed as Person because this would imply assignment of observed behavior to psychological causes internal to other. If, on the other hand, Other is seen as the *cause,* perceiver thus may attribute to him / her certain personal characteristics which may lead to further inferred dispositions.

Geriot thought that certain factors determined a person's perspective at points in time. In other words, perceiving other as "person" rather than as "performer" and vice versa (branching) is related to particular circumstances. Referring to "initial branching," Geriot claimed that the process reflects differential use of cues and categories in identity construction. Factors affecting the process were said to be those affecting the *impressiveness of cues* and those affecting the *categories available for use.* Several of these determinants of branching listed included (1) needs and objectives, (2) expectations concerning the probability of events to be encountered, (3) consequences and value to person of alternative categorization, (4) kinds of cues exhibited, etc. (p. 699). All were thought to stress a functional relationship between perception and action and emphasized the motivational basis of the formulation in general and in particular the causal link between *need, interest* and *selective perception.* The emergent branching could be said to provide Person with instrument ability that would facilitate his or her anticipation of Other's behavior and thus adjustment of his or her behavior. In a previously discussed perspective, it might have been said generally that selective reinforcement determines branching.

The latter statement is not necessarily tongue-in-cheek in view of the following hypothesis advanced by Geriot:

1. When *P's* performance of his own role in a given interaction situation is contingent upon the stranger's role, *P* will tend to view the stranger qua performer and will process information accordingly.
2. *P* initially will tend to view the stranger qua person whenever he anticipates interacting with the stranger in a situation that does not involve the same type of activity system as the one in which the stranger is being observed (p. 699).

These hypotheses relate to attempts to make interaction predictable, but other purposive activity also characterizes person inferences. Geriot illustrates cases where *Person attempts to use identity construction to control Other via altercasting.* (i.e., casting others into an identity which benefits person); and, *where the objectives of Person are anchored in group goals which involve Other.* Clearly articulated goals and roles within a group will result in *Person's objectives eliciting the construction of Other as performer while poorly defined goals and roles lead to a reduction in the tendency to adopt the performer role.* Identity construction also may *resolve expectations about the values of alternative categorizations* as well as reduce *cognitive* dissonance. Finally, *situational demands* can affect which cues are perceived and *perceptual selectivity* may also emphasize certain cues which accentuate differences between others encountered.

Geriot lists a number of implicit assumptions underlying the framework dealing with the role of unconscious processes in identity construction, the characterization of person's inferential perspective of "persons" or "performer," the possibility that the other inferential path can be taken for the one under way, differential initiation of identity construction, etc. However, the implicit gestalt assumption of holism, and preference for good form, remain unidentified even though they are critical aspects of the formulation.

Responsibility and Attribution Theory   Hamilton begins her theoretical essay with a statement of the two most investigated areas of responsibility attribution: Heider's developmental stages of responsibility attribution and "assessment of responsibility attributed for an accidental occurrence" (p. 316). Hamilton eschews the fact that Heider's basic framework had been used uncritically, and feels that social psychological literature is in need of a more adequately social psychological approach to how responsibility is attributed. Recognizing the ancestors of attribution theory as cognitive psychology and the gestalt perspective, Hamilton notes that despite the fact that they were fruitful, they provided an incomplete view of the major determinants of responsibility judgments. While psychological attribution research had emphasized *degree of intent* and *severity of consequences of action* as empirical determinants of responsibility, expectations had not been included. Judgments of actors, according to Hamilton, were functions of causality *and* expectation—*what was done* and *what should have been done*.

Focusing heavily on Heider's model because of its centrality to many conceptions of responsibility attribution, Hamilton first summarizes Heider's formulation. She alludes to Heider's failure to provide an adequate definition of responsibility and the factors Heider suggested as determinants of responsibility—"the extent to which the actor intended, or personally caused, the effect; and, the extent to which the action was caused by environmental factors or pressure." The vagueness of Heider's model of the interplay between *intention* and *environment* is also discussed. Hamilton points out that Heider left unclear whether association, commission, foreseeability, intention and justification (Shaw and Sulzer, 1964) constituted a developmental stage sequence or whether they are different levels of judgment to be used in different situations. She says that the vagueness had not been dispelled with subsequent theoretical work in the area.

Using legal rules as analogs to the above stages, Hamilton concludes that the first few levels seem to mean increasing degrees of intentionality, yet legal judgments of guilt were made in cases representing all four, often with serious consequences. This leads Hamilton to suggest that judgments of "real" adults involve more than levels of causality. For Hamilton, such a conclusion seems buttressed with analyses of common language meanings of responsibility which imply reliability of role performance and social obligations—both "shoulds" rather than "deeds." Hamilton recognizes that social roles as determinants of attributes should be subsumed under external sources of action, but feels that conceptualizing roles in such a manner is inadequate since it implies noninformation about personal dispositions, thus supporting the self-environment attribution dichotomy. Instead, roles are seen by Hamilton as neither internal nor external, but rather internalized. Roles are viewed as the environment acting within us (p. 321).

In her discussion of roles and rules for responsibility, Hamilton argued that roles may modify the rules of responsibility which include blame for rule breaking, reliable performance in role and diffuse obligations to act. Different roles may require different mixtures of the rules. Some may require more reliable performance in roles, others more diffuse obligations to act, and still others more blame for rule breaking. This implies that the actor's social roles may impact responsibility attribution.

Finally, Hamilton discusses the relationship between social structure and attribution processes as a determinant of individual differences in assessing the impact of social roles on attribution. She notes that persons are likely to be in agreement about subordinates who independently broke rules. In-role behavior by subordinates, even when negative, does not usually bring blame for rule-breaking, according to Hamilton. Moreover, role hierarchies operate to remove blame from subordinates for in-role rule-breaking, since the ultimate responsibility lies with those in authority. When there is normative conflict as a result of an authority's instructions exceeding normative bounds, obedience results in conflicting interpretations of the demands among actors and those who judge them. The obedient subordinate is likely to emphasize the role obligations (use the normative motive), the disobedient one is likely to emphasize the expected consequences of obedience. Judges are placed in a dilemma. Also, different definitions of what happened are likely to emerge—one definition might focus on the consequences (consequence grammar) and the other on the motive (motive grammar). "Perceiver conflict over the normative meaning of role thus reveals that roles pervade the description of the action itself" (p. 325). Also, the perceiver's own position in the social structure influences attribution as self-theory would attest. Normative conflict appears to be a setting variable for individual differences among perceivers.

Person Perception and Attribution Theory Person perception has been central to the gestalt perspective in social psychology. In the same year that Heider published *The Psychology of Interpersonal Relations,* Donald T. Campbell published "Common Fate, Similarity and Other Indices States of Aggregates of Person as Social Entities." In this article, Campbell proposed that the organizing principles of gestalt influenced perception of persons in the same manner as they did objects. If this is so, then in all likelihood group "organization" has ramifications for individual members. Some of these consequences for attributions have been explored by David Wilder.

Wilder conducted two experiments yielding data demonstrating that "perception of a person as an individual or group member affects attributions about his or her beliefs and the causes of his or her behavior" (p. 21). Attributions about persons perceived as individuals were different from those about persons who were perceived as members of a group. Other members' behaviors were found to affect attribution when persons were perceived as members of groups. The behavior of others had little effect on attributions when persons were perceived as individuals. Another finding by Wilder supports the gestalt idea that group members are perceived to be more similar than "individuals" despite the knowledge of "no previous contact." There is also more of a tendency to attribute common behavior in group members to the situation than to either *common behaviors in aggregates* or *unique behaviors in aggregates or groups.* Wilder concludes his article by noting that the results showed that "the mere organization of persons into groups and aggregates affects assumptions and attributions made about their behavior."

Just as important as the fact that persons attempt to determine motives and traits of others is the linkage between attribution and social behavior. Increasing numbers of social psychologists are turning their attention to the effects of social perception of person's behaviors. Recent studies have shown that others' perceptions of persons may influence persons' behaviors (Snyder and Swann; Meese et al.). While the answers are not entirely complete regarding the precise process operating when such phenomena occur, it does seem that when persons are perceived in a particular way, a chain of subsequent events may occur. Links in the chain include changes in the behavior directed toward the person by the perceiver. This may be followed by actual changes in the person's behavior which validate the perceiver's perceptions. Subsequently, persons may begin to perceive themselves in a particular way and consequently alter their self-perceptions. Such alterations in self-perceptions, in turn, may then produce alterations in behavior. Baron and Byrne have stated:

> In short, it appears that our perceptions of the traits and behavior of other persons may not simply reflect social reality. To an important extent, they may help to shape it as well (p. 19).

In the 1980s, one line of research in person perception is very likely to be how our perceptions help to shape social reality.

AN EVALUATION OF THE GESTALT PERSPECTIVE IN SOCIAL PSYCHOLOGY

The gestalt perspective arose in protest against other perspectives that were seen as too mechanistic, too analytical, too atomistic, and so on. The emergent perspective also has had its critics. Kanizsa has listed what he calls a "whole host of misunderstandings and trivializations" surrounding the gestalt perspective (p. 71). The list includes (1) inadequate translation of "gestalt," (2) the belief that the gestalt perspective is a psychology of perception; (3) gestalt theory is reductionistic, (4) gestalt theory is nativistic, (5) gestalt theory rejects analysis, (6) gestalt theory is vitalistic, (7) gestalt theory denies the influence of motivation on perception, (8) gestalt theory denies the influence of past experiences, (9) gestalt theory equates regularity with symmetry and (10) gestalt theory relies on "insight" to solve problems.

Kanizsa attributes these misinterpretations of the gestalt perspective to the initial research goals of early gestaltists, terminological problems in the perspective and superficial acquaintance with the gestalt perspective. First, Kanizsa acknowledges that the German word "gestalt" could not be translated adequately into English, French or Italian and that its translation into "form" has led to numerous ambiguities because form was only one of the attributes of gestalt. A more appropriate translation according to Kanizsa would be "organized structure" with an emphasis on "organization."

On the remainder of the "misinterpretations," Kanizsa took the following position: (1) the gestalt perspective is quite general and can be used to study a wide range of experience and behavior; (2) instead of the gestalt perspective attempting to explain psychological phenomena in terms of physiological processes, it only suggests that the same principles of organization existing in the psychological world exist in the world of inanimate nature; (3) the forces that affect humans are not different from those affecting inanimate objects, however, topographical conditions (hereditary constraints) in humans may contribute to the complexity of forces acting on humans; (4) the phenomenological method endorsed by gestaltists *is* an analytic method and stresses studying phenomena under conditions in which they are not distorted, fragmented, etc.; (5) humans do have self-regulating processes that restore functioning when disturbances occur in the same manner that order is restored by self-regulating processes in the physical world, through natural organization; (6) with respect to charges that the gestalt perspective denies the influences of motivational factors and past experience, closer reading of Koffka (1953, p. 355) and Wertheimer (1923, p. 331) clears up these misconceptions; (7) gestaltists consider "good form" to characterize figures that are not symmetrical since they may be stable, simple, cohesive and resistant to transformation—all elements of "good form," but not necessarily geometric regularity; and (8) insight is not proposed as a causal factor in reaching solutions since most problem-solving involves successive discoveries of critical relationships (each discovery being an insight or consequence) through successive restructuring of the problem situation. The laws and causes of restructuring are the causal factors in problem solutions and insight while accompanying solutions, does not produce them (Kanizsa, p. 71).

Most of the above criticisms and rebuttals are related to the gestalt perspective as a unified system. The gestalt perspective as a unified system is practically nonexistent in contemporary social psychology. As a diffuse perspective (some might even say dissipated), gestalt theory is very much a part of social psychology as reflected in the dominant social psychological perspectives and interests today. For example, vestiges of the perspective can be seen in cognitive social psychology, processual symbolic interactionism and even behavior analysis. Gestaltism makes a more prominent appearance in social psychological interests and topics such as "attribution theory" as we have seen. It has been stated by some that the final appraisal of the gestalt perspective has not been made. Hopefully this is the case, since many current social psychological interests and topics remain heavily influenced by gestalt principles and contribute immensely to contemporary social psychology.

CONCLUSIONS

In this chapter, we have been concerned with a perspective which stresses the importance of studying experience and behavior as complex, organized wholes. Key ideas in the perspective founded by Wertheimer, Koffka and Kohler include the notion that the whole of anything exceeds the sum of its parts; that perception is organized; that this organization is as good as stimulus conditions permit; that raw sensation is nonexistent; and, that all stimulation is organized and patterned in the sensory organs.

While it is difficult to call the gestalt perspective a unified system today, it *is* appropriate to call it a *major influence* in contemporary social psychology. Its impact on topics of interest to modern day social psychologists attests to the fact that the bell has not yet tolled for the gestalt perspective.

BIBLIOGRAPHY

Asch, Solomon E. "Forming Impressions of Personality," *Journal of Abnormal and Social Psychology* 41 (1946), pp. 258–290.

———."The Doctrine of Suggestion, Prestige and Imitation in Social Psychology," *Psychological Review* 55 (1948), pp. 250–276.

———."Effects of Group Pressure on the Modification and Distortion of Judgments," in H. Gentzkow, ed. *Groups, Leadership and Men.* Pittsburgh: Carnegie Press, 1951.

Baron, Robert A., and Donn Byrne. *Social Psychology: Understanding Human Interaction.* Boston: Allyn and Bacon, 1981.

Bradley, G. W. "Self-Serving Biases in the Attribution Process: A Reexamination of the Fact or Fiction Question," *Journal of Personality and Social Psychology* 36 (1978), pp. 56–71.

Campbell, Donald T. "Common Fate, Similarity and Other Indices of the Status of Aggregates of Persons as Social Entities," *Behavioral Science* 3 (1958), pp. 14–25.

Carver, C. S., E. DeGregorio and R. Gillis. "Ego-Defensive Bias in Attribution Among Two Categories of Observers," *Personality and Social Psychology Bulletin* 6 (1980), pp. 44–50.

Cohen, A. R. *Attitude Change and Social Influence.* New York: Basic Books, 1964.

Coleman, J. F., R. R. Blake and J. S. Moulton. "Task Difficulty and Conformity Pressures," *Journal of Abnormal Social Psychology* 57 (1958), pp. 120–122.

Deutsch, M. and Krauss, R. M. *Theories in Social Psychology.* New York: Basic Books, 1965.

Eisen, S. V. "Actor-Observer Differences in Information Inferences and Causal Attribution," *Journal of Personality and Social Psychology* 37 (1979), pp. 261–272.

Ellis, W. D. *A Source Book of Gestalt Psychology.* New York: The Humanities Press, 1955.

Geriot, Jean M. "Attribution and Identity Construction: Some Comments," *American Sociological Review* 42 (October 1977), pp. 692–704.

Goldberg, L. W. "Differential Attribution of Trait Descriptive Terms to Oneself as Compared to Well-Liked, Neutral, and Disliked Others: A Psychometric Analysis," *Journal of Personality and Social Psychology* 36 (1978), pp. 1012–1028.

Hamilton, V. Lee. "Who is Responsible? Toward a Social Psychology of Responsibility Attribution," *Social Psychology* 41, no. 4 (1978), pp. 316–328.

Heider, Fritz. "Attitudes and Cognitive Organization," *Journal of Psychology* 21 (1946), pp. 102–112.

——.*The Psychology of Interpersonal Relations.* New York: John Wiley, 1958.

Henle, M. *Documents of Gestalt Psychology.* Berkeley, Ca.: University of California Press, 1961.

Jones, Edward E. and Keith E. Davis. "From Acts to Dispositions: The Attribution Process in Person Perception," in L. Berkowitz, ed. *Advances in Experimental Social Psychology.* New York: Academic Press, 1965.

Kanizsa, Gaetano. *Organization in Vision.* New York: Praeger, 1979.

Katona, G. *Organizing and Memorizing.* New York: Columbia University Press, 1940.

Kelley, Harold H. "Attribution Theory in Social Psychology," in D. Levine, ed., *Nebraska Symposium on Motivation.* Lincoln, Ne.: University of Nebraska Press, 1967, pp. 192–238.

Koffka, Kurt. *Principles of Gestalt Psychology.* New York: Harcourt, Brace, and World, 1935.

Kohler, Wolfgang. *Gestalt Psychology.* New York: Liveright Press, 1947.

Lundin, Robert W. *Theories and Systems of Psychology,* Lexington, Ma.: D.C. Heath, 1979.

Meese, L. A., G. E. Stollak, R. W. Larson and G. Y. Michaels. "Interpersonal Consequences of a Person Perception Process in Two Social Contexts," *Journal of Personality and Social Psychology* 37 (1979), pp. 269–379.

Monson, T. C., and M. Snyder. "Actors, Observers, and the Attribution Process," *Journal of Experimental Social Psychology* 13 (1977), pp. 89–111.

Moore, B. S., D. R. Sherrod, T. J. Liu and B. Underwood. "The Dispositional Shift in Attribution Over Time," *Journal of Experimental Social Psychology* 15 (1979), pp. 553–569.

Neel, Ann. *Theories of Psychology: A Handbook,* Cambridge, Ma.: Schenkman 1969.

Sahakian, W. S. *History of Systems of Psychology*. New York: John Wiley, 1975.

Shaw, M. E. and Costanzo, P. R. *Theories of Social Psychology*. New York: McGraw-Hill, 1970.

Shaw, M. E. and J. L. Sulzer. "An Empirical Test of Heider's Levels in Attribution of Responsibility," *Journal of Abnormal and Social Psychology* 69 (1964), pp. 39–46.

Sherif, M. *The Psychology of Social Norms*. New York: Harper, 1936.

Sicoly, F. and M. Ross. "Facilitation of Ego-Biased Attributions by Mean of Self-Serving Observers Feedback," *Journal of Personality and Social Psychology* 35 (1977), pp. 734–741.

Snyder, M. and W. B. Swann, Jr. "Behavioral Confirmation in Social Interaction: From Social Perspective to Social Quality," *Journal of Experimental Social Psychology* 14 (1978), pp. 148–162.

Turner, Ralph H. "Role-taking, Role Standpoint, and Reference Group Behavior," *American Journal of Sociology* 61 (1956), pp. 316–328.

Watson, Robert L. *The Great Psychologists*. Philadelphia: Lippincott, 1978.

Weiner, Bernard. *Achievement Motivation and Attribution Theory*. Morristown, N.J.: General Learning Press, 1974.

Weiner, Bernard, I. Frieze, A. Kukla, L. Reed, S. Rest and R. Rosenbaum. "Perceiving the Causes of Success and Failure," in E. Jones, et al., *Attribution: Perceiving the Causes of Behavior*. Morristown, N.J.: General Learning Press, 1972.

Wertheimer, Max. *Productive Thinking*. New York: Harper & Row, 1959.

Wilder, David A. "Perceiving Persons as a Group: Effects on Attribution of Causality and Beliefs," *Social Psychology* 41, no. 1 (1978), pp. 13–23.

Wiley, Mary Glenn, K. Crittenden and L. D. Birg. "Why a Rejection? Causal Attribution of a Career Achievement Event," *Social Psychology Quarterly* (1979), pp. 214–222.

Woodworth, R. S. *Contemporary Schools of Psychology*. New York: The Ronald Press, 1948.

Wortman, Camile. "Causal Attributions and Personal Control," in J. Harvey, W. Ickes and R. Kidd, eds., *New Directions in Attribution Research*. Hillsdale, N.J.: Lawrence Erlbaum Associates, 1976.

Zeigarnik, Bluma. "On Finished and Unfinished Tasks," in W. Ellis, ed., *A Source Book of Gestalt Psychology*. London: Routledge, 1938.

THE
FIELD
THEORY
PERSPECTIVE

7

Field theory in social psychology is most often associated with the work of Kurt Lewin (1890–1947) and scholars following in his tradition, including Ronald Lippit, Ralph K. White, Norman Polansky, Sidney Rosen, Leon Festinger, Theodore Newcomb and Dorwin Cartwright. The main features of the perspective originated in the contributions of Lewin, and will be used as a point of departure for this chapter. Let us begin with the founding of the field theory perspective and the contributions of Kurt Lewin.

THE FOUNDING OF THE FIELD THEORY PERSPECTIVE

Kurt Lewin began his career in 1921 at the University of Berlin where he met and established an academic relationship with the gestaltists Wertheimer and Kohler. Both were deeply involved in laying the foundation of the gestalt perspective, and Kurt Lewin was influenced by their interests. Yet Lewin had broader interests than perception and cognition. He was interested in emotions, values, social relationships and motivation among other phenomena. It was because of his interest in motivation that he is credited with the founding of field theory. First, however, attention is directed to Lewin's *approach* to the study of social psychological phenomena, which was radical by that era's standards.

In his book *Principles of Topological Psychology*, Lewin states a goal he considers essential for theoretical psychology. He asserts that "theoretical psychology in its present state must try to develop a system of concepts which shows all the characteristics of a gestalt, in which any part depends upon every other part" (p. 2). With this statement, Lewin places field theory clearly within the domain of the gestalt perspective. But, field theory is different. Let us turn to Lewin's distinctive approach to the structure of science. Lewin endorsed what he considered to be a more scientific approach to social science investigations than that popular during the time in which field theory was developed. He called the latter the Aristotelian mode. Contending that much of psychology seemed prescientific, Lewin questioned the use of *rigid categorizations, the statistical concept of lawfulness, the phenotypic approach to psychology,* and *descriptive methodology.* Alternatively, he suggested the *constructive method* which proposed the following: (1) criterion for lawfulness that does not depend on frequency; (2) an emphasis on relational interpretations of events rather than classificatory ones; (3) a conception of phenomena as existing on a continuum; and (4) a methodology that stresses controlled experimentation and quantitative measures.

With respect to the constructive method (Lewin termed it the Galilean approach), he contended that a lawful relationship between events may very well exist even if only *one* instance of such an event is known. The fact that two events occur together somewhat infrequently does not obviate a lawful relationship between the events. Lawfulness is equated with the establishment of relationships between events. "The proof of a law depends upon the 'purity of the case' and not necessarily upon the frequency with which it occurs" (Chaplin and Krawiec, p. 393). Thus, the importance of the individual case was stressed by Lewin. He observed also that the Aristotelian approach to the structure of science stressed classification of events into discrete groupings. In contrast, Lewin argued that it was more appropriate to emphasize functional relationships between events. Put another way, Lewin felt that it was important to understand *basic relationships* and to observe *function* rather than structure or content. Intimately related to this emphasis was Lewin's suggestion that phenomena should be represented along a continuum. Such a representation, according to Lewin, would show more adequately the similarities and differences among phenomena than discrete categorization. It was within this mode of investigation, then, that Lewin developed a system which was to become known as the field theory perspective.

LEWIN'S FIELD THEORY PERSPECTIVE

As noted earlier, Lewin's system is couched in the gestalt perspective. However, most scholars have considered it sufficiently distinctive in terms of emphasis and conceptualization to warrant distinguishing between the two. Many of the major concepts in field theory were borrowed from mathematics and physics. In fact, Lewin has been criticized for misapplication of the concepts, although others have noted that he only intended to use them as analogies. Let us now examine Lewin's system beginning with the basic concepts which include field, locomotion, life space, dimensions of the life space, force, tension and conflict.

Basic Concepts in Lewin's System

Field   The concept *field* was defined by Lewin as a "totality of coexisting facts which are conceived of as mutually interdependent." "Field theory," in line with this, is "a method of analyzing causal relations and of building scientific constructs." For example, the Lewinian approach assumes that events are the consequences of numerous interacting factors. Such factors cannot be broken down into parts for explanatory purposes. Rather, events must be seen as the result of a series of interacting and co-acting factors which contribute to a pattern—more specifically, a gestalt.

Given the fact that Lewin conceived of complex psychological data in field theory terms, it was necessary for him to develop a methodology congruent with this conception. Lewin responded with the development of a new methodological technique which he called "hodology," or "the science of paths." This science is characterized by the development of geometrical concepts dealing with behavior direction and courses of action within the life space. While the specific nature of Lewin's geometry is beyond the scope of this text, it *is* possible to discuss the resulting development of basic field theory concepts including a second concept, which he termed life space.

Life Space   By life space, Lewin meant "the totality of facts or events by which one's behavior is determined at any given moment" (1936, p.

216). Behavior is seen as *a function of the life space which is a consequence of both the person and his (her) environment.* The person's environment consists of *both his or her temporary or momentary situation and permanent situation.* Lewin's representation of the life space was an egg-shaped subdivided figure. The subdivision represented vectors (which were used to show the kinds of forces acting in and on the individual). The length of the vector represented the *intensity* of the force and the direction of the vector indicated the *line* and point of *application* of the force. If a child's motive is to have fun on a given day, his or her response disposition or similar experiences in the past will not cause him or her to go to an amusement park. In a later section of this chapter, it will be necessary to discuss how past experiences enter into present behavior since Lewin's approach is an ahistorical one.

Important to an adequate understanding of the concept of life space is the fact that Lewin considered life space to be a psychological concept which could be represented by a spatial diagram, but it does not exist as a spatial relationship. This means that life space is a hypothetical construct—an inference about what goes on inside the organism. Important to remember, however, is that what goes on inside the individual is some function of both the individual and his or her environment according to Lewinian thought.

Locomotion   Locomotion was defined as movement within the life space from one point to another point. How does the criminal move from his or her precrime status to a criminal status? Presumably this is done by deciding between alternative courses of action, examining possible courses of action and movement toward certain goals. In a literal sense for Lewin, *locomotion can be either psychological or physical.*

Returning to an example used in preceding chapters, if a man desires sex with a female prostitute, the man is separated from the female prostitute (goal region) by a number of regions enclosed by boundaries. Furthermore, in order to reach the desired goal region, the man must go through all of these regions prior to reaching the prostitute. For example, the man must (1) have the money to buy the prostitute, (2) have the means to get to the prostitute, (3) have the approach necessary to go up to the prostitute, (4) have the place to go to with her, and finally (5) have sex with the prostitute (goal region). One can see that each one of the above regions is cut off from the other, however in order to reach the goal region and have sex with the prostitute, each region specified must be passed through successfully. Lewin would hypothesize that the man could be located somewhere in the life space at any point in his goal-seeking behavior even though there may be no visible indication of this behavior.

The reason why location is thought possible is because the above discussion represents what may be going on inside of the man as well as what his observable behaviors might indicate. According to Lewin, persons have multiple and interacting layers of personality. Some of these layers are readily observable while others (specifically, the core personality) are not accessible to any but intimate associates. They are, at the same time, influenced only minimally by outside forces. Lewin also felt that persons differed in internal structure (personality). Some personalities are more complex, and thus have more regions and greater interaction between regions, than others. These notions led to the development of several additional field theory concepts, referred to here as *dimensions of the life space*.

Dimensions of Life Space   The first dimension of life space to be discussed is the dimension of *differentiation*. The degree of differentiation of the life space is determined by (1) the degree of interaction possible among various aspects of the personality; (2) the number of regions which is some function of the complexity of the personality; and (3) the larger situation in which the individual is functioning. This means that where an individual can be found on the dimension of differentiation is related to personal factors such as age, race, experience, capacity and response salience.

Another dimension of life space is *reality-irreality*. When persons are adjudged to be in contact with the real world, their life spaces are said to correspond with reality; and when persons live in worlds of fantasy, they are said to be irreal. Following this line of thought, adults are thought to be more in contact with reality than children; and, "normal" persons are more realistic than persons who are thought to be psychologically disturbed.

A third dimension of life space according to Lewin is *time perspective*. Because individuals, especially as they become older, can exist in a broad time perspective, Lewin felt that a person's behavior (especially an older person) often is determined by his or her ability to exist in the past, present and future. "Existing in the past" means that there is no need to rely on nonpresent factors as causes of behavior. The ability to exist in the past means that the " past" can be an integral part of an individual's present life space, thus obviating the necessity for "past experiences" explanations of human behavior. To illustrate, the reason why a person may hurry home if he or she is hungry cannot be explained by saying that in the past when the person was hungry he or she satisfied the hunger at home, and that therefore the past experience is the motivation for going home. Rather, any explanation, according to Lewin, must emphasize past experience as a part of the person's current life space. This means that forces within the individual's *present* life space would be responsible for the "going home" behavior. "Past experience" as a *part of the present life space* is only one of *several* causal factors.

Force   Force was another concept vital to Lewin's field theory orientation and was intimately related to the concept locomotion. Force "is a tendency to act in a specific direction" and is more than a drive or excitatory tendency, for it is a *cause* of change, with properties of strength, direction, and point of application. Thus, locomotion within the life space is some function of force. A field of forces with a central field for its structure is a *valence*. An attracting valence is *positive* and a repelling valence is *negative*. Despite the fact that a person may want to move from one part of his or her life space to another, it is entirely possible that the person may find that there is a boundary zone which resists movement. Lewin suggested that these barriers may be social or personal and represent a type of *force*. Let us consider several types of forces as discussed by Lewin.

Five types of forces exist: (1) driving forces, (2) restraining forces, (3) induced forces, (4) need forces, and (5) impersonal forces. Social barriers are examples of *restraining forces*. A woman attending a cocktail party may be very much attracted to a man conversing with his wife and may *want to approach him* (driving force), however, social courtesies will dictate a much more indirect approach (getting a friend who knows the couple to introduce her) than the direct one (simply interrupting the conversation and beginning one with the man) which she might want to follow. Also inherent in the above example is the individual *need* or *wish force;* however, *impersonal forces* may also restrain our amorous woman from directly approaching the man. Such forces as social norms, which are apparent in this case, dictate against the particular kind of intrusion our hypothetical woman would make. Analytically, these forces are *impersonal* and do not necessarily correspond either to the wishes of our woman or to the wishes of the approachable man. What if wishes correspond neither to one's own need nor to the wishes of another person? What happens if they are *induced?* If they are induced, this means that some individuals might be moved toward a particular goal simply because they perceive that movement in a particular direction would benefit a third party. Examples of induced forces include the wishes of a mother for her child, the wishes of a supervisor for his or her workers, and the wishes a teacher might have for his or her students.

Tension   Tension is another concept basic to the field theory perspective in social psychology. Lewin defined it as *a state of a region relative to surrounding regions.* It involves *forces at the boundary of the region which tend to produce changes such that differences of tension are diminished.* For Lewin the *motivation* for much human behavior is not "habit" but rather, tension, which comes from the pressures of wills or needs.

Conflict   A final key concept in the field perspective discussed here is conflict, defined as *the opposition of approximately equally strong field forces.* Lewin distinguished three types of conflict:

1. The person is caught in the middle between two positive valences of near equal strength (approach-approach conflict). An example of this conflict is the newlywed man who finds himself feeling a great deal of love and affection for his mother, who does not want to give up her son, and a great deal of love and affection for his new wife, who does not want to share her husband with any other woman.

2. A second type of conflict occurs when the person stands in the middle between two approximately equal negative valences (avoidance-avoidance conflict). Three subtypes of this conflict can occur: (a) a person may find him or herself in a situation where there are two sets of negative forces with no restraints with respect to locomotion out of the situation. An instance of this type occurs when a student must attend a boring course or drop the course and not graduate, though there is nothing to prevent the student from changing courses during the first week of the quarter. (b) The opposite of the above subtype occurs when the person caught between two negative valences cannot leave the field. What if our student cannot change courses? (c) Finally, there is the situation where a person is in a region of negative valence but can only leave it by going through another region of negative valence. Our student in the boring course may be able to change, but only if he or she goes to the academic dean of the school, and the instructor is actually a friend of the student's.

3. A third type of conflict emerges when a person is exposed to opposing forces derived from a positive and negative valence (approach-avoidance conflict). There are also three forms of this conflict (see Figure 7.1): (a) A situation where there are positive and negative *valences* in a region; (b) A situation where a person attracted to an outside region is encircled by a negative barrier; and (c) A situation where a region of positive valence is encircled by a negative barrier.

With respect to subtype (a), the presidency of the United States is certainly a region which has both positive and negative valences. The social status attached to the position contains most of the positive valences, and the duties and obligations associated with the position may be said to contain most of the negative valences. Situation (b) is

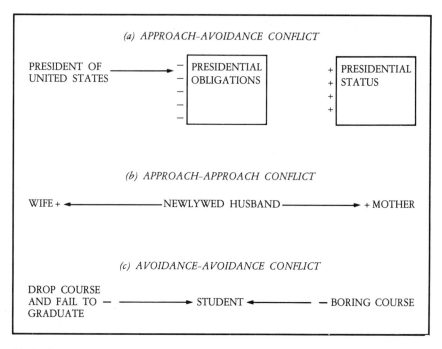

Figure 7.1
Examples of types of conflict in field theory

epitomized by an individual who is attracted to a person outside of his or her marriage, while perceiving the possibility of going through a divorce in a highly negative way. The final subtype can be illustrated by the college student who desires membership in a college sorority; however, in order to become a member he or she must penetrate the initiation barriers surrounding membership.

*Some Basic Theoretical
Statements in Lewin's Field
Theory*

In this section eight theoretical statements basic to Lewin's field theory perspective are discussed. No claim is made to comprehensiveness. They are, however, representative of main features of the system as manifested by the appearances of the fundamental concepts of the perspective, and those interested in a more detailed presentation should turn to *Principles of Topological Psychology*.

1. Behavior has to be derived from a totality of coexisting facts. Implicit in the first statement is the idea that one can identify, study and conceptualize psychological phenomena. For Lewin and his followers an event is a function of several antecedent causes rather than one cause alone. Moreover, usually a number of *interacting* forces result in an event. As we have seen, these forces may be driving, induced, need, impersonal or restraining in nature.

A rapist, for example, does not succeed in his assault only because a woman walks alone on a unlighted street late at night (sometimes thought to be a careless precipitation of the crime). He succeeds because (1) he psychologically and physically locomotes toward the woman; (2) his life space includes particular perceptions of the woman and her environment (rapists rarely assault their own mothers, sisters and other close relatives, nor does the assault usually take place around other people, although there are some exceptions); and (3) his life space includes perceptions about himself and his environment. Regardless of what we might like to think about the rape or the rapist, one thing is certain from the view of field theory: rape is a complex phenomenon resulting from (1) forces, (2) the rapist and (3) his environment, all coexisting and interacting. Explanations of rape as victim precipitated often neglect such coexisting facts, which may be the reason why victim precipitation explanations in most instances lack validity.

2. These coexisting facts have the character of a dynamic field in so far as the state of any part of this field depends on every other part of the field. The reliance of field theory on gestalt social psychology is most apparent in the above assumption. Instead of simply defining gestalt perceptually, field theorists define it dynamically. Lewin's definition is as follows: "A gestalt is a system whose parts are dynamically connected in such a way that a change of one part results in a change of the other parts" (1936, p. 218).

If forces acting upon a person (and his or her environment) can be used as an example of a field, then any change in any one force alters the other forces, the person and the person's environment. What if our hypothetical rapist continues physically and psychologically locomoting toward our woman walking on an unlighted street and suddenly she turns to face him with a gun in her hand? At this point, there has been an alteration in the driving forces of the potential rapist which will affect the restraining forces in the situation, the rapist and his environment. In fact, a boundary zone is now present that resists continued locomotion toward the point of application (the woman) and unless the barrier can be overcome (that is, unless he can render her incapable of protecting herself), the rapist is likely to leave the field. An interesting sideline here is that regardless of most rapists' "violent personalities," leaving the field in the face of resistant barriers is an alternative course of action frequently followed.

3. Behavior depends on the present field. The present field includes forces (point of application and specific direction), the person and the person's environment. Behavior is a function of this present field and not a function of past or future events, because such events "do not exist and therefore cannot have a direct effect now." However, the effect of the past on behavior can be indirect. Historical events are taken into consideration but only as they relate to the present. This occurs because a situation at a given time actually does not refer to a moment without time extension, but to a certain time period.

The fact that a rapist has a history of having committed violent acts in the past cannot be seen as the *cause* of his present assault, nor can the cause be that he was physically battered by his mother as a child. What has caused the rapist's behavior now is present in the rapist's psychological field. It should be noted that determining cause in this instance is a difficult procedure. It involves identifying, exploring and conceptualizing the rape process not as a single isolated fact but as complex processes which are expressions of a concrete situation involving definite persons in definite situations in the present.

4. Some behavior is a function of a state of tension within the individual. This statement is related to Lewin's conceptualizations of "tension," "tension systems," and "locomotion." It was felt that whenever a person experienced a need or an intention, then tension existed within that person. Because a system in a state of tension attempts to achieve equilibrium (tries to change itself in such a way that it becomes equal to the state of its surrounding regions) behavior occurs in the form of locomotion in the person's psychological environment or in his or her perceptions. In such instances, behaviors will *reflect* attempts to move toward a goal region which reduces the tension.

To follow through with the example of the rapist's *intent* upon violating a victim, the rape event itself serves precisely that function (intent of violating the victim). Note that the rapist is conceived here as a person characterized by a system in a state of "tension." Seeing a woman walking alone on an unlighted street induces a positive valence for activity regions in his psychological environment. In other words the woman becomes a goal region toward which the rapist locomotes psychologically as well as physically. The woman's defenselessness heightens his locomotion rather than acting as a restraining force. For the rapist, unlike the nonrapist, defenselessness becomes a positive valence possibly leading to tension-reduction. Moreover, the rapist may also experience a change in the structure of his perceived environment as he moves closer toward his goal, ignoring or not perceiving the woman's defensive nature nor other behavior which would act as a barrier to his goal fulfillment.

5. *Some behavior is a function of nonperception of tension-release.* This proposition also is related to Lewin's "tension," "force" and "locomotion" concepts. While a region of positive valence will result in a certain type of behavior reflecting locomotion toward the region given the existence of tension, nonperception of a goal region will also produce a given type of behavior—*restless behavior.* In such a case, the person may move from one region to another, each time finding the region negative and thus being impelled to locomote.

According to Lewin (1936, p. 62) nonperception of a goal region may not mean that the person does not recognize that a goal region is somewhere but rather that the person does not know the location of the goal region. If the existence of a goal region is known then forces influencing a person's behavior will be directed toward the unknown goal region even if the goal's location *is* unknown. Stated differently, a difference exists between the person who does not know the nature of his or her goals and one who knows what and where his or her goals are but has no idea how to reach them.

Extensive serial monogamy is an example of the first kind of nonperception of tension-release. In extensive serial monogamy (when a person marries and divorces numerous times), the individual really does not have any idea of tension-reduction. The motivating factor which ends and begins each state is the desire to escape the present goal region which is perceived as negative. In contrast, an *extended* divorce state (with or without eventual remarriage) may be characterized by promiscuity, living in, living alone, etc. This epitomizes *search behavior.* The person knows that his or her goal *exists* but does not know where to find it—thus the distinction that Lewin felt was so important in field theory interpretations of behavior motivation.

6. *When there is a need present for a certain goal there is a corresponding force which may cause locomotion toward the goal and thus, equilibrium.* A critical assumption underlying field theory is that needs are accompanied by forces which result in behavior (locomotion). These needs appear to be both physically based and socially based as in the case of hunger and "need" for social power. Regardless of the origin of a need, Lewin felt that it created tension within the person's psychological field leading to a tendency toward locomotion within the field. Locomotion within the field was always toward a goal which would achieve *equilibrium* within the psychological field. *Equilibrium* was thought to exist when the tension level of a given region of the life space is equal to the tension levels of surrounding regions of the life space. This implies that locomotion (behavior) may or may not result

from a "need" or "intention." Locomotion is dependent to some extent upon the degree to which one interpersonal region is in communication with another region. Given that such communication exists, if a need arises in one region, locomotion from that region to the other occurs until a state of equilibrium is reached—that is, until the opposing forces in the two regions are approximately equal in strength.

Shaw and Costanzo have suggested that behavior changes may result from either decreases or increases in absolute tension levels. They point out that an increase in tension in one region or a decrease in tension in one region may result in equilibrium (meaning behavioral change). The only problem with this assertion is that they do not lucidly specify the regional increase. Presumably they mean that if the region close to the region in tension experiences an increase in tension which approximates the "tense" region, then equilibrium has occurred. This is the only logical interpretation one can make of the following statements:

> Change can be produced either by increasing the tension in the region where the behavior originally took place or by decreasing the tension in the region where the behavior originally took place or by decreasing the tension in the region to which locomotion is desired. In the first instance, the overall tension level is increased, leading to dissatisfaction; in the second case, the overall level is decreased and satisfaction is relatively high.
>
> Tension presumably has both general and specific effects. Lewin was never very clear on this point, but apparently the tension is associated with a particular region in some cases, whereas in other cases it is more pervasive and affects the entire system. The degree to which the tension level in one system can affect the tension level in another depends upon the permeability of the boundaries between regions. When the regions are highly differentiated and separated by rigid boundaries, the effects of events in one region on the tension level of another region are minor. However, when the regions are less clearly differentiated and the boundaries less rigid (and therefore more permeable), the interregional effects are great. This interregional exchange of tension reduction is referred to as substitute satisfaction (Shaw and Costanzo, p. 128).

An example of the preceding discussion is necessary at this point. Suppose we have a university student who must remain employed in order to continue his or her university education. Furthermore, let us propose that the student has flunked his or her midterm examination in a course essential to the curriculum being studied, but still has the option of either dropping the course or continuing in the course and maybe receiving a passing grade. In addition, this student has considered full-time employment in order to save money so that he or she might later attend the university on a full-time basis. Shaw and Costanzo's interpretation using the field theory perspective would be that the student has two related regions in the life space—*the student region* and *the occupation region*. One region is in a state of tension following the student's performance on the midterm examination. The other related region (occupation) remains relatively less "tense." Change, however, can occur as a result of decreasing tension in the student region or increasing tension in the occupational region. In the first instance, greater satisfaction is achieved by the student since tension is *low* in absolute terms (the decreased tension may result from more intense study). In the latter instance, while equilibrium has been achieved, satisfaction is likely to be less since tension remains *high* in absolute terms.

7. *The degree of interdependence of two tension systems within a person is some function of the general state of the person; that is, the degree to which the person is fluid or rigid.* Fluidity seems to characterize the following persons: the intelligent, the emotional, the young, the tired, those in fantasy states. The basic idea is that compartmentalization of tension systems in the life space quickly breaks down. While those who are intelligent may "see" things clearly, they also "see" things too clearly and thus fail to discriminate. This failure to discriminate enhances the likelihood that close connections between regions of the life space will be perceived. Those who are tired or under emotional stress are thought to be fluid because they, too, under such conditions may fail to discriminate simply because of the energy required or because they (emotional) cannot *perceive* distinct regions in the life space.

On the other hand, persons who are older, those who are less intelligent, those without emotional stress and those who tend to be more realistic all tend to have rigid regions within the life space with rather distinct lines of demarcation between tension systems. In other words, these are the people who can compartmentalize. The precise interactional results possible when a person is rested, intelligent, older, less emotional, and idealistic are not stated by Lewin and cannot be elaborated here. It would be interesting to know if Lewin felt that certain of these characteristics of a person at a particular time were more or less contributory to the interdependence of tension systems.

8. One activity which reduces tension in one tension system may reduce tension in another system if the two systems are subparts of a larger system. While there is interdependence between all of the regions of the life space, some regions are more closely aligned than others. This means that if there is tension in one region of the life space, this tension may be more related to some regions than others in the person's life space. Therefore, it stands to reason that activities which reduce tension in one region closely related to another region may be used as "substitute" tension reducers for the latter region.

The bisexual is a classic example of a person with two closely related life space (sex) regions, one of which at some point in time may be in a state of tension. The very nature of bisexuality implies that one activity can be easily substituted for another. Specifically, heterosexual relations and homosexual relations are easily substitutable, for the bisexual person, in the general arena of sexual activities. It should be pointed out that for the exclusively heterosexual person, homosexual and heterosexual regions of the life space are *not* related as closely. Usually, only if such an individual's psychological field has irresistible barriers toward heterosexual goal regions will the individual locomote toward a homosexual goal region—a prime example being incarceration for an extended period of time without access to members of the opposite sex.

The bisexual, however, is different from the heterosexual. In his or her case, because the homosexual and heterosexual regions of the life space are so closely related, he or she may engage in homosexual sexual activity as easily as heterosexual sexual activity. The reasons proposed here appear to be somewhat clear cut and are as follows: (1) the bisexual does not perceive great differences between males and females as sexual objects or as sources of sexual pleasure (both are potentially attractive); (2) the true bisexual is usually an individual with a history of substitutable sexual activity—this means that the individual has *not* been exclusively heterosexual or homosexual for long periods of time; and (3) each kind of sexual activity, for the bisexual person, results in sexual gratification (which is the nature of the goal of "doing something sexual"). For heterophilic persons "doing something sexual" automatically means engaging in a heterosexual sexual activity, however, for the bisexual person it may mean heterosexual *or* homosexual sexual activity. In short, for the bisexual person, homosexual sex and heterosexual sex are subparts of a general sex region of the life space. For the heterosexual person, while other sex-related activities may be substitutable (watching pornographic movies and pictures, talking about sex, fantasizing, etc.), homosexual sex is not a part of the sex region of the life space.

A Comment on Lewin's System

To sum up Lewin's system, six characteristics stand out as prominent features based on his approach to science, his basic concepts and theoretical assertions. These characteristics are (1) field theory assumes the use of the constructive method; (2) field theory is a dynamic approach; (3) field theory emphasizes pyschological processes; (4) field theory stresses molar or "whole" analyses; (5) field theory is ahistorical; and, (6) field theory suggests mathematical representations of psychological situations.

Lewin's basic statement of field theory was the forerunner of innumerable research investigations some of which will be discussed later. While the system does not enjoy the popularity it did two decades or so ago, still it remains an important perspective which is reflected in the research and theory of many contemporary social psychologists. Its influence should become apparent in discussions of some of the later developments in social psychology. A cursory examination of the numerous cognitive formulations and group dynamics models substantiates Lewin's present-day influence. Before considering these formulations, some attention will be devoted to other early contributions to field theory by several of Lewin's students and by Edward C. Tolman.

OTHER CONTRIBUTORS TO EARLY FIELD THEORY

Zeigarnik, Mahler, and Lissner: Students of Lewin

Bluma Zeigarnik's work clearly was the most significant of that of the three women whose experimental findings supported Lewin's field theory, although Vera Mahler's and Kate Lissner's works also contributed to the perspective. Zeigarnik, who received her Ph.D. from the University of Berlin in 1927 under the direction of Lewin, published her experimental findings in a paper with the translated title, according to Ellis, "On the Retention of Finished and Unfinished Tasks." The main hypothesis tested by Zeigarnik was Lewin's idea that psychological tension is a source of motivation until the intended task is completed.

Zeigarnik's findings supported Lewin's thesis. She found that when subjects were given a number of tasks to complete and were prevented from completing half of them, if instructed to recall the tasks worked on, recall of the incompleted tasks would be greater than of the completed ones. The results were analyzed and presented as follows:

$$\text{Zeigarnik Quotient} = \frac{\text{the number of incomplete tasks recalled}}{\text{the number of completed tasks recalled}}$$

In order for Lewin's assumption to be supported, the quotient would have to be greater than one. Zeigarnik obtained a quotient of approximately 1.9. However, because many completed tasks were recalled, Zeigarnik felt compelled to interpret her findings further. The interpretation offered was that the experimenter *induced* an additional *force* on the subjects when the subjects were *asked* to recall all of the tasks performed. Thus, the Zeigarnik quotient represents the relative strength of the induced force and the force toward task goals. Deutsch and Krauss state: "As the strength of the induced force increases in relation to the force toward task goals, the quotient should approach one; as it decreases in relative strength, the quotient should increase beyond one. Thus, when the strength of motivation associated with the interrupted task is relatively high, or when the strength of the experimenter's pressure to recall is low, or when the task is interrupted near its end, the Zeigarnik quotient will be high" (1965, p. 40).

Testing another one of Lewin's ideas, Vera Mahler's 1933 paper entitled "Substitute Activities of Different Degrees of Reality" reported findings supporting the contention that quasi-needs (intentions) could be satisfied and therefore tension reduced by substituting activity when the ordinary activity was not available.

Also in 1933, Kate Lissner published her findings on the value of substitute activities for reducing tension. She measured the value of substitute activity by "the amount of decrease in recall of the interrupted activity after a substitute activity had been completed." Lissner found that the *difficulty* of the substitute activity and the *similarity* of the substitute activity to the original one both were positively correlated with substitute value.

Edward C. Tolman and Field Theory

Tolman's "theory of learning," proposed initially in 1932, has been labelled "cognitive field theory" (Lundin, p. 252). It could well have been labelled "behavioral-gestalt-field theory." Tolman himself referred to his system as "purposive behaviorism" but recognized the influence that the gestalt perspective had on his thinking as reflected in basic assumptions and concepts in the formulation (p. 417). Perhaps due to a failure to distinguish between the gestalt perspective and the field theory perspective, Tolman did not *express* an affinity for the latter although *Purposive Behavior in Animals and Men* clearly contains field theory ideas and concepts.

Tolman felt that behavior was *purposive, cognitive* and *molar*. He felt that the emergent patterns and meanings of behavior could be studied objectively by collecting and ordering molar facts. Unfortunately he did not provide guidelines to accomplish this task. With respect to purposes, Tolman contended that they were purely objectively determined complex entities.

Essentially Tolman's system proposed that mental processes intervened (he introduced the concept of intervening variable) between stimuli and responses. These intervening variables had their sources in initiating physiological states, general heredity and past experiences, all of which were referred to as *behavior determinants*. The behavior determinants could be subdivided further into (1) purposes and cognitive determinants, (2) capacities and (3) behavior adjustments, and could be discovered by behavior experiments (p. 414). With respect to learning Tolman felt that it was a function of learning a cognitive map—a "whole," which was thought to be a type of field in the brain which enabled locomotion. Furthermore, learning was related to signs (environmental clues) sign-significates (objects), expectations and confirmation. In learning the organism built up, refined or corrected the expectations of sign-gestalts (wholes) such as signs significates and means-end relations. In later versions of his formulation Tolman discussed types of intervening variables borrowing heavily from Lewin's concepts valence, and life space to classify intervening variables according to *state of drive*, inferred motive and *locomotion (behavior) space*.

Because of Tolman's failure to present a logically integrated system of learning, perhaps his main contribution to the field theory perspective was to demonstrate that certain of its principles and concepts could be applied to interpretations of learning—thus, offering a partial (albeit fragmented) view of socialization from a field theory perspective.

During its formative years, the field theory perspective enjoyed contributions from numerous other investigators who experimentally tested some of its principles which were, in some instances, similar to gestalt principles. Sherif's experiment, mentioned in the gestalt chapter, is an example of the kind of dual perspective experimenting that occurred due to similarities between underlying assumptions in gestalt and field theory. It was during this period that the field theory perspective was recognized as the framework to be used in studying group behavior, and cognitive processes were given attention by scholars with a field theory orientation. The next section is devoted to two substantive areas in social psychology which are affected greatly by field theory—group dynamics and cognitive processes.

FIELD THEORY AND GROUP DYNAMICS

Group dynamics is an area in modern social psychology heavily influenced by field theory principles. Gone from what can be called modern field theory are many of the esoteric Lewinian concepts like valences, vectors, and hodology. Remaining, however, are many of the principles derived from early field theory related to the dynamics of group life. Specifically, principles related to interdependence, tension, molar analyses and the like are applied to groups. Specific questions have arisen when such principles have been used in the study of group behavior. For example, what is the relationship between membership change and stability or change in group functioning? Under what conditions will group changes increase group efficiency? How do groups promote change and/or resist change? The discovery of empirical relations among these phenomena and numerous others has been the focus of investigations in group dynamics.

Kurt Lewin's name has been associated with the origination of group dynamics as a field of specialty within social psychology, and there is good reason for linkage. Group dynamics began its emergence during the middle and late 1930s and emphasized a close relationship between theory and research. Much of the activity surrounding the emergence of group dynamics can be viewed as rebellion against existing conceptions of group life based on personal experiences, historical documents and, in general, speculation. Lewin had already conducted and directed numerous experiments on specific aspects of his field theory system. By the late 1930s, his writing began to reflect a movement away from individual psychology and toward the study of group processes—how groups are formed, how they relate to other groups, group cohesiveness, leadership, etc. In fact, after the early 1940s Lewin devoted most of his attention to group dynamics and applied research. Chaplin and Krawiec credit Lewin and his associates with launching group dynamics, founding action research and laying the foundation for the sensitivity training movement. Furthermore, they feel that Lewin had a greater impact on social psychology than any other individual (p. 585).

Despite Lewin's contributions to the emergence of group dynamics (aside from his theoretical and research contributions, Lewin popularized the concept group dynamics and established the first group dynamics research center), Cartwright and Zander suggest that group dynamics was the result of a convergence of certain trends within the social sciences and society in general (p. 7). More specifically, they refer to society's increasing emphases on human relations and the importance of groups, favorable cultural and economic conditions and many other developments as fostering the emergence of group dynamics.

Certainly the supportive nature of society, the point of development of the social sciences and contributions from other scholars played roles in the emergence of group dynamics as an identifiable field of inquiry. Group dynamics, however, owes a great deal to Kurt Lewin. Its approach has been unmistakably Lewinian. The emphasis in group dynamics on studying the group as a gestalt, the idea that group properties are different from the sum of group parts, the emphases on contemporaneous dynamics and causal interrelations among members of groups and subgroups, cohesiveness, strength of barriers against members leaving the group and forces of attraction within the group all are direct descendents of Lewin's field theory. Several significant publications in the late 1930s and early 1940s contributed to the entrenchment of group dynamics as a field of inquiry in social psychology. The work of Kurt Lewin, Ronald Lippitt and Ralph White conducted at the Iowa Child Welfare Research Station during these years has been referred to as the most influential in regard to group dynamics' emergence (Cartwright and Zander). Yet other important work was under way by scholars such as Theodore Newcomb (1943) and W. F. Whyte. Newcomb's contribution to the emergence of group dynamics and a study reported by Lippitt and White (1943) are discussed below because they are representative of the work conducted during the emerging years of group dynamics. In addition, the influence of field theory during this period should become apparent, as reflected in their works.

Theodore Newcomb's
Bennington Study

During the years 1935 to 1939 Theodore M. Newcomb conducted a study of student attitudes at Bennington College in Vermont which would ultimately show that attitudes are often anchored in social groups. Bennington college had been founded in 1932 and is a small liberal arts college for women that emphasized individual and small group instruction. Faculty-student relations were characteristically informal, democratic and "group-like." In short, Bennington College at that time was a self-contained community meeting most of the needs of its members. Newcomb observed that most of the students had come from conservative backgrounds yet the college atmosphere was liberal. What accounted for this seeming anomaly? Newcomb felt that perhaps there were *properties in the college atmosphere* which affected student attitudes once they arrived at Bennington, and he was correct as we shall see.

Using political and economic attitudinal change as units of cognition, Newcomb found that the "group" contributed to attitudinal change as students progressed from their freshman year to their senior year of college. Generally, conservatism decreased with an increase in the amount of time spent at Bennington. Not only was the senior class found to be more liberal than the freshman classes but as students progressed through the classes, their attitudes became more liberal each year. What caused this attitudinal change? Why did it occur? Newcomb concluded that the nature of information assimilated by students during their stay at Bennington provided a partial answer. Since the college atmosphere was liberal, students were exposed generally to liberal information. He also found that students may have been encouraged to assimilate liberal information since liberal attitudes seemed to be linked with social rewards. In other words, it may have been "socially profitable" for students to adopt liberal attitudes. Because not all students changed their attitudes, Newcomb had to offer an interpretation for these "deviant" cases. He chose to explore individual differences between conservative and nonconservative students and suggested that many of those who remained conservative had formed small interest groups at the outset of their freshman year and may have remained somewhat isolated from the college community. He also noted that some deviant cases had strong family ties with conservative families and this may have served as a buffer against the liberal atmosphere. Thus, the value of social rewards at Bennington would be lessened by the value of social rewards to be gained from maintaining conservative attitudes consistent with those providing social support. Newcomb's study demonstrated the influence of group properties on its individual members—the influence of the "whole" on its "parts."

Lippitt and White's "Social Climate" Study

Following the "social climate" study reported in 1939 by Lewin, Lippitt and White revealing differences in the behavior of childrens' groups under authoritarian and democratic styles of adult leadership, other experimental results such as the famous one by Lippitt and White (1943) were published in the same tradition in the early 1940s. These studies also used a holistic approach and examined the life spaces of subjects. The 1943 experimental results received widespread attention and will be considered here briefly. Lippitt and White experimentally induced three types of "social climates" in five-member children's groups. Attempts were made to match the groups equally on such characteristics as socioeconomic status, personality, patterns of interpersonal relations, intellectual level and physical prowess. The groups were led by adults who had received instruction in either authoritarian, democratic or *laissez-faire* leadership styles and who were moved from one club to another after a six week period and who also changed leadership style. Each club experienced each leadership style under a different leader. The location of the club meetings was the same for all clubs; and, club members engaged in similar activities related to hobby activities. Interviews were conducted with boys and their parents concerning affectivity toward the clubs, reaction to the club and parent-child relationships.

Leadership style was successfully induced as data on leader-behavior in the three different leadership situations revealed. All were statistically significant. *Authoritarian leaders* generally determined all group policy, controlled all group activity by dictating the policy step by step, dictated the work task for each group member and who would work with whom, personalized criticism and praise of the work of group members, and maintained role distance except when showing members how to perform a particular task. *Democratic leaders* made all policy a matter of group decision and encouraged leader-assisted discussion, did *not* make unilateral decisions about steps to be taken in activities (thus allowing choices to be made), allowed members to choose their companion worker, offered objective criticism and praise of group members and did *not* maintain role distances. In the *laissez-faire* climate, leaders, as much as possible, allowed members to make all group or individual decisions, directed activity and supplied information only when asked, did not participate in group activities, and did not criticize or praise member performance.

Lippitt and White concluded after data analysis that the *laissez-faire* social climate produced different characteristics in group members' behaviors than did the *democratic* social climate. They found that the *laissez-faire* climate produced less organization, less completed work, more nontask behavior (playing) and a preference for a democratic climate (*laissez-faire* club members expressed a preference for their democratic leaders). In contrast, a democratic social climate seemed to produce enhanced interest in group activities as suggested by a greater percentage of "work minded conversation" and group members' tendencies to continue working during the temporary absence of group leaders. Group members were also more creative and original in their work. Autocratic climates appeared to create hostility and aggression in some instances and submission in others. Also, club members in autocratic conditions were more dependent and exhibited less individuality. Despite these disadvantages, however, the greatest quantity of work was produced under autocratic conditions. Group dynamics, heavily influenced by the field theory perspective was certainly underway with studies such as this and the emphases on group properties.

Lewin continued to influence the developing area with the publication of "Frontiers in Group Dynamics: Concept, Method and Reality in Social Science; Social Equilibria and Social Change" (1947), in which he outlined a procedure for the analysis of group life. The procedure involved taking into account group goals, group values, group perception of its own situation and the situations of other groups. For Lewin, this meant that a three-step sequence must be followed moving from (1) the separate analysis of the life space of each group to (2) an analysis of group conduct within the total group field to (3) an analysis once again of the effect on the group life space. In this way, it becomes possible to glean changes in the situation caused by action. In other words, the circular causal process that characterizes basic properties of group life is highlighted. Lewin felt that this kind of analysis moved from "perception" to "action" and back again to "perception." For him, perception was important and how perception was changed also was important since it in turn influenced action. In brief, for Lewin, analyses in the social science had to take into account both aspects of the circular process whether groups or individuals were units of analysis.

Morton Deutsch's Theory of Cooperation and Competition

With publications such as these, the focus of group dynamics was clear. It was to be a field of inquiry concerned with the nature of social groups, their development and their interdependence with individuals and other social groups. Prior to the beginning of the 1950s, which was characterized by a flurry of group dynamics activity, two noteworthy publications in field theory appeared, written by Morton Deutsch (one of Kurt Lewin's students). These were entitled "A Theory of Cooperation and Competition" and "An Experimental Study of the Effects of Cooperation and Competition upon Group Process." In his theoretical article, Deutsch proposed a theory concerning the effects of cooperation and competition on group functioning. The hypotheses derived in the theoretical article were tested in the second article and the results reported.

In "A Theory of Cooperation and Competition," Deutsch begins by defining cooperative social situations and competitive social situations. *Cooperative* social situations are defined as those where the goal regions for each individual or subunits of the situation can be entered by any other individual or subunit of the situation. Deutsch uses *promotively interdependent goals* as a nominal concept for the definition. *Competitive* social situations are viewed as those situations where penetration of goal regions of individuals or subunits by any other individual(s) or subunit(s) result in the former individuals or subunits being unable to reach their goal(s) to some degree in the social situation. This situation is called *contriently interdependent goals*. He refers to his concepts as "pure" types and thus not likely to be found in real life situations which he feels are usually characterized by both competition and cooperation with respect to goals and subgoals.

From the above definitions, Deutsch proposes that persons who have promotively interdependent goals with others will have promotively interdependent locomotions in the direction of their goals with others, and those who had contriently interdependent goals with others would come to have contriently interdependent locomotions with others in the direction of their goal. A major assumption made by Deutsch is that persons in cooperative social situations all occupy similar relative positions with respect to their goals and thus, locomotion of any one person results in locomotion in the same direction of others in that situation. In contrast, persons in competitive situations can occupy similar or different positions with respect to their goals and locomotion by one does not necessarily affect locomotion of others although the relative positions of persons could be affected.

Introducing additional psychological assumptions, Deutsch relates the above statements, which he called statements about events in objective social space, to specific events in individual life spaces. Basic hypotheses proposed include two related to perception which suggest that *those persons exposed to cooperative and competitive social situations would perceive themselves as more promotively interdependent and contriently interdependent respectively*. Other hypotheses proposed are related to greater substitutability of actions, more reciprocal liking, more reciprocal rewarding, less self conflict, less obstructing of goals and more helpfulness in cooperative groups than in competitive groups. On a group functioning level, Deutsch hypothesizes greater coordination of effort, more frequent coordination of effort, more homogeneity with respect to amount of individual contributions, greater specialization of functions, more structural stability and more organizational flexibility in cooperative situations than competitive ones. All in all, Deutsch proposes thirty-four hypotheses related (in addition to the above) to motivation, communication, orientation, group productivity, and interpersonal relations.

His second article reports the results of an experiment designed to test hypotheses in the theoretical formulation. Using ten five-person groups, consisting of volunteers from an introductory psychology course, Deutsch experimentally induced cooperation and competition into the groups and concluded that both the perception hypotheses and the group functioning hypothesis were supported.

In the 1950s group dynamics research and theoretical development flourished. Scholars such as Leon Festinger, Stanley Schachter, Kurt Back, Dorwin Cartwright and many others made lasting contributions to social psychology in general and group dynamics in particular. Two classical contributions, by Stanley Schachter and Leon Festinger, are discussed below. These contributions are chosen because of their typicality and their importance to the entrenchment of group dynamics.

Stanley Schachter's "Deviation, Rejection and Communication"

Schachter's point of departure in this significant work was several findings in a study of Festinger, Schachter and Back (1950). In this study (which is also considered to be extremely important to the development of group dynamics), data produced indicated among other things that cohesiveness of the group was positively correlated with the group's ability to influence its members; and that deviation tends to be less in more cohesive groups than in lesser cohesive groups. In other words, the findings supported the hypothesis that uniformity in behavior of individuals is some function of the operation of group standards.

Schachter made a significant contribution to social psychology with "Deviation, Rejection and Communication," which reports findings obtained from an experiment designed to test the empirical adequacy of several propositions including the following: within any group there are pressures toward uniformity of attitudes; the origins of such pressures are in social reality and locomotion; the strength of the pressures toward uniformity that a group can exercise on its members will vary with the cohesiveness of the group and the relevance of the issue to the group; and, if differences of opinions exist within a group, forces will arise for the members to restore uniformity.

Communication was thought to be the mechanism used by groups to exert power over its members and was thought to vary with degree of deviation. In other words extreme deviation from group standards was thought to result in increased communication to the deviate. Specific hypotheses proposed for Schachter's experiment also included the ideas that rejection of deviates would be greater in relevant groups than in nonrelevant groups; and, with relevance held constant, rejection of deviates would be greater in high cohesive than in low cohesive groups.

Schachter designed an experiment in which "cohesiveness" and "relevance" were each dichotomized resulting in four group types. He assigned eight groups consisting of five to seven naive subjects to each group type. Within each group there were three paid confederate subjects who assumed three different roles. One confederate played an extreme deviate role throughout the experiment, another assumed the position that the modal numbers of group members at any time supported, and a third confederate began the experiment by assuming an extreme deviate position but during the course of the experiment moved step by step to the modal position. Subjects were college students who volunteered to be members of four clubs that would meet over time. These consisted of a movie club, editorial club, radio club and a case study club. The clubs were described to the students who then indicated their interest in belonging to a particular club. Students who indicated a high interest in belonging to the case study club and the movie club were assigned to those clubs. The editorial club and the radio club were composed of students who had expressed little, if any, interest in belonging to those clubs. The former clubs were labelled high cohesive groups and the latter clubs were labelled low cohesive groups. Relevance and nonrelevance also were experimentally induced by experimenter statements that the activity to be engaged in either was important to the group or unimportant to the group.

The activity involved the following: each subject was asked to read the life history of "Johnny Rocco," a juvenile delinquent who was to be sentenced for committing a minor crime. Clubs then were asked to discuss and come to some decision about "what should be done with this kid?" The discussion was guided by a seven point scale ranging from "extend love and understanding" to "severely punish him." Because of the design of the life history, most subjects chose a scale position close to the "extend love and understanding" end of the continuum. First, the five to seven naive members of each group were asked to announce their positions and then the three confederate subjects announced theirs. A forty-five minute discussion period followed the announcements during which time observations of who spoke to whom and the length of time persons interacted were recorded. Following the discussion, the experimenter attempted to assess "rejection" through member nominations of others to important or dull commit-tees and a sociometric test.

With respect to communication patterns, Schachter felt that there should be relatively few communications to persons in the modal role; communications to the slider should decrease as the slider moved to the modal role; in higher cohesive-relevant groups, the amount of com-munication addressed to the deviate by those not rejecting the deviate should increase throughout the experiment. Those strongly rejecting the deviate were predicted to reach a peak of communication and then decline continuously. The mild rejectors were predicted to reach a peak later and then decline. Experimental results generally supported Schachter's hypotheses. For example, in high cohesive-relevant groups, communication to deviates decreased near the end of the forty-five minute discussion period and was interpreted by Schachter as rejection because of group pressures toward uniformity. Sociometric test results and committee nomination data produced following the discussion in-dicated that the deviates were rejected but when the same individuals assumed slider and modal roles they were not rejected. Also, rejection seemed to be greater in high cohesive groups than in low cohesive groups but no differences in rejection were found between relevant and nonrelevant groups.

Leon Festinger's Theory of Social Comparison Processes

Another important figure in group dynamics and field theory has been Leon Festinger. A student of Lewin's, Festinger published extensively in group dynamics during the early 1950s. One influential publication was his article ''A Theory of Social Comparison Processes.'' He had already published ''Informal Social Communications'' which had provided an interpretative framework for early group dynamics research such as Schachter's study. His theory of social comparison processes was an at-tempt to extend the latter formulation to other areas including ap-praisal and evaluation of abilities in social groups. Using experimental data derived from three experiments designed to test predictions from the extension of the theory as well as findings from other research in-vestigations as corroborative material, Festinger presented his formula-tion.

Beginning with the hypothesis that *there exists in persons a drive to evaluate their opinions and abilities,* Festinger proposed that the basis for evaluation when objective, nonsocial means are unavailable will be *a comparison of one's own abilities and opinions with others' opinions and abilities.* Two corollaries of this hypothesis were that when no physical or social comparison could be made, subjective evaluations of opinions and abilities were unstable; and, comparisons with others are unlikely when one can evaluate his or her abilities and opinions using objective, nonsocial bases for evaluation. Festinger also postulated that social comparison is related to homogeneity in that increases in differences between a person and those who will be used in the comparison process result in a decrease in the tendency to compare oneself with these divergent others. Corollary statements and derivations included a tendency for persons to choose those close to their own abilities and opinions for comparisons, a tendency for persons to make imprecise evaluations of their opinions and abilities when comparisons were extremely divergent from them. Derivatively, this resulted in *stability of subjective evaluations* of opinions and abilities when others similar to oneself are used for comparison and a tendency to change one's evaluation of the opinion or ability when persons used for comparison are very divergent. In addition, Festinger suggested that persons will be less attracted to those situations where others are very different than to those where persons are felt to be close in terms of abilities and opinions. Moreover, persons within a group will actively attempt to reduce discrepancies with respect to opinions and abilities within the group.

Festinger proposed certain differences between the "behavior" of opinions and abilities. For example, he felt that with respect to abilities, there was a unidirectional drive upward (people attempt to do better and better) which was not the case with opinions (there is no inherent reason for preferring one opinion over another). Also, while there are few nonsocial restraints on changing one's opinions, there may exist many nonsocial restraints on changing one's abilities. Two subderivations of the latter hypothesis proposed by Festinger were (1) a tendency to change one's own position so as to move closer to the group when discrepancies in opinions and abilities exist within a group; and (2) a tendency to change others in the group to bring them closer to oneself. Several other hypotheses and corollaries were advanced by Festinger relating to the field theory concepts of driving, constraining and restraining forces, including statements about pressures toward uniformity of opinions within groups and pressures toward reduction of divergencies in opinions and abilities. Festinger was convinced that his model not only had implications for the behavior of persons in groups but that it also clarified some of the processes of group formation, movement into a group and movement away from a group. The selective tendencies to join some groups and leave other groups, for Festinger, could be located in the drive for self-evaluation.

NEW DEVELOPMENTS IN GROUP DYNAMICS

Deviation and Rejection in Groups

Since the initial studies and theoretical statements in group dynamics, literally thousands of others have been published, many to some degree influenced by Lewin's system. Investigations have revealed much about group formation, group membership, power and influence in groups, structural properties in groups, motivational processes in groups and numerous other dynamics. Using a variety of methodological techniques including laboratory experiments, field studies, natural experiments and field experiments, researchers have focused upon the dynamics of group life. Currently in social psychology investigations are under way to refine and modify knowledge about the functioning of social groups. Within recent years numerous such refinements have been published. For example, Schachter's finding that deviates are likely to be rejected in high cohesive relevant groups has been refined to include other variables. One such variable is *deviate interference with the attainment of a valued group goal* (Suchner and Jackson). The more the deviate's deviation interfered with group goal attainment, the stronger the rejection. In a recent article, Miller and Anderson offer a further refinement. They propose that group decision rules affect the rejection of deviates. In other words, the rule by which a decision is reached affects the extent to which a deviate is rejected in a group. They hypothesize that under majority rule it is impossible for a lone deviate to impede group goal attainment (get his or her way against the opinion of other group members), and thus the deviate should not be rejected too strongly. When the group operates under dictatorship rule two hypotheses emerge. One is that when a deviate is one of the group members other than the dictator (and thus cannot affect group decision), only mild rejection by group members should occur. On the other hand, when the deviate *is* the dictator and makes a decision contrary to group opinion, there should be substantial rejection. In social situations where groups make decisions by unanimity rule, Miller and Anderson also suggested two hypotheses: (1) because situations of unanimity rule usually imply the existence of an alternative (the status quo) which cannot be changed unless there is unanimous support, if the deviate decides in favor of the status quo, rejection is likely to be strong from those opposed to the status quo; (2) if all group members except the deviate support the status quo, because the deviate cannot have his or her own way, rejection is likely to be minimum.

Two hundred and fifty-six female students in an introductory psychology course divided into sixty-four groups of four naive subjects and an experimental confederate were used in an experiment to test the above hypotheses. Groups were informed that because of the cost associated with consulting services and maintaining committees of professional people at correctional institutions for youth which functioned with a parole board, the state of Illinois had to address the issue of possibly lessening cost by using nonprofessionals to make decisions regarding youth confinement and/or release. Groups were told further that the state of Illinois wanted to investigate how these decisions were reached and that they should act as a committee considering further confinement or release. Each group was given the case history of "Tommy," a hypothetical youth confined to an Illinois correctional facility, and asked to read the case history individually and to individually recommend the youth's release or continued confinement. Also, subjects had to indicate whether they were "slightly," "somewhat" or "strongly" in favor of their recommendation. The case history read by the subjects was slanted to induce the subjects to prefer Tommy's release. Following individual recommendations, subjects were asked to discuss the case and arrive at a group decision under one of five conditions assigned by the experimenter: majority rule, dictatorship rule with the deviate as dictator, dictatorship rule with the deviate not the dictator, unanimity rule with the deviate preferring the status quo, and unanimity rule with a deviate who preferred an alternative to the status quo.

Miller and Anderson found that group decision rules had no effect as long as the deviate could not impose her will on the group. Also there were no differences between the conditions in the way group members attributed responsibility for the decision, rejected the deviate or perceived the representativeness of the decision (p. 361). Group members tended to perceive each other as responsible for the group decision and deviates were only mildly rejected. The decision was perceived to be representative and the rule used in decision-making was defined as relatively fair. These results were in contrast to those obtained when the deviate could have her own way despite the preferences of others. Under these conditions, the deviate was held responsible for the decision and also was strongly rejected. Decisions were perceived as unrepresentative and the decision rule was thought to be unfair. However, if the decision were made under dictatorship rather than unanimity rule, group members saw themselves as less responsible and the deviate as more responsible. Deviates were rejected more, decisions were perceived as less representative and the decision rule was felt to be less fair. As Miller and Anderson suggest, their study related to

Festinger's idea (1950) that the desire for group locomotion is an important source of pressure toward uniformity in groups. Their findings lend support to this contention.

That pressures are directed at deviates in social groups to adopt the opinion of the majority or to conform to group norms is supported by findings from numerous studies. The most widely known of such studies was discussed earlier and is the one conducted by Schachter. In the early 1970s, however, publications by Moscovici and Faucheux, and Moscovici and Nemeth, were devoted to minority influence in the absence of particular resources or knowledge. *Behavioral style of the minority* was found to be an important determinant of minority influence. More specifically, Nemeth, Swedlund and Kanki conclude from their study that when minorities are perceived as *consistent* and *confident* in their judgments, they can influence the majority. Nemeth and Wachtler note that the studies from which the above findings emerged were devoid of overt group pressures to change, since subjects were allowed only to state their individual judgments regarding the color of slides and an estimation of their luminosity without discussing their judgmental differences. The question raised by Nemeth and Wachtler is "in a discussion situation where pressures toward uniformity are stressed, can a minority sway the consensus toward his (her) own position or will the majority, if unsuccessful, simply derogate the minority and maintain its own position?" Noting that Schachter's study had provided support for the latter occurrence, Nemeth and Wachtler postulate that the deviate is potentially influential provided there is the appearance of *consistency* and *confidence*. Consistency and confidence are felt to (1) define an alternative position to that of the majority and (2) to inform the majority that uniformity of opinion will not occur through the minority relinquishing their position. Nemeth and Wachtler further propose that the appearance of consistency and confidence in the minority produce conflict in the majority and provided consensus toward which the majority-in-conflict could move. Movement toward the minority position is thought to be likely under conditions of a weakening majority, since a consensus around the minority would be more stable than one around the majority (p. 531).

Nemeth and Wachtler designed an experiment to test effects of a consistent and confident minority on a majority's position. One hundred and sixteen male university students who volunteered for the study were divided into groups of five and brought into a waiting room. A 2 x 3 factorial design with a control was used. A confederate (who served in all six conditions) plus four naive subjects constituted groups in the experiment with the exception of the control group where all five subjects were naive. There were four groups per experimental condition and four groups in the control condition. When a group was brought into the waiting room, subjects were given a case study to read involving a personal injury sustained by "Mr. Smith" while he was at work repairing washing machines. Mr. Smith had already received compensation for hospitalization costs and wages lost during his recuperation. Mr. Smith was suing for the maximum allowable on an insurance policy which was $25,000 to compensate for past and present pain, grief, worry and the possibility of permanent damage since a physician had indicated that the knee would slip out of joint if sudden pressure on the knee was applied. Moreover, Mr. Smith had been told that he might not be able to resume his only recreational activity, bowling. When subjects finished reading the case study, they were instructed to consider, in the manner of jury deliberations, how much they would award Mr. Smith to compensate him for the pain and suffering that he had endured and perhaps would be enduring in the future. Subjects wrote down their initial judgments of the compensation. Pretests had revealed that the vast majority of the subjects gave between $12,000 and $20,000, and none awarded less than $8,000. Subjects then were taken to a discussion room (where they remained standing) and asked to discuss the case (for which they would be paid) for up to forty minutes during which time they should attempt to arrive at a unanimous decision. If unanimity were reached, subjects were told that they would receive an extra 50 cents. The conditions were described by Nemeth and Wachtler:

> In the Chosen conditions, subjects were then asked to take a seat. In the Chosen Head condition, the confederate took the head chair; in the Chosen Side conditions, the confederate took one of two side chairs (each being chosen equally often). In the 'Assigned' conditions, the experimenter assigned subjects to their chairs. In the Assigned Head condition, the confederate was assigned to the head chair; in the Assigned Side conditions, he was assigned to one of the side chairs (p. 533).

During the discussion the confederate took an extremely deviate position, awarding Mr. Smith only $3,000. Six arguments recited from memory were used to support this position, and the deviate talked as much as (but not more than) anyone else. Following the discussion subjects were asked to respond to a questionnaire containing a request for their own opinion once again on the compensation, since no group decision could be reached; a request for their opinion on the case if certain specifics were changed; their perception of other group members;

and, their opinion on another case involving a housewife who suffered injuries in an automobile accident.

Four dependent variables were used to assess confederate influences. They were, first, a change score derived from a comparison of the initial private opinion and the private opinion regarding compensation subsequent to the discussion. A second dependent variable was obtained when subjects were asked to state their opinion on compensation if the maximum allowable were $50,000 and if they alone could decide the amount of damage to award. A comparison of the latter opinions was made with the initial opinions to form a third dependent variable. The fourth one was produced from the opinions stated about the new case. A decrease in compensation following the discussion period was interpreted to mean that there had been confederate influence.

The results presented by the authors showed that the confederate was viewed as more consistent and confident in all experimental conditions as well as more central, strong-willed, more of a leader, more independent and more active than were the naive subjects. He was also seen as less reasonable, fair, perceptive, warm, cooperative, liked, admired and wanted than the naive subjects (p. 537). There were condition differences however. When the confederate occupied head seats he was seen as more consistent, less unfair, less unperceptive, less cold and more active than when he sat in a side chair. Also, when he chose the head chair, the confederate was viewed as more consistent than when he was assigned a head chair, assigned a side chair or chose a side chair. He was also viewed as more confident than when he was assigned a head chair or chose a side seat. *Choosing the head seat* seemed to enhance perceived confidence and consistency. It also seemed to render the confederate effective in influencing majority opinion as indicated by the "change" scores. A final point made by the authors is that *there does not have to be a positive relationship between liking and influence, especially since stability or consistency and confidence can render persons effective in influencing others.* Their findings, interestingly enough, are consistent with those suggesting an association between leadership, high social status and sitting at the head of a table rather than at the side of a table (Dreyer and Dreyer).

The Risky Shifts Phenomenon

"Risky shifts" is another field of inquiry in contemporary group dynamics influenced by the field theory perspective. This is the nominal concept applied to choice shifts that occur in members of a group engaged in risk-taking behavior after they have engaged in the same kind of risk-taking behavior individually. Stoner is credited with initiating research on risky shifts. Subjects were asked to read brief accounts of personal or professional life conflicts. They were then instructed to advise a hypothetical person as to which one of two alternative courses of action should be followed. Lewin, perhaps, would have defined the hypothetical persons as being in a situation of approach-approach conflict. However, in each of the life conflicts, one alternative was more risky than the other. For each situation, after evaluating the risk levels of both alternatives, subjects were instructed to indicate the probability of success level necessary for them to have before suggesting to the hypothetical person the more risky alternative. Following this phase of the experiment, subjects were placed in groups, asked to read and evaluate the same life conflicts, and to arrive at a group decision concerning the probability of success level necessary before advising the hypothetical person to choose the more risky alternative. Findings from this study evoked considerable attention since group decisions were found to significantly shift toward risk—groups containing individuals who had expressed more conservative probability of success levels moved to more liberal probability of success levels.

Since the early 1970s increased attention had been devoted to the mechanisms underlying shifts in risk levels. Explanations of the risky shift phenomenon have included *diffusion of responsibility* (Wallach and Kogan), *task inadequacy, task oriented group discussion* (Cartwright, 1971) and *intraindividual-interindividual processes*. The latter explanation involves both individual familiarization with the task which is reflected in increases in risk-taking and the field theory influenced concept, social comparison process (Blascovich). The intraindividual-interindividual processes explanation appears to be quite plausible, since Blascovich, Veach and Eisenberg report findings indicating risk-taking is some function of group membership. Referring to the interindividual aspect of the pluralistic explanation, Blascovich and Ginsburg propose that "a norm concerning socially acceptable risk levels will emerge when a series of risk taking decisions is made" (p. 207). They further suggest that socially acceptable risk-taking levels are higher in groups because of a latent cultural value favoring riskiness. When persons became members of groups, they often discover that their risk-taking levels are no higher than others, even though they might have speculated otherwise prior to their entrance into the group. Given the cultural value of risk-taking, when persons compare their risk-taking levels, a norm emerges within the group that is higher than average risk-taking levels of individual members and results in accentuating those members' individual levels of risk-taking. In order for the norm to emerge, group members need only to exchange information about their risk preferences.

Blascovich and Ginsburg, in testing some of these ideas, found support for the idea that information-exchange-social comparison process causes group shifts in risk-taking. Moreover, their findings suggest that the process can increase or decrease risk-taking levels of individuals. When risk-taking levels of others within a group are higher than an individual's risk-taking level, that individual conforms by increasing his or her level of risk-taking. When the risk-taking levels of others are similar to one's own, there is a tendency for persons to maintain their levels of risk-taking; and, when the risk-taking levels of others are below one's own risk-taking levels, the individual will lower his or her own risk-taking level. Finally, Blascovich and Ginsburg received support from the data regarding their hypothesis that a group member will increase or decrease his or her level of risk-taking, relative to his or her earlier individual level, in accord with the risk-taking preferences of the other group members (Blascovich and Ginsburg, p. 215).

Undoubtedly, findings such as this provided further support for what became known as "the risky shifts phenomenon." However, as Baron and Byrne report (1981), other findings (for example, those of Knox and Safford) suggest that group discussion produces a shift toward *caution*. These findings have led to a more recent view that group discussion leads members to become more *extreme*. Thus, if a group of individuals is mildly in favor of a cut in federal taxes prior to group discussion, following group discussion they may be expected to be more strongly in favor of a tax cut measure. A similar shift can be expected if a group were initially opposed to a cut in federal taxes prior to group discussion. This phenomenon has been referred to as a *shift toward polarization* and its effects are thought to be broad in scope (for example, courtroom decisions and equity decisions). Simulated jury studies such as those conducted by Myers and Kaplan, and Kaplan, support the evidence of a group polarization effect. Persons in these studies, following group discussion, became more extreme in their judgments about the guilt or innocence of a defendant. More recently, Greenberg found that subjects in group conditions where group discussion followed individual decisions to allocate rewards equitably more strictly invoked the equity norm in allocating rewards after the discussion. This shift did not occur among subjects in the individual condition where group discussion did not occur.

One explanation often cited for group polarization is the *social comparison process* discussed earlier. In Baron and Byrne's words "polarization effects stem from (1) our desire to feel that we are well above average, and (2) the tendency to shift toward extremity that develops when we learn that we do not really occupy this favored, valued position''(p. 437). Another explanation, however, seems just as plausible. Based on research by such scholars as Ebbesen and Bowers, Morgan and Abram, and Vinokur and Burnstein, group polarization may be seen as some function of *persuasive arguments*. Findings from these studies suggest that group shift in the direction of a particular viewpoint is positively related to the *proportion of arguments* in favor of a particular viewpoint. Moreover, when groups consist of two subgroups favoring opposite viewpoints, group discussion seemingly leads to depolarization, each group moving toward the position of the other (Vinokur and Burnstein). At this stage in the development of the group polarization phenomenon two competing explanations are often given. Baron and Byrne have stated in essence that a choice may not be necessary, since both may be operative. Persons may wish to show that their views are above average and may become quite sure that they are the best views when they hear persuasive arguments in favor of their initial views.

"Risky shift" research continues to be popular among social psychologists. Some of its major theoretical explanations have their origins in Lewin's system and in this sense contribute to the persistence of general ideas of field theory in present day social psychology.

Groups and Individual Behavior

That individuals behave differently in group or aggregate situations than they do when alone is well-documented in social psychological literature. Such findings lend support to the field theory holistic approach and to modern day group dynamics. Two studies conducted in the late 1960s have become classics in the field and illustrate how the perceived or actual presence of others affects individual responses in emerging situations. "Presence of others" seems to act as a boundary zone which resists psychological and physical locomotion of persons in the face of emergencies. While impersonal forces such as social norms and values may dictate helping behavior in emergency situations, *fear of social blunders* and *diffusion of responsibility* may act as restraining forces inhibiting *prosocial behavior*. Prosocial behavior is defined as "acts that have no obvious benefit for the person responding, though they benefit some other person and/or conform to a set of moral standards" (Baron and Byron, p. 272).

In the first study, the *critical situation* (a simulated epileptic seizure) was said to create a type of field theory conflict (avoidance-avoidance) for many subjects who vacillated between potential responses to a "victim." Thus, instead of choosing not to help, nonresponders simply were unable to leave the "field" and attempted to reduce their felt stress and conflict by diffusing responsibility for help, although as Darley and Latane suggest nonhelping subjects appear more emotionally aroused than helping subjects—a "sign of their continuing nonresolved conflict" (p. 382).

"Bystander Intervention in Emergencies: Diffusion of Responsibility" is a classic experiment by John M. Darley and Bibb Latane. Beginning their article by recounting the killing of Kitty Genovese in New York City (witnessed by at least thirty-eight nonhelping people from their apartment windows), Darley and Latane posit the idea that factors other than apathy or indifference may have operated against the extension of help to Kitty Genovese. They suggested that the responsibility for helping may have been diffused among onlookers as well as the diffusion of any potential blame for not taking action. Additionally, persons might have perceived that help had already been initiated (p. 377).

In order to test their ideas, Darley and Latane created an experiment similar to the Genovese murder in that in some experimental conditions subjects knew others were aware of an emergency "but were prevented by walls between them from communication . . ." Fifty-nine female and thirteen male students in introductory psychology courses at New York University took part in the experiment. When a subject arrived for the experiment, he or she was taken to a long corridor with several small rooms off it. He or she was then taken to one of the rooms by an assistant and given a pair of headphones with an attached microphone and told to listen to instructions.

The subject was told over the intercom that the purpose of the experiment was to learn about certain personal problems facing college students, and because others with whom he or she would be discussing these problems were strangers, all would remain anonymous. Even the experimenter would be unable to hear the discussion. Further instructions revealed that subjects would talk in turn (for two minutes), and when any one microphone was on, the other would be off—thus only one subject could be heard at one time. Each subject was led to believe that either there was only one other student in the experiment, or two other students, or five other students (in reality, no other student was in the experiment, only the subject and one or more tape recordings made by student confederates) (Baron and Byrne, p. 275; Darley and Latane). Once the discussion began, each individual including the potential victim and the real subject made a brief introductory statement. Then, when it was the victim's turn to talk again, he appeared to have an epileptic seizure. Three conditions existed: a two-person condition where the naive subject perceived that he or she alone knew of the problem; a three-person condition where the naive subject perceived at least one other person knew of the problem; and a six-person condition where it was perceived that five others knew that there was an emergency. What would happen?

What in fact happened was as follows: 85 percent of the subjects who perceived themselves to be alone reported the seizure before the "victim" was cut off; 62 percent of those in the three-person groups and 31 percent of those who thought four others were present did so. In fact, while all of the subjects in the two-person condition reported the incident only 62 percent of those in the six-person groups made a report.

Darley and Latane suggest that their critical situation produced avoidance-avoidance conflict in the sense that subjects worried about the guilt and shame of not helping and they feared making a social blunder by overreacting and spoiling the anonymity of the experiment. For those subjects who perceived themselves alone, the victim's distress quickly resolved the conflict. For those who knew others were present, "the cost of not helping was reduced (pull force for helping) and the conflict they were in more acute." "Caught between the two negative alternatives of letting the victim continue to suffer or the costs of rushing in to help, the nonresponding bystanders vacillated between them rather than *choosing* not to respond" (p. 382). Darley and Latane conclude that bystander nonhelping behavior in the face of emergencies may be a function of the perceived presence of others and the resultant diffusion of responsibility.

In "Group Inhibition of Bystander Intervention" (Latane and Darley) fifty-eight male Columbia University undergraduate students were used to test key ideas: (1) that "an individual faced with the passive reactions of other people will be influenced by them, and will be less likely to take action than if he were alone;" and (2) "compared to the performance of individuals . . . the constraints on behaviors in public coupled with the social influence process will lessen the likelihood that the members of the group will act to cope with the emergency."

Subjects in the experiment were assigned to one of three experimental conditions, described in the following way. Twenty-four subjects were assigned to the *alone conditions* which included a subject being told (either by a secretary or by signs) upon his appearance for the experiment to wait in a room alone and fill out a preliminary questionnaire. During this time the *critical situation* was introduced which consisted of a clearly visible stream of whitish smoke billowing into the room through a small vent in the wall. Ten naive subjects were assigned to the *two passive confederates condition* which involved ten groups of three persons (two confederates in each group) experiencing the critical situation. The third condition involved twenty-four naive subjects assigned to eight three-naive person groups who were exposed to the critical situation.

Results from the experiment were in the direction of the researchers' predictions. Seventy-five percent of the subjects in the alone condition reported the smoke prior to termination of the experimental period while only one subject in the ten two-person confederates condition did so. Just as striking was the finding that in only 38 percent of the eight groups of three naive subjects did *one* subject report the smoke. The others coughed, rubbed their eyes and opened the window but they did not report the smoke. In addition, in post-experimental interviews nonreporters gave a variety of reasons for not reporting the smoke, all centering around the idea that the smoke was interpreted as nondangerous. Baron and Byrne have stated that the inhibitory effect of other bystanders in this experiment appeared to be based on fear of social blunders (p. 279). Thus, even in the absence of group discussion the presence of others can inhibit prosocial behavior. Exceptions to this have been reported when recognized leaders move group members to action or one individual simply acts quickly and serves as a model for others (Firestone, Lichtman and Colamosca).

Findings from the above studies and further investigation into social groups undoubtedly led Bibb Latane to propose a *theory of social impact* in 1973. This basically states that the effects of external forces impinging on a group are divided among the members of the group. In other words the impact of forces on a group *diffuses* among the membership. Size of group, then, determines the impact of external forces on individual members within a group. Thus there is an inverse relationship between group size and external pressures on group members. In the case of external pressures on task-group members this means that as group size increases group members experience decreases in pressures to comply with external pressures. Latane, Williams and Harkins used the theory of social impact to explain the effect of "social loafing." Social loafing refers to the decrease in performance of individual group members which occurs as the size of the group increases. Latane, Williams and Harkins assigned male subjects to an alone condition, two-person groups, four-person groups and six-person groups. Subjects in these conditions were asked to clap their hands and cheer as loudly as possible. The strength of the sounds produced by each subject was measured. The researcher found that the amount of noise made by each subject diminished with increases in group size. The researchers concluded that while groups may be quite efficient and productive, they also may be inefficient as "social loafing" often emerges as group size increases.

While it is impossible in a volume of this kind to review all of the research relevant to field theory, the areas discussed do represent some of those characterizing modern day social psychological research. Now another vestige of field theory is turned to—cognitive processes.

COGNITIVE PROCESSES AND FIELD THEORY

Cognitive processes as a field of inquiry in social psychology is extremely broad. The influence of field theory is felt throughout its theory and research. Yet just as with our discussion of group dynamics and field theory, we must limit ourselves to a consideration of a few representative but significant field theory-influenced contributions and developments in cognitive processes. Two topical concerns heavily affected by field theory and quite contributory to the entire field of social psychology are cognitive dissonance theory and interpersonal attraction theory.

Cognitive Dissonance Theory

In 1957, Leon Festinger published *A Theory of Cognitive Dissonance* containing a set of principles which were to establish him in the social and behavioral sciences for years to come. He developed his formulation from field theory principles, emphasizing the tendencies of cognitive processes toward equilibrium.

The principles set forth by Festinger were concerned with *behavioral motivation*—the chief concern of Kurt Lewin during the founding of field theory. Why do individuals engage in certain types of behavior? What moves them to react in a particular way? Festinger attempted to answer such questions by first of all positing the field theory thesis that "the human organism tries to establish internal harmony, consistency, or congruity among his opinions, attitudes, knowledge and values" (1957, p. 260). From this point of view Festinger developed his theory of cognitive dissonance. A summary of the theory is as follows:

1. There may exist dissonant or nonfitting relations among cognitive elements.

2. The existence of dissonance gives rise to pressures to reduce the dissonance and to avoid increases in dissonance.

3. Manifestations of the operation of these pressures include behavior changes, changes of cognition, and circumspect exposure to new information and new opinions.

4. The maximum dissonance that can possibly exist between any two elements is equal to the total resistance to change of the less resistant element. The magnitude of dissonance cannot exceed this amount because, at this point of maximum possible dissonance, the less resistant element value changes, thus eliminating the dissonance (Festinger, 1957, pp. 28–31).

The concept dissonance is defined as inconsistency between cognitive elements. Consonance obtains when one cognitive element logically follows from another. Cognitive elements refer to opinions, beliefs and knowledge about the environment, the self or about a person's behavior. It is the *relationship* between cognitive elements that gives importance to both consonance and dissonance. The cognitive elements must be related to each other in order to be meaningful in a consonant or dissonant sense. Suppose a middle-class black man living in a predominantly white suburb in a northern state holds the following cognitive elements: (1) a belief that children, regardless of racial or ethnic background, are entitled to an equal education; and (2) an opinion that his neighbor (who is white) is perfectly justified in sending his children to a private school in order for them to escape forced busing to an inner-city, predominantly black, school.

In this example, both cognitive elements are related or relevant to each other, and moreover, many people would agree that they are dissonant. Just how dissonant the cognitive elements are depends on the importance of each cognitive element. An expression of the magnitude of the dissonance for the middle class black man can be illustrated as follows:

$$\frac{\text{Magnitude}}{\text{of}} = \frac{\text{Importance} \times \text{Cognitive Element 2 (his opinion)}}{\text{Importance} \times \text{Cognitive Element 1 (his beliefs)}}$$

Given this instance of dissonance, what could be predicted about the situation from the original formulation? First of all the existence of the discrepant cognitions should be psychologically uncomfortable and motivate tension reduction behaviors (Festinger, 1957, p. 30). Secondly, avoidance of situations and information which would increase the dissonance should be expected, in accordance with another proposition advanced by Festinger which states: *When dissonance is present, in addition to trying to reduce it, the person will actively avoid situations and information which would likely increase the dissonance* (p. 3).

Another crucial variable which must be considered in predicting dissonance reduction by the middle class black is the *strength of the pressures* to reduce the dissonance. Festinger stated that *the strength of the pressures to reduce the dissonance is a function of the magnitude of the dissonance* (p. 18). Given that the *number* and *importance* of both cognitive elements in our example are approximately equal in strength, dissonance for the man should be relatively great in magnitude. The precise way in which he would go about reducing the dissonance could not be specified from the original formulation. However, according to Festinger the man has three options: (1) behavioral change, (2) environmental change, and (3) addition of new cognitions. As illustration, this could mean for our middle class black that he reduce his dissonance by severing his ties with his neighbor, joining the NAACP and working diligently for total integration of inner-city and suburban schools (this would constitute behavior change). Or an alternative option may be pursued, along the lines of environmental change: he may change his social environment by associating exclusively with his white neighbor and internalizing his neighbor's rationale for sending his children to a private school. Another way in which tension reduction might be attempted is through rationalization of his neighbor's behavior: he may convince himself that despite his neighbor's actions, the neighbor is really a good person who is not bigoted but feels that his children should attend a neighborhood school.

Festinger's original formulation implied *behavioral motivation* and quickly became a focal point for numerous investigations. One such investigation, by Festinger and Carlsmith, was an experiment designed to test several predictions from the dissonance formulation. The widely reported finding that *under reward conditions, the smaller the reward used to induce opinion change, the greater the opinion change* evoked considerable interest among experimenters. Three groups of subjects were asked to engage in a dull task for an hour and then to inform future subjects that the task had been enjoyable. A monetary incentive was used in two of the groups. In one group subjects were offered $1 and in the second group subjects were offered $20 to comply. Subjects in a third group constituted the control group and were not offered any monetary incentive. After subjects had informed future subjects about the "enjoyable" nature of the experiment, their attitudes toward the task were measured. Festinger and Carlsmith found that those subjects who had been offered $1 actually rated the task as more enjoyable than those who had been given $20. The finding was interpreted to mean that those subjects in the $1 group had been given just enough of an incentive to cause opposing cognitive elements to be approximately equal in strength and importance. Because post-decision dissonance accompanies attitude-discrepant behavior, justification for compliance becomes important in that dissonance-reduction is based on such justifications. In the $20 group, justification for attitude-discrepant behavior could be based simply on the reward, while in the $1 group justification more likely had to be based on actually believing that the task had been enjoyable (changing cognitions).

Following this experiment, numerous others were conducted in the 1960s and several important dissonance findings were reported. Among those receiving attention were Janis and Gilmore's and Elm's studies that suggested that opinion change was some function of *developing arguments for the attitude-discrepant behavior* rather than due to dissonance-reduction. Another study, by Carlsmith, Collins and Helmreich, reported that *degree of commitment* was a crucial variable related to dissonance. In their study, when subjects had to publicly state a position contrary to their beliefs (high commitment condition), there was the predicted negative relationship between incentive and opinion change. However, a positive relationship between incentive and opinion change was obtained for those subjects who were asked to write an essay stating a position contrary to their beliefs which would be seen only by the experimenter (private condition).

Other experiments on cognitive dissonance have produced findings related to the tendency for persons to expose themselves to selective information following decision-making. Findings have been mixed in this regard. Some subjects apparently do actively avoid post-decision information discrepant with accepted alternatives, while others do not avoid such information.

On still another point, Bem (1967) questioned an essential assumption in cognitive dissonance theory, namely that *dissonance is some function of an inner state that activates reduction attempts and diminishes only after dissonance is reduced.* Tedeschi, Schlenker and Bonoma also questioned Festinger's contention of an inner state and suggested *impression management* was the cause of attitude change— that persons are motivated to present themselves to others as consistent behavers. If behavior *and* attitude are to be made public then a small incentive means that others can attribute responsiblity for the behavior to the person. Thus, in an effort to control what would be viewed as behavior attitude inconsistency in the eyes of others, persons actually change their attitudes in the direction of their behaviors. In instances of high incentive, there is no need to manage impressions since behavior-attitude inconsistency can be attributed by others to an external source (those who provide the incentive) rather than the person himself or herself. Thus a controversy developed surrounding cognitive dissonance theory. The controversy entailed extended arguments over whether *impression-management, interpretations, self-perception interpretations* or *cognitive dissonance interpretations* were appropriate for explaining dissonance effect.

Until recently, the first interpretation had been largely overlooked despite Collins and Hoyt's findings which suggested that when subjects assume personal responsibility for their decisions and when they feel that their decisions will have serious consequences for others, dissonance effects are obtained. Other studies, such as the one by Reiss and Schlenker, have also shown that dissonance effects seem to be some function of socially desirable responses. Sheldon Ungar, in an article devoted to the merits of impression management as an alternative explanatory scheme for what he called "self-perception experiments that are largely irrelevant to dissonance theory," actually sheds additional light on the impression-management-dissonance theory controversy. Ungar examines the proposal of impression-management theory that belief-discrepant behaviors are likely to be related to a person's beliefs about the availability of information to an audience. If the behavior is public and the individual believes it will be perceived as an intrinsic reaction to the stimulus, the individual's attitude response is likely to be managed to create an impression of consistency for the audience; and, "if the behavior is anonymous, individuals should not emit an attitude consistent with that behavior" (p. 82). This means that persons alternate between managing opinions for an audience and managing opinions for themselves. For Ungar the implications are that when behavior is anonymous, persons manage their own belief-behavior consistency which can include activity resisting the implications of belief-discrepant behaviors. Using a 2 x 2 factorial design varying religious behavior (pro vs. anti) and degree of anonymity (public vs. anonymous), ninty-two subjects were assigned to four groups (twenty-one to each of the two public conditions and twenty-five to each of the two anonymous conditions). Under public conditions (when subjects' identities, behaviors, and attitudes were known), proreligious manipulation resulted in more favorable religious attitudes than antireligious manipulation. Under private conditions, subjects did not shift their attitudes following manipulation. Ungar suggests that the findings underscored the extent to which "private" knowledge available only to subjects can be resisted or ignored while public knowledge can *dictate* subjects' responses (p. 88).

It is important to point out that Ungar's findings (as well as others in the past and perhaps others which will be conducted along the same lines in the future) may not settle debates over the superiority of dissonance interpretations, self-perception interpretations or impression-management interpretations of dissonance effects. Ungar's study, however, illustrates the complexity of the controversy and the need for further modification and refinement of dissonance theory, as well as for improved operational definitions of dissonance concepts, taking into account self-perception and impression-management, if dissonance theory is to remain a viable field of inquiry in social psychology. For example, Drachman and Worchel suggest that in order to attempt dissonance reduction by making cognitions more consonant with each other, individuals must accurately attribute the cause of the aversive state to the *existence of* dissonant cognitions. They feel that while alteration of cognitions is one means of reducing dissonance, *misattribution of the aversive state* could be another and thus there may be no drive to alter cognitions. Drachman and Worchel conclude that most people carry around with them dissonant cognitions and when there is an opportunity to misattribute the source of dissonance the individual may do so and consequently adjust to the existence of the *actual* dissonant sources—conflicting cognitions. Whether misattribution can delay individuals focusing on dissonant cognitions long enough for adjustment is felt to be related to the *amount of dissonance* and the *importance of cognitions*. A significant feature of their study is the fact that Drachman and Worchel demonstrate that a person's perception of the *source* of his or her dissonance is an important variable in dissonance reduction. Future research in cognitive dissonance theory will undoubtedly result in even sharper refinement of the formulation.

Interpersonal Attraction Theory

Interpersonal attraction as a field of inquiry in social psychology in particular and of cognitive processes in general owes its existence in large part to gestalt psychology and the field theory perspective. Current competing theoretical explanations in interpersonal attraction all seem to imply the operation of gestalt and/or field theory principles. Moreover, one scholar more than any other single person can be credited with stimulating research in interpersonal attraction, and that scholar is Theodore Newcomb. Two of Newcomb's most influential statements related to interpersonal attraction are considered here.

The Study of Communicative Acts   Newcomb, as may be recalled from an earlier discussion, conducted some of the initial studies in group dynamics. He is also responsible for proposing a statement describing the relationship between molar behavior and molecular behavior—*group properties* and *specific types of communicative acts*. Newcomb's contribution "An Approach to the Study of Communicative Acts," an extrapolation of Heider's POX Model, was a skillful use of field theory assumptions proposed by the founding fathers. Assumptions underlying Newcomb's model were (1) the system (a communication act) is characterized by a balance of forces; (2) a change in any part of the system may effect change in any of the others; and (3) forces impinging upon the system are relatively strong and as a result, there are strains toward equilibrium. All three of these assumptions are important statements in the field theory perspective as we have seen, and leave little doubt as to the importance of field theory in Newcomb's approach to the study of communicative acts. First Newcomb proposed that interdependence between affectivity and cognition was essential to human life. This interdependence was referred to as *coorientation*. Newcomb felt that communication among persons facilitated coorientation in the sense that persons were communicators and objects of communication. A communicative act for Newcomb involved transmitting information from person (*A*) to other (*B*) about something (*X*)—thus, the *ABX* system. The system could be within the life space of *A* or *B* or it could be an objective system inferred from an observation of *A*'s or *B*'s behavior. It contained minimally the following attributes: *A*'s orientation (attitudes and beliefs) toward *X, A*'s orientation (attitudes and beliefs) toward *B; B*'s orientation toward *X;* and *B*'s orientation toward *A*. While Newcomb was aware of the fact that numerous similarities and differences could exist in his system, he presented his model using simple dichotomies in the four relationships (+ + − meaning positively alike or negatively alike in attitude and/or attractions and cognitively alike or unlike on these attributes + − +).

Newcomb felt that orientation was essential because it was conceived of as social, rarely devoid of environmental reference (others' influence), meaning that others' judgments aid persons in social reality testing. Because we depend upon others to aid us in testing reality, we are to some extent dependent upon them and often our behavior will be influenced by them. When our behavior is influenced in this manner, we are *oriented* toward them. Because our orientations either toward *X*, or toward some *B* may be dependent upon *B*'s orientation toward *X*, we are motivated to influence or inform ourselves about *B*'s orientation toward *X*. Generally, we use communication to achieve this goal. Yet, why symmetry of orientation? What is the basis of the assumption of a "strain toward symmetry?" Newcomb suggested two important advantages of symmetry: (1) the case of calculating other's behavior when A's and B's orientations are similar; and (2) validation of one's own orientation toward X when orientations are similar. Both advantages *reward* symmetry and as a result symmetry is likely to acquire *secondary reward value*. Other testable propositions were derived by Newcomb from his general postulate that "the stronger the focus toward A's coorientation in respect to B and X, (a) the greater A's strain toward symmetry with B in respect to X; and (b) the greater the likelihood of increased symmetry as a consequence of one or more communicative acts." Derived propositions included those related to A's judgments of existing symmetry between him or herself and B, likelihood of instigation to and achievement of symmetry and the consequences of increased attraction and intensity of attitudes.

Perhaps the most publicized proposition Newcomb derived from his general postulate related to what he called the *dynamics of coorientation*. First of all, he considered two propositions related to situational variables and strain toward symmetry. They were (1) the less the attraction between A and B, the more nearly strain toward symmetry is limited to those particular Xs, coorientation toward which is required by the condition of association; and (2) under conditions of differentiation of A's and B's role prescriptions with regard to X, the greater the demand for coorientation the greater the likelihood of strain toward symmetry with respect to the role system.

It was Newcomb's discussion of the dynamics of his ABX system given perceived *asymmetry* with regard to X and demand for coorientation toward B and X by A that has received much attention in the literature. What can A do? Newcomb suggested that A could attempt to *achieve symmetry with regard to* X or that he or she could *introduce changes in other parts of the system* or he or she could *tolerate the asymmetry without change*. Regarding the first possibility, A could (1) attempt to influence B toward own orientation, (2) change own orientation toward B, and/or (3) cognitively distort B's orientation. The second possibility suggested that A could (1) alter his or her attraction toward B, (2) alter his or her judgment of own attraction for B, (3) modify evaluation of B's attraction toward himself or herself, and/or (4) alter his or her judgment of B's evaluation of himself or herself. The individual, then, from Newcomb's perspective, could solve problems of asymmetry behaviorally through communicative acts or cognitively by changing his or her perception of own or B's orientation.

Newcomb's theory of interpersonal attraction was a direct extension of his theory of communicative acts and often is referred to as the

ABX theory of attraction. (See Figure 7.2.) Essentially the theory assumes that there is a strain toward balance in persons' attitudes to each other and their attitudes toward some object. (Objects can vary in importance to the persons and in the degree to which they are relevant to the persons in the system.) Concentrating on dyadic relationships, Newcomb proposed that when persons mutually like each other and hold a similar attitude toward some object the system is in a state of *balance*. On the other hand, if persons dislike each other and have similar attitudes toward some object, or if they like each other and have different attitudes toward some object (especially if it was one of common relevance and great importance) then *imbalance* prevailed. Nonbalance occurs when a person dislikes another and attitude similarity or dissimilarity toward *X* is irrelevant. Newcomb postulated that im-

Figure 7.2
Examples of balanced, unbalanced and nonbalanced *ABX* systems

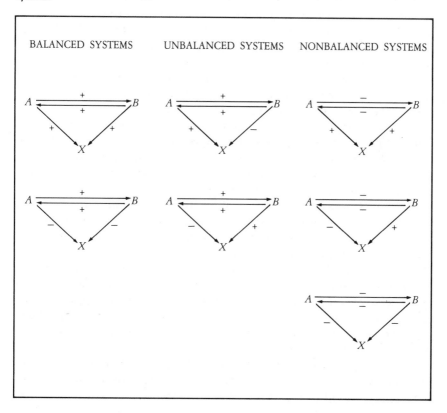

balanced systems were characterized by strains toward balance which would be manifested by change in one or more components of the system. Based on Newcomb's theory, it is axiomatic that there should be a close association between similarity in attitudes and preacquaintance attraction. This generalization has received considerable support (for example, Newcomb, 1956; Byrne et al., 1969). Assuming that most persons like themselves, then they should also like others who are favorable toward them. Curry and Emerson and others have offered strong support for this generalization.

While Newcomb's interpretation of the similarity-attraction phenomenon has been supported by findings from numerous other studies, still other investigators have offered alternative explanations. These explanations include a *balance theory interpretation* (heavily influenced by the gestalt perspective) which stresses intrapersonal consistency or balance in perception of interpersonal relations. This interpretation is different from Newcomb's in that Newcomb proposes that the reasons for preference for balance may include consensual validation and increased ability to predict others' behavior in particular *and* a *secondary reward* value in general. Another interpretation of similarity-attraction effects is *implied evaluation*. Based on Newcomb's finding that liking tends to be mutual, Aronson and Worchel suggest that persons may be attracted toward others similar because they come to believe that sharing similar attitudes means that the other person likes them. A third interpretation is one of the anticipation of rewards on future occasions. Berscheid and Walster suggest that persons are attracted to others similar to themselves because they believe that future interaction will result in rewards for themselves. A fourth interpretation of the similarity-attraction effect according to Layton and Insko is in terms of social comparison theory, which posits that persons have a self-evaluative drive to be in agreement with others.

A quick rereading of Newcomb's theory of communicative acts should reveal that anticipatory reward and social comparison theory interpretations are vital aspects of Newcomb's "strain toward symmetry" explanation. Even Berschied's and Walster's "anticipated rewards of future interaction" can be subsumed under Newcomb's "advantages of symmetry." Finally, the "implied evaluation interpretation" is a special case of "anticipated rewards of future interaction" since there is little reason for one to be attracted to a person who *liked* him or her. Both can be subsumed and are subsumed under Newcomb's "strain toward symmetry" explanation.

A final point to be made about the "state" of interpersonal attraction theory concerns an article written by Richard Santee in which he suggests "a modification of social comparison theory which hypothesizes that similarity of attitudes leads to attraction." He concludes that while this may be so in some cases, in his study, similarity of interpersonal attitudes did not lead to attraction. This conclusion had also been reached by Curry and Emerson. Santee suggests that attitude similarity probably has to be linked with rewards-cost outcome. His findings, in actuality, *support* earlier notions proposed by Festinger (1954) and Newcomb (1953). Simple "similarity of attitudes" was *never* proposed by Festinger and Newcomb as sufficient for reinforcement of interpersonal attraction.

In summary it *is* possible to say that persons often *do* seem to choose their companions and friends on the basis of perceived attitude similarity. Perceived dissimilarity frequently results in interpersonal rejection (Baron and Byrne). The importance of attitude similarity is implied in Geothals, Allison and Frost's finding that persons often overestimate the extent to which they are in agreement with those with whom they identify. Whether the effect of attitude similarity on attraction is due to reinforcement theory ideas or balance theory notions has not been determined in social psychology. Tashakkori and Insko (1979) feel that both explanations have led to important and thought-provoking research. Undoubtedly, both lines of research will continue to be followed by scholars interested in the link between interpersonal attraction and attitude similarity.

FIELD THEORY: EVALUATION AND CONCLUSIONS

Evaluation

Early field theory has been criticized for conceptual vagueness. Neel (1969, p. 6) has pointed out that many field theory concepts such as equilibrium, vectors, boundary, focus, and region, were defined *too* abstractly by Lewin. Others have questioned early and later field theory formulations which have assumed that some internal drive state was responsible for behavior (for example, Bem, 1967). Still another criticism of early field theory has been directed toward its *value-laden* ideas which are thought to have surfaced in field theory interpretations of the "group climate" findings which helped to provide a psychological rationale for democracy when "it was under attack from dictatorial governments."

Yet Lewin's influence in the development of experimental programs in social psychology while he was at the University of Iowa and M.I.T. was profound enough to have an impact on the entire field of social psychology. Social psychology as a discipline remains influenced by Lewin's ingenious research efforts and theoretical contributions. This is so despite the fact that scholars in social psychology presently tend to organize their intellectual activities around a multiplicity of substantive topics rather than around a general orientation to the study of social psychological phenomena (Cartwright, 1979). This tendency, in all likelihood, is what prompted Chaplin and Krawiec to conclude that it is premature to attempt any serious evaluation of Lewin's motivational and/or topological theories since his students and associates continue to propose theoretical statements and programs of research in social psychology that are heavily influenced by Lewin's original theoretical and research contributions (p. 400).

Conclusions

Field theory as the *system* proposed by Kurt Lewin cannot be recognized as part of contemporary social psychology. Yet it continues to be an important influence in the discipline. Many of the principles used in present-day interpretations of social psychological phenomena such as interpersonal attraction, choice shifts and cognitive dissonance have their origins in the initial contributions of Lewin and others like Festinger, Deutsch and Newcomb, to mention a few, who embraced the field theory perspective. To assess the precise impact of the field theory perspective on modern-day social psychology is exceedingly difficult given the state of the discipline which Cartwright (1979) has characterized as lacking theoretical integration. Generally, however, many of the middle range theoretical orientations used in social psychology today such as cognitive dissonance theory, group polarization theory, social comparison theory, and choice theory, have field theory perspective underpinnings. Field theory, in the same manner as the gestalt perspective, remains influential in social psychological theoretical formulations and research investigations. Perhaps the precise nature of this influence will become more apparent when theoretical integration of the discipline is achieved.

BIBLIOGRAPHY

Aronson, E. and P. Worchel. "Similarity versus Liking as Determinants of Interpersonal Attractiveness," *Psychonomic Science* 5 (1966), pp. 157–158.

Baron, Robert A. and Donn Byrne. *Social Psychology: Understanding Human Interaction*, 3rd ed. Boston: Allyn and Bacon, 1981.

Bem, D. J. "Self-Perception: An Alternative Interpretation of Cognitive Dissonance Phenomena," *Psychological Review* 74 (1967), pp. 183–200.

Berscheid, E. and E. H. Walster. *Interpersonal Attraction*. Reading, Ma.: Addison-Wesley, 1969.

Blascovich, J. *Group Risk Taking: A Conceptual Analysis and Experimental Manipulation*. Doctoral dissertation. Reno, Nev.: University of Nevada, 1972.

Blascovich, J. and Gerald P. Ginsburg. "Emergent Norms and Choice Shifts Involving Risk," *Sociometry* 37 (1974), pp. 205–218.

Blascovich, J., T. L. Veach and G. P. Ginsburg. "Blackjack and the Risky Shift," *Sociometry* 36 (1973), pp. 42–55.

Byrne, D. "Attitudes and Attraction," in L. Berkowitz, ed., *Advances in Experimental Social Psychology*. New York: Academic Press, 1969.

Byrne, D., W. Griffitt, W. Hudgins and K. Reeves. "Attitude Similarity-Dissimilarity and Attraction: Generality Beyond the College Sophomore," *Journal of Social Psychology* 79 (1969), pp. 155–161.

Carlsmith, J. M., B. E. Collins, and R. L. Helmreich. "Studies in Forced Compliance: 1. The Effect of Pressure for Compliance on Attitude Change Produced by Face-to-Face Role Playing and Anonymous Essay Writing," *Journal of Personality and Social Psychology* 4 (1966), pp. 1–13.

Cartwright, Dorwin A. "Risk Taking by Individuals and Groups: An Assessment of Research Employing Choice Dilemmas," *Journal of Personality and Social Psychology* 20 (1971), pp. 361–378.

———. "Contemporary Social Psychology in Historical Perspective," *Social Psychology Quarterly* 42 (1979), pp. 82–93.

Cartwright, Dorwin and Alvin Zander. *Group Dynamics*. New York: Harper & Row, 1968.

Chaplin, James P. and T. S. Krawiec. *Systems and Theories of Psychology* 4th ed. New York: Holt, Rinehart and Winston, 1979.

Collins, B. E. and M. G. Hoyt. "Personal Responsibility-for-Consequences: An Integration and Extension of the 'Forced Compliance Literature'," *Journal of Experimental Social Psychology* 8 (1972), pp. 558–593.

Curry, T. J. and R. M. Emerson. "Balance Theory: A Theory of Interpersonal Attraction?" *Sociometry* 33 (1970), pp. 216–238.

Darley, John M. and Bibb Latane. "Bystander Intervention in Emergencies: Diffusion of Responsibility," *Journal of Personality and Social Psychology* 8 (1968), pp. 377–383.

Deutsch, M. "An Experimental Study of the Effects of Cooperation and Competition upon Group Process," *Human Relations* 2 (1949), pp. 199–231.

———. "A Theory of Cooperation and Competition," *Human Relations* 2 (1949), pp. 129–152.

Deutsch, M. and R. Krauss. *Theories in Social Psychology.* New York: Basic Books, 1965.

Drachman, David and Stephen Worchel. "Misattribution of Arousal as a Means of Dissonance Reduction," *Sociometry* 39 (1976), pp. 53–59.

Dreyer, C. A. and A. S. Dreyer. "Family Dinner Time as a Unique Behavior Habitat," *Family Process* 12 (1973), pp. 291–301.

Ebbesen, E. B. and R. J. Bowers. "Proportion of Risky to Conservative Arguments in a Group Discussion and Choice Shift," *Journal of Personality and Social Psychology* 29 (1974), pp. 316–327.

Ellis, W. D. *A Source Book of Gestalt Psychology.* New York: The Hermanities Press, 1955.

Elms, A. C. "Role Playing, Incentive, and Dissonance," *Psychological Bulletin* 68 (1967), pp. 132–148.

Festinger, Leon. "Informal Social Communication," *Psychological Review* 57 (1950), 271–282.

———. "A Theory of Social Comparison Processes," *Human Relations* 7 (1954), pp. 117–140.

———. *A Theory of Cognitive Dissonance.* Evanston, Ill.: Row Peterson, 1957.

Festinger, Leon and J. M. Carlsmith. "Cognitive Consequences of Forced Compliance," *Journal of Abnormal and Social Psychology* 58 (1959), pp. 203–210.

Festinger, Leon, S. Schachter and K. Back. *Social Pressures in Informal Groups.* New York: Harper, 1980.

Firestone, I. J., C. M. Lichtman, and J. V. Colamosca. "Leader Effectiveness and Leadership Conferral as Determinants of Helping in a Medical Emergency," *Journal of Personality and Social Psychology* 31 (1975), pp. 343–348.

Geothals, G. R., S. J. Allison, and M. Frost. "Perception of the Magnitude and Diversity of Social Support," *Journal of Experimental Social Psychology* 15 (1979), pp. 570–581.

Greenberg, J. "Group vs. Individual Equity Judgments: Is There a Polarization Effect?", *Journal of Experimental Social Psychology* 15 (1979), pp. 504–512.

Janis, I. L. and J. B. Gilmore, "The Influence of Incentive Conditions on the Success of Role Playing in Modifying Attitudes," *Journal of Personality and Social Psychology* 1 (1965), pp. 17–27.

Kaplan, M. F. "Judgment by Juries," in M. F. Kaplan, and S. Schwartz, eds., *Judgment and Decision Processes in Applied Settings*. New York: Academic Press, 1977.

Knox, R. E. and R. K. Safford. "Group Caution at the Race Track," *Journal of Experimental Social Psychology* 12 (1976), pp. 317–324.

Latane, Bibb and John M. Darley. "Group Inhibition of Bystander Intervention in Emergencies," *Journal of Personality and Social Psychology* 10 (1968), pp. 215–221.

Latane, Bibb, K. Williams and S. Harkins. "Many Hands Make Light the Work: The Causes and Consequences of Social Loafing," *Journal of Personality and Social Psychology* 37 (1979), pp. 822–832.

Layton, Bruce D. and Chester A. Insko. "Anticipated Interaction and the Similarity-Attraction Effect," *Sociometry* 37 (1974), pp. 149–162.

Lewin, Kurt. *Principles of Topological Psychology*. New York: McGraw-Hill, 1936.

———. "Frontiers in Group Dynamics: Concept, Method and Reality in Social Science; Social Equilibria and Social Change," *Human Relations* (1947), pp. 5–41.

———. *Field Theory in Social Science*. New York: Harper and Brothers, 1951.

Lewin, Kurt, Ronald Lippit and Ralph K. White. "Patterns of Aggressive Behavior in Experimentally Created Social Climates," *Journal of Social Psychology* 10 (1939), pp. 271–299.

Lippit, Ronald and Ralph K. White. "The Social Climate of Children's Groups," in R. G. Barker, J. S. Kounin and H. T. Wright, eds., *Child Behavior and Development*. New York: McGraw-Hill, 1943.

Lundin, Robert. *Theories and Systems of Psychology* 2nd ed., Lexington, Ma.: D. C. Heath, 1979.

Miller, Charles E. and P. D. Anderson. "Group Decision Rules and Rejection of Deviates," *Social Psychology Quarterly* 42 (1979), pp. 354–363.

Morgan, C. P. and J. D. Abram. "The Preponderance of Arguments in the Risky Shift Phenomenon," *Journal of Experimental Social Psychology* 11 (1975), pp. 25–34.

Moscovici, S. and C. Faucheux. "Social Influence, Conformity Bias and the Study of Active Minorities," in L. Berkowitz, ed. *Advances in Experimental Social Psychology*. New York: Academic Press, 1972.

Moscovici, S. and C. Nemeth. "Social Influence 2: Minority Influence," in C. Nemeth, ed. *Social Psychology: Classic and Contemporary Integration.* Chicago: Rand McNally, 1974.

Myers, D. G., and M. F. Kaplan. "Group-Induced Polarization in Simulated Juries," *Personality and Social Psychology Bulletin* 82 (1976), pp. 63–66.

Neel, Ann. *Theories of Psychology: A Handbook.* Cambridge: Schenkman, 1969.

Nemeth, C., M. Swedlund and B. Kanki. "Patterning of the Minority's Responses and their Influence on the Majority," *European Journal of Social Psychology* 4 (1974), pp. 53–64.

Nemeth, C. and Joel Wachtler. "Creating the Perceptions of Consistency and Confidence: A Necessary Condition for Minority Influence," *Sociometry* 37 (1974), pp. 529–540.

Newcomb, T. M. *Personality and Social Change: Attitude Formation in a Student Community.* New York: Dryden Press, 1943.

———. "An Approach to the Study of Communicative Acts," *Psychological Review* 60 (1953), 393–404.

———. "The Prediction of Interpersonal Attraction," *American Psychologist* (1956), pp. 575–586.

———. *The Acquaintance Process.* New York: Holt, Rinehart and Winston, 1961.

Reiss, M. and B. R. Schlenker. "Attitude Change and Responsibility Avoidance as Modes of Dilemma Resolution in Forced-Compliance Situation," *Journal of Personality and Social Psychology* 35 (1977), pp. 21–30.

Santee, R. T. "The Effect on Attraction of Attitude Similarity as Information About Interpersonal Reinforcement Contingencies," *Sociometry* 39 (1976), pp. 153–156.

Schachter, Stanley. "Deviation, Rejection and Communication," *Journal of Abnormal and Social Psychology* 46 (1951), pp. 190–207.

Shaw, M. and P. Costanzo. *Theories of Social Psychology.* New York: McGraw-Hill, 1970.

Stoner, J. A. F. "A Comparison of Individual and Group Decisions Involving Risk," Unpublished Master's Thesis. Cambridge, Ma.: M.I.T. School of Management, 1961.

Suchner, Robert W. and David Jackson. "Responsibility and Status: A Causal or Only a Spurious Relationship?" *Sociometry* 39 (1976), pp. 243–256.

Tashakkori, A., and C. A. Insko. "Interpersonal Attraction and the Polarity of Similar Attitudes: A Test of Three Balance Models," *Journal of Personality and Social Psychology* 37 (1979), pp. 2262–2277.

Tedeschi, J. T., B. R. Schlenker and T. V. Bonoma. "Cognitive Dissonance: Private Ratiocination or Public Spectacle?" *American Psychologist* 26 (1971), pp. 685–695.

Tolman, Edward C. *Purposive Behavior in Animals and Men.* Berkeley, Ca.: University of California Press, 1951.

Ungar, Sheldon. "Attitude Inferences from Behavior Performed Under Public and Private Conditions," *Social Psychology Quarterly* 43 (1980), pp. 81–89.

Vinokur, A. and E. Burnstein. "Effects of Partially Shared Pervasive Arguments on Group-Induced Shifts: A Group Problem-Solving Approach," *Journal of Personality and Social Psychology* 29 (1974), pp. 305–315.

——. "Depolarization of Attitudes in Groups," *Journal of Personality and Social Psychology* 36 (1978), pp. 872–885.

Wallach, M. A. and K. K. Kogan. "The Roles of Information, Discussion and Consensus in Group Risk Taking," *Journal of Experimental Social Psychology* 1 (1965), pp. 1–9.

Whyte, W. F. *Street Corner Society.* Chicago: University of Chicago Press, 1943.

EPILOGUE

A FUNCTIONAL ASSESSMENT OF THEORETICAL PERSPECTIVES IN SOCIAL PSYCHOLOGY

A scheme devised by Gergen, Greenberg and Willis will be used to assess the functional significance of the theoretical perspectives discussed in this volume. The decision to employ this scheme is based upon its ease of application to diverse theoretical perspectives of varying methodological and theoretical scope. In fact, Gergen, Greenberg and Willis employ the scheme to evaluate the theoretical utility of social exchange and portions of their evaluation will be discussed. First, however, let us review briefly major components of the evaluation scheme. Following the review, the scheme is applied to each of the perspectives.

The explanation function. Gergen, Greenberg and Willis refer to two forms of theoretical explanations which theories often provide: descriptive explanations and interpretive explanations. *Descriptive explanation* is said to give a systematic account of what leads to what in social life. It specifies functional relationships between independent and dependent variables. Explanations of this kind do not emphasize why certain functional relationships obtain, rather they stress the necessary and sufficient conditions under which a particular behavior might occur. In contrast, *interpretive explanation* focuses on why certain functional relationships between variables exist—why certain antecedents lead to certain consequences. These types of explanation are thought to lead inevitably to interpretations of a broad array of social life.

The sensitizing function. Does a theoretical perspective direct attention to factors or processes of potential importance? Gergen, Greenberg and Willis feel that this is a vital function of theoretical perspectives (p. 271). They point out, however, that different theoretical perspectives often guide attention in *different* directions, making comparisons between perspectives difficult. Under these conditions, the range of phenomena one hopes to understand and the domain of relevant antecedents for any given range of phenomena can serve as points of comparison for theoretical perspectives.

The organization of experience function. Theoretical perspectives should serve to order social life. To the extent that a perspective can transform a wide array of haphazard phenomena into order and accommodate the multiple and shifting array of human activity as it unfolds over time and situations, a theoretical perspective satisfies the organization of experience function.

The integration function. Theoretical perspectives should strive to integrate disconnected branches of science. When previously disconnected entities are brought together, there is increased sensitization and catalysts for the dissemination and adaptation of novel research procedures and lines of investigation.

The generative function. Because patterns of behavior are constantly emerging, theoretical perspectives that "unsettle" common ways of viewing reality and challenge common assumptions underlying behavior have generative effects. Such perspectives open up new realms of observations, allow differentiated understanding of social actions, and generate intellectual stimulus.

The value-sustaining function. Gergen, Greenberg and Willis feel that one of the major functions of theoretical perspectives is to mold social patterns in valued directions. This means that theoretical perspectives can be judged on the *form* of the good or bad which they happen to sustain. The authors endorse the value-sustaining function of theoretical perspectives and argue that "all theories of human affairs intrinsically are value-laden" (p. 278). The only question that remains, according to the authors, is what form of subjectivity is favored by a particular theoretical perspective.

The above functions are thought to be fundamental for "general" theory in social psychology as well as the other social sciences. Gergen and his colleagues contend that there is no reason why "true value" nor predictive value should be the most important criteria for general theory. Indeed, few, if any, general theories in social psychology would be found adequate since the predictive capacity of theories of social behavior appear to be somewhat limited. The authors imply that theoretical perspectives do play a vital role in social psychology and will continue to do so if they meet the functional criteria specified above. Let us view each of the perspectives discussed in the preceding pages in relation to each of the functions. A comparative illustration of the perspectives on these functions follows each discussion.

The Symbolic Interaction Perspective

The history of symbolic interactionism attests to its far greater emphasis on *interpretive explanations* than on descriptive ones. Even in structural symbolic interactionism, interpretive explanations have abounded. While structural symbolic interactionists have often listed aspects of social structure that influence human behavior, rarely have they been content with simple listings of such phenomena. Instead, they have sought to understand *why* and *how* social structure influences human behavior. Regarding the second branch of symbolic interactionism, processual symbolic interactionism, its very nature has dictated interpretive explanation.

Symbolic interactionism also plays an important *sensitization role.* Processual symbolic interactionism often develops along sensitizing theory lines, as we have seen. Even so, structural symbolic interactionism also has been extremely sensitizing in its role as a branch of a major social psychological perspective. Most areas of social life and most social processes have had to withstand the scrutiny of the probing symbolic interactionist.

Does symbolic interactionism serve to integrate disconnected branches of science, diverse topics and the like? The answer is an unequivocal *yes.* Many scholars would agree that a major unifying force in sociology has been symbolic interactionism. Because sociology covers a wide span of forms of social interaction, the unifying role is a difficult one to play for any perspective. Symbolic interactionism comes as close as any to playing the role successfully. Not only has symbolic interactionism been successful in serving to integrate sociology in general, but it also has provided a unifying framework within which social psychologists, sociologists, political scientists, anthropologists, and many others have been comfortable.

As an organizer of social experience, symbolic interactionism has been one of the main perspectives to give order to diverse social life. The behavior of individuals in bars, on beaches, in homosexual encounters, in marriages, in race riots, in religious organizations, and so on, have been couched within the symbolic interaction perspective and thus given order. The multiple and shifting array of human activity which eludes many perspectives is well-suited for symbolic interactionism, especially processual symbolic interactionism.

Multiple views of the perspective within symbolic interactionism, long a part of the perspective's tradition, have seemed to enhance the generative function of symbolic interactionism. The mere fact that branches of the perspective exist indicates constant challenges by scholars within the perspective to common ways of viewing reality. Symbolic interactionism itself is as dynamic as the units of cognition it proposes to study—constantly changing, and thus fulfilling its generative function.

Does symbolic interactionism serve a value-sustaining function? For example, the value of freedom in our society is sustained in processual symbolic interactionism's dictum that behavior is indeterministic. The perspective also sustains the value of the good of the individual when its structural branch stresses *determinism* in human behavior. Stressing determinism does not negate the value that man or woman is basically good (even the criminal); instead, it attributes those behaviors which would challenge the value of the goodness of humans to social structural variables and their constraining influence. In much the same way as other perspectives, symbolic interactionism seems both to sustain values in the society and to challenge them.

Behavioral Social Psychology

Regarding the *explanatory function* of behavioral social psychology, many would argue that the function is primarily *descriptive*. However, Skinner himself has provided *interpretive* explanations for many of his proposed functional relationships between antecedents and consequences (1974). Moreover, as we have seen, other scholars such as John Kunkel, Sidney Bijou, Donald Baer, Robert Burgess, and many others, have either relatively recently been providing, or are presently beginning to provide, interpretive explanations in behavioral social psychology. In short, behavioral social psychology has traditionally specified necessary and sufficient conditions under which varying behaviors would occur (Gergen, Greenberg and Willis p. 269). More recently, behaviorists in social psychology have begun increasingly to devote attention to developing interpretive forms of explanation. In some instances this has meant elaborating, extending and altering behavioral propositions (for example, Bandura's "learning theory" and Bijou and Baer's "behavior analysis").

In its traditional form, behavioral social psychology has been somewhat limited with respect to the *sensitizing function*. Undoubtedly this is due to the traditionally disproportionate emphasis on descriptive explanation. As interpretive explanation becomes more pronounced in the perspective, behavioral social psychology should become more of a sensitizing device in social psychology.

As an *organizer of experience* behavioral social psychology has functioned well within psychological social psychology. However, its traditional emphasis upon the analysis of the behavior of only one party to social interaction without explicitly analyzing the behavior of other(s) has hindered the scope of its role as an organizer of experiences in social psychology in general (including both psychological and sociological social psychologies). Again, current reformulation, extensions and alterations of behavioral social psychology such as Bijou and Baer's "behavior analysis" in all likelihood will increase the scope of behavioral social psychology's role as an organizer of experience.

The somewhat limited scope of analysis mentioned above also has affected the *integration function* of behavioral social psychology. Only relatively recently (John Kunkel's works are exceptions) have efforts been devoted to employing behavioral social psychology as a means of understanding problems in branches of the social sciences outside of psychology. This limitation is directly related to the mode of analysis previously taken by most behavioral social psychologists, which emphasized the explicit analysis of only one party to social interaction. Just as with the previously discussed function, the integration function of behavioral social psychology is likely to expand in the future.

Gergen, Greenberg and Willis have implied that commitment to any given theoretical perspective within the social sciences may be a dangerous enterprise (p. 277). They suggest further that theoretical perspectives should be sufficiently flexible to "unsettle common ways." In a sense behavioral social psychology has been beset by difficulties with respect to its generative function because of its proponents' unyielding commitment to the perspective. Gergen and his colleagues also state that one reason why behaviorism may have been beset with difficulties regarding the generative function is that its form of externalized hedonism appears cemented to common understanding. Interestingly, however, the generative function of perspectives appears to be related more to the ingenuity and courage of scholars within the field. The rationale for the assertion is found in Gergen, Greenberg and Willis' conclusion that the generative function of Skinnerian behaviorism (a part of behavioral social psychology) has been preserved by examples such as Skinner's *Beyond Freedom and Dignity*, where he extends behaviorism to culturally honored ideals. Skinner's extension *did* "unsettle" common understanding and thus, contributes to the generative function of behavioral social psychology. At this time however, it is difficult to conclude that the perspective has been applied sufficiently to those areas which "most irritate" where perhaps the perspective may be most generative in its effects (Gergen, Greenberg and Willis, p. 278).

A common criticism directed toward behavioral social psychology is that it neglects the roles of cognition, feelings, attitudes, etc. in human behavior. In a sense such criticisms imply that a theory ought to *emphasize* the roles of these phenomena in human behavior. Not to do so implies that humans act inhumanly—that the behaviors of humans are functions of their consequences. Given that one of the functions of theoretical perspectives discussed here is to mold social patterns in valued directions (the value-sustaining function), whether or not behavioral social psychology does this is a relative question, and the answers (affirmative and negative) depend on the audience to whom the question is addressed. If the proportion of those who endorse the perspective among contemporary social psychologists is any indication of those who favor the perspective's value-sustaining function, behavioral social psychology ranks rather low on the value-sustaining function.

The Social Exchange Perspective

Gergen, Greenberg and Willis claim that exchange theory possesses both interpretive and descriptive components but that the greatest emphasis is on interpretation (p. 290). This evaluation of social exchange is in line with my contention, and in addition suggests that one reason why social exchange has gained greater acceptance than behaviorism in social psychology is due to the former's interpretive aspects, which to varying degrees emphasize the importance of motivation, cognition and learning in attempts to explain ongoing social life.

One cannot overemphasize the sensitizing function social exchange has played in social psychology. The stress on patterns of interdependency called attention to how the collectivity sustains various patterns of behavior. Indeed, it is possible that one major distinction to be made between behavioral social psychology and social exchange has been the latter's sensitizing emphasis on *interdependency of persons* rather than the *single* individual. Recently, social exchange theorists have become *sensitized* to conceptual problems in the perspective, such as the difficulty of assessing total rewards and costs, the problem of reducing all outcomes to a common standard, the determination of what is rewarding and costly across individuals, time, and situations. Solutions to these problems in all likelihood will increase the sensitization function of social exchange.

Social exchange is also said to organize a great deal of social experiences. This is so in spite of critics' comments that social exchange is too abstract and only specifies that certain behavior has rewarding and/or costly outcomes. This criticism implies the necessity for developing a model which links specific rewarding and/or costly outcomes with particular types of behavior. Gergen and his colleagues' answer to the criticism is deemed appropriate here:

> because of its highly abstract composition, exchange theory can accommodate the multiple and shifting array of human activity as it unfolds over time. Its terms are sufficiently flexible that, with a modicum of exertion, one can discern their application in almost any encounter. Because of the abstract character of its terms, the theory may be uniquely qualified as a unifying force within contemporary social psychology (p. 273).

The social exchange perspective also seems to rank high on the integration function. To be sure, the framework has been used in a wide array of topical investigations such as legal behavior, organizational behavior, love relationships, etc., and in numerous branches of the social sciences including political science, sociology, anthropology *and* social psychology. Also as a result of its abstract nature the perspective has been especially capable of organizing various and sundry bits of information—thus, its power as an integrator within the sciences.

The social exchange perspective has irritated many, and if irritation is an indication of a perspective's generative function, then the likelihood is that it has performed this function admirably. While the perspective in a sense is congruent with common understanding and common sense with its hedonistic elements, it also has grated on some nerves when applied to humanistic topics such as law, altruism, friendship, and the like. This has more than likely led to the rethinking and reformulation of many traditional ideas in these areas.

For some people social exchange in a sense sustains valued behavior and in another sense it attempts to mold behavior in unvalued directions. Gergen, Greenberg and Willis have stated that in actuality social exchange only leans toward unvalued social patterns (for example, alienation) on a superficial level. Behind this facade, they claim, may be a consciousness-raising experience regarding the interdependency of persons. There is some evidence available for drawing this conclusion. Did not Walster, Berscheid and Walster's work on reward allocation stimulate work by Deutsch, Sampson and Levanthal, to mention a few? Those who are piqued by Walster and his colleagues' approach to reward allocation surely should feel somewhat relieved by Deutsch, Sampson and Levanthal's approach, which questions equity as the only basis of reward allocation.

The Gestalt Perspective

Both forms of explanation, *descriptive* and *interpretive,* can be found in the gestalt perspective. From the founding of the gestalt perspective there has been dual emphasis on descriptive and interpretive explanations. While the descriptive experiment by Wertheimer, later to be called the *phi phenomenon,* led to the emergence of the gestalt perspective, interpretive forms of explanation were also initial aspects of the perspective, as evidenced by gestaltists' early development of basic assumptions and propositions in the perspective emphasizing "tendencies toward organization," "interdependencies among parts," and the like. Finally, while initial experiments in the perspective chiefly dealt with perception, the perspective as it now exists in fragmented form permeates a wide array of social life.

As stated earlier in this volume, the gestalt perspective seems to be dissipated in social psychology. In a very real sense this dissipation has resulted in increased sensitization of the perspective. With the emergence of attribution theory, and its direct link to the gestalt perspective, remnants, at least, of the perspective have been related to a wide range of phenomena.

The gestalt perspective, perhaps because of its fragmented nature, is presently much weaker on the integrative function of theoretical perspectives. While the perspective permeates numerous topical areas in social psychology, because of its fragmented nature, application can only be piecemeal. Thus, the integrative function can only be partially served.

As with the integrative function, the nature of the gestalt perspective dictates limitations with respect to organizing social experiences. While vestiges of the perspective have been shown to have wide applicability (for example, attribution theory in pro-social behavior, attribution theory in allocation of rewards, attribution theory in person perception, etc.), its potential for organizing social experience is severely limited by its current fragmented existence.

With respect to the generative and value-sustaining functions, there is evidence that miniature models derived from the gestalt perspective like attribution theory function to generate novel views of reality, open up new realms of observation, and sustain and mold social problems in valued directions. Even in its fragmented state the gestalt perspective serves some of the functions of a viable perspective in contemporary social psychology.

The Field Theory Perspective

Field theory as a perspective in social psychology was founded on the premise that interpretive explanations were essential in social and behavioral sciences investigations. While field theory, too, is less of a unified system than behavioral social psychology, symbolic interactionism and social exchange, explanations such as those given in cognitive dissonance theory, social comparison theory, impact theory and the risky shifts phenomenon have assumed both descriptive and interpretive forms.

As a sensitizer, the perspective is said to have been extremely *efficient* in giving researchers in a variety of directions. Research in group dynamics, individual processes and individual-group dynamics are examples of the various directions of research in social psychology directly attributable to the field theory perspective.

Field theory enjoyed its most prolific role as an organizer of experience immediately after World War II, when a wide variety of seemingly haphazard phenomena was in need of order. Social psychology as a discipline will be historically indebted to this perspective's functioning in the organizer capacity. Even at present, with the perspective less visible as a working system, field theory spans the scope of both micro and macro processes—thus its integration function is preserved.

The generative and value-sustaining functions of field theory have also been traditional in social psychology. New modes of observation and challenges to common assumptions have been hallmarks of field theory leading to different understandings of social action. Just as important was the role that field theory played in supporting democracy as a value in the United States immediately after World War II. Some have called this role a vital one in sustaining American ideals and values during a chaotic period.

FUNCTIONAL CRITERIA FOR THEORETICAL PERSPECTIVES IN SOCIAL PSYCHOLOGY

THEORETICAL PERSPECTIVES IN SOCIAL PSYCHOLOGY	EXPLANATORY (BOTH DESCRIPTIVE AND INTERPRETIVE)	SENSITIZING	ORGANIZER OF EXPERIENCE	INTEGRATIVE	GENERATIVE	VALUE SUSTAINING
SYMBOLIC INTERACTIONISM	H	H	H	H	H	H
SOCIAL EXCHANGE	H	H	H	H	H	M
BEHAVIORAL SOCIAL PSYCHOLOGY	M	M	M	L	L	M
GESTALT	H	H	M	L	H	M
FIELD THEORY	H	H	H	M	M	H

Figure E.1
Comparative illustration of the current theoretical utility of social psychological perspectives

THE STATE OF THE DISCIPLINE:
THEORETICAL DISORIENTATION
AND TRENDS TOWARD SYNTHESES

One of the most pressing problems in modern day social psychology is the *theoretical* disorientation said to characterize the discipline. Numerous reasons have been given for this disorientation and many can be subsumed under the following three major causes: (1) the concentration of social psychologists on developing "miniature conceptual systems" that bear little explicit relations to each other (Cartwright, p. 90); (2) the failure of social psychologists to develop a distinctive orientation dealing solely with social interactive processes (Cartwright, 1979; Boutilier, Rold and Svensen); and (3) a paucity of attempts made by social psychologists to relate existing theorectical perspectives within the field to each other. Of the three major causes given for disorientation within social psychology today, the latter has the most impact.

"Miniature Conceptual Systems"
and Theoretical Disorientation
in Social Psychology

Currently in social psychology we have "social impact theory," "social comparison theory," "balance theory," "dissonance theory," "equity theory," "attribution theory,"—and the list goes on. West and Wicklund, in their *Primer on Social Psychological Theories,* list and discuss fifteen or so of these "miniature conceptual systems." It seems that Cartwright's observation that many scholars in social psychology organize their intellectual activities around esoteric topics of interest to them is valid. Certainly these microsystems have contributed enormously to social psychology. Yet, as Cartwright states, we need "a more comprehensive theoretical framework" which would give scholars criteria for deciding which problems should be investigated. Moreover, such a framework may obviate the need for a plethora of microsystems since we may discover that many simply are special "cases" of each other.

The Lack of a Distinctive Orientation
and Theoretical Disorientation in
Social Psychology

"Social interaction processes" is a basic unit of analysis in social psychology. Yet recent comments about the unit of analysis suggest that

it suffers from inadequate conceptualization (Cartwright, 1979; Boutilier, Rold and Svendsen). The cleavage between sociological social psychology and psychological social psychology mentioned in Chapter 1,
and the lack of integration between *structure* (both social and
psychological) and *process,* contribute greatly to this theoretical defi-
ciency in social psychology (Boutilier, Rold and Svendsen).

Cartwright has suggested as a cure for the problem that we need to
find "an effective conceptualization of the process by which the
behavior of individuals is converted or transformed into social acts
which have properties of such a nature that they can have consequences
for other people, groups and institutions, or in other words for the
social environment" (1979, p. 92). Boutilier, and his colleagues also
provide an antidote for social psychology's ills with respect to a conceptualization of social interaction processes. Qualifying their proposal,
and seemingly less sanguine than Cartwright, they imply first of all that
the goal of a comprehensive theory of social interaction may be too
lofty. Instead, they suggest, perhaps we should concentrate on elaborating sociological theories and psychological theories in a manner that
makes them become compatible with each other. They state specifically:

> Perhaps we need to elaborate simple models of how individ-
> uals construct and enact societal roles and perspectives while
> simultaneously maintaining their individual identities (p.
> 15).

Precisely how this is to be accomplished is not discussed, although the
authors do emphasize that the effort should be interdisciplinary.

The Lack of Synthesis Between
Theoretical Perspectives and
Theoretical Disorientation in
Social Psychology

The final cause of theoretical disorientation in social psychology to be
discussed deals with the paucity of attempts made by scholars to integrate and/or synthesize existing *perspectives* in the discipline. I suggest that unless divergent perspectives in social psychology can be reconciled, a comprehensive theoretical framework cannot be constructed.
Moreover, even within perspectives much disagreement exists between
proponents over ontological and epistemological assumptions and con-

cepts (social exchange, according to Lindesmith, Strauss and Denzin is one example). This, too, impedes syntheses between perspectives and makes us less sanguine about developing a comprehensive theoretical framework in the near future.

Synthesizing Theoretical Perspectives

On the issue of synthesizing perspectives in social psychology as a step toward theoretical integration of the discipline, a rationale can be provided. The "miniature conceptual systems" Cartwright speaks of can all be couched within several theoretical perspectives in social psychology discussed in the preceding chapters, as has been shown for many of them. In the perspectives discussed, there are certain underlying assumptions which when stated explicity also characterize appropriate miniature conceptual systems. For example, if attribution thoery can be said to be couched in the gestalt perspective (Chapter 6), then the basic assumptions underlying the gestalt perspective also underlie attribution theory, unless it is explicitly stated otherwise.

Moreover, if certain assumptions in the miniature conceptual system violate assumptions in the parent perspective, then there must be some reconciliation between the two sets of assumptions. For example, it is not now possible to reconcile the social exchange perspective with behavioral social psychology based on Skinner's model or Bijou's and Baer's behavior analysis because of the motive assumption explicit in social exchange, and the explicit denial of the motive assumption made by Skinnerian behaviorists and behavior analysts. On the other hand, field theory assumptions seem to be remarkably similar to assumptions made by scholars working within the behavior analysis and/or behavioral social psychology perspective, especially since both emphasize the environment (life space) of the individual and his or her interaction with the environment as causes of human behavior. Differences, however, emerge between field theory and behavior analysis when the role of motive in the perspective is explored, and would have to be reconciled if the two perspectives were to be synthesized.

What has been emphasized thus far is simply that a systematic examination of basic assumptions underlying theoretical perspectives and "miniature conceptual systems" must be undertaken if social psychology is to become an integrated discipline. Hopefully, examinations of this type will facilitate syntheses of extant perspectives in social psychology. Syntheses of theoretical perspectives in the field are not easy, for they involve producing single perspectives from parts of multiple perspectives. A case in point is Peter Singelmann's effort to provide guidelines for synthesizing social exchange and processual symbolic interactionism. He describes his effort as formulating "exchange theory as a process of symbolic interaction." This is precisely what is done but it does *not* produce a synthesis of the two perspectives. From a social exchange stance, some behavior is a function of an "internal psychological state" (Singelmann referred to the state as "hedonistic strivings" (p. 422). This assumption is in direct contrast to most symbolic interaction positions which may explain, partly, why Lindesmith, Strauss and Denzin reject Singelmann's product. While their rejection may not be sufficient reason for stating that Singelmann's attempt falls short, his failure to reconcile underlying assumptions in the two disparate perspectives certainly provides a rationale for such a conclusion. Nevertheless, attempts such as the one made by Singelmann to synthesize symbolic interaction and social exchange must be conspicuous goals of theorizing in social psychology if the discipline is to achieve theoretical integration. Recent trends seem to indicate rudimentary efforts in this direction.

BIBLIOGRAPHY

Blumer, Herbert. "The Problem of the Concept in Social Psychology," *American Journal of Sociology* 45 (1940), pp. 707–719.

———. "What is Wrong With Social Theory?," *American Sociological Review* 19 (1954), pp. 3–10.

———. *Symbolic Interactionism: Perspectives and Methods.* Englewood Cliffs, N.J.: Prentice-Hall, 1969.

Boutilier, Robert G., J. Christian Rold and Ann C. Svendsen. "Crisis in Two Social Psychologies: A Critical Comparison," *Social Psychology Quarterly* 43 (1980), pp. 5–17.

Cartwright, Dorwin. "Contemporary Social Psychology in Historical Perspective," *Social Psychology Quarterly* 42 (1979), pp. 82–93.

Gergen, Kenneth J., M. S. Greenberg, and R. H. Willis. *Social Exchange: Advances in Theory and Research.* New York: Plenum Press, 1980.

Lindesmith, Alfred R., Anselm Strauss and Norman Denzin. *Social Psychology* 5th ed. New York: Holt, Rinehart and Winston, 1977.

Singelmann, Peter. "Exchange as Symbolic Interaction: Convergences Between Two Theoretical Perspectives," *American Sociological Review* 37 (1972), pp. 414–424.

Skinner, B.F. *Beyond Freedom and Dignity.* New York: Knopf, 1971.

West, Stephen G. and Robert A. Wicklund. *A Primer of Social Psychological Theories.* Monterey, Ca.: Brooks/Cole, 1980.

INDEX